## Praise for *Sola*

The great "solas" of Reformation theology have taken on a life of their own, but to be more than slogans they have always needed explication and contextualization. With Volker Leppin's usual combination of erudition and boldness, his new book does just that, both setting out the complex origins of these simple slogans and showing us the richness of the theological and devotional context in which Luther works his way toward them. Again, Leppin shows us a lively, active, creative Luther pushing forward to a deeper and more powerful understanding of God's Word made flesh as the heart of Christian faith.

—Dr. R. Guy Erwin, president and Ministerium of
Pennsylvania Professor of Reformation Studies,
United Lutheran Seminary in Gettysburg and Philadelphia;
former bishop of Southwest California Synod,
Evangelical Lutheran Church in America

Volker Leppin's careful scholarship on Luther's theology is full of historical insight and ecumenical promise, but until now it has largely been available only to German readers. Thankfully, with *Sola*, Leppin's nuanced approach to Luther's thought is introduced to the broader English-speaking world. The Luther that emerges from Leppin's attentive analysis is one deeply embedded in the mystical-monastic theology of his late-medieval context. As such, his thought develops and maintains these broader continuities even as it transforms them into a potent evangelical theology. A welcome and necessary work for all serious students of the Reformation.

—Dr. Erik H. Herrmann, author of
*The Babylonian Captivity of the Church, 1520:
The Annotated Luther Study Edition*

In a historical moment of social polarization and division, *Sola* takes on the conceptual monoliths that define Protestant identity and continue to construct a polemical thought-world that separates "us" (Protestants) from "them" (Roman Catholics): *sola gratia, sola fide, solus Christus*, and *sola scriptura*. With the incisive historical and theological analysis that we've come to expect from Volker Leppin, he shows that these so-called "principles" of the Reformation are actually "vessels for content from the Middle Ages." They demonstrate that Luther and the Wittenberg reformers were engaging theological movements taking shape across Europe in the preceding centuries; the "solas" developed slowly as both distinctive flavors of the emerging Reformation theology and its intended contributions back into those medieval traditions. In this regard, Leppin shows that the "solas" do not define Protestants as intrinsically different than Catholics, but rather point to our "common stock" and reinforce current ecumenical impulses that seek to overcome divide and bring formerly opposing sides back to a common table.

—Dr. Candace L. Kohli, assistant professor of<br>
Lutheran systematic theology and global Lutheranism,<br>
Lutheran School of Theology at Chicago

Leppin's firm command of vital strands of medieval thinking, in both the scholastic and the monastic-mystical traditions, enables him to present effectively how Luther, deeply embedded in these traditions, came to his new understanding of the biblical faith while continuing to use the terminology and insights of several late-medieval theologians. Leppin's careful assessment of key texts, within the context of Luther's time and the framework of recent historical discussions, illuminates the reformer's development of his own agenda and basis for Christian theology.

—Dr. Robert Kolb, professor emeritus of systematic theology,<br>
Concordia Seminary, St. Louis

This collection of essays features Dr. Leppin's research in the context of the Reformation Jubilee of 2017. Individual chapters build a case to challenge conclusions about any singular "reformation breakthrough" in Luther's thought, just as they flesh out the roots, meaning, and later uses of the central Luther-an principles: *solus Christus, sola gratia, sola fide, sola scriptura*. Interpreting Luther as a medieval Christian shaped my monastic, scholastic, and mystical traditions, and in the company of his contemporaries, Dr. Leppin offers a splendid tool for teaching and research.

—Dr. Kirsi Stjerna, professor of Lutheran history and theology, Pacific<br>
Lutheran Theological Seminary, Berkeley, California; core doctoral<br>
faculty, Graduate Theological Union, Berkeley, California; docent,<br>
Helsinki University; author of *Lutheran Theology: A Grammar of Faith*

The famous "sola" formulas of the Reformation are often used as if they were totally new. Grounded in his expertise in late-medieval thinking and piety, Leppin convincingly shows their historical roots, and how they developed and reached their distinctive profile.

—Prof. Dr. Christiane Tietz, University of Zurich;<br>
author of *Karl Barth: A Life in Conflict*

Through this dense book on the Reformation "sola" principles, written into his new American context and presenting works from the years around the Jubilee of 2017, one gets a clear notion of the golden thread in Volker Leppin's yearslong and significant scholarship on Martin Luther. Leppin still pursues his "old experiment" of reading Luther as a medieval human being: it is the Luther of differences and transformations within history, not of opposition to and break from his own time. The book is historical, but it also has a strong and thought-provoking contemporary ecumenical agenda: read it and ponder upon it!

—Dr. Anna Vind, associate professor, University of Copenhagen

# LUTHERAN QUARTERLY BOOKS

### *Editor*

Paul Rorem, Professor Emeritus, *Princeton Theological Seminary*

### *Associate Editors*

Timothy J. Wengert, Professor Emeritus, *United Lutheran Seminary (Philadelphia)*

Mary Jane Haemig, Professor Emerita, *Luther Seminary, St. Paul*

Mark C. Mattes, *Grand View University, Des Moines, Iowa*

*Lutheran Quarterly Books* will advance the same aims as *Lutheran Quarterly* itself, aims repeated by Theodore G. Tappert when he was editor fifty years ago and renewed by Oliver K. Olson when he revived the publication in 1987. The original four aims continue to grace the front matter and to guide the contents of every issue, and can now also indicate the goals of *Lutheran Quarterly Books*: "to provide a forum (1) for the discussion of Christian faith and life on the basis of the Lutheran confession; (2) for the application of the principles of the Lutheran church to the changing problems of religion and society; (3) for the fostering of world Lutheranism; and (4) for the promotion of understanding between Lutherans and other Christians."

For further information, see www.lutheranquarterly.org.

The symbol and motto of *Lutheran Quarterly*, VDMA for *Verbum Domini Manet in Aeternum* (1 Peter 1:25), was adopted as a motto by Luther's sovereign, Frederick the Wise, and his successors. The original "Protestant" princes walking out of the imperial Diet of Speyer in 1529, unruly peasants following Thomas Müntzer, and from 1531 to 1547 the coins, medals, flags, and guns of the Smalcaldic League all bore the most famous Reformation slogan, the first Evangelical confession: The Word of the Lord remains forever.

For the complete list of *Lutheran Quarterly Books*, please see the final pages of this work.

# Sola

# Sola

*Christ, Grace, Faith, and Scripture
Alone in Martin Luther's Theology*

VOLKER LEPPIN

TRANSLATED BY SAMUEL BRANDT

FORTRESS PRESS
MINNEAPOLIS

SOLA
Christ, Grace, Faith, and Scripture Alone in Martin Luther's Theology



Library of Congress Cataloging-in-Publication Data

Names: Leppin, Volker, author.
Title: Sola : Christ, grace, faith, and scripture alone in Martin Luther's theology / Volker Leppin.
Description: Minneapolis : Fortress Press, 2024. | Series: Lutheran quarterly books | Includes bibliographical references and index.
Identifiers: LCCN 2023033170 (print) | LCCN 2023033171 (ebook) | ISBN 9781506491882 (paperback) | ISBN 9781506491899 (ebook)
Subjects: LCSH: Luther, Martin, 1483-1546. | Theology, Doctrinal--History. | Reformed Church--Doctrines.
Classification: LCC BR333.3 .L46 2024  (print) | LCC BR333.3  (ebook) | DDC 230/.41--dc23/eng/20231204
LC record available at https://lccn.loc.gov/2023033170
LC ebook record available at https://lccn.loc.gov/2023033171

Cover design and illustration: Kristin Miller

Print ISBN: 978-1-5064-9188-2
eBook ISBN: 978-1-5064-9189-9

# Contents

# Abbreviations

| | |
|---|---|
| AWA | *Archiv zur Weimarer Ausgabe.* Martin Luther. Weimar: H. Böhlau, 1991–1992. |
| CChr.CM | *Corpus Christianorum: Continuatio mediaevalis.* Turnholt: Brepols, 1966–1967. |
| CChr.SL | *Corpus Christianorum: Series Latina.* Turnholt: Brepols, 1953–1954. |
| CICan | *Corpus Iuris Canonici.* 2 vols. Edited by Emil Friedberg. Leipzig: Tauchnitz, 1879–1881. |
| CSEL | *Corpus Scriptorum ecclesiasticorum Latinorum.* Wien: Verl. d. Österr. Akad. d. Wiss., 1866–1867. |
| DCL | *Dokumente zur Cause Lutheri (1517–1521).* 2 vols. Edited by Peter Fabisch and Erwin Iserloh. Münster: Aschendorffsche Verlagsbuchhandlung, 1988–1991. |
| DH | *Kompendium der Glaubensbekenntnisse und kirchlichen Lehrentscheidungen.* 45th edition. Edited by Heinrich Denzinger and Peter Hünermann. Freiburg: 2017. (Numbers also apply to other editions.) |
| Editio Leonina | *Opera omnia iussu Leonis XIII edita cura et studio Fratrum Praedicatorum.* Thomas Aquinatis. Rom: Typographia Polyglotta, 1882–1883. |
| LW | *Luther's Works.* American Edition. 80 vols. Edited by Jaroslav Pelikan, Helmut Lehmann, and Christopher Boyd Brown. St. Louis: Concordia, 1955–1956. |

Mansi    *Sacrorum conciliorum nova et amplissima collection.* Edited by Johannes Dominicus Mansi et al. Florence: Zatta, 1759–1827.

PL    *Patrologiae cursus completus. Series Latina.* Edited by Jacques-Paul Migne. Paris: Migne, 1841–1864.

WA    *Luthers Werke.* Kritische Gesamtausgabe. 73 vols. Edited by J. F. K. Knaake et al. Weimar: H. Böhlau, 1883–2009.

WA Br    *Luthers Werke.* Kritische Gesamtausgabe. *Briefwechsel.* 18 vols. Weimar: H. Böhlau, 1930–1985.

WA DB    *Luthers Werke.* Kritische Gesamtausgabe. *Deutsche Bibel.* 12 vols. Weimar: H. Böhlau, 1906–1961.

WA TR    *Luthers Werke.* Kritische Gesamtausgabe. *Tischreden.* 6 vols. Weimar: H. Böhlau, 1930–1985.

## Introduction: From Inclusiveness to Exclusiveness. How Luther Transformed Medieval Ideas and Shaped Reformation

2017 was a big year for the Reformation. In fact, it was probably the zenith of interest in Martin Luther and the Reformation in general. In that year, readers of large German newspapers found the Jubilee logo and the face of the reformer confronting them on every copy, less-than-subtly colored to match Germany's national hues of black, red, and gold. International media cameras focused on the service held by Pope Francis in Lund, Sweden on October 31, 2016.[1] But that was just the start: countless other activities and organizations had a veritable blast in that year, be it the international network "Refo500" or the many Lutheran churches that devoted special attention to the Reformation. In the United States, the ELCA observed Reformation Day in Washington with the motto "Looking Back and Called Forward."[2] Luther and the Reformation have probably never received such concentrated attention as in this year, and not only the pessimists have a feeling that this attention will not be matched in the forseeable future. We are now waking up after a very large celebration, and there's something analogous to a hangover in our experience now. The cameras and microphones have disappeared, and researchers such myself, who took full part in the celebrations,[3] must continue their

1. "Home," Joint Catholic-Lutheran Commemoration of the Reformation, Zugriff January 4, 2023, https://www.lund2016.net/.
2. ELCA, "ELCA to Celebrate 500th Anniversary of the Reformation with Public Event in D.C.," Zugriff January 4, 2023, https://www.elca.org/news-and-events/7891.
3. Along with those scholarly works that appeared under my name during that time, as well as the many scholarly conferences I attended (such as the International Congress for Luther Research in Wittenberg from July 30 until August 4, 2017), I want to give special mention to the committee texts in whose formulation I participated: *Rechtfertigung und Freiheit. 500 Jahre*

work without their motivation. This return to cultural and scholarly sobriety is healthy, if only because it leads us back to the basic question of what Luther's contribution really was, is, and will be to a very diverse church and world.

My own biographical and professional path has taken me to two different countries and continents. It ought not to surprise us that this has shaped my approach to this research. The differences pertain to both the scholarship and the churches. While German Lutherans continue to develop their identity within a Protestant framework, which has variously combined Lutherans, Reformed, and the churches of the Protestant Unions into the federation of the "Evangelische Kirche in Deutschland", American Lutheranism has developed in very different and distinct directions. The contrast of various Lutheran scholars has produced some excellent scholarship, as seen in the common projects of Robert Kolb and Timothy Wengert, from whose work I have profited since my days in Germany. I hope to continue to learn from them.

I am rooted in the German scholarly tradition and its strong philological emphasis; these essays certainly bear that mark. Since I was a schoolboy, I have loved Latin, and the reader will see this reflected in the footnotes. Nevertheless, I have taken care to ensure that the main text, including the citations, are all easily accessible in English. German researchers of the Reformation have produced an enormous and rich corpus of work, which has almost grown to be too much. This grand tradition, however, has always been shaped by certain presuppositions that have never been thoroughly questioned. One of the major ones is that Protestant Luther research in Germany has always taken place in a confessionally binary context, in which Protestant theology and churches "faced" Roman Catholic theology and churches. This "showdown" can be seen in the building at the University of Tübingen, which houses my previous office: it had a confessional, organizational, *and* architectural boundary running through it. Protestant and Catholic thinkers did and do both find a home there, but such boundaries have led to a tendency in German research to emphasize the differences between Luther and Catholicism. The Middle Ages have usually been lumped together with the latter. These strict categories have

---

*Reformation 2017. Ein Grundlagentext des Rates der Evangelischen Kirche in Deutschland (EKD)* (Gütersloh: Gütersloher Verlagshaus, 2014; 4th ed., 2015); *Erinnerung heilen—Jesus Christus bezeugen. Ein gemeinsames Wort zum Jahr 2017*, ed. Evangelische Kirche in Deutschland and Deutsche Bischofskonferenz (Hannover: Linden, 2016); *Reformation 1517–2017. Ökumenische Perspektiven*, ed. Volker Leppin and Dorothea Sattler (Freiburg: Herder; Göttingen: Vandenhoeck and Ruprecht, 2014) (the last book including an English translation of the document). The latter texts emphasize my ecumenical perspective.

been softened by researchers such as Heiko Oberman, Berndt Hamm, and Ulrich Köpf, but we can still feel them. The following essays owe a lot to these researchers who have helped to transform Luther's purported "break" with the Middle Ages into a gentle transformation.[4]

The other dominant figure in the German discussion is Gerhard Ebeling. No other Luther researcher has done more to shape our picture of the reformer than he, and the twenty-first century has not yet brought forth his equal. His main accomplishment was a structured presentation of Luther's hermeneutics, in a time of extremely high German interest in hermeneutics in general. He arrived at Luther's high estimation of Holy Scripture due to the predominance of word-of-God theology around the Second World War. This naturally had its boundaries, most prominently in Ebeling's tendency to detach Luther from his historical context (although Ebeling *did* have a solid foundation in medieval studies) and to emphasize his uniqueness instead of placing him in a conversation with his contemporaries.[5] It is difficult for non-German readers to estimate just how large of an effect this had in Germany. It has to do with the German understanding of academic education, seen in the fact that the standard biography on Gerhard Ebeling was written by his last academic student.[6] The teacher ensured that his own understanding of his legacy was captured by his student. The essays in this book thus belong in a context of international Luther research "after Ebeling."[7] They bind together my

---

4. For more on this concept, cf. *Reformation als Transformation? Interdisziplinäre Zugänge zum Transformationsparadigma als historiographische Beschreibungskategorie*, ed. Volker Leppin and Stefan Michels (Tübingen: Mohr Siebeck, 2022).

5. For my critique and admiration of Ebeling, cf. my two articles: Volker Leppin, "Der Verlust des Menschen Luther: Zu Ebelings Lutherdeutung," *Journal for Early Modern Christianity* 1 (2014): 29–50; Leppin, "Hermeneutik und Seelsorge. Gerhard Ebelings Vermächtnis für die Lutherforschung," in *Neige dein Ohr . . . Beiträge zur ökumenischen Theologie: FS Christian Schad*, ed. Paul Metzger, Andreas Rummel, and Wolfgang Schumacher (Leipzig: Evangelische Verlagsanstalt, 2021), 123–30.

6. Albrecht Beutel, *Gerhard Ebeling. Eine Biographie* (Tübingen: Mohr, 2012).

7. The difficulty experienced by German researchers to separate themselves from the Ebeling paradigm can be seen in the grotesque critique levied at me by Ulrich Köpf (himself a student of Ebeling and a scholar whom I otherwise greatly respect) in a long article devoted almost solely to my theses. (Ulrich Köpf, "Martin Luther und Tauler," in *Frömmigkeitsgeschichte und Theologiegeschichte. Gesammelte Aufsätze* [Tübingen: Mohr, 2022], 515–39). For reasons I cannot understand, he has greatly distorted my argumentation in Volker Leppin, *Die fremde Reformation. Luthers mystische Wurzeln*, 2nd ed. (Munich: Beck, 2017), where I employed the gentle metaphor of Luther deriving "a certain melody for the later Doctrine of Justification" from Tauler (Leppin, *Die fremde Reformation*, 25), Köpf draws the inappropriate conclusion that I wanted "to trace the central doctrine of the reformer to a singular source" (Leppin, *Die fremde Reformation*, 522). On the very same page (Leppin, *Die fremde Reformation*, 25) employed by Köpf to justify his argument, I also list out various other important sources, such as "that, what

German formation with the perspectives of American research shaped by Oberman. Vincent Evener,[8] Christine Helmer,[9] Anna Marie Johnson[10] and Ronald Rittgers[11] are representatives of a generation of American Luther scholars who have successfully worked to present Luther situated in his medieval context.

Every such attempt requires an understanding of Luther's core theology.

> Interpreters of Luther's thought are [. . .] challenged to identify the central theme of his theology. A popular candidate has been 'theology of the cross', since Luther once said that 'the cross alone is our theology'. But Luther also wrote in 1532 that the proper subject of theology is the human being guilty of sin and condemned, and God who is justifier and saviour. Other candidates for the centre of his theology are the hidden and revealed God, Christ, the Word of God, law and gospel, and justification.[12]

With this, Scott Hendrix has neatly captured the core challenge of Luther research. Never did Luther produce a systematic overview of his thought, and yet there has never been a theologian with such internal coherency to their theology. Every text of his can be derived from a few basic sentences, every thought is connected to the others. It *does* always pertain to cross, sin, justification, or some other core moment. However, these moments were not always present altogether and were certainly not without their shifts in definition. We can see this with the example of justification, which, since the "Luther Renaissance" of the early twentieth century, has stood in the center of German-speaking Luther research. Dozens of scholars following the Luther Renaissance have attempted to

stands out here [intended is Luther's reading of Tauler], was still by no means fully developed into a system. Luther would use it later to develop the basic structure of his thought. He was helped in this endeavor by reading Paul and Augustine, who did not contradict his reading of Tauler." Köpf's article devotes great energy to attacking an opinion that is simply not mine. Nevertheless, I still recommend reading it because it provides a helpful collection of material for understanding Luther's usage of Tauler.

8. Vincent Evener, *Enemies of the Cross: Suffering, Truth, and Mysticism in the Early Reformation* (Oxford: University Press, 2021).

9. Christine Helmer, *The Trinity and Martin Luther*, 2nd rev. ed. (Bellingham: Lexham, 2017); *The Medieval Luther*, ed. Christine Helmer (Tübingen: Mohr, 2020).

10. Anne Marie Johnson, *Beyond Indulgences: Luther's Reform of Late Medieval Piety, 1518–1520* (Kirksville: Truman State University Press, 2017).

11. Ronald R. Rittgers, *The Reformation of Suffering: Pastoral Theology and Lay Piety in Late Medieval and Early Modern Germany* (Oxford: University Press, 2012). Cf. also Rittgers, *Protestants and Mysticism in Reformation Europe*, ed. Vincent Evener and Ronald K. Rittgers (Leiden: Brill, 2018).

12. Scott Hendrix, "Luther," in *Cambridge Companion to Reformation Theology*, ed. David Bagchi and David Steinmetz (Cambridge: Cambridge University Press, 2004), 39–56, 40.

establish Luther's "breakthrough" on justification.[13] But these historical reconstructions always had a very clear idea of what they would find before they started their work. The dizzying array of debates in the sixteenth century pertaining to justification show us that this concept did not enjoy a clear consensus in Luther's time (or today).[14] And we cannot forget that the historical studies of the twentieth century certainly did not take place in a vacuum! The Luther Renaissance was only one library desk or seminar room away from Dialectical Theology.[15] The latter's development of a theology of the word of God certainly shaped scholars' understanding of Luther, as we have already seen above with Ebeling. Word-of-God theology helped Ernst Bizer (1904–1975) find a focal point in the *promissio*, in the event of justification.[16] His brief approach to this would be developed further by Oswald Bayer[17] (born 1939) and has deeply shaped our understanding of the trajectory of Luther's thought. Many of these portraits of Luther have produced very *pleasant* depictions of his theology—but scholarship, which inverts the usual order of investigation and result, is still not satisfying.

A historical focus has other difficulties as well. A historical reconstruction errs when it works teleologically, starting with the end of a development (in this case reformational theology at the end of Luther's life and following his death) and then making sure that everything leading up to that final result neatly falls into the expected categories. In Luther's case, the developments were not at all linear. He employed quite a bit of trial and error in his theological trajectory. As far as we can tell, the mystical spirituality of his cloister was important for him throughout his life. His abbot and confessor John Staupitz († 1524) greatly formed his thought. Of course, he was not untouched by the influence of the scholastic theology he received during his studies in Erfurt from Joducus Trutvetter († 1319) and Bartholomeus Arnoldi of Usingen († 1532). His own reading of Gabriel Biel († 1495) deepened this as well. Biel's explanation of the mass and his *Collectiorium* on the Sentences of Peter Lombard († 1160) left a

13. Cf. the anthology *Der Durchbruch der reformatorischen Erkenntnis bei Luther*, ed. Bernhard Lohse (Darmstadt: Wissenschaftliche Buchgesellschaft, 1968); *Der Durchbruch der reformatorischen Erkenntnis bei Luther: Neuere Untersuchungen*, ed. Bernhard Lohse (Stuttgart: Zabern, 1988).
14. Cf. Charles P. Arand, Robert Kolb, James A. Nestingen, *The Lutheran Confessions: History and Theology of The Book of Concord* (Minneapolis: Fortress Press, 2012), 159–215.
15. *Luther, Barth, and Movements of Theological Renewal (1918–1933)*, ed. Heinrich Assel and Bruce McCormack (Berlin: De Gruyter, 2020).
16. Ernst Bizer, *Fides ex auditu: Eine Untersuchung über die Gerechtigkeit Gottes durch Martin Luther*, 3rd ed. (Neukirchen: Neukirchener Verlagsanstalt, 1966).
17. Oswald Bayer, *Promissio: Geschichte der reformatorischen Wende in Luthers Theologie*, 2nd ed. (Darmstadt: Wissenschaftliche Buchgesellschaft, 1989).

deep impression on the young Luther. Finally, Luther read the humanist authors of his age. Perhaps the most important of them was Erasmus of Rotterdam († 1536), whose edition of the Greek New Testament came to Luther's attention during his lectures on Romans. This brings us to the most profound impact of Luther's reading on his thought: his early lectures on the Psalms, Romans, Galatians, and then his second round of lectures on the Psalms cast his thought into a biblical form. This biblical formation is the object of comparison with the later development of a scriptural principle—but it is not identical with it.

That brings us to the actual topic of this volume. The Scriptural Principle is one of the so-called "exclusive particles" of the Reformation. The others are *Solus Christus*, *Sola gratia*, and *Sola fide*. These four concepts form a network of interdependent hermeneutical poles. They require each other for their definition, but none of them are as clearly defined as are the presuppositions for the concept of justification. As Eberhard Jüngel (1934–2021) has emphasized, it is not possible to talk about justification without referring to these concepts in some way.[18] They are thus very central to the Reformation and have the distinct advantage of being a *group* of concepts, limiting the danger of reducing reformational theology to any one of them. Such intrinsic multidimensionality has a very good chance of doing justice to the multifaceted nature of reformational theology, including that of Luther. This high degree of flexibility is the reason why these concepts will be used as "shafts" to get to the roots of reformational theology.

There are occasional voices which point out that the exclusive particles were "discussed in this form by a restorative dogmatic only in the nineteenth century."[19] Is it really the case that using them undercuts any effort to be historically precise? This question does have its merits—but it is a question fundamental to any historical investigation. Historical descriptions and explanations are never restricted to recounting but always blend in ideas from the present. This is also true for the concept of justification—it was never used "in this form" in the sixteenth century because the sixteenth century line of questioning was different than the twenty-first century's. There is both a temporal distance of about five centuries and a large distance in worldview created by the Enlightenment. These are more of a barrier than helpful tools when trying to understand the Reformation's doctrine of justifications. Historical reconstruction therefore must consist of holding distance and proximity in proper balance

---

18. Eberhard Jüngel, *Justification. The Heart of the Christian Faith: A Theological Study with an Ecumenical Purpose* (London: Bloomsbury, 2014), 147–259.
19. Martin Honecker, "Martin Luthers Theologie im Reformationsgedenken," *Theologische Rundschau* 81 (2016): 35–47, 44.

so that the past is not only recounted but also analyzed; that historical thought is not flooded by anachronistic concepts but that it constantly works to find the appropriate language and concepts.

Thus, it is certainly correct that treating all of the exclusive particles in a volume such as this one carries a measure of ambiguity with it. Eberhard Jüngel (whom I have just drawn upon to justify the approach of this book) actually preferred the concept of *"solo verbo"* to *"sola scriptura."*[20] Others have utilized both in their models and ended up with a group of five exclusive particles.[21] These models usually harbor certain ideas about the theology of the word, which are often more the result of twentieth-century debates than the result of a stringent model of the sixteenth century. And yet, this very fact makes clear that the canon of exclusive particles has not been closed. That is not a drawback! We are not trying to nail down a dogmatic concept but are seeking to elucidate what justification actually means for the sixteenth century with the help of other supporting concepts. This group of "exclusive" particles is anything other than anachronistic: Philip Melanchthon describes the *sola* in *Sola fide* as a *particula exclusiva* in his work on the concept of faith.[22] The "exclusive" concept was present in the sixteenth century and the implied demarcation as well. In fact, we can find the thrust of the idea in this word. We *are* dealing with a rather bellicose language that is particularly well-suited to highlight the difference between reformational theology and the Middle Ages.

It is, therefore, all the more surprising that the studies in this volume seek to demonstrate an affinity of these exclusive particles to the Middle Ages. These essays stick closely to source texts to describe this, but they did not have the thoughts of this introduction as their goal. In fact, they were all written independently for various occasions (mostly conferences leading up to the Reformation Jubilee in 2017) and have only been lightly modified since then.[23] But they did continue in the spirit of the "experiment" that I announced in the first edition of my German-language Luther biography:

> [Luther] should be considered a man of the Late Middle Ages for as long as possible, who discovers (often quite slowly) and who does not want to depart from his roots—and in the end perhaps did not depart fully from them.[24]

---

20. Jüngel, *Justification*, 148.
21. *Rechtfertigung und Freiheit.*
22. Philipp Melanchthon, *Argumentum epistolae Pauli ad Romanos* (*Melanchtons* Werke, ed. Robert Stupperich, vol. 5 [Gütersloh: Gütersloher Verlagshaus, 1965], 42:29).
23. I have especially shifted the focus of the bibliography away from German research instead of allowing it to balloon with new additions.
24. Volker Leppin, *Martin Luther* (Darmstadt: Wissenschaftliche Buchgesellschaft 2006; 3rd ed., 2017), 12. A highly reduced version of this biography in English can be found as: Volker Leppin, *Martin Luther: A Late Medieval Life* (Grand Rapids: Baker Academic, 2017). Actually,

I have tried to use exacting philological means to further develop this point in the following essays. One of the results of admitting this idea of gradual development in Luther's thought is that we start to see the "reformational breakthrough," a long cherished topos in Reformation studies, as being inaccurate. This image does have a compelling drama and *puissance*, but it also simply ignores a lot of historical facts. It would, however, also be wrong to claim that Luther was doomed to go down this path from the beginning. This sees Luther as the goal of history, a sort of "all roads led to Luther" idea. This teleology is not only a theological one but also a personal one too. Such approaches to history are by no means only fiction. It remains the standard approach to the Middle Ages in Luther research that one sees them as the precondition that brought forth Luther. This is precisely where the basic thesis of my experiment gains its validity: everything *could* have developed differently. In 1516, nobody—including Luther—had the faintest idea that this monk who was holding a lecture on Paul's letter to the Romans would be anybody worth mentioning half a century later, and certainly not as a Reformer. Of course, we will find the seeds of later developments and conflicts. But Luther's contemporaries in 1516 did not regard him as the great foil to the pope as they would at the end of his life. We have to see the world of this time period with their eyes in order to really take in the surprise of the Reformation. The first way to do this is to explore Luther in his medieval situation, as a traditional and time-bound person.

Such a perspective also means recognizing that medieval thought and life already knew a fair amount of what we consider to be innovation in the Reformation. It remains an astonishing fact that very little is known

my categorization as presented there (Leppin, 42) must be seen as somewhat oversimplified in light of these studies. There, I suggested the following chain of developments: "Luther had been steered by Staupitz around 1513 toward an understanding of *solus Christus*, or Christ alone. His increased reading of Augustine in the period around 1516–17 reveals an obvious focus on *sola gratia*. An important moment in the development of the principle of *sola fide*, by faith alone, can be seen at the disputation of Heidelberg in 1518. And now in 1519 *sola Scriptura*, Scripture alone, was added to the equation." It would be more precise to see the various Solus-formulations as constituting certain steps in Luther's development, which made him increasingly likely to exclude himself from other theologies. In this sense, one will have to take autumn of 1519 as the point of no return, both because of Luther's theological insights and because he now saw the pope as the antichrist (for more on this, cf. Volker Leppin, "Luthers Antichristverständnis vor dem Hintergrund der mittelalterlichen Konzeptionen," in *Transformationen: Studien zu den Wandlungsprozessen in Theologie und Frömmigkeit zwischen Spätmittelalter und Reformation*, 2nd ed. (Tübingen: Mohr Siebeck, 2018), 471–86). In such a context, the various exclusive particles floating around in his theology found a new binding power.

about the late-medieval critique of indulgences (chapter 1), which was expressed for both economic and theological reasons. In this critique, we see a symptom of the late-medieval tension between internal and external forms of spirituality—indulgence is contrasted with God's effect on the internal person. The Reformation picked up right as this divergence had set in and continued the development of the internal form. John of Staupitz is a key figure for this with his idea that salvation depends entirely on Christ (chapter 2). He once told his protégé Luther that God "wants to be uncomprehended beyond Christ"[25] (see below, p. 31), a statement that proved to be invaluable for Luther in his spiritual crises. This word of solace from his confessor is only comprehensible when we see Staupitz as a representative of a broad current in the late Middle Ages, which immersed itself in the passion of Christ. This current had shaped and led Luther during his early lectures. The concentration on Christ is very difficult to separate from the idea of the singular effect of God's grace, which in turn was present at virtually every turn of medieval theology. Much like *Solus Christus*, *Sola gratia* cannot be pitted against the Middle Ages and chalked up as paradigm shift for the Reformation. But the formulation of this thought in such pithy phrasing *would* require some theological work, especially an intense reading of Augustine. This work is essential for Luther's own journey toward a theological critique of indulgence (chapter 3). It took place as Luther intensely read the sermons of John Tauler († 1361), the pupil of Meister Eckhart, in 1515/1516. The marginalia written by Luther contain the peculiar formulation that only *nuda fides in deum* remains for a person (see below, p. 75). This is not yet the exclusive particle *sola fide*. But with it, we see that the latter formulation, held dearly as a marked distinction from medieval theology, was in fact developed in a late-medieval horizon (chapter 4). This chapter will explore how this exclusive particle included and excluded medieval thought. All transformations take place in a tension of continuity and innovation, and this is certainly true for Luther's reformational development. The *difference* of reformational theology to medieval theology does not necessarily mean a break between the two. It is better to speak of preserving certain medieval content. We can only see this by taking a really granual look at the stages of development within the new reformational theology. The shift often can be seen in the *regrouping of given views* and as the *intensification of individual developments* instead of a complete break with the past. That also applies to the

---

25. WA TR 2, No. 1490 [112.9–15–16]).

fourth exclusive particle presented here, *Sola scriptura* (chapter 5). It is only adequately understood against the backdrop of wrestling with the validity of authorities before and after the Leipzig Disputation. The supreme significance of Scripture was never contested by the reformers. But it was also never contested by the medieval world. The *disjunction* known in the Protestant world between Scripture and everything else is the product of the debate concerning the new doctrine of justification. If we follow the still very popular opinion of August Twesten (1789–1876), then we hear a familiar refrain: the formal principle of Protestant dogmatics, the Doctrine of Scripture, had to be created after the material principle, the Doctrine of justification, had taken shape—and after it had become controversial.[26] The development of the Scriptural Principle meant, on the one hand, finding common ground in a singular source, but on the other, it meant that you could demonstrate the peculiarity of a new position in contrast to earlier ideas. When Scripture takes on the function of an argumentative bolster, it then becomes very important to consider how Luther expands the Scriptural Principle. As the debate with the Roman authorities heated up, he came to the conclusion that Scripture explains itself (chapter 6). Only when we follow this development in which Luther defended himself against the pope's suppression do we see the paradoxical similarity of his hermeneutics to medieval-monastic understandings of Scripture, but we also see the yawning gap between his understanding of Scripture and the historical-critical approach familiar to us today. That proximity-distance question makes it hard for us to classify Luther and his theology today. Narrow studies of Luther can be very helpful here, including, I hope, the final chapter of this book: Luther's explanation of 2 Corinthians 3:5 (chapter 7). I have chosen this study because it neatly presents the contrast of spirit and letter, a common topic for Luther and his fellows in Wittenberg as they read Augustine's *De spiritu et littera* and applied it to biblical texts. Luther's explanation of 2 Corinthians 3:5 gives us an example of how Luther distinguishes himself from the Middle Ages and how he continues it. The Lutheran transformation finds its particular telos in its explanation of the Bible.

All essays presented here have in common that they portray Luther as a deeply medieval man in his theology and spirituality. They therefore reduce the exclusive character of the *particulae exclusivae*. The appearance

---

26. August Detlev Christian Twesten, *Vorlesungen über die Dogmatik der Evangelisch-Lutherischen Kirche, nach dem Compendium des Herrn Dr. W. M. L. de Wette*, 3rd ed. (Hamburg: Friedrich Perthes, 1834), 274.

of paradox may not deceive the reader! Yes, we *are* questioning (and sometimes correcting) Lutheran self-presentation. The exclusive character of the *particulae exclusivae* became a useful, polemical devise to define the newly formed Wittenberg movement: self-definition is particularly easy and satisfying when it involves distinguishing yourself *from* someone else. "I am this and not anything else—and most certainly not you!" is a form of self-definition that we know very well in our own media-shaped day and age. It is clear and performs useful work in shaping identity. But it is often also subtly aggressive and reductive because it makes opposition out of difference. This constitutes a major theme of this book: how differences were turned into opposition, and how opposition can be traced back to mere differences.

The following historical investigations have in common that their objects—Christ, grace, faith, and Scripture—were not pitted by Luther against medieval theology but rather that their definition was a slow and gradual process. The opposition expressed in the polemics thus appears to be less exclusive and gradual—if we allow ourselves to look closely at its emergence and formulation. Luther continued according to the logic of the Middle Ages gradually, eventually reaching a point where he could understand his theology as special and new. That is not wrong. There was no "Lutheran" theology in the Middle Ages. With it came into being a church with its own special character.

Being particular and well-defined does not necessarily mean negating or repelling difference. The studies presented here are also intended to contribute to a model of Lutheran theology that softens the exclusive character of the *Sola*-formulations, allowing the intrinsically Lutheran content to remain but also giving attention to the efforts by the "others" to be authentic Christians as well. This book is directed into today's ecumenical context and thus does not limit itself to a historical reconstruction of the emergence of the exclusive particles. These particles will hopefully lose a bit of the exclusivity if the arc of this book (seen in the ordering of the essays) has any truth to it.

The ecumenical implications can be neatly summarized in this development: Luther discovered *Solus Christus* from his teacher Staupitz; we can detect its presence as early as his first lectures on the Psalms from 1513. He followed his mentor's theological focus but certainly did not find himself in opposition to the theology of the Middle Ages or to today's Catholicism. The ecumenical compatibility is not only true because Luther was a pupil of Staupitz, who did not join the Reformation and died as a highly regarded abbot in Salzburg. It is even more true because the central significance of Christ in the theology and spirituality of the time was so blatantly self-evident. The idea that the concentration on Christ stands in opposition to all other options for salvation naturally brought Christ to the fore. However, it only follows the intention of medieval teaching on salvation in which the saints did not somehow present an "alternative" to Christ but derived their saving power from him. We see a similar dynamic with grace. Luther develops *Sola gratia* in the context of his lectures on Paul's epistles and while intensely reading Augustine (especially *De spiritu et littera*), but in so doing he was taking up a basic message of the Middle Ages: everything depends on God's grace. This message is an ecumenical commonality, just like that of Christ as an indispensible mediator. The Middle Ages saw a human contribution as part of this. With *Sola fide*, Luther removed that from the picture. This may be the move that gives his theology its clearest reformational focus, the most extreme form of alternatives and exclusivity. And it has not lost its poignance: *Sola fide* remains one of the most marked differences between Lutheran and Roman Catholic theology. This difference is certainly more pronounced than Doctrine of Scripture, even though *Sola scriptura* is a product of the Reformation and the 1519 Leipzig Disputation. This doctrine is much less controversial than it appeared for many generations. Today, Lutheran theology understands Scripture to have emerged in a tradition and that its interpretation never occurs without the interpreter's own situation playing a role. During the Second Vatican Council, Roman Catholic theology arrived at a dogmatic constitution, *Dei verbum*, which Joseph Ratzinger, the later Pope Benedict XVI, could summarize as a *Sola scriptura (. . .) totum in traditione*.[27]

Regardless of the level of coherency in today's ecumenical discussions, these essays advise us to regard these differences as more gradual than exclusive. The 1999 Joint Declaration on the Doctrine of Justification says about *Sola fide* that whatever differences might remain on this topic ought not to separate the church bodies.[28] That brings us to the perspective behind this investigation: exclusive particles help us to discern more than to separate. These formulations did lead to and cement confessional separation from the sixteenth century onward. But their historically sensitive examination yields the insight that they are vessels for content from

---

27. Joseph Ratzinger, "Kommentar zu *Dei verbum* Kap. 1–2," in *Lexikon für Theologie und Kirche. Ergänzungsbd. 2* (Freiburg: Herder, 1967), 497–528, 524.

28. *Joint Declaration 26–27.* (cf. "Joint Declaration on the Doctrine of Justification," Lutheran World Federation, accessed April 1, 2023, https://www.lutheranworld.org/content/resource-joint-declaration-doctrine-justification).

the Middle Ages, the common stock of both Catholic and Protestant churches. If we understand their formation as the result of transformations, then that means they still contain a common legacy while denoting difference. They are not absolute sentences of truth but members of a living, shifting theological language that continues to develop today. May these studies, which examine the transformations leading to confessional separation, also contribute to further gradual transformations to overcome that separation.[29]

29. I wish to extend special thanks to Samuel Brandt, for translating this manuscript, to Kyle Sorkness, for his assistance in identifying quotations throughout, and to Maia de Bourcier for editing.

1.

# Critique of Indulgences in the Late Middle Ages

The critique of indulgences in the late Middle Ages is a topic that cannot be treated as if one could just forget that the indulgences and their critique was a prominent topic at the beginning of the Reformation. One of the most important questions pertaining to Luther's own critique of indulgences is to what extent it was rooted in a medieval tradition of spirituality.[1]

Ascertaining this heuristic difficulty, however, does not mean that we ought to adopt a model of the decades leading up to the Reformation, such as that of Carl Ullmann,[2] who spoke of "pre-reformers" as if those whom he labeled this way did not have their own place in history but only paved the way for Luther. Even though both Ullmann and I find that persons such as John Ruchrath of Wesel did in fact play a decisive role in the development of reformational spirituality, the goal of our investigation cannot be to make the late Middle Ages into a simple explanation for the Reformation.

But the paradigms developed for the historical investigation of the Reformation *can* be helpful for understanding the critique of indulgences. One robust model of the late Middle Ages has emerged that refuses to understand the late Middle Ages as a one-dimensional linear development. This period is thus neither a pious, holy Middle Ages that would be confronted with the Reformation, nor is it that period of legendary

---

1. Wilhelm Ernst Winterhager, "Ablaßkritik als Indikator sozialen Wandels vor 1517: Ein Beitrag zu Voraussetzungen und Einordnung der Reformation," *Archiv für Reformationsgeschichte* 90 (1999): 6–17 has pointed out the plenty of evidence that both criticism of indulgences was common in 1517 *and* that the income from indulgences had sharply declined.
2. Carl Ullmann, *Reformatoren vor der Reformation: Vornehmlich in Deutschland und den Niederlanden*, 2 vols., 2nd ed. (Gotha: Perthes, 1866).

decadence for which only Luther could provide salvation.[3] Instead, the Middle Ages is characterized by innumerable degrees and directions of tension—these could be held together during the Middle Ages but took on a diversified institutional form in the Reformation. But there are three tensions which we can identify that have great potential to help our understanding: the tension between the participation of laymen and the clerical estate; the tension between a decentralized ecclesial leadership by means of councils/secular authorities or by the singular person of the pope; and finally, the tension between external and internal spirituality.

The following investigation will be roughly delineated according to these three tensions. The tension between laypersons and the clerics will give special focus to anti-clericalism, and the tension of centrality will focus on critique of the papacy. The tension between internal and external spirituality is reflected very directly in the writings critical of indulgences. A measure of protection against narrowly focusing on explaining the Reformation is provided by the fact that the chosen sources in the following text are drawn from all over Europe. Methodologically, this means that the individual testimonies are detached from their original contexts in favor of a consolidation of the history of spirituality, but this brings with it the benefit of grasping indulgence criticism as a pan-European phenomenon that shaped piety in the fifteenth and sixteenth centuries in great breadth and diversity.

## MOTIFS OF CRITICISM OF THE CLERGY

One of the reasons why investigations into indulgence criticism can be so misleading is because some of what appears in retrospect as a critical argument was actually formulated in the course of a lively development of the doctrine of indulgences itself. That means in particular: some of what was formulated before the bull *Salvator noster* expresses opinions and teachings that, at the time of their publication, was still in conformity with papal doctrine. That would change in 1476. As is well known, the bull Sixtus IV (1471–1484) effected an extension of papal power to grant indulgences to the afterlife *per modum suffragii* (by way of suffrage),[4]

---

3. Cf. Volker Leppin, "Die Wittenberger Reformation und der Prozess der Transformation kultureller zu institutionellen Polaritäten," in *Transformationen: Studien zu den Wandlungsprozessen in Theologie und Frömmigkeit zwischen Spätmittelalter und Reformation,* 2nd ed. (Tübingen: Mohr, 2018), 31–68.

4. Heinrich Denzinger, *Compendium of Creeds, Definitions, and Declarations on Matters of Faith and Morals,* 43rd ed., ed. Peter Hünermann, Robert Fastiggi, and Anne Englund Nash (San Francisco: Ignatius Press, 2012), 1398.

thereby confirming and strengthening the hope that indulgences could also be applied to souls in purgatory.

Therefore, when the Parisian theologian Jean Gerson, in a French sermon on All Souls' Day in 1401,[5] preached about the souls of the deceased, he excluded the possibility of indulgences for them.[6] Gerson was still operating within a theological framework that was not forced to assume such a transferability of indulgences to the deceased. It was not until 1502 when Wimpfeling published this sermon (*Sermo II Pro defunctis*) as part of the edition of Gerson's works in Latin that the argument Gerson was making here had, in effect, become one that again reduced papal power relative to the expansion made possible by Sixtus IV. In a series of questions on how to help souls, there was also a concise treatise on indulgences:

> Can indulgences be acquired for the deceased? Answer: I do not think so, for indulgences have been instituted for the sake of merciful care which has its place here until death, but not after death. And the days of indulgence are calculated based on the days of imposed penance.[7]

Gerson utilized solely the logic of the Sacrament of Penance, which provides for a punishment appropriate to the deed but also intends for this punishment to be performed here and now. The transfer of indulgence to the deceased would undo the correspondence of penance and punishment. Gerson regards it as theologically impossible. As mentioned before, in the early fifteenth century, this was completely unproblematic. But it does belong to a large-scale development within indulgence theology; in the sixteenth century, it would mean a *de facto* criticism of the extension of papal and clerical power beyond the boundaries of this world. In this context, it made sense that Gerson would express himself positively toward indulgences and would even consider it plausible that the church's Office of the Keys might also reach until purgatory, but only *per indirectum, propter communionem in caritate* (indirectly because

---

5. See Louis Mourin, *Jean Gerson, Prédicateur français* (Brugge: De Tempel, 1952), 122–23; Nikolaus Paulus, *Geschichte des Ablasses am Ausgang des Mittelalters*, 2nd ed. (Darmstadt: Wissenschaftliche Buchgesellschaft, 2000), 6, assigns 1396–99 as the date.
6. Jean Gerson, *Oeuvres complètes*, ed. Palémon Glorieux, vol. 7/2, No. 344 (Paris: Desclée, 1968), 549–60, 557.
7. *Quarta pars operum Johan-|nis Gerson prius non impressa* (Strasbourg 1502), M 4ʳ: "*Possuntne acquiri indulgentie pro mortuis? Responsio: Teneo quod non: quia indulgentie ordinate sunt curie misericordie qui hic est et durat vsque ad mortem, non autem post mortem. Et sumuntur dies indulgentie pro diebus penitentie iniuncte.*" My translation.

of communion in love).[8] With these words, he was clearly paving the way for the later language employed by Sixtus IV, although still under the pretense of highly restricted ecclesial power. Within the same tract, he clearly emphasized that the extensive authority to bind and dissolve resided only with *papa supremus, scilicet Christus* (the supreme Pope, who is Christ).[9] It was on this basis that he could cautiously recommend the acquisition of indulgences:

> It is sober and healthy council, toward which a pious person ought to work according to his vocation, which encourages the acquisition of indulgences without curious discussion of the exact, apparent and certain quantities or measurability.[10]

Despite these qualifications from Gerson, we can see just how intensely the question of the efficacy of indulgences in the afterlife was discussed in the immediate run-up to *Salvator noster* in the *Floretum* of the Spanish theologian Alfonso Fernández (Tostado) of Madrigal († 1455), a participant in the Council of Basel. In q. 60 on Matthew 16—whereby verse 19 the question of the power of binding and loosing was to be addressed, he explicitly stated that there was no possibility of granting indulgences directly to the deceased:

> Granting indulgences is an act of jurisdiction. The jurisdiction of the church, however, does not extend directly to the dead.[11]

Again, this is by no means a fundamental critique of indulgences but rather a definitional limitation of the scope of indulgences. It takes into account their connection to the Sacrament of Penance and their personalized attribution to the penitent.[12] However, despite the criticism of such applicability to the deceased, Alfonso's treatise also already contained

8. Gerson, *De indulgentiis* (Jean Gerson, *Oeuvres complètes*, ed. Palémon Glorieux, vol. 9, No. 473 (Paris: Desclée, 1973), 654–58, 656; Paulus, *Ablass am Ausgang des Mittelalters* (cf. n. 5), 7.

9. Gerson, *De indulgentiis* (cf. n. 8), 655.

10. Gerson, *De indulgentiis* (cf. n. 8), 656: "*Consilium est ergo sobrium et sanum quod absque curiosa discussione de praecisa vel evidenti ac certa quantificatione seu mensuratione hujusmodi indulgentiarum, studeat homo pius tales acquirere secundum qualitatem suae vocationis.*" My translation.

11. *El tostade sobre sannt matheo. Floretum sancti mathei* (Hispali: Paulus de Colonia, 1491), o.P., c. 16 q. 60: "*Nam concessio indulgentiarum est actus iurisdictionis. Et tamen iurisdictio ecclesie non se extendit directe ad mortuos.*"

12. Alfonso, *Floretum* (see n. 11), c. 16 q. 60 emphasizes that *semper imponitur aliquid opus ei cui indulgentia conceditur*, which can only be applied for the glory of God or for the *utilitas ecclesiae*. Therefore, it is impossible for indulgence to apply to the deceased, who cannot be expected to perform more works.

arguments that would later support the establishment of *Salvator noster*; referring to Thomas Aquinas, he explained that at least some scholars were of the opinion that this transfer was indeed possible if it was true that granting indulgences at a pilgrimage church opened a way for the transfer of indulgences to the deceased.[13] Others, however, he countered, were of the opinion that this was not possible because the indulgence could then be applied to all deceased persons, and thus the order of punitive justice created by God himself would be completely emptied of its intentions.[14] Thus, Alfonso cannot simply be counted among the critics of indulgences. However, he provided arguments that were to become of particular importance for the discussion of indulgences, especially where the limitation of clerical and papal power was at stake.

The most immediate form of indulgence critique was certainly the one that attacked the blatant greed associated with indulgence. This can be neatly categorized with classical anti-clericalism. We find this in a highly developed form with the Lenten sermons from the Franciscan Olivier Maillard († 1502), which were printed in Paris in 1498. On the Festival of the Cathedra Petri (celebrated on February 21 in Paris at the time), he preached on Exodus 24:12, where God says to Moses, "Come up to me on the mountain," (*Ascende ad me in montem*) and used this together with the festival as a hook to speak about the degrees of dignity in the church, giving special attention to the question of the Office of Keys. This led him to treat the matter of the abuse of official privileges—and ultimately indulgence. He posed a rhetorical question asking if it was correct that a usurer could attain the forgiveness of their sins simply by giving money for indulgences. Maillard did not want to believe that and certainly did not want to preach it.[15] He classified the entire phenomenon of indulgence as simony[16] and demanded of the laypersons that they pray to God for an improvement in all areas of the church.[17] This sort of critiquing abuse of power found its way into university teaching. John Major († 1555, taught in Paris starting in 1493) explored the question in the

13. Alfonso, *Floretum* (see n. 11), c. 16 q. 60.
14. Alfonso, *Floretum*, c. 16 q. 60: *tunc posset liberare omnes qui sunt in purgatorio quod non videtur conveniens: quia sic evacuaret ordinem pugnitionis a deo institute*—the verb *evacuare* is worthy of note here; we encounter it in the indulgence discussion with both John Eck and Luther. For more on this, see: Volker Leppin, "Der Einfluss Johannes Ecks auf den jungen Luther," *Luther* 86 (2015): 135–47.
15. *Sacre theologie magistri: necnon | eloquii preconis celeberrimi | fratris oliuerii ordinis milnorum professoris opus quadragesimale | perutilissimum* (Paris, 1508), 26ʳ b.
16. *Sacre theologie magistri*, 26ᵛ a.
17. *Sacre theologie magistri*, 26ᵛ a.

fourth book of his 1509 commentary of Lombard's *Sentences* (d. 20 q. 2) in the context of the Doctrine of Penance "if indulgences are valid" (*an valeant indulgentiae*).[18] As for Alfonso of Madrigal, he found in Matthew 16:19 a decisive biblical passage that argued for the possibility of indulgences.[19] It was also beyond doubt for him that there was a basis for the church's administration of indulgences in the "treasure of the church" (*thesaurus ecclesiae*).[20] He fundamentally affirmed indulgence. But he warns of the abuses of the *quaestores* (those selling indulgences), as well as those who forged the "seal of the church's prelates" (*sigilla praelatorum ecclesie*).[21] The parallels drawn between these two groups highlight a general skepticism toward the sale of indulgences lurking in the background of his thought. He was not alone. In his addition to the Chronicle of Dietrich Engelhaus, Matthias Döring reports in 1451 that many individuals had hoped to acquire indulgence from the relics left in Rome during the Jubilee Year of 1450. He also mocks those who hoped for a complete absolution and refers to others who despise this praxis and its association with the unbridled greed of the Roman Curia.[22]

## MOTIFS OF CRITICISM TOWARD THE PAPACY

It ought not to surprise us that we find a fundamental criticism of indulgences with John Wycliffe. In the debates concerning the papacy of his time, he was increasingly obsessed with curtailing its area of effect. Virtually all papal claims were annulled. For Wycliffe, the pope could only ever hope to be the head of a particular church, namely the earthly one, in contrast to the *ecclesia triumphans* (church triumphant) in heaven. And even here, it was questionable if he could be really considered a member of the church since the church consisted of the community of the predestined and one cannot say with any certainty that he (or any individual for that matter) belonged to this heavenly host.[23] Accordingly, Wycliffe concluded that the pope could exercise no jurisdiction over heavenly matters. Thus, the pope had nothing lasting to effect in purgatory.[24] He

18. For more on this, see: Paulus, *Ablass am Ausgang des Mittelalters* (see n. 5), 71–72.
19. Johannis Maioris, *Quartus Sententiarum* (Paris, 1509), 124ᵛ b.
20. Maior, *Quartus Sententiarum*, 124ᵛ b.
21. Maior, *Quartus Sententiarum*, 125ᵛ a.
22. Matthiae Doeringii *Continuatio Chronici Theodorici Engelhusii, in I. B. Menckenii | Scriptores | rervm | Germanicarvm | praecipve | Saxonicarvm*, vol. 3 (Leipzig, 1730), 1–30, here col. 17.
23. For more on this, see: Volker Leppin, "Der Primat des Papstes im langen 15. Jahrhundert," in *Die Päpste der Renaissance. Politik, Kunst und Musik*, ed. Michael Matheus et al. (Regensburg: Pustet, 2017), 353–80, 354–59.
24. Iohannis Wyclif *Tractatus de ecclesia*, ed. Johann Loserth (London: Trübner, 1886), 565, 26–29.

embedded this idea in c. 23 of his tractate *De ecclesia*, which contained an extensive treatment of the question of the possibility and legality of indulgences. Wycliffe argued that the basic meaning of *indulgentia* meant nothing other than forgiving one of their guilt *gratis*.[25] In this sense, only God could dispense indulgence.[26] If humans want to be part of this, they can, in the sense of the petition of the Lord's Prayer, "forgive us our sins as we forgive those who have sinned against us."[27] Both laypersons and priests could do this.[28] Indeed, God's forgiveness is more likely found in a forgiving layperson than in a cleric who buys or sells indulgences and purports to have authority over that which only God can administer.

But the real thrust of Wycliffe's criticism lays in the question of the pope, for it was only the canonists who had ascribed to him alone the significance of the absolution of sin.[29] No other medieval theologian goes to such lengths to undermine this doctrine. His first step is to declare the entire doctrine of *merita supererogata* (supererogatory merits) to be a human invention, and with it also the treasure of the church (*thesaurus ecclesiae*).[30] Those merits that went beyond what was required, the *merita supererogata*, were what were said to accrete in the treasure trove of merit in the church, and the church could tap this reserve to dispense merit in the form of indulgences. But according to Wycliffe, this was impossible for simple logical reasons. The merits performed by Christ and the saints belonged to the past and thus could not be somehow deposited, stored or distributed in the present.[31] If God were to decide to allow the merits of a saint to benefit another person, the decision of a pope could affect nothing about it.[32]

However, Wycliffe went even further in his criticism. He criticized the idea that indulgences could be sold, denoting it as blasphemy. Since salvation was found ultimately in Christ, this would mean that God did not sell righteousness but, since he is righteousness itself, that he would make himself a product.[33] Thus, whoever claimed to be able to transfer indulgence in the name of God perpetrated blasphemy. The giving of indulgence—and Wycliffe was not only speaking of *selling* indulgence—is

25. Wyclif, *Tractatus de ecclesia*, 549, 6–15.
26. Wyclif, *Tractatus de ecclesia*, 576, 30–31.
27. Wyclif, *Tractatus de ecclesia*, 551, 6–12.
28. Wyclif, *Tractatus de ecclesia*, 575, 14–577, 17.
29. Wyclif, *Tractatus de ecclesia*, 549, 20–21.
30. Wyclif, *Tractatus de ecclesia*, 551, 6–12.
31. Wyclif, *Tractatus de ecclesia*, 564, 11–15.
32. Wyclif, *Tractatus de ecclesia*, 569, 23–25.
33. Wyclif, *Tractatus de ecclesia*, 560, 34–561, 10.

nothing other than proof that the pope does not belong to Christ.[34] After all, if he was really the successor to Peter, he would not purport such things but would follow Peter's example of humility.[35] Accordingly, the discussion of indulgence led Wycliffe to his basic argument against the papacy: Christ alone is the head of the church.[36]

What Wycliffe could handle as a theoretical tract (albeit a very pointed one) took on concrete, present significance when Jan Hus adopted his thought in a disputation criticizing (Anti-)Pope John XXIII's 1412 call for a crusade against King Ladislaus.[37] In this context, the question of indulgences also played a decisive role: Hus by no means denied that priests could grant a full indulgence, and that of guilt as well as punishment. But this was permissible only on the basis of a special revelation[38]—even for the pope. A similar tension between the general rule and the possibility of going beyond it is also evident in Hus's statement that sacramental penance is necessary—even if *contritio* is sufficient for Christ,[39] who is present everywhere. Thus, according to Hus, the sacramental event gains its primary significance from the fact that it intensifies the *contritio* as a necessary part. The high weight of this disposition is then also shown in the fact that an indulgence can only be given to the one who is in a proper relationship with God.[40] Then it does not even need a specific form—as Hus underlines with the example of the sinner (traditionally equated with Mary Magdalene) whom Jesus Christ forgave (Luke 7:36–50).[41] Here, we can clearly see how the contemporary, ecclesiologically relevant dispute with the pope concerning obedience (according to Council of Pisa) and an emphasis on internal piety intertwine to form a poignant argument in the given situation.

Such new criticism had lasting effects. The ecclesiological question was further developed by John Ruchrath of Wesel along the lines of Wycliffe's argumentation into a fundamental question of the authoritative basis for

34. Wyclif, *Tractatus de ecclesia,* 561, 19–30.
35. Wyclif, *Tractatus de ecclesia*, 562, 5–18.
36. Wyclif, *Tractatus de ecclesia*, 563, 2.
37. *Quaestio disputata de indulgentiis, in Historia | et | monumenta | joannis hus | atque | hieronymi | pragensis,* vol. 1 (Nürnberg: Montanus, 1715), 215–35; see also: Hus, *Contra cruciatam,* CCHr. CM 238, 133–44; for the context, see: Pavel Soukup, "Jan Hus und der Prager Ablassstreit von 1412," in *Die mittelalterlichen Ablasskampagnen: Luthers Thesen von 1517 im Kontext,* ed. Andreas Rehberg (Berlin: De Gruyter, 2017), 485–500, 489; for a comparison between the thought of Hus and Wycliffe, see: Herbert B. Workman, *John Wylif: A Study of the English Medieval Church,* vol. 2 (Oxford: Clarendon, 1926), 7.
38. Hus, *Quaestio disputata,* 216–17, cf. n. 37.
39. Hus, *Quaestio disputata,* 217.
40. Hus, *Quaestio disputata,* 217.
41. Hus, *Quaestio disputata,* 217.

church doctrine. However, he had to answer for this also before ecclesiastical authorities.[42] He wrote a treatise *De indulgentiis*, which started from a clear biblical position: in all the writings of Jesus Christ, there was no mention of an indulgence, nor any mention in the other apostolic writings of the New Testament or in the church fathers.[43] In fact, Ruchrath of Wesel took the argumentation even further: from the Holy Scriptures, it is clear that God forgives guilt, including the eternal punishment deserved by original sin,[44] but not the temporal punishment that one incurs in the course of one's life.[45] Conversely, the pope and the priests are able to remit punishments imposed by man through positive justice, but not those imposed by God.[46] Therefore, indulgences could be considered valid as such only when they remove *humanly* imposed punishments.[47] But for life and faith, only what is made known by revelation can be considered binding. Ruchrath saw nothing about indulgences in the revelation of Scripture.[48] Therefore all indulgences, which are proclaimed beyond the narrow framework described here, are nothing but pious deception of the faithful (*pie fraudes fidelium*),[49] as Wesel explained with reference to Petrus Cantor. In an ironic twist of his argument, he then repeated the argument of Peter of Tarentasia, who had tried to refute the view that the church had no right to grant indulgences by arguing:

> If the church does not absolve the punishments dealt by God when it gives out indulgences, then the church does more damage than it helps because by means of absolution it leads from the satisfaction of sins to even graver punishments in purgatory.[50]

Indulgences as deception of the faithful and harm to all: this was a plausible criticism of indulgences, combined with an implicit *sola scriptura* idea. And, at the time, Ruchrath was not alone with such considerations.

---

42. Markus Wriedt, "Johannes Rucherath," in *Religion in Geschichte und Gegenwart*, vol. 4, 4th ed. (Tübingen: Mohr, 2001), 530–31.

43. Johann Ruchrath von Wesel, "De indulgentiis," in *Reformtheologen des 15. Jahrhunderts: Johann Pupper von Goch, Johann Ruchrath von Wesel, Wessel Gansfort*, ed. Gustav Adolf Benrath (Gütersloh: Gütersloher Verlagshaus, 1968), 39–60, 39.

44. Wesel, "De indulgentiis," 48.

45. Wesel, "De indulgentiis," 51, with reference to 40.

46. Wesel, "De indulgentiis," 41.

47. Wesel, "De indulgentiis," 51.

48. Wesel, "De indulgentiis," 52.

49. Wesel, "De indulgentiis," 58.

50. Wesel, "De indulgentiis," 59: "*Si ecclesia dando indulgencias non absoluit a penis taxatis a deo, ergo ecclesia dando indulgencias pocius nocet quam prosit, quia a penis satisfactoriis absoluendo ad grauiores purgatorias transmittat*"; subsequently, (Wesel, "De indulgentiis," 60) refers to earlier material with the comment: "*Ad secundum argumentum respondetur totum concedendo.*"

The idea he developed that indulgences were a fraud spread widely: in his 1470 Christenspiegel, Dietrich Kolde of Münster wrote that those who participate in indulgences sin against the second commandment; they "carry out false lists[51] and immodest indulgences for a number of prayers through which they deceive many people and dishonor God."[52]

Gerson's above-mentioned criticism of indulgence for the deceased also had an aspect of a paranesis of confession: no one should find comfort in the idea that someone could acquire indulgence for them after their death. To the contrary, he states:

> I also say that absolution from punishments and guilt frees from purgatory and a person can desire, attain and use it if it comes into effect. This is true even if a person is in the hour of their death and seeks grace—they will be freed from purgatory and their prayer will be heard.[53]

A post-mortem indulgence, which was too easy to attain, would erode the desire for absolution in the Sacrament of Penance. We know Gerson primarily as the author of an *ars moriendi*, and he is true to that here, reminding the reader of the proper attitude as they draw toward their death. The proper usage of clerical transmission of penance takes place through the proper attitude of penance (so the train of thought), and, in the last idea, this attitude can be expressed through sincere prayer. Such prayer can even substitute the Sacrament of Penance. Gerson thus opens a path to an internalized form of salvation from the pains of purgatory, which is no longer coupled to indulgence but rather with the internal attitude toward God. This form of criticism that used internal penitent spirituality to criticize externalized indulgence constituted a significant current of late-medieval criticism of indulgence.

## INTERNAL AND EXTERNAL ACTS

We also see this with the above-mentioned Parisian teacher John Major. He explicitly warns of the idea that an external act can add to an internal

---

51. Determined by Paulus, *Ablass im Ausgang des Mittelalters* (cf. n. 5), 254, most likely as lists.
52. *Der Christenspiegel des Dietrich Kolde von Münster*, ed. Clemens Drees (Werl: Dietrich-Coelde-Verlag, 1954), 91: "*die valsche rolkens ende onbescheidelicken aflaten* [Ablässe] *voer sommige gebeden schriuen daer si vele menschen mede Bedrieghen ende got onteeren*".
53. Gerson, *Quarta Pars* (cf. n. 7), M 4ʳ: "*Dico etiam quod absolutio a pena et culpa liberat a purgatorio et eam homo desiderare potest / impetrare et eay vti. Si habita fuerit. Etiam si in postrema hora mortis persona petat gratiam vt liberata sit a purgatorio, oratio sua exauditur.*" My translation.

one.[54] Accordingly, he repeatedly emphasized that an indulgence can only be considered valid if you truly regret and confess. He further deepens the internal components with his addition that this was even true if you felt *contritio* and had previously had the will to confess.[55] His theology of penance made *satisfactio* and the reductive indulgence completely dependent on internal regret. This results in interesting considerations for a theology of indulgence that argue against the characteristic quantification that we know of indulgence. For example, if you traveled from Paddington to Rome in a jubilee year, you received the same amount of indulgence as someone who came from Viterbo just a few kilometers away.[56] A wealthy man, who might tithe three times the required sum, would not receive more than a poor woman.[57]

Strictly speaking, this was not all criticism of indulgence but can all be seen as various facets of the then contemporary theology of indulgence. However, this facet begins to get more pronounced in the late Middle Ages. Olivier Maillard developed a much sharper criticism, ultimately calling into question any legitimacy of indulgences whatsoever. Referring to Durandus of St. Portiano, he explained that *nichil* [. . .] *certum in sacra scriptura* (nothing certain in Holy Scripture) could be found about indulgence and nothing was to be read in the church fathers either.[58] This sets the stage for a fictitious woman in a parish who says, "Father, I do not know if they are good" (*Pater, nescio si sint bone*),[59] to which his own voice denies the "necessity or a justified and rational reason" (*necessitas aut iusta et rationabilis causa*) for indulgences.[60] He considered the only true indulgence to be to stop sinning in one's life.

In the context of mysticism and the *Devotio moderna*, the emphasis on internal experience became more fundamental. Arnold Angenendt has pointed out that the exact moment when Clemens IV lays a legal framework for indulgence in the bull *Unigenitus Filius* is also the moment when Henry Suso is pushing his own understanding of indulgence, which understands indulgence to be entirely founded in mystical union with

---

54. Major, *IV Sent* (cf. n. 19), 125ʳ a: "*nec tamen consequens est quod actus exterior aliquid boni superaddit actui interiori.*"
55. Major, *IV Sent*, 125ʳ a.
56. Major, *IV Sent*, 125ʳ a–b.
57. Major, *IV Sent*, 125ʳ b.
58. Maillard, *Opus quadragesimale* (cf. n. 15), 26ʳ a.
59. Maillard, *Opus quadragesimale*, 26ʳ a.
60. Maillard, *Opus quadragesimale*, 26ʳ b.

Christ.[61] In chapter 14 of the *Büchlein der ewigen Weisheit*, Suso begins his argumentation with the insight that God's justice demands that every sin must be atoned for and that *die ungeleisten Büsse in dem heissen eitoven dez grimmen vegfúres muste leisten* ("the unaccomplished atonement has to be performed in the scorching furnace of grim purgatory").[62] Due to "how long this would last"[63] for the soul, Christ opened a different path:

> It can easily do penance and make amends through my innocent and noble suffering. The soul can simply reach into the precious treasure of the merit I earned and draw on it for itself. Even if it were supposed to burn in purgatory for a thousand years, it has removed its guilt and done its penance in a short time so that it enters into eternal joy without any purgatory.[64]

It is not only the substitution of purgatory that brings Suso into conflict with the blossoming Doctrine of Purgatory. His language of the "treasure" may have been an even greater problem for him. It sounds blatantly like the formula of *thesaurus ecclesiae* that Clemens IV adopted. According to Suso, the treasure of Christ's merits is not transmitted sacramentally through the penitential three-step of *contritio, confessio,* and *satisfaction* (contrition, confession, and satisfaction). Instead, the faithful receive these merits by means of an existential penitent connection to Christ, which Suso explains with the concept of *grifen* (sorrow):

> It is accomplished as follows: 1. A person considers with a sorrowful heart very carefully and often the seriousness and number of his offenses, for which he has so clearly deserved angry looks from his heavenly Father. 2. He should then consider as nothing his own acts of atonement because, compared to his sins, they are a drop in the ocean. 3. He should then joyfully consider the immensity of my atonement because the smallest drop of my precious blood that flowed abundantly all over out of my loving body could atone for the sins of a thousand worlds. And yet each person draws this atonement to himself only to the extent that he identifies himself with me by suffering along with me. 4. Finally, a person should humbly and beseechingly sink his small self into the immensity of my atonement and cling to it.[65]

---

61. For the following argumentation, cf. Arnold Angenendt, "Seuse Lehre vom Ablaß," in *Reformatio ecclesiae: FS Erwin Iserloh*, ed. Remigius Bäumer (Paderborn: Aschendorff, 1980), 143–54, 145. 148; see also Angenendt's comparison of Suso and Luther in Angenendt, "Seuse Lehre vom Ablaß," 152–53.

62. Henry Suso, "Little Book of Eternal Wisdom," in *The Exemplar, with Two German Sermons*, trans. and ed. Frank Tobin (Mahwah, NJ: Paulist Press, 1989), 252.

63. Suso, "Little Book of Eternal Wisdom," 252.

64. Suso, "Little Book of Eternal Wisdom," 252.

65. Suso, "Little Book of Eternal Wisdom," 252.

What Suso describes here is a form of internalization that is founded entirely in *contritio*. Works have been replaced with a scorning and destructive attitude. An individual finds comfort solely in the humility of Jesus Christ—and therein a rapaciously quick salvation from the fires of purgatory. When Arnold Angenendt speaks here of a doctrine of indulgence, he is being far too cautious. Suso developed a form of spirituality that skips indulgence altogether. Of course, he knows the basic doctrine of indulgence and does not call it into question,[66] but what he develops here removes the "middlemen" (and things) from penitence, which leaves very little room for purgatory or for indulgence. Angenendt has appropriately pointed out that Suso's arguments were anything but marginal for the medieval world. The *Horologium sapientiae* (a Latin version of the *Büchlein*) could be counted among the bestselling books of the Middle Ages, and, as Angenendt emphasizes, it contains the idea embedded within the salvatory clauses concerning orthodox doctrine of indulgence that individual human works must be made irrelevant for the process of salvation.[67] The quantitative spirituality of indulgence was anything but the normal piety of the late Middle Ages. It was directly confronted with a persistent, latent, and yet also explicit criticism of indulgences and their proclamation and sale.

Suso clearly had an effect on a great number of individuals, including John of Staupitz. In one of his sermons (probably held in Nurnberg in spring of 1517, only extent in summary),[68] he developed a concept of penitence with very close similarities to Suso's. They nearly cite the statements from the *Büchlein*:

> And this is true that a person who feels sincere regret does not only escape hell but also the punishment of Purgatory entirely, even if he passes away in bad behavior and without the Christian sacraments.[69]

---

66. Heinrich Seuse, *Deutsche Schriften*, ed. Karl Bihlmeyer (Stuttgart: Kohlhammer 1907), 525, 22–23.

67. Pius Künzle, ed., *Heinrich Seuses Horologium Sapientiae* (Freiburg: Universitätsverlag, 1977, 497, 16; cf. Angenendt, *Seuses Ablasslehre* (cf. fn. 61), 149; Berndt Hamm, "Wollen und Nicht-Können als Thema der spätmittelalterlichen Bußseelsorge," in *Spätmittelalterliche Frömmigkeit zwischen Ideal und Praxis*, ed. Berndt Hamm and Thomas Lentes (Tübingen: Mohr, 2001), 111–46, 142–43; Hamm, *Ablass und Reformation: Erstaunliche Kohärenzen* (Tübingen: Mohr, 2016), 188–89.

68. Joachim Carl Friedrich Knaake, ed., *Johann von Staupitzens sämmtliche Werke/Iohannis Staupitii Opera, quae reperiri potuerant omnia*, Erster Band: Deutsche Schriften (Postdam: A. Krausnick, 1867), 15; for more on the indulgence criticim of Staupitz, cf. Berndt Hamm, *Ablass und Reformation* (cf. n. 68), 228–30.

69. Staupitz, *Operae* (cf. n. 68): "*Vnd dis ist war das ein mensch ein so hertzliche rew furnemend mag nit allein der hellen entpfliehen, Sonder auch domit die pein des fegfeurs, ob er gleich in vngeperligkait Vnd un die Christenlichen Sacrament wurd verfarn, genntzlich ablegen.*" My translation.

It was this intensified understanding of piety that he brought even more clearly and sharply against the papal praxis of indulgence:

> And it is not of the kind, as the simple people often have been told by many, that a person receives forgiveness of sins by earnestly confessing and participating in the temporal delivering of the papal indulgence, but the sound of a golden coin falling into the till does not relieve a sinner of their sins but rather the most important thing is that it is preceded by a contrite heart.[70]

What might appear here as a reminder of the proper manner of dealing with indulgence as contained in the official instructions—namely that indulgence without prior concrete, sacramental penance and without true *contritio* can have no effect—is then developed even further by Staupitz in the following passage. A regretful, penitent heart can even replace sacramental penance—and with it, indulgence:

> It is entirely without doubt that a person can receive forgiveness of their misdeeds through right and proper contrition, even without any indulgence which they might use, but it is unbelievable and groundless that a person can find the same [forgiveness] even with the highest papal pardon where there is no true, sincere regret about their sins.[71]

In 1517, the mystical intensification of penitent spirituality would become a strong factor for the extensive relativization of the power of indulgences.

★ ★ ★

At the end of this essay, we will examine an orientation toward the Reformation. Such a clear statement by Staupitz containing a theological critique of indulgence, as well as his formulation of a sharp attack from spring of 1517 on the idea that "as soon as a coin in the coffer rings, a soul from

---

70. Staupitz, *Operae*, 18: "*VNd hat nit die weyse wie durch etliche In das einfeltig volcklein zu offtermalen gepildet wirdet, So der mensch seine sunden vleissig peicht vnd sich dann der Bapstlichen indulgentz durch sein zeitliche handtraichung tailhaftig mach das er domit vergebung der sunden erlang, dann der klangk des guldens so der In die geld kisten felt, wirdet den sunder seiner sunden nit entledigen Sondern dem allem muss furnemlich vnd zuvorderst ein recht berwet hertz vorgeen.*"

71. Staupitz, *Operae*, 18: "*Ist auch gantz onzweiffenlich, das der mensch durch ain rechtgegrundte ordentliche rew, auch on allen ablas des er sich mocht geprauchen vergebung seiner missethat erlangen kann, aber vnglaublich vnd on allen grundt, das ein mensch auch mit der hochsten babstlichen begnadung, Wo nit zuvor ain ware hertzliche rew uber seine sunden mitlaufft verzeihung derselben mag befinden.*"

purgatory springs" (also attacked by Luther),[72] indicate just what deep roots Luther's own criticism of indulgence has in the medieval indulgence criticism handled here. But even the Reformation will not have the last word.

An examination of medieval spirituality yields widely disparate examples of indulgence criticism. Taken together, they indicate just how inappropriate it would be to understand indulgence as a singular identifying marker of the Middle Ages. Indulgence certainly belonged to the pronounced features of this period, but it was never simply accepted without contradiction. Powerful criticism was derived from the lived faith of the Middle Ages itself. With mysticism—seen poignantly with Suso, one of the most-read medieval authors of the late Middle Ages—we get an insight into a cultural current that tended to relativize or even devalue indulgence. Others gave utterance to an even more blunt criticism when they decried the greed of the indulgence merchants or the pope's claims to power. Indulgence was a given for the Middle Ages but also a permanent object of contention.

72. WA 1:234.9–10: *Hominem praedicant, qui statim ut iactus nummus in cistam tinnierit evolare dicunt animam.*

# 2.

# "Solus Christus" from Late Medieval<br>Passion Piety to Reformation Faith

I complained once to my dear Staupitz regarding the delicacy of predestination. He stated that predestination is understood and found in the wounds of Christ, nowhere else; as it is written: Hear him! The Father is too high. But the Father has said, "I will give you a way to come to me, namely, Christ. Go, believe, cling to Christ, so that you will find who I am in due time." But we don't do this, therefore God is incomprehensible for us, unthinkable; he is not understood, he does not want to be grasped outside of Christ.[1]

The famous confessional counsel that Staupitz gave Luther, probably in 1516,[2] reflects how deeply the exclusive particle of *solus Christus* is rooted in late-medieval passion piety. Specifically, it shows that the centrality of Christ, at least for Luther's superior and confessor,[3] was very closely

---

1. "*Ego semel conquerebar de sublimitate praedestinationis Staupitio meo. Respondit mihi: In vulneribus Christi intelligitur praedestinatio et invenitur, non alibi, quia scriptum est: Hunc audite. Der vater is zu hoch, sed dixit Pater: Ego dabo viam veniendi ad me, nempe Christum. Ite, credite, hengt euch an den Christum, so wirts sichs wol finden, quis sim, suo tempore. Das thun wir nicht, ideo Deus est nobis incomprehensibilis, incogitabilis; er wirt nicht begriffen, er will ungefast sein extra Christum.*" WA TR 2:112.9–16 (No. 1490).
2. In any case, this dating is valid if one can connect the advice concerning predestination with being frightened by the body of Christ at Eisleben, as in Wilhelm-Ernst Winterhager, "Martin Luther und das Amt des Provinzialvikars in der Reformkongregation der deutschen Augustiner-Eremiten," *Vita religiosa im Mittelalter: Festschrift für Kaspar Elm zum 70. Geburtstag*, ed. Franz J. Felten and Nikolas Jaspert (Berlin: Duncker & Humblot, 1999), 707–38, 736.
3. On Staupitz, see Berndt Hamm, "Johann von Staupitz (ca. 1468–1524)—spätmittelalterlicher Reformer und 'Vater' der Reformation," *Archiv für Reformationsgeschichte* 92 (2001): 6–41; Berndt Hamm, "Staupitz, Johannes von," *Theologische Realenzyklopädie* 32 (2001): 119–27.

connected to elements of passion piety. It is in the wounds of Christ that the young Martin Luther is supposed to seek salvation.

The counsel Staupitz gives here stands in the context of a particular inward piety oriented toward the person and, above all else, the suffering of Christ. This had become a central theme of spiritual and theological reflection, particularly in those circles that Berndt Hamm has classified as "theologians of piety," a category that includes the *Devotio moderna*.[4]

## CHRISTOCENTRIC SOTERIOLOGY IN THE DEVOTIONAL THEOLOGY OF THE LATE MIDDLE AGES

Perhaps the clearest expression of devotion to Christ in the late Middle Ages is found in the *Imitation of Christ* by Thomas à Kempis, considered the basic reference point of the *Devotio moderna*. The old question of whether á Kempis was the author or merely the editor of this work can be set aside due to the current state of research,[5] which has disentangled itself from the strong concept of authorship of the nineteenth century.[6] What is certain is that the text compiled by à Kempis was completed by 1441[7] and that it was initially named by him after the opening citation of John 8:12,[8] "Qui sequitur me . . . "[9] Not only was the title later replaced by *De imitatione Christi*[10] but the order of the four books was also rearranged to conform with the traditional order of these chapters of this work. The

On his theology, see also David Steinmetz, *Luther and Staupitz: An Essay in the Intellectual Origins of the Protestant Reformation* (Durham: Duke University Press, 1980).

4. See Berndt Hamm, "Frömmigkeit als Gegenstand theologiegeschichtlicher Forschung. Methodisch-historische Überlegung am Beispiel von Spätmittelalter und Reformation" in Berndt Hamm, *Religiosität im späten Mittelalter: Spannungspole, Neuaufbrüche, Normierungen*, eds. Reinhold Friedrich and Wolfgang Simon (Tübingen: Mohr Siebeck, 2011), 85–115; Berndt Hamm, "Was ist Frömmigkeitstheologie? Überlegungen zum 14. bis 16. Jahrhundert," in Hamm, *Religiosität im späten Mittelalter*, 116–53.

5. See Cebus C. de Bruin, "Ist Geert Groote der Verfasser des Büchleins *De imitatione Christi*? Kritische Randbemerkungen zu Van Ginnekens Hypothese betreffs der Autorschaft der Imitatio," in *Altdeutsch und altniederländische Mystik*, ed. Kurt Ruh (Darmstadt: Wissenschaftliche Buchgesellschaft, 1964), 462–96.

6. See Rudolf van Dijk, "Spiritualität der 'inicheit.' Mystik und Kirchenkritik in der Devotio Moderna," in Mariano Delgado, ed., *Die Kirchenkritik der Mystiker: Prophetie aus Gotteserfahrung*, vol. 2 (Stuttgart: Kohlhammer, 2005), 9–38, 26.

7. On the possible time of writing, see Marinus K. A. van den Berg, "Thomas van Kempen," *Ons Geestelijk Erf* 77 (2003): 9–29, 25–26.

8. Thomas à Kempis, *De imitatione Christi* 1. I c. 1, *Thomae Hemerken a Kempis Opera Omnia*, ed. Joseph Pohl, vol. 2 (Freiburg: Sumptibus Herder, 1904), 5, 7–8.

9. Dijk, "Spiritualität."

10. Dijk, "Spiritualität," 27.

book on the Eucharist, which originally had been the third, was made the fourth, and given the additional weight of being the conclusion, this change gave the impression that the booklet culminated in Eucharistic piety.[11] In fact, the original version had the *Liber internae consolationis* at the end. In its reception, as Rudolf van Dijk states, this rearrangement "led to an underemphasis on mysticism."[12] Read in the original order, the *Imitatio Christi* culminates in an immersion in God. The last chapter is entitled: "That all hope and confidence must be fixed on God alone."[13] The exclusive formula *solo Deo*, as well as the affective concept of *fiducia*, indicate the basic orientation of this theology as related to God. This affective path that leads exclusively to God begins with Christ: "Let our highest concern be this: to meditate on the life of Jesus Christ."[14] This disposition leads to humility,[15] and finally, through the total suppression of one's heart, to a true *libertas*. According to á Kempis, one can only achieve this in the fear of God,[16] a freedom that consists of freedom from everything created.[17] Humans reach this in a double movement[18]—the despising of oneself and the love for Jesus—who "above all wants to be loved."[19] This love is carried out in turn with an intensity that á Kempis gains from the materials of mysticism:

> Come, faithful soul, prepare your heart for this bridegroom, so that he may deign to come to you and dwell in you. For thus he says: If anyone loves me, he will keep my word, and we will come to him and make our home with him.[20]

It is therefore the bridal encounter with Jesus that leads to the *solus Deus*. But this way, which according to John 14:6 is Jesus Christ himself,[21] is a way of the cross where Jesus Christ not only has proceeded but is also still proceeding.[22] The ascent to God can only be realized through suffering, grounded in the meditation of Christ. In this way, the *crux* becomes the

11. Dijk, "Spiritualität"; see Kurt Ruh, *Geschichte der abendländischen Mystik. Vierter Band: Die niederländische Mystik des 14. bis 16. Jahrhunderts* (Munich: C. H. Beck, 1999), 189.
12. Dijk, "Spiritualität," 29.
13. Thomas á Kempis, *De imitatione Christi* 1. III c. 59, 261, 12–13.
14. Thomas á Kempis, *De imitatione Christi* 1. I c. 1, 5, 13–14.
15. Thomas á Kempis, *De imitatione Christi* 1. I c. 2, 7.
16. Thomas á Kempis, *De imitatione Christi* 1. I c. 21, 39, 17–19.
17. Thomas á Kempis, *De imitatione Christi* 1. II c. 8, 73, 7–9.
18. Thomas á Kempis, *De imitatione Christi* 1. II c. 7, 71, 4–7.
19. Thomas á Kempis, *De imitatione Christi* 1. II c. 7, 70, 6–7.
20. Thomas á Kempis, *De imitatione Christi* 1. III c. 56: 253, 4.
21. Thomas á Kempis, *De imitatione Christi* 1. III c. 56: 39, 17–19.
22. Thomas á Kempis, *De imitatione Christi* 1. III c. 56: 254, 8–25.

actual *gloria* of human beings.[23] The rich distribution of manuscripts that the *Imitatio Christi* soon enjoyed indicates that such Christocentricity found rich soil in late-medieval piety[24]—even if, in addition to these forms of inner devotion to Christ, there was also a stronger and contrasting idea of the path to God, as seen in the equally widespread *Himmelsstraß* of Stephan of Landskron, which primarily sought to lead the way to heaven through learning and heeding the articles of faith and the Ten Commandments.[25]

This same deepening and introspection can be found in the writings of John of Paltz, in particular his *Coelifodina*, preceded a few years earlier by a much more concise German edition of the *Heavenly Mine* (himmlische Fundgrube), which was reprinted more than twenty times between 1490 and 1521.[26] This popular book went back to sermons that Paltz had given to Frederick the Wise at his request.[27] Published by Kachelofen in Leipzig in 1490, it begins with a reference in which we hear what Staupitz advised Luther a few years later, at the same time making clear its anchoring in Bernard's mysticism:[28] "The holy, sweet teacher Saint Bernard says in his book on The Song of Songs, that there is neither a more useful nor sturdier thing to heal the wounds of sin than contemplating the wounds of Christ."[29]

23. Thomas á Kempis, *De imitatione Christi* 1. III c. 56: 254, 25–26.
24. See also the overall assessment of Robert Rosin, "Reformation Christology: Some Luther Starting Points," *Concordia Theological Quarterly* 71 (2007): 147–68, 159, which refers to Thomas à Kempis, Tauler, and Bernard, as well as the *Theologia Germanica*.
25. Stephan von Landskron, *Die Hymelstrazs: Mit einer Einleitung und vergleichenden Betrachtung zum Sprachgebrauch in den Frühdrucken* (Augsburg: Gerardus Johannes Jaspers, 1484, 1501, 1510; Amsterdam: Rodopi, 1979), especially 3ʳ.
26. Cf. Johannes von Paltz, *Werke. Vol. 3: Opuscula* (Berlin: De Gruyter, 1989), 158; Berndt Hamm, *Frömmigkeitstheologie am Anfang des 16. Jahrhunderts: Studien zu Johannes von Paltz und seinem Umkreis* (Tübingen: Mohr Siebeck, 1982), 110–11; Christoph Burger, "Die Passionsharmonie des Augustinereremiten Johannes von Paltz (ca. 1445–1511)," in *Evangelienharmonien des Mittelalters* (Asson: Royal Van Gorcum, 2004), 123–38, 125–28.
27. Paltz, *Werke* 3, 202, 1–15; Hamm, *Frömmigkeitstheologie*, 111–12.
28. Franz Posset, *The Real Luther: A Friar at Erfurt & Wittenberg* (St. Louis: Concordia, 2011), 86–87, in a way correctly, but a bit unilaterally, speaks of a "Bernard Renaissance" Luther took part in. Wolfhart Pannenberg, "'Extra nos'—Ein Beitrag Luthers zur christlichen Frömmigkeit" in Albert Raffel, ed., *Weg und Weite: Offene Wege: Festschrift für Karl Lehmann* (Freiburg: Herder, 2001), 197–205, 200–01, construes a line of development from late-medieval mysticism to Luther by ascribing, on the one hand, mysticism of benevolence to the first, and on the other, mysticism of faith to the Reformation. However, this simplifies the actual developments considerably.
29. Paltz, *Werke* 3, 202, 18–20, which seems to allude to Bernard of Clairvaux's *Sermon in canticum canticorum* 62, 7. Bernard of Clairvaux, *Sämtliche Werke. Lateinisch/Deutsch*, ed. Gerhard B. Winkler, vol. 6 (Innsbruck: Tyrolia Verlaganstalt, 1995), 332, 24–26.

It is precisely this contemplation of the sufferings of Christ, with reference to a citation of Pseudo-Albert,[30] that is contrasted with external forms of piety.[31] Paltz opens the way to this contemplation very practically by advising meditation on a painted crucifix, on which the viewer should contemplate the five wounds, especially the side wound.[32] It is obvious that the text is intertwined with the iconographic tradition of the late Middle Ages.

Correspondingly, a Cologne manuscript from 1508 with illustrations attributed to the Master of the St. Bartholomew Altarpiece offers a depiction of the *arma Christi* and the five wounds of Christ at the beginning, after a miniature of Christ's entry into Jerusalem.[33] This pattern of depicting the wounds of Christ resonates with a whole number of images of suffering in the late Middle Ages.[34] Along with the *arma Christi* (instruments of Christ's suffering),[35] the Man of Sorrows is probably the most widespread,[36] and there is also an example in this manuscript.[37] A look at this type of art points us again to the Wittenberg context. Around 1515, Lucas Cranach painted a Man of Sorrows that concentrates on the upper body of the sufferer, that is, it does not show the wounds on the feet, and it alludes to the motif of the *arma Christi* by a scourge on Christ's lap.[38] As in Paltz's text, the special focus here, as was common in the genre of Jesus as the Man of Sorrows, lies on the side wound above all. This picture is particularly remarkable because it was reproduced again in 1537 with

30. Paltz, *Werke* 3, 202–03. The quotation seems to follow the model of John of Dorsten, *De celebratione missae* (Erfurt, c.1488), unpaginated (fol. 15ᵛ–16ʳ): "*Dicit namque Albertus Simplex memoria passionis christi maioris est meriti. quam si quotidie ieiunares in pane et aqua. aut quotidie psalterium integrum decantares. Aut te quotidie usque ad effusionem sanguis disciplinares*" (For Albert Simplex says that the memory of Christ's passion is of greater merit than if you fast daily on bread and water, or daily chant the entire psalter, or even if you practice a daily discipline so far as to shed your own blood). See on identification, Paltz, *Werke* 3, 202–03, fn. 8; there is also proof of a German version in a Nuremberg manuscript, which explains the three lists used by Paltz.
31. Paltz, *Werke* 3, 202, 20–203.
32. On devotion to the side wound of Christ in the late Middle Ages, see Berndt Hamm, "Die 'nahe Gnade'—innovative Züge der spätmittelalterlichen Theologie und Frömmigkeit," in Hamm, *Religiosität im späten Mittelalter*, 544–60, 554–55.
33. Paltz, *Werke* 3, 188; on the image of the wounds, see especially illustration 2.
34. S. E. Sauser, "Wunden Christi," in *Lexikon der christlichen Ikonographie*, vol. 1 (Freiburg: Herder, 1968), 540–42.
35. See Anon., "Arma Christi" in *Lexikon der christlichen Ikonographie*, vol. 1 (Freiburg: Herder, 1968), 183–87.
36. On the history of the motif, see Martin O'Kane, "Picturing the 'Man of Sorrows': The Passion-Filled Afterlives of a Biblical Icon," *Religion and the Arts* 9 (2005): 62–100, esp. 62–84.
37. Paltz, *Werke* 3, 188; see esp. illustration 3.
38. Rainer Stamm, ed., *Lucas Cranach der Schnellste* (Bremen: Hachmannedition, 2009).

only slight modifications, but now as a work probably by the younger Cranach in Wittenberg.[39] What Bodo Brinkmann and Gabriel Dette ascribe to this later work with Reformation origins also applies *mutatis mutandis* to the earlier example, which presumably dates back to the time before Luther's public appearance:

> The pictorial form has been very popular since the 14th century. The achievement of the Cranach workshop is that it has been sharpened by consistent, pictorial logic while at the same time reducing and concentrating the image: Cranach's realization of the subject does not contend with assisting angelic figures with their gestures of mourning or with a full assembly of the *arma Christi*—the instruments of suffering—but with a precise depiction of the martyred body, in which every detail deliberately evokes certain aspects of the Passion.[40]

In devotional literature, as well as in art, there is a concentration on the person and the suffering of Jesus. Here, "Christ hanging on the cross" becomes the "book of life,"[41] and the image of the Man of Sorrows shows what an amazing continuity this devotion to Christ has through the beginning of the Reformation movement.[42]

39. See Bodo Brinkmann, ed., *Cranach der Ältere* (Ostfildern: Hatje Cantz Verlag, 2007), 240–41; Stamm, *Cranach*, 77, n. 23. At the same time, another Man of Sorrows of the same type was created by Cranach the Elder (Stamm, *Cranach*, 81, n. 24). The portrait by the younger Cranach was still used intensively in the devotional culture of the seventeenth and eighteenth centuries, as evidenced by a later inscription that quotes Ludemilie Elasbeth Gräfin of Schwarzburg-Rudolstadts on the image, Stamm, *Cranach* (see n. 38); on Gräfin, see Susanne Schuster, *Aemilie Juliane von Schwarzburg-Rudolstadt und Ahasver Fritsch: Eine Untersuchung zur Jesusfrömmigkeit im späten 17. Jahrhundert* (Leipzig: Evangelische Verlagsanstalt, 2006), 176–79. The fact that individual motifs—such as the representation of the Holy Family or St. Bonaventure's ladder to heaven—were changed by the Reformation remains unaffected by the obvious continuity seen in the case of the Man of Sorrows motif.
40. Brinkmann, *Cranach*, 240.
41. Paltz, *Werke* 3, 231, 10.
42. So also says Stamm, *Cranach*, 74, of numerous variants in the Man of Sorrows motif by Cranach—but precisely not of those that had been influenced by the theology of the Reformation. The traditional character of these motifs in certain commissioned contexts has long been observed in Andreas Tacke, *Der katholische Cranach: Zu zwei Großaufträgen von Lucas Cranach d.Ä., Simon Franck und der Cranach-Werkstatt (1520–1540)* (Mainz: von Zabern, 1992). Stephen Ozment, *The Serpent and the Lamb: Cranach, Luther, and the Making of the Reformation* (New Haven: Yale University Press, 2011), 79–88, speaks of Cranach "anticipating Luther," both in terms of depictions of piety and in terms of church criticism, based on the depiction of the cleansing of the temple in 1510. Richard Viladesau, *The Triumph of the Cross: The Passion of Christ in Theology and the Arts, from the Renaissance to the Counter-Reformation* (Oxford: Oxford University Press, 2008), 158, describes Cranach's Reformation style as being above all "didactic"—on the basis of a detailed examination of his depictions of the crucifixion.

This christological concentration is by no means limited to the Wittenberg context. In 1514, a description appeared in Nuremberg of the life of Mary and Christ with the admonition that the reader should ask Christ "that he may share his mercy with you, that you may follow him according as you are able and make a firm resolve to follow him."[43] Anyone paying attention to the differences with Reformation doctrine will find the aspect of merit more emphasized here than in the other late-medieval texts.[44] But this is precisely what is remarkable if we observe the accumulation of this kind of text. These texts still intertwine in a broad stream of devotion towards Christ, all concerned with "compassion," whereas the Reformation would make some distinctions.[45] However, compassion concentrates all hope on Jesus Christ, as shown in a text from ten years earlier (also printed in Nuremberg) about the contemplation of Christ's suffering. Christ is effusively addressed: "O you, my true lover, my Lord / my helper / my refuge / my consolation / my hope / my issue / my guardian / my redeemer / and all my desires."[46]

Luther's superior Staupitz also took part in this passion piety. The sermons he gave in Salzburg in 1512 are particularly striking.[47] In them, the focus on Christ, evident in many late-medieval contexts, is noticeably sharpened: "Release your spirit to him alone, complain to him alone."[48] Staupitz sometimes emphasized a theology of grace: "and he gives you grace for free."[49] Wolfram Schneider-Lastin, to whom we owe the edition of these sermons, rightly points out that they, preserved in only one

43. Anon, *Das leben vnsers erle | digers Jesu Christi / nach lauttung des hey-|ligen Ewangeli / mit vil andechtiger be-| trachtung / Auch mit beylauffung des | lebens der junckfrawen Marie / von | einem Parfuesser der obseruantz | Also zusamen gezetz / von anfang | der kindthait Cristi / biß auff | sein himelfart / vol suesser | vnd andechtiger leer | vnd betrachtung* (Nuremberg: Stuchs, 1514).

44. Anon, *Das Leben unsers Erledigers*, 3ʳ: "So du wilt ansehen vnn bedencken verdienlich das leben deines gots vnd erledigers" ("So you will look at and think on the life of your God and liberator").

45. Anon, *Das Leben unsers Erledigers*, 3ᵛ.

46. Anon, *Das ist ein schonner | Passion von dem leyden vnsers | lieben herren Jhesu Christi| (This is a Beautiful Thing | Passion of the Life of Our Lord | Dear Jesus Christ|)* (Nuremberg: Hieronymus Huber, 1504), Y 4ᵛ–5ʳ.

47. Johann von Staupitz, "Salzburger Predigten: Eine textkritische Edition," ed. Wolfram Schneider-Lastin (Diss. Phil. Tübingen, 1990). On these sermons, see Franz Posset, "Preaching the Passion of Christ on the Eve of the Reformation," *Concordia Theological Quarterly* 59 (1995): 279–300, 282–95; Franz Posset, *The Front-Runner of the Catholic Reformation: The Life and Works of Johann von Staupitz* (Aldershot: Ashgate, 2002), 135–56; Richard Wetzel, "Staupitz und Luther. Annäherung an eine Vorläufer-Figur," *Blätter für pfälzische Kirchengeschichte und religiöse Volkskunde* 58 (1991): 369–95, 381–83.

48. Staupitz, "Salzburger Predigten," 43, 49.

49. Staupitz, "Salzburger Predigten," 55, 195. In light of such formulations, Lothar Graf zu Dohna, "Staupitz und Luther. Kontinuität und Umbruch in den Anfängen der Reformation,"

manuscript, "reduce the delicate source gap between the Latin Tübingen sermons of 1497/98 and the 1515 publication *Following the Worthy Death of Christ*."[50] In fact, in the latter treatise, which appeared in Leipzig in 1515,[51] Staupitz developed the thoughts of this sermon further. In terms of genre, this is an *ars moriendi*, albeit one that is deeply Christocentric. Additionally, the text is linked to Luther in some respects—if only by the dedication to Countess Agnes of Mansfeld. A year later, at the Corpus Christi procession, the conversation about Luther's fright at the monstrance with the body of Christ would take place in Mansfeld.

At first, however, the text had nothing to do with Luther, presenting advice for Agnes and then, by its publication, for the wider public. Physical death had hereafter lost its horror because through Christ it "became an instrument of life."[52] This is precisely why Staupitz combined the way of the *ars moriendi* with elements of meditation on the passion. Conformity with Christ should accordingly be the only way for the believer to die rightly, and this in contrast to the saints:

> Whoever wants, might learn from St. Peter or some other saint how to die or might see how the pious chose to live their lives. I want to learn from Christ and no one else. He is given to me as a model from God, according to which I shall act, suffer, and die. He is the serpent on the rod, at the sight of which the poison of death dies. He is the only one whom all people shall follow, in whom all good living, suffering, and dying is modelled for everyone and anyone, so that no one does anything right, can suffer or die right if it does not happen in conformity to the living, the suffering, the dying of Jesus Christ, in whose death all other death is swallowed up.[53]

Thus, Christ is depicted here as an effective example: discipleship is only possible when death is swallowed up in Christ—and it can only pertain to Christ. In contrast to the Nuremberg print, in this context all activity of the human being is taken up in Christ and from Christ. In mystical language, the soul becomes the bride through Christ's blood, but only in the way "that it [. . .] above all is not acting, but suffering

---

*Pastoraltheologie* 74 (1985): 452–65, 460, maintains, with a degree of truth, that in these sermons Staupitz shows "the essential elements of his Reformation theology."

50. Staupitz, "Salzburger Predigten," V.

51. Joachim Carl Friedrich Knaake, ed., *Johann von Staupitzens sämmtliche Werke/Iohannis Staupitii Opera, quae reperiri potuerant omnia*, Erster Band: Deutsche Schriften (Postdam: A. Krausnick, 1867), 50–88.

52. Staupitz, *Werke*, 60.

53. Staupitz, *Werke*, 62.

alone."[54] Already this emphasis on Christocentricity and the passivity of the follower of Christ indicates a proximity to ideas usually associated with the Reformation.[55] So it is no surprise that Luther, as late as 1519, when he was asked to write an *ars moriendi*, first pointed out that this was not necessary since Staupitz's *Following the Worthy Death* already existed[56] and only hesitantly began drafting his *Sermon on Preparing to Die*.[57] Like Staupitz, here Luther preached dying in Christ[58] and also referred to the model of the bronze serpent.[59] That was the central message that Luther had taken and carried on from his father confessor and that he was still able to formulate, though at this point less pronounced than Staupitz himself, in such a way that Christ and his saints were praised as a model.[60]

## THE CHRISTOCENTRIC HERMENEUTIC IN LUTHER'S EARLY LECTURES

The latter remark is all the more striking since Luther himself had already declared in 1514 that he was always preaching Christ.[61] This was not an adversarial polemic but merely a basic idea of preaching where Luther in no way differed sharply from his contemporaries. On the contrary, he took part in that Christocentric piety and theology that he observed all around him. This also applies to his academic work on the text of Scripture. As is well-known, he used the *Quincuplex Psalterium* of Jacques Lefèvre

54. Staupitz, "Salzburger Predigten," 78; see also Berndt Hamm, *The Early Luther: Stages in a Reformation Reorientation* (Minneapolis: Fortress Press, 2017), 205–09.

55. In recent discussion, Bo Kristian Holm, "Justification and Reciprocity: 'Purified Gift-Exchange' in Luther and Milbank," in *Word—Gift—Being*, ed. Bo Kristian Holm, Peter Widmann (Tübingen: Mohr Siebeck, 2009), 87–116, 88–94, draws attention to the fact that Luther's doctrine of giving by no means presupposes pure passiveness on the part of people as one-sidedly as is often presupposed, especially in German-language Luther research; as a definitive example of this, see Ingolf U. Dalferth, "Mere Passive. Die Passivtiät der Gabe bei Luther," in *Word—Gift—Being*, ed. Bo Kristian Holm and Peter Widmann (Tübingen: Mohr Siebeck, 2009), 43–71.

56. WA Br 1:381.17–18 (No. 171).

57. Its strong involvement in the late-medieval piety literature is also emphasized in Hamm, *The Early Luther*, 116; see also the emphasis on the "great differences," Hamm, *The Early Luther*, 118.

58. WA 2:689.14–15 LW, 42:99–115.

59. WA 2:689.17–19; LW 42:104–05.

60. WA 2:689.28–29; LW 42:106–07. On this, see Marc Lienhard, *Martin Luthers christologisches Zeugnis: Entwicklung und Grundzüge seiner Christologie* (Göttingen: Vandenhoeck & Ruprecht, 1979). See also Hamm, *The Early Luther*, 148–50.

61. WA 1:31.3–4.

d'Étaples[62] for his first lectures on the Psalms.[63] With its collation of five Latin versions, the work was a philological masterpiece, but it was also a hermeneutically important one. Over against the rabbinic historical exegesis in particular, Lefèvre found a deeper historical meaning opened through Christ as the "key of David."[64] With it, according to his claim, he felt able to unlock the actual spiritual message of the Old Testament. This resonates in his explanation of Psalm 1:

> A Psalm of our Lord Jesus Christ. For there is one who has the key of David: he who shuts, and no one opens/ opens, and no one shuts. The prophet speaks in the spirit[ual sense]. Blessed is the man: this applies to Christ.[65]

Now this method also unlocked the meaning of the Psalms for Luther in the described Christocentric horizon of the theology of piety. Luther used this quotation from the French humanist almost verbatim in his *Praefatio Ihesu Christi*, which was published in the Wittenberg Psalter by the Rhau-Grunenberg printer and inspired his lecture.[66] As given in the introduction, "Holy and true is the one who has the key of David / he who opens, and no one shuts."[67]

For Luther, following Lefèvre's hermeneutics[68] meant "every prophet has to be understood as talking about Christ,"[69] and it was in this sense that

---

62. On d'Étaples, see Jean-Pierre Massaut, "Lefèvre d'Étaples d'exérgèse au xvi^e siècle," *Revue d'histoire ecclésiastique* 78 (1983): 73–78. For an interesting study comparing Lefèvre and Luther with special reference to the Epistle of James, see Guy Bedouelle, "Lefèvre d'Étaples et Luther: Une recherche de frontières. 1517–1527," *Revue d'histoire et de philosophie religieuses* 63 (1983): 17–31.

63. See Luther's notes on this in WA 4:466–526.

64. Henricus Stephanus, *QVINCVPLEX | Psalterium | G allicum. | R omanum. | H ebraicum. | V etus. | C onciliatum* (Paris: 1509), aᵛ.

65. Jacques Lefèvre d'Étaples, *Quincuplex Psalterium* (Genève: Droz, 1979), b 1ʳ.

66. See especially WA 55/I:L with n. 1; for detail about this printing, see Gerhard Ebeling, "Luthers Psalterdruck vom Jahre 1513," in Gerhard Ebeling, *Lutherstudien*, vol. 1 (Tübingen: Mohr Siebeck, 1971), 69–131.

67. WA 55/I:6.5–7: "*Sanctus et verus qui habet clauem Dauid / qui aperit et nemo claudit / claudit et nemo aperit.*" My translation. This literal reference shows that Luther wanted to stand out far less from the tradition than Ebeling's interpretation suggests, which often used the confessionally overriding term *ausschließlich* (exclusively); see Ebeling, "Luthers Psalterdruck," 280–81. For example, the adjective "omnis" in WA 55/I:6.25–8.1 used by Ebeling for his purpose in n. 24 does not mean exclusivity but only universality. On the roots of Luther's christological interpretation far back into patristics, see Kurt-Victor Selge, "Mittelalterliche Traditionsbezüge in Luthers frühe Theologie," in *Die frühe Reformation in Deutschland als Umbruch*, ed. Bernd Moeller (Gütersloh: Gütersloher Verlagshaus, 1998), 149–56: 153–53.

68. In view of the popular appeal, one must say in contrast to Ebeling, "Luthers Psalterdruck," 126, that actually "Faber's special influence can be seen."

69. WA 55/:6.25.

he interpreted the individual Psalms. So Psalm 6 became for him a "prayer of Christ about his suffering and the sins of his members."[70] Compared to Lefèvre, it is striking that Luther focuses more on the second part of the statement—on the meditation for believers—than on the sufferings of Christ.[71]

It was precisely this hermeneutical approach that the entire Scripture was to be understood through the perspective of Christ, which Luther carried on in his later interpretations. In Romans 1:3, within the context of his *Lecture on Romans*, he saw it confirmed that "the whole [of Sacred Scripture] is to be understood as concerning Christ, especially where it is prophetic. But it is everywhere prophetic, although not in the superficial, literal sense."[72]

This basic hermeneutical choice—in which Lefèvre's delimitation of a strict, literal sense still reverberates—also gives Romans a clearly christological reading that harmonizes with mystical interpretations. The apostle wrote the epistle exclusively to destroy our wisdom and to show that we need Christ and his righteousness.[73] The relationship between Christ and righteousness goes so far that Luther can declare that *solus Christus* is the righteousness of God.[74] The centering on Christ, taken from the devotional literature of the late Middle Ages, is enriched here with Pauline vocabulary and thus begins to take on the specific shape in which it became an indelible mark of the Reformation. Already in his interpretation of Romans, Luther began to develop this Christocentrism in contrast to human works:

70. WA 55/I:38.3–5: "*oratio Christi pro suis passionibus et peccatis membrorum suorum.*"
71. d'Étaples, *Quincuplex Psalterium*, 11ʳ.
72. WA 56:5.10–11; see also WA 56:414.15–16: "Scripture is everywhere and only about Christ."
73. WA 56:3.6–11. For the mystical background of the "destroy" terminology used here by Luther, see his marginal notes on Tauler: "*Et si sciamus, quod deus non agat in nobis, nisi prius nos et nostra destruat (i.e. per crucem et passiones), tamen adeo stulti sumus, ut eas velimus tantum suscipere passiones quas nos elegimus vel quas in aliis factas vidimus vel legimus.*" [And if we know that God does not act in us unless he first destroys us and ours (i.e., through the cross and our passions), yet we are so stupid that we want to receive only those passions that we have chosen, or that we have seen or read done in others.] WA 9:102.10–13 with my translation. However, Luther likely only got to know Tauler in the time of his lectures on Romans; see Karl-Heinz zur Mühlen, *Nos extra nos: Luthers Theologie zwischen Mystik und Scholastik* (Tübingen: J. C. B. Mohr, 1972), 97. Very cautious in dating, but leaning toward the same period, is Henrik Otto, *Vor- und frühreformatorische Tauler-Rezeption: Annotationen in Drucken des späten 15. und frühen 16. Jahrhunderts* (Gütersloh: Gütersloher Verlaghaus, 2003), 183. Therefore, one can speak of a linguistic and conceptual proximity here, but not of a genesis of the thought in the course of Luther's mystical reading. Rather, it is evidently the other way around, a note on Tauler's reading arising from what was learned from Paul.
74. WA 56:247.1; LW 25:233.

Thus, for example, Job was afraid of all his actions. And the apostle was not conscious of any wrong he had done, but yet he did not think that he was thereby justified. And thus righteousness must be left to Christ alone, and to Him alone the works of grace and of the Spirit. But we ourselves are always under the works of the Law, always unrighteous, always sinners, as it says in Ps. 32:6, "Therefore let everyone who is godly offer prayer to Thee."[75]

This idea of Christ as our righteousness—and as judge, of course—also occurs in the *Disputatio de viribus et voluntate hominis sine gratia disputata* of 1516[76] and thus became a key conviction of the Wittenberg theology before it became public.

## CHRISTOCENTRISM IN VERNACULAR DEVOTION

This orientation of Luther's hermeneutic toward Christ also allowed him, in the spring of 1517, to relate the Sixth Psalm as the first penitential Psalm for the individual to whom Christ speaks in the words of the Bible.[77] He did so in his first publication in German, *The Seven Penitential Psalms*.[78] There, in a way that is characteristic of Luther, academic activity and edifying writing flow into one another with a christological focus. Thanks to Staupitz, at no point does Luther, who simultaneously praises the newness of his own Augustinian theology in his famous letter to Lang,[79] have to deviate from the devotional context in which he found his home. The centrality of Christ is part of this milieu rather than opposed to it. To put it bluntly, one could say that Luther himself initially remained—at least in a certain area of his activity—a preacher and writer oriented toward the theology of the passion, even after the indulgence controversy had begun and was consuming some of the young scholar's energy.

Two sermons that Luther probably delivered on Good Friday in 1518 show his theological orientation toward the passion.[80] He develops in them the idea based on Augustine[81] that Christ is both *exemplum* and

---

75. WA 56:252.29–253, 2; LW 25:239. To understand the use of *iustitia* in the lectures on Romans, see zur Mühlen, *Nos extra nos*, 129–40.
76. WA 1:149.33–34.
77. WA 1:159.33.
78. Luther had previously published the *Theologia Germanica*; see WA 1:152–53. For more on this publication before the Ninety-Five Theses, see now Timothy J. Wengert, "Martin Luther's First Major Publication," *Lutheran Quarterly* 36 (2022): 166–80.
79. WA Br 1:99.8–13 (No. 41); LW 48:41–42.
80. WA 1:335.
81. See Erwin Iserloh, "Sacramentum et exemplum—ein augustinisches Thema lutherischer Theologie" in *Reformata reformanda: Festgabe für Hubert Jedin zum 17. Juni 1965*, ed. Erwin

*sacramentum.*[82] As in Staupitz's *Following the Worthy Death*, Christ is a model for us to imitate[83] and the effective cause of our salvation. Christ's sufferings and the suffering of the believer should flow into one another.

> The one who does not yet understand the passion of Christ, who does not perceive that he is depicted in it, and who has not thereby learned to suffer with Christ, he suffers in vain with Christ. For you are a fool if you go along secure about yourself while Christ is grieving over you and suffering for you without desiring to suffer with him. In Christ, you suffer alongside him personally.[84]

The way Staupitz colors these thoughts is remarkable not only because of the mentioned reference to his *Following the Worthy Death* but also because of the fundamental importance that he ascribes to suffering with Christ here. This emphasis on suffering with Christ was also a central part of his devotional theology. Suffering becomes the central reference point through which Christ becomes the believer's own, so that in him *exemplum* becomes *sacramentum*. At a time when the reformulation of the theology of justification is already evident in the *Lectures on Romans*, this process of thought is Luther's contribution to a thoroughly traditional discourse of christologically centered devotion to the passion.[85] The strong devotion of the cross also belongs to this outlook. This also entails a mystical exchange: "You suffer because you deserve it; Christ suffers for your sake and innocently bore not his own but your sins on the cross."[86] Luther paired this theology of the passion with Christocentrism in his writings while reflecting on the rule of Christ in his interpretation of the 109th (110th) Psalm. According to his interpretation, published in

Iserloh and Konrad Repgen (Münster: Aschendorff, 1965), 247–64. In connection with Iserloh, but with special importance for the mediating function of faith, see Erik Kyndal, "Christus, 'Sakrament' und 'Gabe.' Einer terminologische Präzisierung von Luthers Christologie 1521," in *Kirche zwischen Heilsbotschaft und Lebenswirklichkeit: Festschrift für Theodor Jørgensen zum 60. Geburtstag*, ed. Dietz Lange and Peter Widmann (Frankfurt: Lang, 1996), 197–216, esp. 207–08. Assuming a special traceability of the *theologia crucis* to the *Imitatio Christi*, H. Rix, "Luther's Debt to the Imitatio Christi," *Augustiniana* 28 (1978): 91–107, 95–96, probably goes too far in light of the widespread devotion to the cross in the Middle Ages, especially since Luther nowhere quotes this writing expressly. Even the remarkable abundance of similarities that Rix lists cannot definitively prove such a use of the *Imitatio Christi* by Luther.

82. WA 1:337.14; 339.17–21; on this pair of concepts in Luther and his Augustinian background, see Lienhard, *Martin Luthers christologisches Zeugnis*, 64–66.

83. See WA 12:338.1; LW 30:117 on the term *imitari*.

84. WA 1:338.12–15. My translation.

85. The importance of mystical piety in the late Middle Ages to Luther's Christology is also mentioned in Lienhard, *Luthers christologisches Zeugnis*, 27–31.

86. WA 1:339.28–29. My translation.

the summer of 1518, the psalm is about "the kingdom and the priestly creation of our Lord Jesus Christ,"[87] and this in turn consists of the word and the Gospel.[88] In fact, Luther already had explained *virga* as being the *Evangelium* in verse 2 in the *Dictata super Psalterium*,[89] the first lecture on the Psalms mentioned above. But the interpretation at that time still lacked that clear word-theological emphasis that can now be found in the text from the year 1518. Now Luther is particularly concerned with clarifying that the way this word works is determined "solely by God."[90] He strives for a theological and christological interpretation of the *Solus Deus*. A close look at the program of reform emerging in 1518 shows at the center of its message a focus on salvation through Christ, whose mediation is understood theologically as suffering. The emphasis on God alone in the work of salvation does not contradict passion piety; rather, in Luther's eyes, such piety gives salvation its only appropriate framework.

This is also clarified by the central devotional text of the following year:[91] the *Sermon on the Contemplation of Christ's Holy Passion*.[92] The woodcuts on the title page that were added to this text changed their motifs. The depiction of Christ on the cross was dominant, but individual printers also used the traditional motif of the Man of Sorrows,[93] which we can surmise is derived from John of Paltz's *Instructions on Meditation*. At least from the perspective of the printer, this new publication by the monk from Wittenberg on his way to fame—which, with twenty-two printed editions by 1522 and a Latin translation in 1521,[94] was extremely successful—fit perfectly with the need of the devout public for an inwardly oriented piety.[95] This corresponded to the table of contents,

---

87. WA 1:690.26.

88. WA 1:693.33–34.

89. WA 55:278–79. For *virga* (branch) as related to the word of God, see the interpretation of 1518, specifically WA 1:694.26.

90. WA 1:34.

91. On the fundamental importance of this text as the basis for Luther's later proclamation of Christ, see Manfred Seitz, "Luthers Christologie in seinen Predigten" in *Jesus Christus—Gott für uns*, ed. Friedrich-Otto Scharbau (Erlangen: Martin-Luther-Verlag, 2003), 43–57, 54.

92. On this, see Martin Brecht, "Luthers reformatorische Sermone," in Christian Peters and Jürgen Kampmann, eds., *Fides et pietas: Festschrift Martin Brecht zum 70. Geburtstag* (Münster: Lit, 2003), 15–32, 23–24.

93. See WA 2:131–32. I owe thanks to Timothy Wengert, for the hint that a depiction of the Man of Sorrows with *arma Christi* can also be found in a print of *On the Freedom of a Christian* from 1522: *Von der freyheit | eynes Christen | menschen. | Martinus Luther* (Coburg: Feilenfürst, 1522) (VD 16 L 7204), C 3ᵛ.

94. WA 2:131–35.

95. On Luther's involvement in an "interiorized religious iconography based on the *Sermon on Preparing to Die*, see Hamm, *The Early Luther*, 131.

which nevertheless shows a particular emphasis. As previously mentioned, John of Paltz had referred to a pseudo-Albertine quotation on the inner devotion to Christ:

> Whoever meditates on Christ's passion, even skimming superficially like selecting peas or beans, gains more benefit than from fasting all year. Even more, it benefits more than practicing a discipline every week that would make him shed blood all year. Thirdly, it benefits more than praying the psalter every week all year.[96]

Luther obviously reacts to this tradition when he explains, "There is a saying ascribed to Albertus about this, that it is more beneficial to ponder Christ's passion just once than to fast a whole year or to pray a psalm daily, etc."[97] Luther's critical turn—very much in tension with the iconographic appeal of the printed editions—goes against the use of pictures and crosses, and therefore against a piety conveyed through images and media.[98] These statements refer to Luther's intensive opposition to the use of images in the mystical context of the idea of de-imaging.[99] In the same year as the sermon based on Staupitz mentioned above, Luther formulated the following with great ambiguity:

> You shall not look at the sin in sinners, or in your conscience, or in those who abide in sin to the end and are damned. If you do, you will surely follow them and also be overcome. You must turn your thoughts away from that and look at sin only within the picture of grace. Engrave that picture in yourself with all your power and have it before your eyes. The picture of grace is nothing else but that of Christ on the cross and of all his dear saints.[100]

For the devout reader of such instructions, here it is difficult to decide whether Luther is speaking in terms of an exclusively spiritual, inner

---

96. Paltz, *Werke* 3, 202, 20–203, 5.
97. WA 2:136.12–14; LW 42:7.
98. WA 2:136.16–17; LW 42:7–8.
99. See Meister Eckhart, *Werke*, ed. Nikolaus Largier, vol. 2 (Frankfurt: Klassiker-Verlag, 1993), 326, 23–29: "*Nû sprechent die meister, daz, sô man bekennet die crêatûre in ir selber, daz heizet ein âbentbekenntnisse, und dâ sihet man die crêatûre in bilden etlîcher underscheide; sô man aber die crêatûre in gote bekennet, daz heizet und ist ein morgenbekantnisse, und alsô schouwet man die crêatûre âne alle underscheide und aller bilde entbildet und aller glîcheit entglîchet in dem einen, daz got selber ist*" (Now the masters say, that, if one perceives the creature for itself, this is called an evening perception, and one sees the creature in images with a number of differences; but if one perceives the creature in God, this is called and is a morning perception, and then one sees the creature without any difference and de-imaged of all images, and de-equalized of all equality in the one that is God himself.)
100. WA 2:689.24–29; LW 42:104.

image or whether "have it before your eyes" also refers to a visible image. Admittedly, it is striking that the first prints of this treatise, also widely distributed, did not have a woodcut on the title page,[101] as we still find on the front page of his *Meditation on Christ's Passion* despite that sermon's critical turn against images.

Here, however, the instruction was that the suffering of Christ is considered righteous when one is afraid of the wrath of God.[102] The contemplation of the passion is thus turned into a self-reflection by those who discover themselves to be the cause of Christ's suffering; human sinfulness is revealed by and in Christ.[103] The basic Reformation form of law and gospel can undoubtedly be intuited here, albeit in the characteristic form that the knowledge of God's wrath is derived from Christ, such that the independent function of the law can only emerge as christologically mediated. Above all, Luther's involvement in traditional spirituality remains striking at this point. The recognition of one's own sinfulness as "self-awareness" corresponds to that mystical imperative: "Be aware of yourself" (*Nim din selbes war*). Alois Maria Hass has identified this as the central theme of Eckhartian mysticism,[104] and in the same context Luther takes up the idea that a person must conform (*gleych formig*) to Christ,[105] which he with Staupitz opposed.[106] And it is precisely on this basis that Luther can accept the pseudo-Albertine quotation and explain it as follows:

> We say without hesitation that he who contemplates God's sufferings for a day, an hour, yes, only a quarter of an hour, does better than to fast a whole year, to pray a Psalm daily, yes, better than to hear a hundred masses. This meditation changes man's being and, almost like baptism, gives him a new birth.[107]

The recalling of fasting for a year and praying the Psalter every day shows that Luther wants to make the Albert quotation adoptable. His initial

---

101. See WA 2:681.
102. WA 2:137.10–12; LW 42:8.
103. WA 2:137.22–23; LW 42:8–9.
104. See Alois Maria Haas, *Nim din selbes war: Studien zur Lehre von der Selbsterkenntnis bei Meister Eckhart, Johannes Tauler und Heinrich Seuse* (Freiburg: Universitätsverlag, 1971).
105. WA 2:138.19; "conformable" in LW 42:10. On the occurrence of this thought in the interpretation of the Psalms, see Florian Schneider, *Christus praedicatus et creditus: Die reformatorische Christologie Luthers in den Operationes in Psalmos (1519–1521), dargestellt mit beständigem Bezug zu seiner Christologie* (Neukirchen-Vluyn: Neukirchener, 2004), 211–99.
106. Concerning the doctrine of *conformitas* in Staupitz, see details in Markus Wriedt, *Gnade und Erwählung: Eine Untersuchung zu Johann von Staupitz und Martin Luther* (Mainz: von Zabern, 1991), 145–86.
107. WA 2:139.11–15; LW 42:11.

criticism does not prove to be a fundamental rejection of this approach but rather an indication of a necessary spiritual correction directed to deepen the inner perspective. Pseudo-Albert is still insufficiently understood and transposed when the rejection of certain external forms leads to new externalities; only the deep inner understanding of Christ represents an appropriate dealing with himself and salvation.

This understanding then leads to a change in the human being that Luther described as "essential," which is striking when compared to the later forensic interpretation of the doctrine of justification. It is not solely about a relational reorientation of human existence but about a new reshaping affecting its substance.[108] The opening discourse on equality, based on Staupitz, is to be understood in the sense that *forma* as an essence is liable to change. This change forms the basis for the new Christian everyday reality. In a notable shift in emphasis compared to Staupitz, Luther makes it clear simply through the arrangement of the text that Christ's exemplary character can only be adequately understood with respect to salvation. Only in the last of the fifteen bullet points of the treatise does Luther change over from the description of Christ as *sacramentum*, allowing people to participate in suffering and resurrection, to the dimension of *exemplum*.[109] For Luther, an ethically realized passion piety can only follow after devotional immersion in the passion.

The emphasis on the exclusivity of God's and Christ's work in salvation rings clearly here, also with an eye toward the spiritual shaping of life. Luther does not entirely contradict his medieval forerunners, but he gave accents in his own specific way. Scripture is not a guide for everyday life but instead points to the reordering of the ground of the Christian's everyday reality. These remarks shed a clear light on the agglomeration of convictions within which the relationship to Christ alone allowed Luther's message of justification to grow. In the *Sermo de duplici iustitia*, he clearly states, "The first is alien righteousness, that is the righteousness of another, infused from without. This is the righteousness of Christ by

---

108. See Simo Peura, "Die Teilhabe an Christus," in Simon Peura and Antti Raunio, eds., *Luther und Theosis: Vergöttlichung als Thema der abendlandischen Theologie* (Helsinki: Luther-Agricola-Gesellschaft, 1990), 121–62, 148–60; and Mark Totten, "Luther on *unio cum Christo*: Toward a Model for Integrating Faith and Ethics," *Journal of Religious Ethics* 31 (2003): 443–62, 447–52. They rightly point out such effective moments in Luther's doctrine of justification. For a critical examination of those philosophical presuppositions in interpretations of Luther that pushed these effective elements into the background, see Risto Saarinen, *Gottes Wirken auf uns: Die transzendentale Deutung des Gegenwart-Christi-Motivs in der Lutherforschung* (Stuttgart: Steiner Verlag Wiesbaden, 1989).

109. WA 2:141.8–13; LW 42:13–14.

which he justifies through faith."[110] The context of the sermon on how to contemplate Christ's suffering shows that the *infusion* treated here should be given a lot of weight. Luther is really concerned with change in people that fundamentally affects them. His new concept of justification permeates both texts, but each is formulated with different terminology: the first with the language of medieval piety, and the second with the aid of Augustinian-Pauline vocabulary.[111]

## ON SOLUS CHRISTUS AS A MARK OF SEPARATION FROM THE OLD CHURCH

The preceding undertaking has shown how deeply the Reformation idea of *solus Christus* is anchored in the culture of late-medieval devotion. Even where there are indications of later idiosyncrasies, Martin Luther as author remained involved in the genre of devotional literature as it was cultivated in his environment, especially by Staupitz. However, *solus Christus* also became an exclusive formula in a demarcating sense, parallel to its positive development. The distinction from the church of the pope was already taking place in the *signum* of *solus Christus*, even while elsewhere Luther still participated in the discourse of the tradition and did not break from it.

The indulgence controversy in general, although not the Ninety-Five Theses themselves, made this happen. At their spiritual core, these theses are still plainly a result of the reorientation of the devotional theology that Martin Luther received within the late-medieval landscape of belief from Staupitz and, as mediated through him, John Tauler.[112] The appeal

---

110. WA 2:145.9–10; LW 31:297.

111. These thoughts developed into the idea of the marital exchange in his writing *On Christian Freedom*, an idea Luther elaborated over a long period beginning with the first Psalm lectures; see Walter Allgaier, "Der "fröhliche Wechsel" bei Martin Luther: Eine Untersuchung zu Christologie und Soteriologie bei Luther unter besonderer Berücksichtigung der Schriften bis 1521" (Diss., Erlangen, 1966), on the proximity of Staupitz, see 142–44. See also Oswald Bayer, "Das Wort ward Fleisch. Luthers Christologie als Lehre von der Idiomenkommunkation," in *Jesus Christus—Gott für uns*, ed. Friedrich-Otto Scharbau (Erlangen: Martin-Luther-Verlag, 2003), 58–101, 61–62; Reinhold Rieger, *Von der Freiheit eines Christenmenschen / De libertate christiana* (Tübingen: Mohr Siebeck, 2007), 180–95. Holm, "Justification" makes clear that it is precisely this image of marriage, rooted in mysticism, that typifies the felicitous exchange between Christ and sinful humanity.

112. See Volker Leppin, "'*Omnem vitam fidelium penitentiam esse voluit:*' Zur Aufnahme mystischer Traditionen in Luthers erster Ablassthese," in *Transformationen* (Tübingen: Mohr Siebeck, 2015), 261–27.

to Christ as "our Lord and Master"[113] simply expressed that positive reference to Christ that Luther developed from years of passion theology.[114] However, in his arguments with his opponents, Luther soon realized that his critique of indulgences had a soteriological impact which emphasized the power of Christ so strongly that, from this perspective, other theological models of grace seemed inadequate.[115] Thus to John Eck's objection that Christ looks at the heart and the will,[116] Luther replied in his *Asterisci* that, in the soul, Christ is the ruler and the will is wholly subservient.[117] In this context, the *passio Christi* repeatedly played a role in the argument as well.

In this way, and unlike in the Ninety-Five Theses themselves, Luther was now able to contrast faith in Christ and the willingness—as suggested in his clarifying works—to follow his example with a piety that relied on indulgences.[118] This still belongs to the tension between inner and outer piety, which can be observed elsewhere. But the contrast within the *Asterisci*, spurred on by Eck's challenging argumentation, heightened to a point that increasingly contradicted not just any arbitrary stance on piety but the mainstream one of the medieval church. With respect to Luther's thirty-fourth thesis, which explained that the indulgences confirmed by the pope can only remit the penalties of sacramental satisfaction as people used them,[119] Eck had to refer to the formula for absolution ("For what I have not imposed, may the bitter passion of Christ supply")[120] and so brought the direct liturgical application of passion theology into the debate. Luther countered this by saying that the passion of Christ was thereby devalued as Eck was only focusing on the punishments, not on the guilt of the people.[121] Luther began to suspect that he was doing this on

---

113. "*Dominus et magister noster*," WA 1:233.10; LW 31:25.
114. On the implicit christological background of the Ninety-Five Theses, see Rosin, "Christology," 160.
115. This is aptly noticed in Athina Lexutt, "Christologie als Soteriologie: Ein Blick in die späten Disputationen Martin Luthers" in *Relationen—Studien zum Übergang vom Spätmittelalter zur Reformation. Festschrift zu Ehren von Karl-Heinz zur Mühlen*, ed. Wolfgang Matz and Athina Lexutt (Münster: Lit., 2000), 201–16, 202: "Christology as soteriology—this is the short-form of the Reformation's insight."
116. WA 1:283.3.
117. WA 1:283.19–20.
118. WA 1:306.22–25.
119. WA 1:235.3–4; LW 31:28; for reference to Eck's sixteenth *Obeliscus*, see DCL 1:429, note y.
120. WA 1:301.1; on this formula, see also Ludwig Rapp, "Die Statuten der ältesten bekannten Synode von Brixen im Jahre 1511," *Zeitschrift des Ferdinandeums für Tirol und Vorarlberg* 22 (1878): 1–46, 43.
121. WA 1:301.13–15.

the basis of his piety toward Christ, risking a deviation from the medieval consensus: "Perhaps it has not been safe for me to say that this practice of the priests would not be acceptable to me, lest he should say again that I sow the Bohemian virus."[122] There is therefore an inkling that, given the same basis for emphasizing the passion of Christ, the weight attached to it can lead to a gap, one that Luther also related to different ways of theology in his *Asterisci*. He thought that the path he followed was opposed to the Aristotle-oriented,[123] scholastic thinking of Eck.[124] The connection of the *solus Christus* principle with a new theological model was already becoming apparent as Luther would then express it most clearly in the Heidelberg Disputation. He even went so far as to question the truth claim of scholastic theology: "I admit that all these things are true, if the scholastics are right. What Eck asserts, I reject."[125]

A little later, this contrast culminated in the famous confrontation in Thesis 21 of the Heidelberg Disputation between the *theologus gloriae* and the *theologus crucis*.[126] Even the mention here of the *crux* points directly to the passion-Christology background.[127] This applies even more so to the determination of the content of the teaching of the *theologus crucis*,[128]

122. WA 1:301.13–15.

123. On the contrast between Christ and Aristotle, see WA 1:304.10–11.

124. WA 1:282.12.

125. WA 1:303.19–20; see also 306.9–10: "Should Christ and his word be with me, I will not be afraid, no matter what the whole world may do to me."

126. WA 1:354.21–22; LW 31:40; Martin Luther, *Studienausgabe*, ed. Hans-Ulrich Delius, vol. 1 (Berlin: Evangelische Verlagsanstalt, 1987), 215, 14–15. Luther developed this distinction further in his explanations of the theses on indulgences: "A theologian of glory does not recognize, along with the Apostle, the crucified and hidden God alone [1 Cor 2:2]. He sees and speaks of God's glorious manifestation among the heathen, how his invisible nature can be known from the things which are visible [See Rom 1:20] and how he is present and powerful in all things everywhere. This theologian of glory, however, learns from Aristotle that the object of the will is the good and the good is worthy to be loved, while the evil, on the other hand, is worthy of hate. He learns that God is the highest good and exceedingly lovable. Disagreeing with the theologian of the cross, he defines the treasury of Christ as the removing and remitting of punishments, things which are most evil and worthy of hate. In opposition to this the theologian of the cross defines the treasury of Christ as impositions and obligations of punishments, things which are best and most worthy of love." WA 1:614.17–25; LW 31:227. See Jens-Martin Kruse, *Universitätstheologie und Kirchenreform: Die Anfänge der Reformation in Wittenberg 1516–1522* (Mainz: von Zabern, 2002), 133.

127. Essential to this, see Graham Tomlin, "The Medieval Origins of Luther's Theology of the Cross," *Archiv für Reformationsgeschichte* 89 (1998): 22–40; see also Lienhard, *Luthers christologisches Zeugnis*, 74.

128. See also the references to the deep anchoring of Luther's *theologia crucis* in his interpretation of the Psalms in Michael Kreuzer, *"Und das Wort ist Fleisch geworden:" Zur Bedeutung des Menschseins Jesu bei Johannes Driedo und Martin Luther* (Paderborn: Bonifatius, 1998), 212–22. Very appropriately, see Lienhard, *Luthers christologisches Zeugnis*, 37: "We want to express the

which argues in terms of passion theology, when Luther says that he looks at the *visibilia et posteriora Dei* through suffering and the cross.[129] In his *Probatio*, the Reformer explained that this is about seeing the humanity of Christ against all of humanity's own wisdom.[130] At least the basic idea clearly corresponds to the mystical passion-Christology found in Bernard of Clairvaux, who wrote:

> I think that this was the chief reason for the invisible God, that he wished to be seen in the flesh, and to be communicating as a man with men; namely, he drew all the affections of the carnal men, who only could love carnally, back to the saving love of his flesh, and thus gradually led them to spiritual love.[131]

The conflict between monastic and scholastic theology, occasionally having been located as originating in the twelfth century[132] (though not undisputed),[133] is found here with Luther as a version sharpened at the point of passion-Christology. It is one medieval tradition that the Wittenberg monk brings forward against another—the scholastic one. The mystical orientation of his argument becomes even clearer if one includes Bucer's account of the Heidelberg Disputation, which, based on his own eyewitness testimony and a subsequent conversation with Luther about several theses, gives more detailed explanations.[134] Characteristic here is Thesis 1 on the law of God. The *probatio* prepared by Luther in writing[135] deals primarily with the deadly character of the law based on biblical and

fact that Luther's writings do not offer treatises on Christology. However large the space that Christ occupies in them, they do not offer any elaborate Christology."

129. WA 1:354.19–20; LW 31:40; Luther, *Studienausgabe* 1, 215, 12–13.

130. WA 1:362.4–14; LW 31:52–53; Luther, *Studienausgabe* 1, 208, 4–13.

131. Bernhard von Clairvaux, *Sämtliche Werke. Lateinisch/Deutsch*, ed. Berhard G. Winkler, vol. 5 (Innsbruck: Tyrolia-Verlag, 1994), 118, 21–26. On the background of Luther's *theologia crucis* in Bernard, see Tomlin, "Origins," 33–37; Ulrich Köpf, "Wurzeln reformatorischen Denkens in der monastischen Theologie Bernhards von Clairvaux," in *Reformation und Mönchtum*, ed. Athina Lexutt, Volker Mantey, and Volkmar Ortmann (Tübingen: Mohr Siebeck, 2008), 29–56, 54–55; on Luther's use of Bernard at the time of the Heidelberg Disputation, see Theo Bell, *Divus Bernhardus: Bernhard von Clairvaux in Martin Luthers Schriften* (Mainz: von Zabern, 1993), 127–33.

132. Available in various editions and translations, see Jean Leclercq, *The Love of Learning and the Desire for God: A Study of Monastic Culture* (New York: Fordham University Press, 1961).

133. Ingo Klitzsch, *Die "Theologien" des Petrus Abaelardus: Genetisch-kontextuelle Analyse und theologiegeschichtlich Relektüre* (Leipzig: Evangelische Verlagsanstalt, 2010), 589.

134. See the reference to this in WA 9:162.6–7 and 14–15; see Thomas Kaufmann, *Der Anfang der Reformation: Studien zur Kontextualität der Theologie, Publizistik und Inszenierung Luthers und der reformatorischen Bewegung* (Tübingen: Mohr Siebeck, 2012), 341.

135. On the preparatory character of the *probationes*, see Helmar Junghans in Luther, *Studienausgabe* 1, 188.

patristic evidence.[136] According to Bucer's report however, Luther, following Augustine's *De spiritu et littera*, also developed the positive meaning of the *lex spiritus* and stated that this is placed in the hearts of people so that no longer they but Christ lives in them, according to Paul (Gal 2:20).[137] This indicates that for Luther, at the time of the Heidelberg Disputation, epistemological Christocentricity went hand in hand with a more soteriological one, according to which the law condemns everything that does not happen in Christ.[138] Christocentricity here gave Luther the strongest possible opposition to a kind of university theology he perceived to be as dominant as it was erroneous. This formation of *solus Christus* as the clarion call for his fight against the medieval church was reached a good year earlier than that of *sola scriptura*, which only emerged in its full form in the Leipzig Disputation.[139] This disputation became highly relevant for the ecclesiological impact of the opposition used back in Heidelberg, insofar as the question Eck and Luther were decisively arguing was about Christ as the head of the church.[140] This brought the orientation toward Christ in opposition to the leadership of the church by way of the pope, and in this respect it was quite obvious that, shortly after the Leipzig Disputation, Luther came to the conclusion that the antichrist ruled the church.[141]

The development of the principle of *solus Christus* had a definite conclusion now. In retrospect, this gives a picture of how Luther's convictions gradually differed from those of his environment, although not in such a way that one could speak in terms of a simple progression. Rather, in this transformation of late-medieval devotion to Christ and to the passion, continuity and discontinuity were inextricably linked. On the one hand, Luther worked for a long time as a devotional writer within the framework of devotional literature as he was familiar with it from John of Staupitz. On the other hand, he simultaneously developed, especially in confrontation with John Eck, an increasingly critical application of the principle of *solus Christus* against the medieval church. In both threads, we find distinct concepts and formulations—positive and devotional, as

136. WA 1:355.32–356.4; Luther, *Studienausgabe* 1, 200, 10–15.
137. WA 9:162.37–43.
138. WA 1:354.35–36; Luther, *Studienausgabe* 1, 3–4.
139. See Volker Leppin, "Die Genese des reformatorischen Schriftprinzips: Beobachtungen zu Luthers Auseinandersetzung mit Johannes Eck bis zur Leipziger Disputation," in *Transformationen: Studien zu den Wandlungsprozessen in Theologie und Frömmigkeit zwischen Spätmittelalter und Reformation*, 2nd ed. (Tübingen: Mohr Siebeck, 2018), 355–97.
140. WA 59:437.131–37.
141. WA 6:429.33–430.6; LW 44:165.

well as critical—that refer to their close connection. The principle *solus Christus* simultaneously became an integrative, continuous idea, as well as an exclusive, delineating one. It remains inextricably linked to Luther's late-medieval background, even when Luther felt he had to go down a path that would lead him out of the medieval church.[142]

142. Translated, with permission, by Miles Hopgood from the author's slightly revised "Solus Christus. Zur Genese einer reformatorischen Exklusivpartikel aus der spätmittelalterlichen Passionsfrömmigkeit," *Transformationen: Studien zu den Wandlungsprozessen in Theologie und Frömmigkeit zwischen Spätmittelalter und Reformation* (Tübingen: Mohr Siebeck, 2015), 279–301, using the original title "'Solus Christus.' Von der spätmittelalterlichen Passionsfrömmigkeit zum reformatorischen Glauben," in *Jesus Christus. Von altestamentlichen Messiasvorstellungen bis zur literarischen Figur*, ed. Thomas Fornet-Ponse (Münster: Aschendorff, 2015), 91–107. The text translated by Miles Hopgood appeared in LQ 37 (2023). 1–26.

# 3.

# "Sola Gratia." Penitence and Grace in Luther's Early Theology

"When our Lord and Master Jesus Christ said, "Repent" [Matt 4:17], he willed the entire life of believers to be one of repentance."[1] This admonition is found at the very beginning of the theses concerning indulgence, whose posting on October 31, 1517, has been considered as the symbolic beginning of the Reformation. Nowadays, we know that the yearly celebration of this date has attached far more significance to it than is necessary.[2] And yet, this day seems a bit counterintuitive when we contextualize it within late-medieval spirituality. On the eve of All Saints Day in 1517, the monk and professor Martin Luther made known nothing other than a further development of the intense debate raging in the late Middle Ages concerning the theology of penance.

## THE FIRST LECTURES ON THE PSALMS IN THE HORIZON OF LATE MEDIEVAL SCHOLASTICISM

In the printed edition of his *Enarratio Psalmi LI [quinquaginti primi]*, the fourth penitential Psalm, Luther looked back at his previous struggle to understand penance:

1. Luther, *Disputatio pro declaratione virtutis indulgentiarum* (WA 1:233.1–2): *"Dominus et magister noster Iesus Christus dicendo 'Penitentiam agite &c.' omnem vitam fidelium penitentiam esse voluit."* Cited after LW 31:25: "Ninety-Five Theses *or* Disputation on the Power and Efficacy of Indulgences."
2. The question of whether Martin Luther actually posted his Ninety-Five Theses on the door of Wittenberg's Castle Church remains open. A study of the central arguments can be found in: Volker Leppin and Timothy Wengert, "Posting of the Ninety-Five Theses," *Lutheran Quarterly* 29 (2015): 373–98.

Yes, in the use of the Sacraments and in confession we teach men to look mainly at the Word, so that we call everything back from our works to the Word. . . . The hearing of gladness is in confession, or, to call it by its more proper name, in absolution and the use of the keys: "Have faith. Your sins are forgiven you through the death of Christ." Though we urge the people to the Sacraments and to absolution, still we do not teach anything about the worthiness of our work or that it avails by the mere performance of the work, as the papists usually teach about the Lord's Supper, or rather about their sacrifice. We call men back to the Word so that the chief part of the whole action might be the voice of God itself and the hearing itself. / On the other hand, the pope omits the Word and argues about the form and power of the Sacraments or about contrition and attrition. In the schools I was so corrupted by this teaching that only with great labor, by the grace of God, was I able to turn myself solely to the hearing of gladness.[3]

In this text, Luther distances himself from late-medieval scholastic debates. This belongs in the context of a confrontation that he had very clearly formulated during the reception of his theses concerning indulgence in 1518. In that year (probably during Lent[4]), Luther held a sermon on penance and explained:

Secondly, that you never place your trust in attaining your absolution through contrition (then you would be trusting in your works which means in the worst possible way), but rather in the words of Christ who spoke to Peter: whatever you loose on earth will be loosed in heaven.[5]

Much like his later writings, Luther is handling and interpreting a contrite heart in the event of penance as the activity of the individual. Or perhaps it is better to describe it as a necessary attitude for the individual to have. He contrasts this emphasis with an emphasis on the activity of God, which

---

3. "*Quin in Sacramentorum usu et confessione docemus ad verbum potissimum respiciendum esse, ut omnia revocemus a nostris operibus in verbum. (. . .) In Confessione seu, ut rectius appellemus, in Absolutione et clavium usu est Auditus gaudii: Crede, remissa sunt tibi peccata tua per Christi mortem. Etsi igitur hortamur ad Sacramenta et ad absolutionem, tamen non docemus aliquid de dignitate nostri operis, quod ex opere operato valeat, sicut Papistae de Coena Domini seu suo sacrificio solent. Sed revocamus homines ad verbum, ut caput totius actionis sit ipsa vox Dei et ipse auditus.*" Cited after LW 12:369, 369–70.

   "*Contra Papa obmisso verbo de forma et virtute sacramentorum disputat, Item de contritionibus et attritionibus. Hac doctrina sane ita sum ego in scholis corruptus, ut vix magno labore, Dei gratia, me ad solum Auditum gaudii potuerim convertere*" (Luther, *Ennarratio Psalmi LI.* [WA 40/2:411.21–23.28–38]).

4. WA 1:317.

5. Luther, *Sermo de poenitentia* (WA 1:323.23–26): "*Secundum vide, ne ullo modo te confidas absolvi propter tuam contritionem (Sic enim super te et tua opera confides, id est, pessime praesumes), sed propter verbum Christi, qui dixit Petro: Quodcunque solveris super terram, solutum erit et in caelis.*"

takes place in the word of absolution. Research into the late-medieval background of this debate has been skewed by the dialectic of "contritionism" and "attritionism."[6] The first attitude was said to denote an interpretation of penance that made complete *contritio* a necessary precondition for the effect of penance and absolution.[7] "Attritionism," on the other hand, considered *attritio*—the simple fear of God and his punishments—sufficient; this was then transformed into true *contritio* through the Sacrament of Penance and thus brought into play for an effective process of penance.[8]

Luther's recourse to the concepts of *contritio* and *attritio* allows us to discern that he really did know a distinction between them. However, the descriptors "contritionism" and "attritionism" have proven to capture the theological phenomenon only partially. In particular, its historical development has not been treated with the precision that is necessary. Such a conceptualization uses the precondition for the Sacrament of Penance as the nomenclature but excludes the holistic, functional process of penance.[9] For most theories formulated with these descriptors, this total context is actually very important. If we consider the total context, then several conceptions that have previously been described with "contritionism" can better be described as *subjective penance theory*. In the center of the successful act of penance is—especially in the early Middle Ages—an event internal to the person. In the late Middle Ages, this is doubly shifted. On the one hand, the subjective attitude was so tightly coupled with the Sacrament that one can now speak of a *sacramental-subjective penance theory*. On the other hand, the late-medieval binding of the subject led

6. Cf. Heiko Augustinus Oberman, *The Harvest of Medieval Theology: Gabriel Biel and Late Medieval Nominalism* (Cambridge: Harvard University Press 1963), 146–60.

7. Cf. Eva-Maria Faber, "Kontritionismus," in *Lexikon für Theologie und Kirche*, vol. 6, 3rd ed. (Freiburg: Herder, 1997), 333. The concept of *contritio* came about with Anselm of Canterbury and his interpretation of Ps 50:19 ("cor contritum et humiliatum Deus non spernet") auf. Before that, *compunctio* was far more commmon (cf. Bernhard Poschmann, *Handbuch der Dogmengeschichte IV/3: Buße und Letzte Ölung* [Freiburg: Herder, 1951], 87).

8. Cf. Anton Ziegenaus, "Attritionismus," in *Lexikon für Theologie und Kirche*, vol. 1 (Freiburg; Herder, 1993), 1168–70. This question has attained such significance because it continues Early Modern debates. The Council of Trent accepted an attritionist attitude (DH No. 1678), although it must be said that it made this decision not entirely unsatisfied (cf. Ziegenaus, "Attritionismus," 1169). The seventeenth century saw the conflict flare up again and was explicitly declared to be open by Pope Alexander VII in a decree on May 5, 1667, with the possibility left open of a later decision by the Holy See.

9. At this point, it is also worth considering what Reinhold Seeberg, *Die religiösen Grundgedanken des jungen Luther und ihr Verhältnis zu dem Ockhamismus und der deutschen Mystik* (Berlin: De Gruyter, 1931), 5 ascertained (with a bit of overemphasis): "Western Christendom has always concentrated itself on the concept of penance. In penance, all fundamental concepts of religion come together: sin and the guilt that comes of it, God with his punishments and grace, faith, contrition, and justification, the church's authority and good works." My translation.

to self-examination and self-observation (this is where Luther's criticism begins), which is entirely focused on whether the act of heartfelt contrition was sufficient. Put another way, was humility before God and self-criticism to a sufficient extent integral, or was the person merely led by fear of God's punishments? In some cases, this profound introspection could be considered appropriately as "contritionism."

The attitude usually meant under the nomenclature that "attritionism" can be best captured in its high-medieval origins as *sacramental-objective penance theory*. The proponents of this theory had the theological priority of securing penance as a clear-cut, objective act that gives security to an individual. It need not even rely on a person's own individual efforts for their salvation. But the more one considered the pastoral perspective, the more it became necessary to take the subjective disposition of the penitent into account. That meant admitting that the means of grace cannot be denied to an individual with a contrite heart so that in the context of the spiritual theology of the late fifteenth century, it can be appropriate to speak of "attritionism."

With Peter Lombard, *subjective penance theory* became the standard theory for twelfth-century scholasticism.[10] His theology of penance developed in a sacrament-skeptical direction. In Sent. IV d. 17 c. 1, he asks "if sin is be forgiven without confession."[11] After reviewing various authorities that spoke for a spectrum of answers, he concluded:

> [. . .] that the sins are destroyed without oral confession and external punishment by means of contrition and humility of the heart. That is why he purports that God forgives him who confesses his sins with a demeaned mind; for that is truly confession of the heart and not only of the mouth through which the soul is internally purified from the stains and contamination of sin.[12]

10. For more on this representative character, cf. Berndt Hamm, *The Early Luther*, 7–8. Poschmann, *Buße und Letzte Ölung* (cf. n. 7), 84–85 presents us with the background of this theory for Abelard, who ascribed "the forgiveness of sins unequivocally to the subjective factor." While he did generally define penance as *contritio* and *satisfactio* in his ethics (Peter Abelard, *Ethics: An Edition with Introduction*, English translation and notes, ed. D. E. Luscombe [Oxford: Clarendon Press, 1971], 76.20), he then restricted proper penance to "dolor animi super eo in quo deliquit" (Abelard, *Ethics*, 76.22–23); for more on Abelard's understanding of penance, cf. Tobias Georges, *Quam nos divinitatem nominare consuevimus: Die theologische Ethik des Peter Abaelard* (Leipzig: Evangelische Verlagsanstalt, 2005), 248–53.
11. Petrus Lombardus, Sent IV d. 17 c. 1 (Petri Lombardi, *Sententiae in IV libris distinctae*, vol. 2 [Grottaferrata [Rom]: Coll. cf. *Bonaventurae Ad Claras Aquas*, 1981], 342, 15–16): "*an sine confessione dimittatur peccatum.*"
12. Petrus Lombardus, Sent IV d. 17 c.1 (Lombardus, *Sententiae 2* [cf. n. 11], 345, 19–23): "*quod sine confessione oris et solutione poenae exterioris peccata delentur, per contritionem et humilitatem*

This approach to the theory of penance brought about an enormous destabilization of the priestly transmission of salvation. In the second chapter, Lombard expressly adds that, when faced with the question of whether it is enough to bring one's sins to God alone, he is inclined to agree with the authorities that "all the faithful of either sex . . . should individually confess all their sins in a faithful manner to their own priest at least once a year."[13] Their authority to bind and to loose was accordingly only a *declarative* authority: the authority was "the power to bind or loose, which means to show individuals that they are bound or loosed."[14]

This problem was bound to become virulent when the Fourth Lateran Council intensified the requirement to go to confession and intensified the priestly execution of the Sacrament of Penance. It was explicitly ordered *"All the faithful of both sexes shall (. . .) faithfully confess all their sins at least once a year to their own (parish) priest."*[15] That brought with it an objectification of the moment of penance that would soon be taken up and further developed by Thomas Aquinas.

Aquinas did this in the *Summa theologiae*, characteristically avoiding the usage of the *attritio*-concept. Instead, he concentrated on the effectivity of the Sacrament in the priest's word. In ST III q. 84 a. 3, he treats the question of the form, which is to say the essence-imparting portion of penance, and then divides the aspects of the Sacrament according to Aristotelian categories, with the preconditions being material in the penitent but the *forma* being constituted by the word of the priest, "Ego te absolvo."[16] In contrast to the usual division of *contritio*, *confessio*, and *satisfactio*, the priest's word of absolution would become the center of the event of penance. This was analogous to the Sacraments of Baptism and the Eucharist, for which Aquinas also found the word to be the form that constituted the Sacrament.[17]

---

cordis. *Ex quo enim proponit, mente compuncta, se confessurum, Deus dimittit; quia ibi est confessio cordis, etsi non oris, per quam anima interius mundatur a macula et contagio peccati commissi."*

13. Petrus Lombardus, Sent IV d. 17 c.2 (Lombardus, *Sententiae* 2 [cf. n. 11], 348.9–10): *"qui sufficere contendunt Deo confiteri peccata, sine sacerdote."*

14. Petrus Lombardus, Sent IV d. 18 c.6 (Lombardus, *Sententiae* 2 [cf. n. 11], 361, 3–4: *"potestatem ligandi et solvendi, id est ostendendi homines ligatos vel solutos."* My translation.

15. DH No. 812: *"Omnis utriusque sexus fidelis (. . .) omnia sua solus peccata saltem semel in anno fideliter confiteatur proprio sacerdoti."* Translation Medieval Sourcebook, accessed October, 3, 2023, https://sourcebooks.fordham.edu/sbook.asp

16. Editio Leonina 12:289. In his commentary, Cajetan made the matter all the more precise: "Sacramentaliter absolvo te" (Editio Leonina 12:290).

17. Editio Leonina 12:289; cf. Poschmann, *Buße und Letzte Ölung* (cf. n. 7), 91. Against this background, it is actually plausible to consider absolution as the fourth element of the medieval doctrine of penance (Charles Morerod, "Le manque de clarté de Gabriel Biel et son impact sur la Réforme" *Nova et Vetera* 75 [2000]: 15–32, 21). Of course, it is easy to identify a close parallel to the later Reformation's emphasis on absolution. However, one must exercise caution as it is

Against this background, the effect of the sacrament could not be thought of as dependent from a special sort of *contritio*. Thus, in his commentary on Lombard's *Sentences*, Aquinas presented a version of the doctrine that one can classify as sacramental-objective or even as attritionism.[18] In Sent IV d. 22 q. 2 a. 1 ad 3., he explains:

> The forgiveness of sins is in both cases the cause of the sacrament of penance: sometimes, that forgiveness is granted temporally before the external sacrament, sometimes it occurs through the sacrament itself. For when somebody goes to confession with a penitent heart (*attritus*), but not a fully contrite one (*contritus*), then grace and forgiveness of sins are granted to them by means of confession and absolution as long as they does not present an obstacle to this.[19]

Here, we see the idea of a transformation of *attritio* to *contritio* within the Sacrament bound up with a certain, limited disposition of the penitent. It is to be found in the missing obstacle to forgiveness itself. Just as in the *Summa*, the real accent is found in the external word of absolution. The activity of the penitent is dramatically reduced.

Duns Scotus shifted the accent of the argumentation in a different direction from that of Aquinas in that he used the disposition of the penitent as the starting point of his entire theory. Thus, his ideas provided a foothold for a theory of *attritio* and further to a conceptual framework of attritionism. In his comprehensive sentence commentary, the *Ordinatio* from around 1300,[20] he treats the question in Sent IV d. 14 q. 2 "Utrum actus poenitendi requisitus ad deletionem peccati mortalis, sit actus alicuius virtutis?" ("Is the act of penance, which is necessary for the destruction

---

not entirely clear if Luther actually knew of Aquinas (cf. Stefan Gradl, "Inspektor Columbo irrt: Kriminalistische Überlegungen zur Frage: 'Kannte Luther Thomas?'" *Luther* 77 [2006]: 83–99). Notwithstanding, the above historiography is not attempting to present Aquinas's complete theology of penance, which Poschmann, *Buße und Letzte Ölung* (cf. n. 7), 90, considers to be a "rather complicated structure" laden with "certain unclarities and dissonances." My translations.

18. For more on Aquinas's doctrine of penance, cf. Anton Ziegenaus, *Umkehr, Versöhnung, Friede: Zu einer theologisch verantworteten Praxis von Bußgotttesdienst und Beichte* (Freiburg: Herder, 1975), 110–11.

19. Thomas Aquinas, Sent IV d. 22 a. 1 ad 3: "*remissio peccatorum utroque modo est res ipsius poenitentiae sacramenti: quae aliquando tempore praecedit sacramentum exterius, aliquando autem in ipso sacramento efficitur; quia quando aliquis accedit ad confessionem attritus, non plene contritus, si obicem non ponat, in ipsa confessione et absolutione, sibi gratia et remissio peccatorum datur.*" (See Thomae Aquinatis, *Scriptum super Sententiis*, ed. Maria Fabian Moos, vol. 4 [Paris: P. Lethielleux, 1947], 1097). My translation.

20. For more on the various versions of the commentary on the sentences, see: Thomas Williams, "Introduction: The Life and Work of John Duns the Scot," in *The Cambridge Companion to Duns Scotus*, ed. Thomas Williams (Cambridge: University Press, 2003), 1–14, 6–7; 9–10.

of mortal sin, also a virtue?")[21] At this point, he found occasion to speak about *attritio*, which he classified in his theology of grace as a *meritum de congruo*,[22] a merit that God sees as such although it is none at all. Such a penitent heart, *attritio*, is transformed into *contritio* through grace.[23] With the transformation of *attritio* to *contritio*, the question follows: is sin taken away?[24] The answer was yes. The objectivity of the Sacrament had such a weight for Scotus that he explained that even if *attritio* is not present in the form of a *meritum de congruo* but only as a simple will "to receive the sacrament of penance,"[25] God can allow penance to take effect in this penitent by the power of his covenant with which he supports the sacrament. This is the reason for the institution of the sacrament in the first place.[26] Much like Aquinas, it is interesting to see how the sacramental act gets concentrated on the word of absolution. "The Sacrament of Penance is that 'priestly absolution which takes place by means of certain words.'"[27] Thus, despite Aquinas's tendency to overemphasize certain aspects, Duns Scotus did share his interest in sacramental objectification as was strengthened in the prescriptions of the Fourth Lateran Council.

The new concentration of *contritio* reacted to Duns Scotus's developments by calling on doctrine from the early Middle Ages. William of Ockham gave great attention to his position in his commentary of the fourth book of the Sentences.[28] That these debates were not concerned with a juxtaposition of "contritionism" and "attritionism" but rather the question of the effectivity of God's grace and its sacramental connection can be seen in Ockham's first rebuttal to Duns Scotus. It is only possible *de potentia absoluta*[29] that God justifies an unbeliever "without any good

21. Duns Scotus, Ordinatio IV d. 14 q. 2 (Ioannis Duns Scoti, *Opera omnia*, vol. 13, [Vatican: Typ. Polyglottis Vaticanis, 2011], 21:527–28): "Utrum actus poenitendi requisitus ad deletionem peccati mortalis, sit actus alicuius virtutis?" My translation.

22. Duns Scotus, Ordinatio IV d. 14 q. 2 No. 134 (Duns Scotus, *Opera* 13 [cf. n. 21], 34.886–89).

23. Duns Scotus, Ordinatio IV d. 14 q. 2 No. 137 (Duns Scotus, *Opera* 13 [cf. n. 21], 35.910–14).

24. Duns Scotus, Ordinatio IV d. 14 q. 2 No. 146 (Duns Scotus, *Opera* 13 [cf. n. 21], 37.963–64): "sic debet concedi in sensu divisionis, quod per actum, qui est contritio, deletur peccatum."

25. Duns Scotus, Ordinatio IV d. 14 q. 4 No. 218 (Duns Scotus, *Opera* 13 [cf. n. 21], 54.391–92): "recipere Sacramentum peonitenti sicut dispensator in Ecclesia."

26. Duns Scotus, Ordinatio IV d. 14 q. 4 No. 218 (Duns Scotus, *Opera* 13 [cf n. 21], 54.395–97).

27. Duns Scotus, Ordinatio IV d. 16 q. 1 No. 25 (Duns Scotus, *Opera* 13 [cf. n. 21], 136.151–52) "Poenitentia-sacramentum est illa 'absolutio sacerdotalis facta certis verbis.'" My translation.

28. William of Ockham, Sent IV q. 10–11 (Guilelmi de Ockham, *Opera Theologica*, vol. 7, *Quaestiones in librum quartum sententiarum [Reportatio]*, ed. Rega Wood and Gedeon Gál [St. Bonaventure, NY: St. Bonaventure University, 1984], 216.19–218.8).

29. For the history of the *potentia absoluta* concept, cf. William J. Courtenay, *Capacity and Volition: A History of the Distinction of Absolute and Ordained Power* (Bergamo: Pierluigi Lubrina,

motion of the will and without contrition or attrition concerning sin."[30] But in fact, this did not match up with the conception of the sacred.[31] Ockham's answer was found in an intensification of *contritio*, which he emphasized as being new: "And therefore, I say without any other example that mortal sin cannot be remitted by means of a sacrament without some form of contrition."[32] That a medieval thinker would sell his own idea as being without precedent is quite unusual.[33] But it is not unwarranted in this case. What Ockham does here is to combine conceptually the sacramental side found in the understanding of the Fourth Lateran Council with the subjectivity-oriented direction of early medieval doctrine. He transfers the subjective, sacrament-skeptical doctrine of penance of someone like Lombard (whom he repeatedly references at this point[34]) into a subjective-sacramental theory centered in an understanding of penance as an *actus poenitentis* ("penitential act").[35] The effectivity of the sacraments was not substituted by the subjective experience of the penitent (there was a potential for that with Lombard). Rather, it was made dependent on those subjective conditions. Ockham more precisely determined the conditions for this disposition: legal maturity, knowledge of the conditions and a free will.[36] Such a person stood under the conditions—"their sins will not be forgiven without a good movement in their own will."[37]

As is typical for his *Collectorium*, Gabriel Biel extended Ockham's considerations even further but argued in a doubled fashion. Heiko Augustinus Oberman has aptly summarized this argument based on the distinction within penance "as virtue and as sacrament."[38] Biel introduces the

1990); for Ockham, cf. Volker Leppin, "Does Ockham's Concept of Divine Power Threaten Man's Certainty in His Knowledge of the World?" *Franciscan Studies* 55 (1998): 169–80.

30. Ockham, Sent IV q. 10–11 (Ockham, *Opera Theologica* 7 [cf. n. 28], 218, 10–12): "sine omni bono motu voluntatis et sine contritione vel attritione de peccatis." My translation.

31. Ockham, Sent IV q. 10–11 (Ockham, *Opera Theologica* 7 [cf. n. 28], 218, 14; 220, 18; 222, 11).

32. Ockham, Sent IV q. 10–11 (Ockham, *Opera Theologica* 7 [cf. n. 28], 220, 6–8): "Et ideo dico sine omni praeiudicio aliorum quod per nullum sacramentum potest remitti peccatum mortale sine omni contrition in generali vel speciali."

33. Ockham himself undertook such a self-interpretation as a renewer in another prominent case: the doctrine of universals (cf. Volker Leppin, *Wilhelm von Ockham: Gelehrter—Streiter—Bettelmönch*, 2nd ed. [Darmstadt: Wissenschaftliche Buchgesellschaft, 2012], 66–68).

34. Ockham, Sent IV q. 10–11 (Ockham, *Opera Theologica* 7 [cf. n. 28], 218, 12–13).

35. Ockham, Sent IV q. 10–11 (Ockham, *Opera Theologica* 7 [cf. n. 28], 221, 7–8).

36. Ockham, Sent IV q. 10–11 (Ockham, *Opera Theologica* 7 [cf. n. 28], 220, 8–10).

37. Ockham, Sent IV q. 10–11 (Ockham, *Opera Theologica* 7 [cf. n. 28] 220, 14–15): "non remittitur sibi peccatum sine motu bono propriae voluntatis."

38. Oberman, *Harvest*, 157. This double character "as both virtue and sacrament" ascribes Maria C. Morrow, "Reconnecting Sacrament and Virtue: Penance in Aquinas's Summa Theologiae," *New Blackfriars* 91 (2010): 304–20, 306 to the doctrine of penance of Aquinas; for more on the

distinction between penance as an act of habit and penance as an act of the absolving priest.[39]

In the sense of *poenitentia* as a virtue (the first sense), Gabriel Biel describes in Sent IV d. 14 q. 1 that for a person who has fallen into a mortal sin after their baptism, a formal or virtual act of penance is required *de potentia ordinata*.[40] A virtual act of penance is to be understood as an act of penetrant love of God; a radical acceptance of God allows for the forgiveness of sins without formal penance.[41] The special thing about Biel's conception is that he foresees this possibility expressly as an event *de potentia ordinata*.[42]

Although the event of penance belongs in the realm of proper actions by God, Biel cannot extricate himself from a contradicting position that sees *poenitentia* as a virtue[43] and is *opinio communis* according to which the Sacrament of Penance blots out sin. The conflict only pertained to the question of how exactly this blotting was to be done.[44] After drawing in the ideas of Duns Scotus, Aquinas, and a few others, he comes to the conclusion that mere *attritio*, as long as it is discernable from *contritio*, is not sufficient for the pouring out of grace.[45] The required *contritio* could not be considered a simple disposition toward grace but collaborated with grace for the good of the person.[46] In a classic sense, this position can be termed synergistic: sacramental grace—consisting of the "proclamation by a priest of certain words over a human who confesses his sins"[47] (which is to say absolution[48])—is bound to a subjective event within an individual person. And *this* brings with it the consequence that, just like Ockham's

emphasis of the "penitent virtue" by Biel, cf. Reinhard Schwarz, *Vorgeschichte der reformatorischen Bußtheologie* (Berlin: De Gruyter, 1968), 125.

39. Biel, *Collectorium* d. 14 q. 1 a. 1 Notabile 1 A, Z. 8–11 (Gabrielis Biel, *Collectorium circa quattuor libros Sententiarum. Libri quarti pars prima [dist. 1–14]*, ed. Wilfried Werbeck and Udo Hofmann [Tübingen: Mohr, 1975], 418); for more on the significance of Biel's understanding of penance, cf. Morerod, *Manque de clarté* (cf. n. 17), 22.

40. Biel, *Collectorium* d. 14 q. 1 a. 2 concl. 3 M, Z. 1–3 (Biel, *Collectorium* [cf. n. 39], 428).

41. Biel, *Collectorium* d. 14 q. 1 a. 2 concl. 3 M, Z. 50–54 (Biel, *Collectorium* [cf. n. 39], 430).

42. Cf. also Biel, *Collectorium* d. 14 q. 1 a. 2 concl. 2 L, Z. 15f (Biel, *Collectorium* [cf. n. 39], 427).

43. Cf. here Biel, *Collectorium* d. 14 q. 1 a. 3 dubium 3 (Biel, *Collectorium* [cf. n. 39], 441–43): According to this, *poenitentia* is to be seen as a virtue and, more precisely, as a theological virtue, as far as it concerns the love of God. However, as concerns the stain of sin, it is rather to be considered a moral virtue (AA, Z. 17–19).

44. Biel, *Collectorium* d. 14 q. 2 a. 1 Notabile 2 D, Z. 1f (Biel, *Collectorium* [cf. n. 39], 449).

45. Biel, *Collectorium* d. 14 q. 2 a. 1 Notabile 2 L, Z. 9f (Biel, *Collectorium* [cf. n. 39], 465).

46. Biel, *Collectorium* d. 14 q. 2 a. 1 Notabile 2 L, Z. 14–16 (Biel, *Collectorium* [cf. n. 39], 465).

47. Biel, *Collectorium* d. 14 q. 2 a. 1 Notabile 1 C, Z. 47–48 (Biel, *Collectorium* [cf. n. 39], 449). My translation.

48. Cf. Biel, *Collectorium* d. 14 q. 2 a. 1 Notabile 1 A, Z. 11–15 (Biel, *Collectorium* [cf. n. 39], 445).

theory, the application of grace is dependent on a precondition within the person. That precondition consists of the human doing what is in them (*facere quod in se est*).[49] In the course of the entire argument where sacramental-theological ideas follow virtue-theoretical considerations, Biel's argument homes in on a sacramental interpretation. In its most pure form, his thought can be described by our well-known subjective-sacramental theology of penance.

Thus, Gabriel Biel is essential for our understanding of Luther's own ideas concerning penance. So is John of Paltz, who is usually described with the language of attritionism, but also demonstrates extensive similarities to Biel in his application of *facere quod in se est*.[50] In his *Coelifodina* (compiled from various parts of the *Heavenly Treasure*, written for Elector Friedrich and Herzog Johann between 1490 and 1502),[51] he extensively explored the relationship between *attritio* and *contritio*, developing an extensive vocabulary in the process. According to his definition, *attritio* could be considered an incomplete *detestatio peccati* that was founded in a simple *timor servilis* (servile fear) of death and hell.[52]

Paltz appears to have known something about Duns Scotus.[53] In any case, he radicalized certain aspects of his theology, staunchly subscribing to the idea that such an *attritio* could be transformed into *contritio* by God, even before one went to a priest. The basis for this divine recognition is that sinners simply do what is in them (*facere quod in se est*).[54] Here, we come across the same concept that was so central to Biel—a closeness, which Adolar Zumkeller has drawn attention to.[55] This nearness is what creates a difference for the concepts *contritio* and *attritio*. While Biel basically believes that the former is experienced by the person, Paltz tends toward the latter. He even rigorously defines what this action consists of: calling upon Christ and the saints, trusting in the intercessory prayers of others, and giving alms.[56] *Attritio* was thus redefined from a certain

49. Biel, *Collectorium* d. 14 q. 1 a. 2 Concl. 5 U, Z. 32 (Biel, *Collectorium* [cf. n. 39], 437).
50. Cf. Hamm, *Frömmigkeitstheologie* (cf. n. 6), 277. For background information on his doctrine of *facere quod in se est* in the "Compendium theologicae veritatis" from Hugo Ripelin of Straßburg, cf. Adolar Zumkeller, *Erbsünde, Gnade, Rechtfertigung und Verdienst nach der Lehre der Erfurter Augustinertheologen des Spätmittelalters* (Würzburg: Echter Verlag, 1984), 408.
51. For more on how this came to be, cf. Johannes von Paltz, *Werke*, vol. 1, *Coelifodina*, ed. Christoph Burger and Friedhelm Stasch (Berlin: De Gruyter, 1983), XV–XXI.
52. Paltz, *Coelifodina* (Paltz, *Werke* 1 [cf. n. 51], 260, 7–8. Paltz followed in the footsteps of his teacher John of Dorsten concerning his particular distinctions and examples (cf. Zumkeller, *Erbsünde* [cf. n. 50], 416–18; Hamm, *Frömmigkeitstheologie* [cf. n. 6], 275).
53. Zum Bezug von Paltz auf Duns Scotus. For more on Paltz's relation to Duns Scotus, cf. Hamm, *Frömmigkeitstheologie* (cf. n. 6), 276.
54. Paltz, *Coelifodina* (Paltz, *Werke* 1 [cf. n. 51], 260, 23–26.
55. Zumkeller, *Erbsünde* (cf. n. 50), 411.
56. Paltz, *Coelifodina* (Paltz, *Werke* 1 [cf. n. 51], 260, 31–36).

attitudinal form to a certain behavior and activity, enabling one to follow instructions and, despite recognizing one's own deficiency before God, to achieve the proper form of regret. The securing went even further. For those not able to do what was in them but only *aliquo modo*, the Sacrament of Penance was ready for them. Absolution would transform *attritio* into *contritio*.[57] And, according to Paltz, even for those who did not even do *aliquo modo*, what was in them could hope for sacramental salvation. They still had the option of Extreme Unction in order to be saved from eternal damnation.[58] Despite his strongly pastoral orientation toward the subjective disposition of the individual, Paltz ultimately roots the story of salvation in a sacramental horizon where it was still possible to attain salvation by means of a sufficiently sacramental lifestyle, even if one lacked the desired personal disposition.[59]

If we distance ourselves from an oversimplified model that wants to pit attritionism against contritionism, then we can detect a double movement in the theology of penance at the close of the fifteenth century. On the one hand, it was honing an understanding of penance as a sacrament that was administered by a priest. On the other hand, it placed a great emphasis on the subjective capabilities of the individual person to do what was in them. Taken together, they form the background for Luther's own theology of penance a few decades later. As we see with theologians such as Ockham and Gabriel Biel, the debates about the various individual positions were far less relevant than the web of possibilities they created together. Luther's great challenge was found in confronting the heavy emphasis on the internal disposition of the individual, especially in the form provided by Biel. If one were to read Biel's theory of a collaboration between *contritio* and absolution, then the unavoidable conclusion was that sacramental penance was dependent on an internal posture of the person and dependent on their natural capabilities.

Luther gave very little time and attention to his commentary of Book IV of the Sentences.[60] His first real foray into the topic of penance took place with his first lectures on the Psalms, the *Dictata in Psalterium*, held in Wittenberg in 1513–1515. Leif Grane's conclusion that Luther "speaks here as a theologian of the *via moderna*"[61] is accurate, at least for

37. Paltz, *Coelifodina* (Paltz, *Werke* 1 [cf. n. 51], 261, 9–13).

58. Paltz, *Coelifodina* (Paltz, *Werke* 1 [cf. n. 51], 262, 31–263, 12).

59. For more on the meaning of the "guarantee function of the sacraments," see Hamm, *Frömmigkeitstheologie* (cf. n. 6), 275.

60. Cf. Martin Luther, *Erfurter Annotationen 1509–1510/11*, ed. Jun Matsuura (AWA 9): 557–58.

61. Leif Grane, *Contra Gabrielem: Luthers Auseinandersetzung mit Gabriel Biel in der Disputatio Contra Scholasticam Theologiam 1517* (Copenhagen: Gyldendal, 1962), 309, my translation; adopted by Berndt Hamm, *Promissio, Pactum, Ordinatio: Freiheit und Selbstbindung Gottes in der*

his theology of penance. In one of his latest lectures on Psalms 115 (113), he explained:

> Therefore the doctors teach rightly that God gives grace infallibly to those, who do what is in them. And even if a person cannot prepare themselves for grace in a dignified manner because they do not stand in a proper relation to it, they can nevertheless prepare themselves congruently because of God's promise and the covenant of mercy.[62]

Thus, Luther succinctly summarizes the path to salvation as we can find in Gabriel Biel's theory of penance, including the idea of a *pactum* made between God and a believer in order to execute his *potentia absoluta* for the believer's salvation.[63] That *promissio*,[64] which is read

*scholastischen Gnadenlehre* (Tübingen: Mohr, 1977), 377. Grane's conclusion is part of his theory of a late dating for Luther's "breakthrough." This understanding must be taken carefully with all of its nuances: the observations concerning Luther's doctrine of penance are only a small component in a general development for Luther, which has to depart from the sort of "scholarly construction" that Leif Grane took as the state of research in his time (cf. Berndt Hamm, "Impending Doom and Imminent Grace: Luther's Early Years in the Cloister as the Beginning of His Reformation Reorientation," in *The Early Luther: Stages in a Reformation Reorientation* [Minneapolis: Fortress Press, 2017], 26–58, 27). In fact, it is more accurate to speak of a slow development that took place at different speeds for each theological topic, often moving back and forth between various conceptions and gradually transforming given theological ideas than it is to speak of a radical break with them (see Leppin, *A Late Medieval Life*, 42.)

62. Luther, *Dictata in Psalterium* (WA 55/2:876.92–877.95): "*Hinc recte dicunt Doctores, quod homini facienti quod in se est, Deus infallibiliter dat gratiam, Et licet non de condigno sese possit ad gratiam preparare, quia est incomparabilis, tamen bene de congruo propter promissionem istam Dei et pactum misericordie.*" Thus, we cannot reject the thought of internal disposition for the late phase of the First Psalm Lectures as does Erich Vogelsang, *Die Anfänge von Luthers Christologie nach der Ersten Pslamenvorlesung insbesondere in ihren exegetischen und systematischen Zusammenhängen mit Augustin und der Scholastik dargestellt* (Berlin: De Gruyter, 1929), 124. And, in contrast to Hamm, *Promissio* (cf. n. 61), 380, Luther does not fill *facere* exclusively through "self-judgement" and "supplication" but he also speaks of *Iuste et sobrie et pie vivere* and *sancte vivere*—and in fact, he says about all of this that "*vix*" is a sort of *dispositio*. This devaluing serves to emphasize that we are dealing with merits *de congruo*, not *de condigno* (cf. 877, 95–98). That *facere* includes acts of sanctification is not affected by this. However, we can identify a specific transformation of Biel's thought when Luther writes, "totum tempus gratie preparatio est ad futuram gloriam" (877, 103–04). Hamm, *Promissio* (cf. n. 61), 381, strongly emphasizes the "new approach" in this. And indeed, Luther does have Biel's idea here that an *actus diligendi* of grace, understood as a *dispositio*, precedes penance according to nature but not time. (Biel, Collectorium III d. 27 a. un a. 3 Dubium 2 [Gabrielis Biel, *Collectorium circa quattuor libros Sententiarum. Liber tertius*, ed. Wilfried Werbeck and Udo Hofmann {Tübingen: Mohr, 1969}, 506, R1–3]). Over time, it becomes a temporally permanent condition.

63. Heiko Augustinus Oberman, "Wir sein pettler. Hoc est verum. Bund und Gnade in der Theologie des Mittelalters und der Reformation," in *Die Reformation: Von Wittenberg nach Genf* (Göttingen: Vandenhoeck & Ruprecht 1986), 90–112, 101–12.

64. Cf. Oswald Bayer, *Promissio: Geschichte der reformatorischen Wende in Luthers Theologie*, 2nd ed. (Darmstadt: Wissenschaftliche Buchgesellschaft, 1989).

as a keyword in later contexts, makes clear what diverse and multi-faceted transformations Luther's thought experienced over the years. Even when Luther is handling penance head-on, Biel's mark on his thought can still be discerned. Biel had defined penance primarily as a virtue, namely the willing suffering of a just punishment,[65] and had described its process in five steps: (1) the punishment of the sin (*vindicare seu punire peccatum*), (2) *contritio* as *detestatio* of sin, (3) sadness and pain (*dolor*), (4) the acceptance of sadness and pain and the new attainment of favor in the eyes of God, and (5) the acceptance of an external punishment.[66] This paradigm makes clear how Biel saw the proper collaboration of *contritio* and grace. And with Luther, we encounter precisely these concepts again (sometimes in a less-clear state of affairs), sometimes even in a word-for-word citation in the description of penance, especially when describing statements of *nostri theologi* or *nostri Scholastici* concerning penance, bringing them all together with the biblical text. What the Bible describes as *iudicium*, he interpreted as the acts of penance while laying out Psalms 1:5 ("Therefore the wicked will not stand in the judgement,"): "Being irate about oneself, feeling pain, being ashamed, detesting, punishing,"[67] and he summarized all of this with a citation from Proverbs 18:17, "The one who first states a case seems right."[68] In the *Dictata*, he finds the immediate consequence of seeing Christ to be self-detestation.[69] Throughout his entire first lectures on the Psalms, Luther appears to have favored a theory of penance largely compatible with that of Biel, where trust in the powers of an individual person—*faciens quod in se est*—was connected with a self-critical, negative interpretation of the *contritio*-concept.

65. Biel, *Collectorium* d. 14 q. 1 a. 1 Notabile 1 A, Z. 35–37 (Biel, *Collectorium* [cf. n. 39], 419).
66. Biel, *Collectorium* d. 14 q. 1 a. 1 Notabile 1 B, Z. 1–12 (Biel, *Collectorium* [cf. n. 39], 419).
67. Luther, *Dictata in Psalterium* (WA 55/2:32.21–25):
"{*Irasci sibi*
{*dolere*
*vt* {*pudere*
{*detestari*
{*vindicare*," my translation; cf. also WA 55/2:36.10–14: "*Item, Quod nostri Scolastici theologice vocant actus penitentie, scil. displicere sibi, detestari, condemnare, accusare, velle vindicare, punire seipsum, castigare et cum effectu odire malum et irasci sibi, vno verbo appellat Scriptura Iudicium.*"
68. Luther, *Dictata in Psalterium* (WA 55/2:33.1).
69. Luther, *Dictata in Psalterium* (WA 55/2:75.27): "*Omnis qui cepit agnoscere Christum et veritatem, mox incipit detestari suam vanitatem.*" (All who are captivated by a doubt of Christ and truth quickly begin to doubt their own vanity.) My translation.

## THE ALTERNATIVE TO SCHOLASTIC DEBATE: LUTHER'S DISCOVERY OF PENANCE

It is against this context of a deep formation through Biel's understanding of penance that we must read an account that Luther gave in the dedicatory letters for his confessor Staupitz. It accompanied the publication of the *Resolutiones*, the extensive explanation of the indulgence theses:

> Reverend Father: I remember that during your most delightful and helpful talks, through which the Lord Jesus wonderfully consoled me, you sometimes mentioned the term "*poenitentia*." I was then distressed by my conscience and by the tortures of those who through endless and insupportable precepts teach the socalled method of confession. Therefore I accepted you as a messenger from heaven when you said that *poenitentia* is genuine only if it begins with love for justice and for God and that what they consider to be the final stage and completion is in reality rather the very beginning of *poenitentia*.[70]

The shift in Luther's understanding of penance is thus decisive. A negative perspective becomes a positive one, and for Luther, "now no word sounds sweeter or more pleasant to me than *poenitentia*."[71] As I have argued elsewhere,[72] it is probable that Luther developed his new understanding of penance (toward which Staupitz had pushed him) while reading John

---

70. Luther, *Widmungsschreiben zu den Resolutiones disputationum de indulgentiarum virtute* (WA 1:525.4–14): "*Memini, Reverende pater, inter iucundissimas et salutares fabulas tuas, quibus me solet dominus Ihesus mirifice consolari, incidisse aliquando mentionem huius nominis 'poenitentia', ubi miserti conscientiarum multarum carnificumque illorum, qui praeceptis infinitis eisdemque importabilibus modum docent (ut vocant) confitendi, te velut e caelo sonantem excepimus, quod poenitentia vera non est, nisi quae ab amore iusticiae et dei incipit, Et hoc esse potius principium poenitentiae, quod illis finis et consummatio censetur.*" Cited after LW 48:65, to John of Staupitz: Wittenberg, May 30, 1518. Even though the significance of the doctrine of penance was increasingly overshadowed by the doctrine of justification, Jack E. Brush, *Gotteserkenntnis und Selbsterekenntnis. Luthers Verständnis des 51. Psalms* (Tübingen: Mohr 1997), 126 still finds a central significance for Luther's understanding of theology in his 1532 exegesis of Psalm 51. Cited after LW 48:65.
71. Luther, *Widmungsschreiben zu den Resolutiones disputationum de indulgentiarum virtute* (WA 1:525.20–21): "*nunc nihil dulcius aut gratius (…) sonet quam 'poenitentia'.*" Cited after LW 48:66.
72. Volker Leppin, "'omnem vitam fidelium penitentiam esse voluit:' Zur Aufnahme mystischer Traditionen in Luthers erster Ablaßthese," in *Transformationen: Studien zu den Wandlungsprozessen in Theologie und Frömmigkeit zwischen Spätmittelalter und Reformation*, 2nd ed. (Tübingen: Mohr Siebeck, 2018), 261–77. For my response to Ulrich Köpf's critique of my interpretation of Luther's Tauler-reception, see above in the introduction, n. 7. Vincent Evener, *Enemies of the Cross: Suffering, Truth, and Mysticism in the Early Reformation* (Oxford: University Press, 2021), 44–62 has offered an excellent interpretation of the marginalia written into Tauler's works by Karlstadt and Luther.

Tauler. He was reading Tauler while holding his lectures on Romans.[73] And here it really does make sense that Luther was interested in penance.[74]

John Tauler did not participate in the scholastic discourse. However (or, perhaps, therefore), we encounter an understanding of penance with him that smacks of the subjective, sacrament-skeptical tones of Peter Abelard. On the day of the Elevation of the Cross, he spoke of the continuous relapse of the person into sin:

> Even if you fall seventy times a day, every time you should return and come back to God. And merge again with God, so that your sin will be omitted. When you go to confession with it, you do not know how to say it. This should not scare you. You have not noticed that it [i.e., your deed] could damage you, just confess your nothingness. And respond to your own disdain with calmness, not with melancholy. [. . .] St. Paul says: Everyone who loves God will be successful. In the gloss it says that this also refers to the sinner. So, sinner, be silent and take refuge in God, and contemplate your nothingness. And keep it inside; do not run to the confessor with it.[75]

This text is obviously close to the negative understanding of penance that we encountered with Biel. Yet, right next to the passage pertaining to self-detestation, Luther wrote, "remember this!"[76] A few lines later, where the text advises against going directly to a confessor with sins, he scribbled: "an extremely helpful bit of advice!"[77]

He clearly got a lot out of his reading. The reason for that becomes apparent when we see that both of Luther's marginalia in the Tauler text surround Paul's text of Romans 8:28, "We know that all things work together for good for those who love God, who are called according to his purpose." And in fact, this passage starts with a positive relation to God at the beginning of penance. Thus, self-detestation is but one side of the coin, with the other being a deep love of God.

Luther was led to a shift in his understanding of penance—by his reading of Tauler[78] as well as by Staupitz, who may have pressed Tauler

---

73. See below for the exact dating.

74. Cf. Leppin, "omnem vitam," (cf. n. 72) 13–20.

75. Sermones: *des hoch\ geleerten in gnaden erleüchten do\ctoris Johannis Thaulerii sannt \ dominici ordens die da weißend \ auff den nächesten waren weg im \ gaist zů wanderen durch überswe\ bendenn syn. Von latein in teütsch \ gewendt manchem menschenn zů \ såliger fruchtbarkaitt* (Augsburg: Hans Otmar, 1508), fol. 192ᵛ. Cited after: John Tauler, *Johannes Tauler: Sermons*, trans. Maria Shrady, Classics of Western Spirituality (Mahwah, NJ: Paulist Press, 1985), 166.

76. Luther, *Randbemerkungen zu Taulers Predigten* (WA 9:104.11): "*Hoc nota tibi.*"

77. Luther, *Randbemerkungen zu Taulers Predigten* (WA 9:104.12): "*Utilissimum consilium.*"

78. Henrik Otto, *Vor- und frühreformatorische Tauler-Rezeption: Annotationen in Drucken des späten 15. und 16. Jahrhunderts* (Gütersloh: Gütersloher Verlagshaus, 2003), 183–214.

into his hands. On the one hand, this had to do with an orientation toward a positive basic attitude as the basis for penance. It most likely also had to do with a creeping desacramentalization of penance. This is demonstrated fundamentally in the idea that proper regret before God makes external confession superfluous, as well as in the idea that life as a whole is a grand, comprehensive path of penance, just as Tauler presents on the previous page of the edition used by Luther. Even if there is no marginalia on said page, we can assume that Luther had intensely studied this sermon and thought through the lines that read, "is not the work of a day or two. Thou must set thyself to constantly search thy soul and overcome thyself in all things."[79]

In his lectures on Romans, Luther had not yet adopted and developed this double desacramentalization, but he had made remarkable changes to his understanding of penance as compared to his early adherence to the *Via moderna*. Where once a *facere quod in se est* stood at the beginning of penance, now there was a radical self-detestation and, in a scintillating dialectic, a radical trust in God. Such a dialectic could actually make the Sacrament of Penance irrelevant. The deeply felt *contritio* was not thought of as a step in the trio of *contritio, confessio,* and *satisfactio* but rather stood alone and as the cornerstone of a direct communicative relation to God. This relation had no direct need for a priest—as was the case for Peter Lombard.

> After this it happened that I learned—thanks to the work and talent of the most learned men who teach us Greek and Hebrew with such great devotion—that the word *poenitentia* means metanoia in Greek; it is derived from *meta* and *noun*, that is, from "afterward" and "mind." *Poenitentia* or metanoia, therefore, means coming to one's right mind and a comprehension of one's own evil after one has accepted the damage and recognized the error. This is impossible without a change in one's disposition and [the object of one's] love. All these definitions agree so well with Pauline theology that, at least in my opinion, almost nothing could illustrate Paul's theology better than the way they do.[80]

---

79. Tauler, *Sermones,* (cf. n. 75) fol. 192[r+v]: "*Diß sol nichtt sein aines tages. vnd des anderen nicht. Sunder es sol one vnderloß sein alltzeit. vnd nymm dein selb war in allen dingen.*" Cited after John Tauler, *The Sermons and Conferences of John Tauler,* ed. and trans. Walter Elliott (Washington, DC: Apostolic Mission House, 1910), 696.

80. Luther, *Widmungsschreiben zu den Resolutiones disputationum de indulgentiarum virtute* (WA 1:525.24–30), "*Post haec accessit, quod studio et gratia eruditissimorum virorum, qui nobis graeca et hebraea officiosissime tradunt, didici, idem verbum graece 'Metanoea' dici a 'meta' et 'noyn', id est a 'post' et 'mentem', ut sit poenitentia seu metanea resipiscentia et post acceptum damnum et cognitum errorem intelligentia sui mali, quod sine mutatione affectus et amoris fieri est impossibile, quae omnia*

If we read this in the context of Luther's engagement with Tauler in 1515/16, then this statement fits very well to the situation in which Luther got to know Erasmus's *Novum Testamentum*.[81] Erasmus commented Matthew 3:2, where the word μετάνοεῖτε first appears in the New Testament as a cry from John the Baptist:

> μετάνοεῖτε. (. . .) But our people believes that doing penance consists of washing away our sins with some form of penance. By the way, μετάνοια is derived from μετάνοεῖν and means understanding something after the fact (a posterius intelligendo), such as when some lapsed individual recognizes their error after completing their deed (. . .) In my opinion, it can be conveyed appropriately with "Be aware" or "Return to your senses!"[82]

It is obvious that Luther wants to refer back to this insight from Erasmus. It signaled the clear departure from the scholastic understanding of penance, brought to its fullest, punishment-focused one-sidedness by Biel. Now the movement started to make the *mens* the true content of penance. While it would be foolish to understand Luther's own account as corresponding perfectly with how events transpired,[83] we can nevertheless discern elements in his account that testify to his intense engagement with late-medieval and humanistic literature on penance. Luther will go on to develop the philological argumentation even further by analyzing additional possibilities for the translation of μετά, taking both *post* and *trans* into consideration. Ultimately, he will settle on the primary translation of the word μετάνοια as being *transmutation* in the spirit.

> Then I progressed further and saw that metanoia could be understood as a composite not only of "afterward" and "mind," but also of the [prefix]

*Paulinae Theologiae ita respondent apte, ut nihil ferme aptius Paulum illustrare possit, meo saltem iudicio.*" Cited after LW 48:66–67.

81. Luther first mentions Erasmus concerning the latter's annotations to Rom 9:19 (WA 56:400.15).
82. *NOVVM IN-| strumentum omne, dilgienter ab ERASMO ROTERDAMO| recognitum et emendatum non solum ad græcam ueritatem, ue-| rumetiam ad multorum utriusque linguæ codicum, eorumque ue-| terum simul et emendatorum fidem (. . .)* (Basel: Froben, 1516), [Annotationes] 241: "μετάνοεῖτε. (. . .) *At nostrum uulgus putat esse pœnitentiam agere, præscripta pœna quapiam luere commissa. (. . .) Alioqui* μετάνοια *dicta est a* μετάνοεῖν, *hoc est, a posterius intelligendo, ubi quis lapsus, re peracta, tum demum animadvertit erratum suum. (. . .) Meo iudicio commode uerti poterat, Respicite, siue ad mentem reddite.*" My translation. Cf. also Martin Brecht, "Luthers neues Verständnis der Buße und die reformatorische Entdeckung," *Zeitschrift für Theologie und Kirche* 101 (2004): 281–91, 284, who considers this explaination to be a decisive reference point for Luther. Erasmus summarized this explanation in his comments on Jesus's call to repentance in Mark 1:15 (Brecht, "Luthers neues Verständnis," 296).
83. For more on his character as an autobiographical stylization, cf. Leppin, *omnem vitam* (cf. n. 72), 266.

"trans" and "mind" (although this may of course be a forced interpretation), so that metanoia could mean the transformation of one's mind and disposition. Yet it seemed to express not only the actual change of disposition but also the way by which this change is accomplished, that is, the grace of God.[84]

In a gradual process (so his later accounts), he developed a concept of penance after Staupitz gave him food for thought. We can broadly identify this concept as being holistic and certainly a mental replacement of a sacramental event.

While Luther's own reconstruction of the actual events is certainly very complicated, it is very interesting to note that Luther's own reconstruction of events *over a lengthy period of time* flies in the face of the commonly held thesis that Luther experienced a breakthrough concerning penance. Luther later writes of a breakthrough concerning *iustitia*, his "Grand Self-Testimony."[85] We can identify a palpable influence from his time spent reading Tauler at the latest in the Scholia explanation to Romans 8:26 since he mentions Tauler here for the first time. We can date that to spring of 1516.[86] The editors of Romans compared both Tauler's and Luther's marginalia to this letter much earlier, in fact starting with Romans 1:1.[87] It is possible that Luther's first encounter with Tauler took place earlier—spring of 1516 only serves as our first concrete bit of evidence. And in the course of that year, Luther also came to a significant revision of his own

84. Luther, *Widmungsschreiben zu den Resolutiones disputationum de indulgentiarum virtute* (WA 1:526.1–4), "*Denique profeci et vidi, 'Metanoean' non modo a 'post' et 'mentem', sed a 'trans' et 'mentem' posse deduci (sit sane violentum), ut 'Metania' transmutationem mentis et affectus significet, quod non modo affectus mutationem, sed et modum mutandi, id est gratiam dei, videbatur spirare.*" Cited after LW 48:67.

85. For more on this problem, cf. Leppin, "omnem vitam" (cf. n. 72). The late character of the recollection and the parallels in the early recollection of a discovery of *poenitentia* allow us to understand the report from 1545 (WA 54:185.12–186.20) as ahistorical, and certainly much more so than the dedicatory text for Staupitz. The experience with his interpretation does require us to exercise caution against interpreting his early recollections too graciously. Luther may have been closer to the events, both temporally and in his thoughts—but this is still no account of real events!

86. For the dating of the lecture, cf. WA 56:XXIX. According to this passage, the lecture took place in the final weeks of the winter semester. My previous dating of Luther's reading of Tauler—developed on the basis of Karl-Heinz zur Mühlen, *Nos Extra Nos: Luthers Theologie zwischen Mystik und Scholastik* (Tübingen: Mohr, 1972), 97, which came to spring of 1515 (cf. Leppin, *omnem vitam* [cf. n. 72], 276), must be thus corrected on the basis of further research to spring of 1516. However, the first mention of Tauler could have taken place before Luther actually read him, which would make a lot of sense, especially for the arguments developed around Rom 8:7.

87. Luther, *Römerbriefvorlesung* (WA 56:157 comment to l. 3).

conception of penance; toward the end of the lecture, he scribbled in a notebook (without, however, copying into his lecture script):[88]

> Hence it is most absurd and gives strong support to the error of Pelagius to use the commonly accepted statement: "God infallibly pours His grace into him who does what is within his power," if we understand the expression "to do what is within his power" to mean that he does something or can do something.[89]

That is a stark difference to the earlier citation from Psalms 115 (113), and it exists without forcing us to speak of a radical inflection point[90] and does not even imply an indissoluble dependence on Augustine. The criticism of Pelagianism was so common to the Middle Ages that we need not assume that Luther is obliquely referencing to Augustine's anti-Pelagian texts, even though he naturally did know *De spiritu et littera*.[91]

Even if we detect some Augustinian influence here, Tauler still looms large, as we see in a further transition. At Romans 13:13, Luther explained, "Repentance is sweet sorrow and sorrowful sweetness."[92] The very thing that he would describe two years later in a dedicatory text for Staupitz— that penance had become sweet to him—appears in the Romans lectures, and indeed it takes the form of a typically mystical element. Since the early Middle Ages, sweetness is closely connoted with mystical spirituality.[93] When we look at the development of penitential spirituality and theology

88. Luther, *Römerbriefvorlesung. Mitschriften* (WA 57:228.7–12).

89. Luther, *Römerbriefvorlesung* (WA 56:503.1–4): "*Ideo absurdissima est et Pelagiano errori vehementer patrona Sententia Vsitata, Qua dicitur: 'Facienti, quod in se est, Infallibiliter Deus infundit gratiam', Intelligendo per 'facere, quod in se est', aliquid facere Vel posse.*" Cited after LW 25:497, "Lectures on Romans".

90. For the critique of this, cf. Hamm, "Naher Zorn und nahe Gnade" (cf. n. 62).

91. For more on the usage of "De spiritu et littera" in the Lectures on Romans, cf. Bernhard Lohse, "Die Bedeutung Augustins für den jungen Luther," in *Evangelium in der Geschichte: Studien zu Luther und der Reformation*, ed. Leif Grane et al. (Göttingen: Vandenhoeck & Ruprecht 1988), 11–30, 22–30. The earlier usage is far more controversial. We have no clear reference for the time in Erfurt (cf. Luther, *Erfurter Annotationen* [cf. n. 60], CIII–IV), and Lohse 1.1.O.18 must admit that there are no clear references in the Lectures on the Psalms; for further references, which also do not reach back to the earliest years, cf. Hans-Ulrich Delius, *Augustin als Quelle Luthers: Eine Materialsammlung* (Berlin: Evangelische Verlagsanstalt 1984), 171–74. Thus, it seems that Gerhard Ebeling, "Die Anfänge von Luthers Hermeneutik," in *Lutherstudien*, vol. 1 (Tübingen: Mohr 1971), 1–68, 16 is correct when he assumed that Luther "got to know [. . .] *De spiritu et litterta* [. . .] only after the first Lectures on the Psalms." My translation.

92. Luther, *Römerbriefvorlesung* (WA 56:491.18–19): "*penitentia Est dulcis dolor et dolens dulcedo.*" Cited after LW 25:484.

93. Friedrich Ohly, "Geistige Süße bei Otfried," in *Schriften zur mittelalterlichen Bedeutungsforschung* (Darmstadt: Wissenschaftliche Buchgesellschaft, 1977), 93–127; Ohly, *Süße Nägel der Passion: Ein Beitrag zur theologischen Semantik* (Baden-Baden: Koerner, 1989).

with Luther, then it is apparent that there is no antagonism between Pauline Augustinianism and the Middle Ages. Together with mystical spirituality (especially in the form conveyed to Luther by Staupitz), medieval theology formed the lever that Luther would use to dislodge scholastic penitential theology (as he had learned it from Biel). The joyful tone heard here is found elsewhere in the Romans commentary, even before the first mention of Tauler: in Romans 8:7, Luther emphasizes that fear and terror ought not be preached to a penitent but rather the joy of the final days.[94] Love will rescue one from God's wrath.[95] This is an idea that is at least compatible with his recollection of Staupitz and emphasizes precisely what Luther places in the center of his theology.

The development; which Luther subsequently made while immersed in Tauler, Paul, and Augustine; led to another consequential shift in his doctrine of penance. For Romans 11:29, he explained:

> For the counsel of God is not changed by either the merits or demerits of anyone. For He does not repent of the gifts and calling which He has promised, because the Jews are now unworthy of them and you are worthy. He is not changed just because you are changed, and therefore they shall turn back and be led again to the truth of the faith. . . . Hence it is not a matter of our repentence, but of God, who repents of what He changes and destroys.[96]

With this explanation of the verse "Sine penitentia enim sunt dona eius" ("For God's gifts and calling cannot give him cause to regret"), the absolute dependency of salvation on God comes to expression. This corresponds to an equally absolute passivity for the human, which cannot attain any merits and is directed completely toward faith. Again, the parallel to Tauler's annotations jump off the page at us. In the fourth sermon, he states:

> It is God's way not to reward any works other than His own. In Heaven, He will bestow on thee a crown for His works and not for thine. Whatsoever work of thine God does not work in thee, counts for nothing.[97]

---

94. Luther, *Römerbriefvorlesung* (WA 56:365.12–20).

95. Luther, *Römerbriefvorlesung* (WA 56:365.8–9).

96. Luther, *Römerbriefvorlesung* (WA 56:440.1–8): "*Nullius meritis neque demeritis mutatur consilium Dei. Non enim penitet eum sui doni et vocationis promisso, Quia illi nunc sunt indigni et vos digni. Non mutatur vobis mutatis, ideo reuertentur et adducentur tandem ad veritatem fidei. (. . .) Non ergo ad nostram penitentiam refertur, Sed ad Deum, quem penitet eius, quod mutat ac perdit.*" Translation after LW 25:432.

97. Tauler, *Sermones* (cf. n. 75), fol. 10ʳ. Cited after: John Tauler, *The Sermons and Conferences of John Tauler*, ed. and trans. Walter Elliott (Washington, DC: Apostolic Mission House, 1910), 105.

This fits very well with the mystical-Augustinian macrostructure of Luther's theology, and he was reminded of an apparently popular saying that summarized Augustine. He had already used it in his Sentences commentary at d. 27 c. 7[98] and wrote it again here:

> Whatever you have of merit preempting grace has given to you, God has crowned nothing in us other than his gifts.[99]

This contestation of individual works had an early impact on Luther. But he draws a new consequence in the cited passages of the commentary on Romans and in the marginalia for Tauler. Much like in Romans, Luther also notes in the margins of Tauler:

> Therefore the entirety of salvation is resignation of the will in everything as he teaches here in either the spiritual or the temporal domains. And it is simple faith in God.[100]

The mystical, Augustinian, Pauline thought complex that moved and inspired Luther in these years led to an utter passivity of the human and God's exclusivity in matters pertaining to salvation, making faith the junction between them. This theory of faith should not be unscrupulously identified as a mature *sola fide* theology, but it does make clear

98. Luther, *Erfurter Annotationen* (cf. n. 60), 470, 10–11. The saying can be seen as early as Albertus Magnus (*Summa theologiae* II tr. 16 q. 100 membr. 1 [Alberti Magni *Opera Omnia*, ed. Steph., Caes., Aug., and Borgnet, vol. 33 [Paris: Vivès, 1895], 246: "*Quidquid habes meriti praeventrix gratia donat. Nil Deus in nobis praeter sua dona coronat*") and is most likely based on Augustinian sentences, especially Augustine, *Epistola 194*: "*Quod est ergo meritum hominis ante gratiam, quo merito percipiat gratiam, cum omne bonum meritum nostrum non in nobis faciat nisi gratia et, cum deus coronat merita nostra, nihil aliud coronet quam munera sua?*" (CSEL 57:190.12–15). Biel used this verse at the tricky passage: "*cum Deus coronat nostra merita, sua coronat munera*" (as God crowns our merits, he also crowns his gifts). Gabrielis Biel, *Collectorium circa quattuor libros Sententiarum. Liber secundus*, ed. Wilfred Werbeck and Udo Hofmann [Tübingen: Mohr, 1984], 508.11); even closer to the language of this saying is: Augustine, *In Johann 3*, 10 (CChr.SL 36:25.25–26): "*Coronat autem in nobis Deus dona misericordiae suae Hamm, reformato Rechtfertigungslehre!*"
99. Luther, *Randbemerkungen zu Taulers Predigten* (WA 9:99.28–29) "*Quicquid habes meriti praeventrix gratia donat, Nil deus in nobis praeter sua dona coronat.*" My translation.
100. Luther, *Randbemerkungen zu Taulers Predigten* (WA 9:102.34–36), "*Igitur tota salus est resignatio voluntatis in omnibus ut hic docet sive in spiritualibus sive temporalibus. Et nuda fides in deum.*" It is important to consider that *fides* was for Luther primarily a hermeneutically deficient concept when compared to *visio* (cf. Leif Grane, "Christus finis omnium: Eine Studie zu Luthers erster Psalmenvorlesung," in *Caritas Dei: Beiträge zum Verständnis Luthers un der gegenwärtigen Ökumene. FS Mannermaa*, ed. Oswald Bayer [Helsinki: Luther-Agricola-Gesellschaft, 1997], 170–91, 186, with reference to Luther, *Dictata super Psalterium*: "*Que visio excedit fidei claritatem septies et amplius*" [WA 3:469.3]).

the situation that Luther could develop such a transformation in. In the Romans commentary, we see a new, far more mystical interpretation of penance than we did during the lectures on the Psalms. The main moment of this new interpretation is contesting the emphasis on human *facere quod in se est* as found by Biel and Paltz.[101] These insights led Luther toward his paradoxical formulation of Christian existence as *simul iustus et peccator* around this time. He introduces it in his Romans commentary as a description of the process of penance, "Therefore if we always are repentant, we are always sinners, and yet thereby we are righteous and we are justified; we are in part sinners and in part righteous, that is, we are nothing but penitents."[102] The development of his theology of penance leads directly into the mystic-Augustinian transformation of those very basic concepts that later became decisive characteristics of later reformational theology. The fact that these new statements are concentrated in the last third of the Romans lectures ought to provide evidence to us that Luther developed them relatively late and, most likely, under the influence of his reading of Tauler (at the latest in 1516). In any case, there is a high congruence between the text of the lectures and his marginalia of his edition of Tauler.

## THE RADICALIZATION OF THE MYSTICAL UNDERSTANDING OF PENANCE AND ITS APPLICATION TO THE QUESTION OF INDULGENCE IN SERMONS

The question of indulgence undergoes a certain development in the lectures on Romans. Along with a few instances of *indulgentia* in singular as a parallel concept to *gratia*,[103] there is also the occasional usage of the plural for indulgences. In the course of his explanations of Romans 4:7, this takes place quite objectively and neutrally. Luther transfers Augustine's statements about the comprehensive effectiveness of love[104] from baptism

---

101. Zumkeller, *Erbsünde*, (cf. n. 50) 411, has discovered that Paltz and Biel were actually dealing with a similar and by no means forced understanding of *facere quod in se est* that accorded grace a very minor participation in this action so that this interpretation "caused Martin Luther to sharply protest against this in his Lectures on Romans from 1515/1516 because he saw a Pelagian element in it."
102. See, for example, Luther, *Römerbriefvorlesung* (WA 56:442.20–22): "*Si ergo semper penitemus, semper peccatores sumus, et tamen eoipso et Iusti sumus ac Iustificamur, partim peccatores, partim Iusti i. e. nihil nisi penitentes.*" Cited after LW 25:434.
103. Luther, *Römerbriefvorlesung* (WA 56:112.18; 262.13)
104. Augustine, *Epistle167* (CSEL 44:603.4–6).

to penance and indulgences.[105] But the tone has shifted dramatically in Romans 10:4—shortly before we have our first definitive evidence that Luther has been reading Tauler. There is a certain probability that his reading is well underway at this point. Here, Luther adopts the mystical-Augustinian opposition with its positive concentration on the concept of faith, defining the intention of the apostle Paul to be the statement that: "the total righteousness of man leading to salvation depends on the Word through faith and not on good works through knowledge."[106] According to Luther, insufficient understanding of this state of affairs resulted in far too much emphasis being placed on the deeds of the saints,[107] and the doctrine of indulgence became out of control:

> This is where so many promises of indulgences come from and so many permits for building and ornamenting churches and for multiplying ceremonies.[108]

105. Luther, *Römerbriefvorlesung* (WA 56:289.12–13). In this point, the otherwise extremely helpful article from Lothar Vogel, "Zwischen Universität und Seelsorge: Martin Luthers Beweggründe im Ablassstreit," *Zeitschrift für Kirchengeschichte* 118 (2007): 187–212, 194 n. 27 appears to fall short as it refers only to a few indulgence-critical places in the lectures on the Psalms, which lack clarity (cf. also David Bagchi, "Luther's Ninety-Five Theses and the contemporary criticism of indulgences," in *Promissory Notes on the Treasury of Merits. Indulgences in Late Medieval Europe*, ed. Robert N. Swanson [Leiden: Brill 2006], 331–55, 332). Luther, *Dictata in Psalterium* WA 55/2:384.15–19 criticizes the very human attitude ("nos"!) of allowing oneself to be convinced of an easy path to God by means of convenient doctrine and indulgences ("*Et hoc fit totum, quia putamus nos aliquid esse et sufficienter agere, ac sic nihil conamur et nullam violentiam adhibemus et multum facilitamus viam ad celum, per Indulgentias, per faciles doctrinas, quod vnus gemitus satis est.*"); Luther, *Dictata in Psalterium*, 395.339–43 is actually a critique of the praxis of the mendicant orders and not a fundamental critique of indulgence ("*Et hoc fit totum, quia putamus nos aliquid esse et sufficienter agere, ac sic nihil conamur et nullam violentiam adhibemus et multum facilitamus viam ad caelum, per Indulgentias, per faciles doctrinas, quod vnus gemitus satis est.*").
106. Luther, *Römerbriefvorlesung* (WA 56:415.22–23): "*Quod tota Iustitia hominis ad salutem pendet ex verbo per fidem. Et non ex opera per scientiam.*" Cited after LW 25:407.
107. Luther, *Römerbriefvorlesung* (WA 56:417.20–23).
108. Luther, *Römerbriefvorlesung* (WA 56:417.23–25): "*Inde veniunt tot indulgentiarum promissa et permissa pro templis edificandis, ornandis, ceremoniis multiplicandis.*" Cited after LW 25:409. This sort of criticism of indulgences is common (Erasmus's critiques are particularly blistering) to an era that sought to calculate an individual's stint in purgatory with obsessive precision. Indulgences served a sort of calculator for that: "*Nam quid dicam de iis, qui sibi fitis scelerum condonationibus, suavissime blandiuntur, ac Purgatorii spatia veluti clepsydris metiuntur, saecula, annos, menses, dies horas, tamquam e tabula mathematica, citra ullam errorem demetientes.*" Erasmus, *Laus stultitiae*, 40 (Erasmus von Rotterdam, *Ausgewählte Schriften*, ed. Wener Welzig, vol. 2 [Darmstadt: Wissenschaftliche Buchgesellschaft 1975], 94).

As Gabriele Schmidt-Lauber has emphasized, Luther generally did not use his lectures as a platform for criticizing the state of the church.[109] He did not include this comment (which apparently targeted the Peter Indulgence from 1515)[110] in the oral presentation of his lectures, as it is missing in all of the notes taken by his students.[111]

And yet, the young theologian soon found fame with his criticism of indulgence. As a preacher, Luther dared to say things that Luther the lecturing exegete would not. In a sermon from as early as September 21, 1516,[112] Luther declared that he understood penance to be a process entirely effected by God. The true believers trust that it is not their penitential work but rather God's grace that absolves their sin.[113] This is just like Tauler, who recognized the validity of confession before God and without a priest. Thus, it is probable that Luther could fit the entire process of this internal confession under the term *contritio*,[114] and as such a real *contrition* that was distinct from the "fear of the noose,"[115] Luther's derisive term for *attritio*.

109. Gabriele Schmidt-Lauber, *Luthers Vorlesung über den Römerbrief 1515/16: Ein Vergleich zwischen Luthers Manuskript und den studentischen Nachschriften* (Köln: Böhlau, 1994), 156.

110. For more, cf. Nikolaus Paulus, *Geschichte des Ablasses am Ausgang des Mittelalters*, 2nd ed. (Darmstadt: Wissenschaftliche Buchgesellschaft, 1923), 149–48.

111. However, we certainly do see theologically decisive polemics against trusting in mere works in the remarks on Rom 10:6; cf. Luther, *Römerbriefvorlesung* (WA 57:208.22–209.4).

112. Wolfgang Breul, "Luthers Visitation im Augustinerkloster Grimma und seine frühe Ablasskritik: 'Nun will ich der Pauke ein Loch machen,'" *Herbergen der Christenheit* 32/33 (2008/2009): 7–27 claims that Luther's *Decem praecepta* (WA 1:424.1–10) was a sermon from the end of July 1516—however, what is extant is in fact a printed version that had been prepared for printing in 1518 (see WA 1:394), which can be regarded as a reliable account of his preaching in 1516/1517 only with great precaution.

113. Luther, *Sermo in Die sancti Matthaei* (WA 1:86.31–32): "*Hi non sua poenitentia sed Dei gratia peccatum sanari confidunt.*" It is precisely this human passivity Luther expresses as the main content of the *Theologia deutsch*, from which one can learn "*ne homines in aliud quicquam confidant quam in solum Ihesum Christum, non in orationes et merita vel opera sua*" (Luther an Staupitz, March 31, 1518 [WA Br 1:160 {No. 66, 10–11}]); cf. also Heiko Augustinus Oberman, "Simul gemitus et raptus: Luther und die Mystik," in *Kirche, Mystik, Heiligung und das Natürliche bei Luther: Vorträge des Dritten Internaionalen Kongresses für Lutherforschung* (Göttingen: Vandenhoeck & Ruprecht, 1967), 20–59, 39; for the mystical critique of *merita*, cf. Bengt Hägglund, "Luther und die Mystik," 84–93, 93.

114. Luther, *Sermo de indulgentiis* (WA 1:98.26–29).

115. Luther, *Sermo de indulgentiis* (WA 1:99.10) for the usage of *galgen rew* (regret/fear of the noose); for *attritio*, see Luther, *Grund und Ursach aller Artikel* (WA 7:365.34); The term *galgen rew* for this can already be found with Staupitz (Johann von Staupitzens, *sämmtliche Werke*, ed. J. K. F. Knaake, vol. 1, *Deutsche Schriften* [Potsdam: Krausnick, 1867], 16). For information on Luther's criticism of the idea that *attritio* can be transformed into *contritio*, cf. Steffen Kjeldgaard-Pedersen, *Gesetz, Evangelium und Buße: Theologiegeschichtliche Studien zum Verhältnis zwischen dem jungen Johann Agricola (Eisleben) und Martin Luther* (Leiden: Brill, 1983), 245.

Luther continued this critical theological posture in a sermon probably held on January 16, 1517.[116] In this sermon, we observe both the application of Luther's new insights concerning indulgences and an increasing radicalization of Luther's own theology of penance; he is now clearly following Tauler in the non-sacramental-subjective focus. Luther's increasing vehemence in his attacks on indulgence can be understood as the fruit of his anti-attritionism posture as he had learned from Biel.[117] And indeed, on February 24, 1517, he explained in a sermon for the Festival of St. Matthew:

116. Luther, *Sermo pridie Dedicationis* (WA 1:94–99). The editors of the WA assumed that the *dies Dedicationis* had to do with a festival for the dedication of a church, with a sermon held the evening before. They therefore precluded the idea that this could have taken place around the time of the indulgence theses and correct the Löscher's date of "1517" to 1516, and more precisely, October 31 of that year. Norbert Flörken, "Ein Beitrag zur Datierung von Luthers sermo de indulgentiis pridie Dedicationis," *Zeitschrift für Kirchengeschichte* 82 (1971): 344–50, 349 has found good reasons—especially the temporal proximity to Tetzel's sermons—that this sermon by no means had to have been held for the church dedication festival of the Allerheiligenkirche (whose dedication celebration was anyways January 17). It is somewhat more plausible that this sermon was held at Luther's regular preaching station, the Stadtkirche of Wittenberg, whose dedicatory festival was May 31. If this is true, then we can accept Löscher's year and date of the sermon to May 31, 1517. Of particular interest is that Luther mentions an indulgence-critical sermon held in the Castle Church when reflecting in "Wider Hans Worst": "Now when many people from Wittenberg went to Jütterbock and Zerbst for indulgences, and I (as truly as my Lord Christ redeemed me) did not know what the indulgences were, as in fact no one knew, I began to preach very gently that one could probably do something better and more reliable than acquiring indulgences. I had also preached before in the same way against indulgences at the castle and had thus gained the disfavor of Duke Frederick because he was very fond of his religious foundation." (WA 51:539, 4.10, cited after LW 41:231–32: *Agaist Hanswurst*); Joachim Ufer, "Luther und Tetzel," *Blätter für pfälzische Kirchengeschichte und religiöse Volkskunde* 46 (1979): 166–76, 168, has coherently bound this with the sermon *pridie Dedicationis*—Luther's own reference makes it unnecessary to imagine him as preaching *only* in the Stadtkirche. If we take Luther's statement as being reliable, then he must have preached in the Castle Church at least once. If we take the dedication festival from Flörken, then January 16, 1517, is indeed the most plausible date, and it also fits well to Tetzel's appearance in Jüterbog (most likely on April 10, 1517; see Nikolaus Paulus, *Johann Tetzel, der Ablaßprediger* [Mainz: Kirchheim, 1899], 41). However, the one drawback is that there is no direct reference in the sermon for the dedication to Tetzel's proclamation of the Indulgence of St. Peter. This proclamation took place only a few days later. (See the above n. 110). But a direct reference to Tetzel is not necessary to understand the sermon—especially when one considers that he had been preaching indulgence as a representative of Arcimbolds since 1516 (s. Paulus, *Johann Tetzel*, 29–30; Ufer, "Luther und Tetzel," 168).

117. In fact, the criticism that we hear from Staupitz at the same time has a very different emphasis: he did not relativize *satisfactio* in light of *contritio* but explained in his "Libellus de exsecutione aeternae praedestinationis," which is based on his sermons in Nurnberg from 1516/17: "*hinc commendabilior et utilior est liberatio a peccatis per propriam satisfactionem quam per indulgentiam*" (Johann von Staupitz, *Sämtliche Schriften*, vol. 2, *Lateinische Schriften II*, ed. Lothar Graf zu Dohna, Richard Wetzel, and Albrecht Endriss (Berlin: De Gruyter, 1979), 254; cf. also Breul, *Luthers Visitation* [cf. n. 112], 22–23). It is possible that this hints toward the gradual disassociation of Luther from Staupitz: while Luther did receive the basis for his doctrine of

Then in addition, the very profusion of indulgences astonishingly fills up the measure of servile righteousness. Through these nothing is accomplished except that the people learn to fear and flee and dread the penalty of sins, but not the sins themselves. Therefore, the results of indulgences are too little seen but we do see a great sense of self-security and licentious sinning; so much so that, if it were not for the fear of the punishment of sins, nobody would want these indulgences, even if they were free.[118]

This is a clear demarcation to what we know as attritionism. But, it is worth emphasizing here that Luther was still ambivalent regarding other late-medieval positions. We can understand the fact that he still understood internal penance as only the *res* of the Sacrament and granted the externally performed *confessio* and *satisfactio* the status of external signs[119] (and thus they would remain constitutive of the sacrament) as a continuation of the subjective-sacramental interpretation of Gabriel Biel. More precisely, Luther's sermon had to do with an emphasis on *poenitentia* as a virtue. That is also present with Biel, notwithstanding his dogmatic systematization of contritionism. But reading Tauler had slightly twisted *poenitentia* into a non-sacramental direction. Now Luther directly opposed private oral confession, arguing that James 5:16 understands confession to be the mutual confession of sins of the faithful, but that Holy Scripture knows nothing of private confession.[120] And reparation was not to be understood as an certain act determined in private confession but rather as a task for the entirety of Christian life ("*totius vitae Christianae officium*").[121] The external acts that follow the divinely effected event of penance were de-sacramentalized. This meant that they were removed from the context of the priestly administration of salvation. In his sermon from February 24, 1517, Luther was prepared

penance from Staupitz, his conclusions were certainly much more radical than his confessor's, especially after his engagement with Tauler. However, according to Scheurl's notes from Staupitz's sermons from Lent 1517, he had expressed himself in a way that Luther could have seen as a confirmation of his opinions: "*Ist auch gantz onzweiffenlich, das der mensch durch ain rechtgegrundte ordenliche rew, auch on allen ablas des er sich mocht geprauchen vergebung seiner missethat erlangen kann*" (Staupitz, *Sämtliche Werke 1* [cf. n. 115], 18).

118. Luther, *Sermo Die S. Matthiae A. 1517* (WA 1:141.22–26): "*Adhuc servilem iustitiam mire perficiunt ipsae effusiones indulgentiarum, quibus nihil agitur quam ut populus discat timere, fugere, horrere poenam peccatorun, non autem ita et peccata. Ideo parum sentitur fructus indulgentiarum, sed magna securitas et licentia peccandi, Ita sane ut, nisi timerent poenam peccatorum, nullus vellet optare gratis istas indulgentias.*" Cited after LW 51:31.

119. Luther, *Sermo de indulgentiis* (WA 1:99.8–9).

120. Luther, *Sermo de indulgentiis* (WA 1:98.30–31).

121. Luther, *Sermo de indulgentiis* (WA 1:98.34).

to utilize an anti-clerical idiom when he decried the "snoring priests" ("*O stertentes Sacerdotes*"[122]).

In this sermon, all of Tauler's major moments leap out at us. Or perhaps it is better to say that Tauler's major ideas *as processed by Luther* are neatly assembled here: penance as a way of life, the concentration on the internal event, and the conviction that *fides* is the central anthropological moment of penance[123] all come together in Luther's sermon from May 30, 1517. And as Luther develops his understanding of penance in a non-sacramental direction, he starts honing its anti-indulgence edge. According to his systematics, indulgences belong in the domain of tasks decided in the area of private confession for *satisfactio*[124] and are thus merely external signs, not essential to penance. This sermon exposes Luther's thought at a stage of its development when it is separating itself from "attritionism" and sharpening its focus on non-sacramental *contritio* as he learned it from Biel and Tauler. The critique of indulgences is a rigorously derived product of this development.

We have reconstructed this conviction in 1517 as a gradual transformation of Biel's thought by means of reading Tauler. Soon thereafter (actually in the following year), Luther will describe this in his dedicatory writings as an abrupt shift in his understanding of penance. A characteristic phrase shows how this memory has an objective reason in the statements described here. A year later, Luther would write to Staupitz that he learned from him that nothing can be considered true penance "[unless] it begins with love for justice and for God." [125] Precisely this phrase is found in a sermon from May 30, 1517: true penance is the penance that "hates sin through love of justice and of punishment" ("*amore iustitiae et poenarum*

---

122. Luther, *Sermo Die S. Matthiae A. 1517* (WA 1:141.37); for the problem of anti-clericalism, see: Peter A. Dykema and Heiko Augustinas Oberman, *Anticlericalism in Late Medieval and Early Modern Europe*, ed. Peter A. Dykema (Leiden: Brill, 1993). Cited after LW 51:31.

123. Luther, *Sermo de indulgentiis* (WA 1:96.15): "*Ecce fides distinguit inter Abel et Cain*"; see also Luther, *Sermo in die Purificationis Mariae* (WA 1:13.1–2): "*cum tamen omnes Scriptura sanare videtur unico verbo de indulgentiis, quod est, credere in Christum.*"

124. Luther, *Sermo de indulgentiis* (WA 1:98.37–38).

125. Luther, *Widmungsschreiben zu den Resolutiones disputationum de indulgentiarum virtute* (WA 1:525, 12), cited after LW 48:65. The idea that love is the origin of penance can be found in the High Middle Ages: "*Haec autem paenitentia tum ex amore Dei accidit et fructuosa est*" (Abaelard, Ethics [cf. n. 10], 76.23–24); for similar passages by Paltz, see Hamm, *Frömmigkeitstheologie* (cf. n. 6), 276; by Biel, cf. Schwarz, *Bußtheologie* (cf. n. 38), 130. This idea can be found most clearly with Staupitz in his "Büchlein von der Nachfolgung des willigen Sterbens Christi," where in the ninth chapter Staupitz counts, "*allein die ewige frewde bey Christo suchen vnnd bitten*" ("to search only for eternal joy with Christ and to pray"; my translation) as one of the characteristics of true penance (Staupitz, *Sämtliche Werke* 1 [cf. n. 115]: 71; for more on this, see Schwarz, *Bußtheologie* (cf. n. 38), 155.

*odit peccatum*").[126] This understanding cannot be nailed down to a temporally precise moment in Luther's theology, although Luther will claim to do just that later. But we do find it peppered through Luther's thought in this early phase, a clear demonstration of the intensity with which Luther adopted the ideas of Staupitz and Tauler.

## THE ACADEMIC CONFRONTATION

By early summer of 1517, Luther had developed his theology of penance and a corresponding critique of indulgence. The latter was developed with a specifically theological interest (and less of a socioeconomic one) and a pastoral intention. On October 31, 1517, he wrote to Albrecht of Mainz with a very defensive-exculpatory tone, explaining:

> Now, I do not so much complain about the quacking of the preachers, which I haven't heard; but I bewail the gross misunderstanding among the people which comes from these preachers and which they spread everywhere among common men. Evidently the poor souls believe that when they have bought indulgence letters they are then assured of their salvation.[127]

This explanation indicates that there was a pastoral development taking place that led to the indulgence theses of October 31, 1517. By this point, Luther knew the *Instructio Summaria* from Cardinal Albrecht,[128] which did in fact include a passage stating that the purchase of an indulgence would not only replace the stational pilgrimage to Rome but also even private

126. Luther, *Sermo de indulgentiis* (WA 1:99.10–11); cf. the thoughts developed by Luther as early as *Sermo Die S. Matthiae A. 1517* (WA 1:141.26–27): "*Cum potius populus ad poenam amandam esset exhortandus et crucem amplectendam*" ("whereas the people ought rather to be exhorted to love the punishment and embrace the cross," LW 51:31). The idea of *amor iustitiae* as a consequence of the Gospel can be found in *Operationes in psalmos*, WA 5, 563, 20; for more, see: Kjeldgaard-Pedersen, *Gesetz* (cf. n. 115), 240, 244. Considering these reliably appearing citations from May 1517 until May 1518, it is not entirely unproblematic when one attempts to connect a divergence between faith as love of God and regret with the theses in "Pro veritate" (as did Hamm, *The Early Luther* [cf. n. 10], 22). Theses 8, 9, and 18 from this series of theses (WA 1:631.3–6. 23–24) only say that faith cannot be founded in *contritio*. Thesis 25 allows for *contritio* and a firm faith in the word of absolution to exist as an indistinguishable act: "*Evidentia contritionis signa satis habet sacerdos, si peccatorem sentit petere et credere absolutionem*" (Luther, *Pro veritate* [WA 1:631, 37–38]).

127. Luther, *Brief an Albrecht von Mainz, 31. Oktober 1517* (WA Br 1:111 [No. 48, 16–20]): "*In quibus non adeo accuso praedicatorum exclamationes, quas non audiui, Sed doleo falsissimas intelligentias populi ex illis conceptas, quas vulgo vndique iactant. Videlicet, Quod credunt infelices anime, si literas indulgentiarum redemerint, securi sint de salute sua.*" Cited after LW 48:46, *To Cardinal Albrecht, Archbishop of Mainz: Wittenberg, October 31, 1517.*

128. Mentioned in Luther, *Brief an Albrecht von Mainz, 31. Oktober 1517* (WA Br 1:111 [No. 48, 47]).

confession, being in itself sufficient to attain access to all of the goods of the church.[129] It is probable that what Luther describes as a "falsissimas intelligentias" actually refers to this passage, which would mean that his critique is going straight for the *Instructio* and its author. But these remarks also make clear that Luther's criticism of indulgences as a phenomenon was both an "expression of a Wittenberg university theologian"[130] and a reflex in a situation that Luther felt to be pastorally problematic.[131]

However, this does not explain why he chose the form of an academic disputation to handle the question of indulgence. A different series of discussions is important here. When Luther held his sermon on May 30,

129. Cf. DCL 1:269: "*Declaramus etiam, quod pro dictis duabus gratiis principalibus consequendis non est opus confiteri seu ecclesia saut altaria visitare, sed duntaxat confessionale redimere.*" Since the purchase of a confessionale (an indulgence letter) is denoted as the second *gratia principalis* (DCL 267), the connection to the two other main graces—the first being "*remissio omnium peccatorum*" (DCL 264) and the third being "*participatio omnium bonorum ecclesie universalis*" (DCL 268)—remains unclear. But we can understand it with the help of Albrecht's text, the *Avisamenta Johannes Arcimboldis*: "*Quas quidem duas principales gratias confessionalium & participationis omnium bonorum ecclesie pro maiori christi fidelium commodo prefatus dominus commissarius statuit, pro vna quota concedi debere, & in litteris confessionalibus comprehendi*" (*Johann Erhard Kappens* (. . .) | *Kleine* | *Nachlese* | *einiger, größten Theils noch ungedruckten,* | *Und sonderlich* | *zur Erläuterung* | *Der* | *Reformations-Geschichte*| *nützlichen Urkunden.*| *Dritter Theil* (Leipzig: Friedrich Brauns Erben, 1730), 186–87.

130. See the apt thesis of Lothar Vogel, "Zwischen Universität und Seelsorge: Martin Luthers Beweggründe im Ablasstreit," *Zeitschrift für Krichengeschichte* 118 (2007): 187–212, 196. My translation.

131. Vogel, *Zwischen Universität und Seelsorge* (cf. n. 130), 187–88. 204–11, however, rightly emphasizes that the pastoral situation ought not to be placed in relation to concrete processes of confession, as did Friedrich Myconius, *Geschichte der Reformation*, ed. Otto Clemen (Leipzig: Voigtländer, 1954), 20–21, where he describes for the year 1517: "In the same year, many came to Wittenberg with valid letters of indulgence and confessed before Doctor Martin for their grace." Even more important is the observation from Wilhelm Ernst Winterhager, "Ablaßkritik als Indikator historischen Wandels vor 1517: Ein Beitrag zu Voraussetzungen und Einordnung der Reformation," *Archiv für Reformationsgeschichte* 90 (1999): 6–71, 14, that Luther repeatedly referred to the criticism of indulgences, which had its home in the general populace. He even claims that "the indulgence-critical discourse must be located before his [Luther's] theses on indulgence." Winterhager concludes quite understandably, "The popular frustration with indulgences, which had permeated every single layer of society, was the primed reactant for Luther's success." (Winterhager, "Ablaßkritik," 20, my translation). Winterhager's idea only requires further development with the observation that these developments did not emerge out of a vacuum shortly before 1517 but in fact brought to expression old tensions from the late Middle Ages. We can see an indication of the deeply rooted character of this tension in the fact that Winterhager, "Ablaßkritik," 34, considers the indulgence criticism in the *Narrenschaft* by Sebastian Brant to be an exaggeration, while the indulgence campaign of "Peraudi" continued to enjoy success. In fact, we are not dealing with a juxtaposition of reality and exaggeration but rather with a broad spectrum of late-medieval forms of spirituality with a high degree of tolerance for each other (cf. also the indication of criticism of those critiquing indulgences from John of Paltz in 1490, "Ablaßkritik," 35); For more on the theologically motivated criticism of indulgences in the late Middle Ages, see chap. 1 of this book.

he had already been in posession of a collection of disputations from John Eck for several weeks. This collection was heavily skewed toward the latter's disputations held in Vienna in 1516.[132] This edition also contained a collection of theses (long neglected in scholarship) from a disputation held by Eck in Bologna on July 12, 1515.[133] Previous scholarship has given attention to these theses mostly because of their relevance for the Upper-German Rent Conflict (Germ. *Oberdeutsche Zinsstreit*).[134] The other theses appear to consist of a somewhat random mixture. Eck arranges them roughly in the same way that he later would in his confrontation with Luther in Heidelberg: first those pertaining to theology, then those belonging to philosophy.[135]

The theological theses do not treat a singular topic. Eck handles the doctrine of indulgence alongside the Doctrine of the Trinity[136] and the relation between faith and science.[137] His opponent in Bologna had given him cause to think about this[138]—John Fabri had arrived at the topic of

132. *Disputatio Joan. Ec|kij Theologi Viennae Pannoniae ha-| bita cum Epistola ad Reuerendis-| simum Episcopum Ei-|stettensem.| (. . .)* (Augsburg: Miller, 1517) (VD 16 E 314); cf. Johannes Eck, *Disputatio Viennae Pannoniae habita (1517)*, ed. Therese Virnich (Münster: Aschendorff, 1923), XXII–XXIV; Christoph Scheurl likely send this collection of disputations to Luther on April 1, 1517 (Christoph Scheurl to Martin Luther, April 1, 1517 [WA Br 1:91 {No. 36, 2–4}]: "*Amicum meum Iohannem Eckium de virtute tua feci certiorem, unde amicitiae tuae percupidus nedum ad te literas dedit, sed et libellum cum disputationibus suis mittit*").

133. These theses also appeared in a different edition in the previous year; cf. *AVDI LECTOR | johannes Eccij Theologi In-| goldstadiensis. orationes accipe tres non | inelegantes (. . .)* (Augsburg: Miller, 1515), F 2ᵛ–F 3ᵛ.

134. Cf. Heiko Augustinus Oberman, *Werden und Wertung der Reformation: Vom Wegestreit zum Glaubenskampf*, 2nd ed. (Tübingen: Mohr, 1979), 161–64. 174–96.

135. Eck, Disputation of Bologna (Eck, *Disputatio Viennae habita* 46:6): "*Impertinentia theologica*"; (Eck, *Disputatio*, 47, 29): "*Impertinentia philosophica.*"

136. Eck, *Disputation von Bologna* (Eck, *Disputatio Viennae habita* 46:7–9): "*Sicut Pater genuit Filium, sic Deus genuit Deum. Essentia tamen divina nec generat, nec egeneratur; a Patre tamen essentia realiter non dustinguitur, sed formalitert.*" The tricky questions pertaining to the Doctrine of the Trinity would become characteristic for the Vienna Disputation in 1516; cf. Eck, *Disputatio*, 26–30.

137. Eck, *Disputation von Bologna* (Eck, *Disputatio Viennae habita* 46:10–11): "*Fides scientiae non est incomprehensibilis; itaque fidem in aeterna beatitate manere cum visione, non est improbabile.*"

138. However, Eck had been interested in penance for quite some time by this point. In 1512, he published a woodcut of the "Schiff des Heils" (Ship of Salvation), which he repeatedly named the "Ship of Contrition." (*Das schiff des heils| Auff das aller kürtzest hie vß geleget | Nach der figur die doctor Johannes von Eck gemacht hat zů Ingolt| stat. bewegt auß den predigten des wirdigen Herren doctor Johannes gei-| ler von Keisersperg [. . .]* [Straßburg: 1512], 1ᵛ u.ö.; cf. Jonathan Reinert, *Passionspredigt im 16. Jahrhundert: Das Leiden und Sterben Jesu Christi in den Postillen Martin Luthers, der Wittenberger Tradition und altgläubiger Prediger* [Tübingen: Mohr, 2020], 125–32. Based on the sermions from Geiler of Kaysersberg, he also proposed various grada-tions of contrition. These consisted of "*Mißfalhaben von vergangener sünd*" (feeling aversion

usury while treating the collection of interest and bound the problematic side of indulgence to it, stating in a thesis:

> To claim that the Pope is not capable of granting a plenary indulgence for the souls in Purgatory and satisfaction for all of his [the Pope's] punishments by his temporal guardianship, as established to God's praise and glory, namely by means of supplication (*per modum suffragii*) is godless, criminal and entirely opposed to all holy doctors. Instead it is not opposed to faith but rather pious to believe that the Pope can give indulgence to the souls who are in Purgatory on the basis of his authority if this actually takes place for the cases, which is expressed in the Bull.[139]

Fabri was probably referring to a Bull published by Pope Leo X on March 31, 1515. It declared the Indulgence of St. Peter.[140] The doctrine of *modus suffragii* ("by means of supplication") constituted the further context. Pope Sixtus IV had created the possibility of delivering the church's treasure of grace to the souls imprisoned in purgatory with his bull "Salvator noster" from August 3, 1476, also intended to raise funds for St. Peter's in Saintes.[141] It was here that the pope provided "plenary indulgence by way of suffrage be effective for the mitigation of sufferings and for the benefit of those souls in purgatory."[142] It was not entirely clear what was meant by this—the pope had to explain *modus suffragii* a year later. An indulgence provided *per modum suffragii* was applied "in such a way, however, that the faithful themselves should make suffrage for those souls that those souls of the dead cannot achieve for themselves."[143] But this also did not ensure full clarity; it

to comitted sins), "*sich selber straffen vner die sünd*" (punishing oneself for sin) and "*fürsatz die sünde fürhin zů meyden*" (resolving not to comit sin) (Reinert, *Passionspredigt*, 4ʳ). He especially emphasized the comforting words of the priest in sacramental penance (Reinert, *Passionspredigt*, 7ʳ).

139. "*Asserere papam non esse pro temporali subsidio, ad laudem et honorem Dei ordinato, indulgentias plenarias pro expiatione omnium penarum suarum animabus in purgatorio, saltem per modum suffragii, concedere, impium, scelestum ac sanctis doctoribus omnino contrarium est. Immo nihil fidei contrarium, sed potius pie credendum Papam etiam per modum auctoritatis animabus in purgatorio existentibus indulgentias posse dare, si id fiat pro eis quod in Bulla est expressum.*"; cited after Nikolaus Paulus, *Die deutschen Dominikaner im Kampfe gegen Luther (1518–1563)* (Freiburg im Breisgau: Herder, 1903), 296 n. 4.

140. *Text in DCL 1* (cf. n. 129), 212–24.

141. For the context of this bull, cf. Bernd Moeller, "Die letzten Ablaßkampagnen. Der Widerspruch Luthers gegen den Ablaß in seinem geschichtlichen Zusammenhang," in *Die Reformation und das Mittelalter: Kirchenhistorische Aufsätze*, ed. Johannes Schilling (Göttingen: Vandenhoeck & Ruprecht, 1991), 53–72, 59.

142. DH 1398: "*plenariam remissionem per modum suffragii ipsis animabus purgatorii.*"

143. DH 1406: "*ita tamen, ut fideles ipsi pro eisdem animabus suffragium darent, quod ipsae defunctorum animae per se nequaeant adimpere.*"

at least seemed plausible that an intercessory prayer from the pope could be necessary. Fabri now used the proclamation of the Indulgence of St. Peter to extend the authority of the pope even more. The vague *modus suffragii* was declared to be the certainty found in all teachers of the church, and it was supposed to be probable that the pope had authority to adjudicate in purgatory. Eck picked up this point and explained:

> Just as the works of satisfaction are useful for bringing about satisfaction for deadly sins, so can indulgences be given by the Pope to the dead not only by means of supplication but also with authority.[144]

Eck extended this radically papist theory even further: the occupants of purgatory were actually pilgrims of the church[145] and therefore under the authority and power of the pope. Thus, the pope could provide indulgence to an individual who had never undertaken penance, regardless of word, deed or even intention.[146] In a later thesis, Eck developed the idea that would drive Luther crazy:

144. Eck, *Disputation von Bologna* (Eck, *Disputatio Viennae habita* 47:9–11): "*Sicut opera satisfactoria etiam in peccato mortali utiliter satisfaciunt, ita et indulgentiae mortuis non tantum per modum suffragii sed autoritative a papa dari possunt.*" My translation. Eck gradually departs from this understanding. In *ENCHI-| RIDION LOCO-| RVM COMMVNIVM IOAN-| nis Eckij, aduersus Martinum Lu-| therum & asseclas eius (. . .)| Interiecta sunt passim quaedam ha| ctenus impressa (. . .) per ve-| nerabilem virum F. Tilmannum Siber-| gensem (. . .)* (Köln: Fuchs & Quentel 1532), I 4ʳ, the text reads: "*Applicat autem papa eis indulgentias non autoritate absoluendo, sed per modum suffragii.*" However, as Heinrich Schauerte, *Die Bußlehre des Johannes Eck* (Münster: Aschendorff, 1919), 231 n. 1 assumes, we may well be dealing with additions made by Tilman Smeling, the Dominican Prior from Cologne who is named on the title page (cf. the section *De indulgentiis in Enchiridion locorum | communium aduersus Lutteranos.| joanne Eckio Autore* (Landshut: Weißenburger, 1525), I 2ʳ⁺ᵛ und auch noch in der 1533 erschienen deutschen Ausgabe (Johannes Eck, *Enchiridion. Handbüchlin gemainer stell unnd Artickel der jetzt schwebenden Neuwen leeren. Faksimile-Druck der Ausgabe Augsburg 1533*, ed. Erwin Iserloh [Münster: Aschendorff, 1980], 132–34). Later, Eck only employs these phrases in a modified form. The cited sentence can be found in the edition from 1536 (*ENCHI| RIDION LOCORVM | communium adversus Lu| therum & alios ho-| stes ecclesiæ.| Ioan. Eckio authore.| AVTHUR IAM SEPTI-| mo recognouit & pluribus lo-| cis illustrauit, adnotatonib.| P. Tilmanni acco-| modatis* (Augsburg: Weissenhorn, 1536), 151ᵛ, but here expressly under the title "Appendix Tilmanni." We can therefore speak cautiously of Eck adopting the popular teaching at the time that the pope could not intervene in the matters of purgatory.

145. Eck, *Disputation von Bologna* (Eck, *Disputatio Viennae habita* 47:15–16): "*Existens in purgatorio est quodammodo viator et ita super terram, sicut et sanctus Paulus in raptu fuit viator simpliciter.*"

146. Eck, *Disputation von Bologna* (Eck, *Disputatio Viennae habita* 47:17–19): "*Eadem ratione non confesso et non contrito actu vel proposito indulgentiae dari possunt, licet non nisi super contritis et confessis.*"

This is why the Pope can empty most of Purgatory through his plenipotency but not all of it as Christ did in his resurrection. But he can be useful for those left over by means of supplication.[147]

When these theses were read in Wittenberg in mid-April 1517, they must have confirmed the deepest dread of Luther and his fellow theologians. They consisted of precisely the doctrine that Luther had identified as erroneous. This was no longer a case of erroneous ideas among the common people, nor some voice shrilly clamoring for attention in the marketplace of academic ideas. Now it was being espoused by a theologian with standing and substance. Eck understood this to be an intentionally formulated academic position. The sermon from May 30, 1517, which we have extensively treated above, is almost certainly a reaction to Eck's theses.

Luther was not the first to take an academic swing at Eck's argument. That was Karlstadt. Only a few days after April 26, 1517 (the best date we have given the evidence with Christoph Scheurl's letter),[148] Karlstadt presented 151 theses in Wittenberg that treated questions of grace and justification. He had clearly adopted Eck's form for his own theses.[149] It is not certain to what extent we can determine a reaction to the *content* of Eck's theses, especially those from Bologna. Karlstadt did not reach the topic of indulgences in this series,[150] although his careful treatment of *contritio* and *attritio* could have given him the means to contest their dispensational character.[151] Luther did, on October 31, 1517, with his

147. Eck, *Disputation von Bologna* (Eck, *Disputatio Viennae habita* 47:20–22): "*Quare papa pro maiori parte de plenituine potestatis purgatorium evacuare posset, non tamen totum, sicut Christus fecit in resurrectione, attamen residuis per modum suffragii prodesse potest.*" My translation. This thesis was numbered as the tenth although the seventh was missing.
148. For this dating (instead of September 25, considered by Theodor Kolde, "Wittenberger Disputationsthesen aus den Jahren 1516–1522," *Zeitschrift für Kirchengeschichte* 11 [1890]: 448–71, 450–51, n. 1), cf. Hermann Barge, *Andreas Bodenstein von Karlstadt. Bd 1: Karlstadt und die Anfänge der Reformation*, 2nd ed. (Nieuwkoop: Adamant Media Corporation, 1968), 463–64.
149. Cf. Volker Leppin, "Der Einfluss Johannes Ecks auf den jungen Luther," *Luther* 86 (2015): 135–47.
150. Karlstadt, *Conclusiones de natura, lege et gratia* (*Kritische Gesamtausgabe der Schriften und Briefe Andreas Bodensteins von Karlstadts. Vol. 1/1*, ed. Thomas Kaufmann [Gütersloh: Gütersloher Verlagshaus 2017], 485–511). In the German version of this essay, I erroneously referred to the sentence "*Sunt qui dicunt/ indulgentias non prodesse/ Nos autem miramur cur id dicere audeant/ quando sonitus campanarum (quibus ad ecclesiam vocatur populus) prosit,*" which can be found in the Parisian edition of the theses but actually belongs to a later list of theses: Karlstadt, *Conclusiones De tribulationis et praedestinationis materia* [*Kritische Gesamtausgabe der Schriften und Briefe Andreas Bodensteins von Karlstadts*, ed. Thomas Kaufmann, vol. 3 (Gütersloh: Gütersloher Verlagshaus 2020), 370, 7–8.
151. Karlstadt, *Conclusiones de natura, lege et gratia* (Karlstadt, *Kritische Gesamtausgabe 1/1*, 505.5–6).

Ninety-Five Theses against indulgences. They accompanied a letter to Cardinal Albrecht along with an extensive earlier tract,[152] *De indulgentiis*, where Luther devoted attention to Eck's statements. He also reacted to rumors he had heard about the indulgence preachers, and complained that they were demanding people to donate money instead of teaching them what indulgence really was.[153]

Having established a clear and extensive definition of penance, Luther takes up the topic of *contritio* and *attritio*.[154] But his main argumentation was poimenic. It was impossible for an individual to have certainty that they were sufficiently penitent,[155] nor could they be certain of whether it

152. Cf. the mention of a "tractat vnd conclusion" and "tractat, conclusiones vnd andere schriefte" in the letter from Albrecht of Mainz to his college of vicars in Halle (published in Ferdinand Körner, *Tezzel, der Ablaßprediger: Sein Leben und sein Wirken für den Ablaß seiner Zeit, mit besonderer Rücksicht auf katholische Anschauungen neu untersucht und möglichst nach den Quellen, mehrfach nach bisher noch ungedruckten, dargestellt* [Frankenberg: Roßberg, 1880], 148–49; information on the letter found Körner, *Tezzel*, 89). The text was identified by Löscher as a sermon and was correspondingly printed in WA 1:65–69. The mention of the tract and its delivery to Mainz make it clear that this is about a standalone text. Current scholarship, while still assuming that there was a printed edition of the *95 Theses* sent to Albrect of Mainz (Bernd Moeller, "Thesenanschläge," in *Luthers Thesenanschlag—Faktum oder Fiktion*, ed. Joachim Ott and Martin Treu [Leipzig: Evangelische Verlagsanstalt 2008], 9–31), is not terribly concerned that such an extensive and important text would have been sent by Luther only as a handwritten text. It is more important that we have a text that can be reliably dated to just before October 31, 1517. The dating "between March and October 1517" (Bagchi, *Luther's Ninety-Five Theses*, 338) is therefore too imprecise. The above-described relation to Eck's theses argues strongly for the text having been written only after Scheurl's letter. It therefore is likely to have been written in summer 1517 at the earliest; Hans Volz, *Martin Luthers Thesenanschlag* (Weimar: Böhlau, 1959), 18 presents the most plausible suggestion that the tract was written at the same time as the Ninety-Five Theses on indulgence.

153. Luther, *Tractatus de indulgentiis* (WA Br 12:5 [No. 4212a, 7–11]); cf. Luther, *Sermo habitus X. post Trinit. A. 1516* (WA 1:65, 12–17). Luther explicitly refers to news he has heard about the indulgence dealers: "*Nunquam enim commissarii et ministri aliud praedicant, quam quod commendent indulgentias et populum provocent ad dandum.*" He had also treated the topic in his sermon on Candlemass Day from February 2, 1517, in which he explained: "*Ecce purgationis ordo atque praescriptio. Hactenus populo praedicatum est de maximis indulgentiis, per quas homo ipse a seculi huius miseriis, passionibus laboribusque liberetur*" (Luther, *Sermo in die Purificationis Mariae* [WA 1:130, 27–29]). This corresponds closely to Tetzel's first day of work with Albrecht on January 22, 1517 (*DCL* I:247–48); he held his first sermon about indulgences on January 24 in Eisleben (Volz, *Thesenanschlag*, 11). We also know of sermons held in Berlin (October 5, 1517) and Halle (December 12 and 14, 1517), which treated the indulgence theses (Winterhager, *Disputation* [see n. 131], 132). Winterhager does not believe, however, that Tetzel stayed in Frankfurt on the Oder in November 1517, as some have deduced from a remark from Cochlaeus (Winterhager, *Disputation*, 140).

154. Luther, *Tractatus de indulgentiis* (WA Br 12:6 [No.4212a, 53]); cf. Luther, *Sermo habitus Domin. X. post Trinit. A. 1516* (WA 1:66, 26).

155. Luther, *Tractatus de indulgentiis* (WA Br 12:6 [No.4212a, 44–45]); Luther, *Sermo habitus Domin. X. post Trinit. A. 1516* (WA 1:66.17–19).

was possible for imperfect contrition to be "boosted" to sufficiency with an indulgence[156]—one ought to take pains to ensure that indulgence not bring people into a false sense of security.[157] He juxtaposed both approaches with an intensification of subjective understandings of penance while emphasizing its non-sacramental nature. Any and every mitigation of punishment (which was the effect of *poenitentia* according to Biel's classical understanding) constituted merely an *external* grace and did not heal the *morbus naturae* (sickness of nature).[158] Such a healing could only take place through internal grace and a truly authentic contrition. This was enjoyed only by a very few individuals.[159] According to Luther, this true penance would immediately grant the human person their salvation. Without it though, salvation was impossible.[160]

It is here that Luther fully develops the consequences of the Augustinian-mystical insights he had made during the Romans lectures and his confrontation with the biblical texts. At this point, he had reached a subjective, sacrament-sceptical opinion similar to that of Lombard or John Tauler. The sacrament was not effective per se, only the *contritio*. Luther hammers his opinion home in the same way that the representatives of so-called contritionism had done. But he goes even further: he removes the sacramental context altogether.

This has implications for all sorts of other areas. With his sermon finding increasing popular resonance, Luther started radically restricting the boundaries of papal power, even in this early phase of his theology. The pope could only administer his own penance and that commended to his priests. Luther refers to the penitential formulation that stated the forgiveness of sins reached "as far as the keys of the Mother Church extend,"[161]

---

156. Luther, *Tractatus de indulgentiis* (WA Br 12:6 [No.4212a, 53–54]); Luther, *Sermo habitus Domin. X. post Trinit. A. 1516* (WA 1:66.25–27).

157. Luther, *Tractatus de indulgentiis* (WA Br 12:9 [No.4212a, 152–53]); Luther, *Sermo habitus Domin. X. post Trinit. A. 1516* (WA 1:69.4–5).

158. Luther, *Tractatus de indulgentiis* (WA Br 12:5–6 [No.4212a, 19–22]); Luther, *Sermo habitus Domin. X. post Trinit. A. 1516* (WA 1:65.25–28; here: *morbus animae*).

159. Luther, *Tractatus de indulgentiis* (WA Br 12:6 [No.4212a, 38–42]); Luther, *Sermo habitus Domin. X. post Trinit. A. 1516* (WA 1:66.11–15).

160. Luther, *Tractatus de indulgentiis* (WA Br 12:7 [No.4212a, 64–69]); cf. Luther, *Sermo habitus Domin. X. post Trinit. A. 1516* (WA 1:66.37–67.4).

161. Luther, *Tractatus de indulgentiis* (WA Br 12:6 [No.4212a, 30–31]); cf. Luther, *Sermo habitus Domin. X. post Trinit. A. 1516* (WA 1:66.3–5), where he cites the text of the bull: "*in quantum claves sanctae matris Ecclesiae se extendunt, et de iniunctis poenitentiis misericorditer relaxamus.*" This is clearly referring to the *Instructiones confessorum* ("*[. . .] dando tibi plenissimam omnium peccatorum tuorum veniam et remissionem remittendoque tibi penas purgatorii, inquantum claves sancte matris ecclesie se extendunt*"; DCL I:239, and also the *Instructio summaria Albrechts von Mainz* ("*[. . .] remittendoque tibi penas purgatorii et restituendo te illi innocentie, in qua eras, quando*

and he concluded that "it is very audacious to preach that souls are saved from purgatory through these indulgences because this sentence is obscure and does not explain how we are to understand it."[162] Otherwise, one would have to regard the pope as an extortionist monster who arbitrarily refused to grant poor souls that which he did for money.[163] Of course, this happens right around the time when Eck was preaching the idea that the pope can empty purgatory if he so wanted. Luther's statements *could* be referencing that.

And Luther addressed another point from Eck: the doctrine of *modus suffragii*. It was Eck's claim of an authoritative efficacy of the papal indulgence that brought Luther to this question in the first place. The main problem for him was the *suffragium*, no matter if it pertained to the pope representing the church or the complete alienation between the individual subject seeking God and the individual subject experiencing punishment. According to this logic, if someone had died in sin, enough grace could be accredited to them despite not having been truly penitential in their heart.[164] The extreme emphasis on a subjective grounding of penance (just like Luther read in Tauler) became a central thrust of the attack on the usual penitential praxis. Luther continues this line of reasoning on May 30, 1517, with a christological focus.[165] While preaching on the pericope from the tax collector Zachaeus in Luke 19:1–10, Luther states his conclusion at the beginning of the sermon, "For those to whom Christ is anything, everything is nothing; for those to whom Christ is nothing, then everything continues to be important."[166] The background of this radical alternative between Christ and the world was a new understanding of sin that, just as he had preached a year prior, juxtaposed the radicality of internal *contritio* with an external-sacramental event. But Luther still saw this through the lens of classical sacramental theory as described by

*baptizatus fuisti, in quantum claves sancte matris ecclesie se extendunt*"; *DCL* I:280); for more on Luther's reading of the *Instructio*, cf. Volz, *Thesenanschlag*, 17; Moeller, *Ablaßkampagnen*, 69.

162. Luther, *Tractatus de indulgentiis* (WA Br 12:6 [No.4212a, 32–33]); cf. Luther, *Sermo habitus Domin. X. post Trinit. A. 1516* (WA 1:66.5–7): "*Quare nimis temerarium est praedicare, per istas indulgentias redimi animas a purgatorio, cum hoc sit obscure dictum nec, quomodo intelligi velit, exponat.*" My translation.

163. Luther, *Tractatus de indulgentiis* (WA Br 12:6 [No.4212a, 34–35]); cf. Luther, *Sermo habitus Domin. X. post Trinit. A. 1516* (WA 1:66.7–9).

164. Luther, *Tractatus de indulgentiis* (WA Br 12:7 [No.4212a, 93–95]); cf. Luther, *Sermo habitus Domin. X. post Trinit. A. 1516* (WA 1:67.28–30).

165. For more on the Christocentrisim conveyed by Staupitz, cf. Leppin, *A Late Medieval Life*, 23.

166. Luther, *Sermo de indulgentiis* (WA 1:94.8–9): "*Quibus Christus aliquid est, illis omnia nihil sunt quibus autem Christus nihil est, continuo illis omnia grandia sunt.*"

Lombard: the distinction between *res* and *signum*.[167] Luther described penance in these categories according to his own manner—the *res* of penance was the *contritio*, both confession and atonement in the spirit.[168] The actual content was therefore an internal event in which confession was interpreted as confession in the heart and *satisfactio* interpreted as self-disdain.[169]

By summer of 1517, Luther had developed his thought with a tract and had come to the attention of John Eck. His own teaching was now sharply critical of indulgence. This brought forth the famous theses against indulgence in October. They were not initially intended for a broader public but did in fact possess an academic character. Luther summarized his previous development of his theology of penance.[170] The Ninety-Five Theses presented the implications of Tauler's intensified *contritio*-understanding for an understanding of indulgences and the Sacrament of Penance. He had already developed the basic structure earlier, seen clearly in the double-theses at the beginning:

> 1. When our Lord and Master Jesus Christ said, "Repent" [Matt 4:17], he willed the entire life of believers to be one of repentance. 2. This word cannot be understood as referring to the sacrament of penance, that is, confession and satisfaction, as administered by the clergy.[171]

167. Luther, *Sermo de indulgentiis* (WA 1:98.24); for more on the adoption of this distinction in medieval theology, cf. Peter Lombard Sent IV cf. 1 c. 2 (*Magistri Petri Lombardi Sententiae in IV libris distinctae*, vol. 2 [Quaracchi: Rome, 1981], 232, 3).

168. Luther, *Sermo de indulgentiis* (WA 1:98.24–26). Luther speaks here about an *interior cordis et sola vera poenitentia* as the *res* of penance, but later defined *poenitentia interior* as *vera contritio, vera confessio, vera vonfessio in spiritu* (Luther, *Sermo*, 99, 1–2).

169. Luther, *Sermo de indulgentiis* (WA 1:99, 2–5).

170. Bagchi, *Luther's Ninety-Five Theses*, 353–54, offers an excellent comparison of Luther's statements in the Ninety-Five Theses with his earlier theology—his text from October 31, 1517, really does constitute only a small degree of innovation compared to earlier texts (Bagchi, *Luther's Ninety-Five Theses*, 355).

171. Luther, *Disputatio pro declaratione virtutis indulgentiarum* (WA 1:233.10–13): "*1 Dominus et magister noster Iesus Christus dicendo 'Penitentiam agite &c.' omnem vitam fidelium penitentiam esse voluit. 2 Quod verbum de penitentia sacramentali (id est confessionis et satisfactionis, que sacerdotum ministerio celebratur) non potest intelligi.*" Cited after LW 31:25: "Ninety-Five Theses or Disputation on the Power and Efficacy of Indulgences." The statement "*Vulgaris autem tripartita scholasticorum poenitentia frigida est usque ad verae poenitentiae internitiem*" further homes in the critique on the threefold sacramental understanding of penance. However, it does not yet evidence the later threefold understanding of absolution, grace, and faith Luther will present in the autumn of 1519 in his *Sermon von dem Sakrament der Buße* (WA 2:715.21–30). Thus, the sermon *Nymmer thuen die hochste buß* (WA 4, p. 612, 31–613, 5) would seem to be best dated to sometime in 1518; placing it in the period of Luther's occupation with Erasmus (Brecht, "Luthers neues Verständnis," 285) appears to be too early.

Once again, the statements coined by Tauler (we saw them in the sermon from May 30) are brought into even sharper focus.[172] Now, the *res* and *signum* of the Sacrament are no longer distinguished. Instead, Luther homed his critique in on what he had said in the sermon: external penitential acts were not rooted in Scripture. He described the biblical penance as being only the *poenitentia vera*, the internal *contritio*.[173] The non-sacramental, subjective theory of penance á la Tauler had thus been completely developed. Applying this theory to the system of indulgences lent the theory a burning relevance, especially among those who had heard his sermons.

Luther was able to make extensive use of his earlier thought. Thesis 82 shows that he was considering Eck. It also shows that he was trying to convey questions that could be held by laypersons:[174]

> Why does the pope not empty purgatory for the sake of holy love and the dire need of the souls that are there if he redeems an infinite number of souls for the sake of miserable money with which to build a church?[175]

---

172. A basic convergence between Luther's indulgence theses with those of late-medieval spirituality is conceded by Hamm, *The Early Luther* (cf. n. 10), 96, although he insists ultimatetly that they constitute a reformational text. The idea of *odium sui* in thesis 4 is quite peculiar here. We find Luther's annotations to a Tauler passage that speaks of *"ainer verschmehunge dein selber"*—a dishonoring of yourself (Tauler, *Sermones*, [cf. n. 75], fol. 192ᵛ; cf. above p. 69), which ought to adequately convey the idea of *odium sui*. We find similar ideas in Staupitz, who explains that Christ's promise of paradise to the thief crucified with him applies to everyone, *"der sich selb vordampt, Christum in allemr echtfertiget, vnnd alle weldt vorachtet"*—who condemns himself and honors Christ with all means and despises the world (Staupitz, *Von der Nachfolgung* [Staupitz, *Sämtliche Werke*, 1:71]). It is the case that one can understand certain positions held by Luther as a return to Scholasticism as embodied by Peter Lombard. In this particular case, it is worth considering that Luther himself wrote about the indulgence theses to Staupitz: *"Ego sane secutus theologiam Tauleri et eius libelli, quem tu nuper dedisti imprimendum Aurifabro nostro Christianno"* (Luther and Staupitz, March 31, 1518 [WA Br 1:160 {No. 66, 8–9}]). After his own recent understanding, Luther developed his decisive ideas on the indulgence theses from Tauler and *Theologia deutsch* (meant with the *"eius libelli"*).
173. Thus, the *satisfactio* is less discernable in internal penance (as Bizer, *Fides*, 80, has it); for more on the emphasis of internal penance, see Bayer, *Promissio* (cf. n. 64), 165. However, there are effects of penance in the suffering experienced in faith; for more, see the interesting statements of Ronald R. Rittgers, "Embracing the 'True Relic' of Christ: Suffering, Penance, and Private Confession in the Thought of Martin Luther," in *A New History of Penance*, ed. Abigail Firey (Leiden: Brill 2008), 377–93.
174. Luther, *Disputatio pro declaratione virtutis indulgentiarum* (WA 1:237.20–21).
175. Luther, *Disputatio pro declaratione virtutis indulgentiarum* (WA 1:237.22–25): *"Cur Papa non evacuat purgatorium propter sanctissimam charitatem et summam animarum necessitatem ut causam omnium iustissimam, Si infinitas animas redimit propter pecuniam funestissimam ad structuram Basilice ut causam levissimam?"* Cited after LW 31:32.

The term *"evacuare purgatorium,"* which Luther uses here to describe the emptying of purgatory, had already come across our path when we examined Eck's Bologna Disputation. Just like in the tract *de indulgentiis,* in which Luther had asked why the pope only used his power over purgatory on the basis of payment and not as a free gesture of kindness, we see Luther also developing a potent anti-papal argument here. Allowing hypothetical laypersons to pose the question serves only as a mild distraction. This can be explained with the concentration on *modus suffragii,* which had been developed in Eck's theses. It is only the claim, made in the footsteps of Fabri, that the pope did in fact have a definitive authority to bind and loose sins, extending even beyond the boundaries of death itself. This provides the background for properly understanding Luther's 26th thesis, in which he explains:

> The pope does very well when he grants remission to souls in purgatory, not by the power of the keys, which he does not have, but by way of intercession for them.[176]

These statements targeting papal power would later play an important role in the process against Luther. Silvester Prierias, the *Magister Sacri Palatii,* became crucial for this.[177] He was tasked with providing a thorough evaluation of the *causa Lutheri,* whose main points can be seen in the *"Dialogus"*[178] written in three days in spring of 1518. Prierias described his goal as defending the church against Luther's attacks "on truth itself and this Holy See."[179] He assumed four *"fundamenta"* for his text[180] that created new conditions for the debate. These *fundamenta* were not primarily concerned with the doctrine of penance but rather Prierias devoted his

---

176. Luther, *Disputatio pro declaratione virtutis indulgentiarum* (WA 1:234.27–28): *"Optime facit papa, quod non potestate clavis (quam nullam habet) sed per modum suffragii dat animabus remissionem."* Cited after LW 31:27.
177. For more on the amplified degree of power of the Magister Sacri Palatii in questions of censorship, cf. the decree: *Inter sollicitudines: "statuimus & ordinamus, quod de cetero perpetuis futuris temporibus nullus librum aliquem seu aliam quamcumque scripturam, tam in urbe nostra, quam aliis quibusvis civitatibus & diœcesibus imprimere seu imprimi facere praesumat, nisi prius in Urbe per viacrium nostrum & sacri palatii magistrum, in aliis vero civitatibus & diœcesibus per episcopum vel alium habentem peritiam scientiæ libri, seu scripturæ hujusmodi imprimendæ ab eodem episcopo ad id deputandum, ac inquisitorem hæreticae pravitatis civitatis sive diœcesis, in quibus librorum impressio hujusmodi fieret, diligenter examinentur, & per eorum manu propria subscriptionem, sub excommunicationis sentenia gratis & sine dilatione imponendam, approbentur."* (Mansi 32:913)
178. For the development of this document, cf. DCL I, 38.
179. DCL 1:52: *"in veritatem ipsam et sanctam hanc Sedem."*
180. Cf. DCL 1:53–56.

attention to ecclesiology, especially the Doctrine of the Pope. He found the universal church to be the Roman church according to its internal power (*virtualiter*);[181] the pope was the head of the church, even if in a different fashion than Christ.[182] Thus, the doctrines of the Roman church and the pope were to be followed as an infallible rule (*regula fidei infallibilis*).[183] Prierias took two sets of ideas—Luther's critique, rooted in penitential theology, of the pope's overreach, as well as his critique of a papalistic ecclesial structure—and rejected them with the sentence, "Whoever says about indulgences that the Roman church cannot do what it actually does is a heretic."[184] Regarding Luther's thesis 26, where he states that the pope himself had said his power only extends beyond this life in the sense of supplication, Prierias argued that the pope did in fact have power in purgatory in a jurisdictional sense.[185] In the blink of an eye, *modus suffragii*—formulated by Fabri, adopted by Eck, and contested by Luther—had become the official statement of the *Magister Sacri palatii*. What had started as a theological and poimenical effort to establish a biblically founded understanding of penance now boiled over and threatened to change the very structure of the church.

＊　＊　＊

This development took place in about half a year. During this period, Martin Luther himself changed from an adherent of late-medieval, scholastic penitential doctrine to a dissident accused of heresy.

In fact, Luther was a committed proponent of the "contritionist" or subjective-sacramental understanding of penance á la Gabriel Biel. He even adopts the idea of *facere quod in se* in an affirmative sense. As Luther works on his Romans lectures, this attitude starts to shift, and we have good evidence to believe that it did so in the context of his reading Johann Tauler's sermons. Here, Luther got to know a subjective-non-sacramental doctrine of penance, and he eagerly adopted it. Its full radicality is not quite visible in the Romans lectures, but it is definitely a preamble to later conflicts, especially Luther's critical take on *facere quod in se est*. Throughout 1516 and 1517, Luther's sermons develop a strong preference

---

181. DCL 1:53: *"Ecclesia vero universalis virtualitzer est ecclesia Romana."*
182. DCL 1:53.
183. DCL 1:55.
184. DCL 1:56: *"Qui circa indulgentias dicit, ecclesiam Romanam non posse facere id quod de facto facit, hereticus est."*
185. DCL 1:74: *"papa habet clavem iurisdictionis secundum sanctos, etiam min purgatorio applicative."*

for inner penance. It was this subjective-non-sacramental Theology shaped by Tauler that led to a burgening critique of indulgences.

This critique was honed and terminologically focused in the spring of 1517 when Luther was confronted with John Eck's own interpretation of indulgence. From this point onward, he developed a sharp criticism of *modus suffragii* and pertinant papal forms of the indulgence system. He sent these new ideas to the bishops on October 31, 1517, and also offered them to his friends for discussion. But one cannot claim that his understanding of penance had reached its final form at this point. That would come about when Luther generally recast his own theology into a theology of the word. At the end of this development, he came to the formulation found in his 1519 "Sermon on the Sacrament of Penance" that the elements of sacramental penance are absolution, grace, and faith.[186] The emphasis on faith was a logical product of Tauler. His concentration on absolution meant that he was accepting ideas from Aquinas and other medieval thinkers. But he now gave absolution a new contour: it was a clear proclamation of the word full of promise. Theology of penance thus became an integral part of the emerging reformational theology with its concentration on the Doctrine of Justification and the word of God.

186. Luther, *Sermon von dem Sakrament der Buße* (WA 2:715.21–30).

4.

# *Sola fide* and Monastic Existence. The Amalgamation of Paul and Mysticism in Luther's Romans Lectures

According to Berndt Hamm's stark description, Luther "replaced the medieval centerpiece of love with the centerpiece of faith."[1] This draws our attention to Luther's engagement with various understandings and concepts of faith in his early lectures. One of his first duties as a professor[2] at the University of Wittenberg was to lecture on the Psalms. At various points in the *Dictata in Psalterium*, Luther made comparisons to Romans,[3] and upon finishing this project, he directed his attention to that book. His Romans lectures began at Easter 1515.[4] Johann Oldecop has provided us with a quite exact report of how Luther prepared the text so that his students could follow him and his notes: "The Doctor went over to Johan Grunenberg the book-printer and ordered him to print the letters of Paul with the columns spaced far apart for the sake of glosses."[5]

---

1. Berndt Hamm, *The Early Luther*, 22.
2. Ulrich Köpf, "Martin Luthers theologischer Lehrstuhl," in *Frömmigkeitsgeschichte und Theologiegeschichte: Gesammelte Aufsätze* (Tübingen: Mohr, 2022), 540–55, has demonstrated that this was not a professorship specifically intended for biblical studies.
3. References can be found in WA 56:XII, n. 1.
4. Karl Euling, ed., *Chronik des Johan Oldecop* (Tübingen: Litterarischer Verein, 1891), 45:71–72 (No. 87): "*Im jare 1515 des mandages na dem witten sondage, in Quasimodo geniti, kam ik Johannes Oldecop to Wyttenberge (. . .). Und umme de tit hof an doctor Martinus Luther epistolas Pauli ad Romanos to lesende*" (cf. WA 56:XII). In 1515, the Sunday Quasimodogeniti fell on April 15.
5. Oldecop, *Chronik* 45:12–15 (No. 87). My translation.

The printed edition, which Luther used for his lectures, has been preserved and serves as the source text for the Weimar Edition.[6] Additionally, various sets of notes from the students have been preserved and published.[7] They generally exhibit a high degree of congruence, indicating that Luther's students were taking very precise notes.[8] Gabriele Schmidt-Lauber has demonstrated that Luther went on excourses from his lecture notes during the oral presentation.[9] The lectures likely ended in early September 1516.[10] Taken together, Luther's own text and the notes of his students offer us an excellent source for reconstructing Luther's theological considerations in the midst of his reformational development.[11] We will avoid a "pivot-construct" or "breakthrough-model" when reassembling the evidence.[12] The quest for a certain point in his theological development where he is definitively different than before cannot be a guideline for understanding Luther's theology. It is far more appropriate to speak of a gradual development with a clear reformational theology at the end. But there are many stages along the way with frequent superpositions of ideas. When we reconstruct Martin Luther's theological development using today's standards of scholarship, we find no abrupt "before" and "after." As clear as it is that Luther began as a late-medieval theologian who was

6. For more on the manuscript, cf. WA 56:XII–XV.

7. WA 57 (I: Röm).

8. Gabriele Schmidt-Lauber, *Luthers Vorlesung über den Römerbrief 1515/16: Ein Vergleich zwischen Luthers Manuskript und den studentischen Nachschriften* (Köln: Böhlau, 1994), 10–11.

9. Schmidt-Lauber, *Vorlesung*.

10. In a letter sent to Spalatin; which is best dated to September 9, 1516; Luther speaks of having ended the lectures on Paul ("Now, however, having finished lecturing on Paul"; WA Br 1:56 [No. 21, 8], cited after LW 48:19). But the dating is unsure as Luther himself occasionally writes: "altera nativitatis hora duodecima 1516" (WA Br 1:56 [No. 21, 8], line 16). "Altera" can refer either to the day following *dies nativitatis* or the following Monday. The birthday could be either that of Mary or of Jesus. Thus, there are four plausible dates based on Luther's text: September 9 or 15, 1516 (if we take the birthday to be Mary's) or December 26 or 29, 1516 (and if we take Christmas to be the beginning of the year, then it could even be December 26 or 31, 1516) (cf. the thorough work performed by Clement in WA Br 1:53–54). But Luther surely finished his work by the beginning of the Galatians lectures, which we know to have started on October 27, 1516 (WA Br 1:73 [No. 28, 27–28])—that excludes all December dates in 1516 and in 1515, since we would have to accept a long pause between the lectures on Romans and those on Galatians. Thus, the September dates are the most plausible and September 9 does seem most likely. Luther would have ended the Romans lectures shortly before this date.

11. For more on the question brought by the terms "breakthrough" and "development," cf. the classic essays by Otto Hermann Pesch, "Zur Frage nach Luthers reformatorischer Wende: Ergebnisse und Probleme der Diskussion um Ernst Bizer, Fides ex auditu," *Catholica. Jahrbuch für Kontroverstheologie* 20 (1966): 216–43, 264–80; "Neuere Beiträge zur Frage nach Luthers 'Reformatorischer Wende,'" *Catholica. Jahrbuch für Kontroverstheologie* 37 (1983): 259–87; 38 (1984): 66–133.

12. Hamm, *Früher Luther* 27; cf. above 72.

deeply shaped by John of Staupitz[13] and that he represented a theology by 1520 that no longer conformed with a late-medieval framework, it remains an impossible desideratum to find clear steps between these stages.

However, such an approach favoring a continuous development assumes that Luther's own memory was faulty[14] when he spoke about his great reformational discovery in his "Grand Self-Testimony"[15] in 1545. It is quite peculiar that this very memory pertains to the interpretation of Romans 1:17 and the understanding of faith contained therein. This famous passage, which has been subjected to countless interpretations, allows us to infer how Luther understood himself in 1545 as he wrote this. But it says precious little about the actual development of the

13. Cf. Luther's own statement: "*Staupicius hat die doctrinam angefangen*" ("Staupitz is the one who started the teaching [of the gospel in our time]." (WA TR 1, 245, 12 [No. 526], trans. after LW 54:97).

14. For more on the research of memory, cf. Jan Assmann, *Religion and Cultural Memory: Ten Studies* (Stanford: University Press, 2005).

15. "*Interim eo anno iam redieram ad Psalterium denuo interpretandum, fretus eo, quod exercitatior essem, postquam cf. Pauli Epistolas ad Romanos, ad Galatas, et eam, quae est ad Ebraeos, tractassem in scholis. Miro certe ardore captus fueram cognoscendi Pauli in epistola ad Rom., sed obstiterat hactenus non frigidus circum praecordia sanguis, sed unicum vocabulum, quod est Ca 1: Iustitia Dei revelatur in illo. Oderam enim vocabulum istud 'Iustitia Dei', quod usu et consuetudine omnium doctorum doctus eram philosophice intelligere de iustitia (ut vocant) formali seu activa, qua Deus est iustus, et peccatores iniustosque punit. (. . .) Donec miserente Deo meditabundus dies et noctes connexionem verborum attenderem, nempe: Iustitia Dei revelatur in illo, sicut scriptum est: Iustus ex fide vivit, ibi iustitiam Dei coepi intelligere eam, qua iustus dono Dei vivit, nempe ex fide, et esse hanc sententiam, revelari per euangelium iustitiam Dei, scilicet passivam, qua nos Deus misericors iustificat per fidem, sicut scriptum est: Iustus ex fide vivit. Hic me prorsus renatum esse sensi, et apertis portis in ipsam paradisum intrasse.*" (Meanwhile, I had already during that year returned to interpret the Psalter anew. I had confidence in the fact that I was more skilful, after I had lectured in the university on St. Paul's epistles to the Romans, to the Galatians, and the one to the Hebrews. I had indeed been captivated with an extraordinary ardor for understanding Paul in the Epistle to the Romans. But up till then it was not the cold blood about the heart, but a single word in chapter 1[:17], "In it the righteousness of God is revealed," that had stood in my way. For I hated that word "righteousness of God," which, according to the use and custom of all the teachers, I had been taught to understand philosophically regarding the formal or active righteousness, as they called it, with which God is righteous and punishes the unrighteous sinner. . . . At last, by the mercy of God, meditating day and night, I gave heed to the context of the words, namely, "In it the righteousness of God is revealed, as it is written, 'He who through faith is righteous shall live.'" There I began to understand that the righteousness of God is that by which the righteous lives by a gift of God, namely by faith. And this is the meaning: the righteousness of God is revealed by the gospel, namely, the passive righteousness with which merciful God justifies us by faith, as it is written, "He who through faith is righteous shall live." Here I felt that I was altogether born again and had entered paradise itself through open gates.) (WA 54:185.12–20; 186.3–9, trans. after LW 34:336–37); for more on this so-called Grand Self-Testimony (großes Selbstzeugnis), cf. Ernst Stracke, *Luthers großes Selbstzeugnis 1545 über seine Entwicklung zum Reformator historisch-kritisch untersucht* (Leipzig: Eger & Sievers, 1926).

previous thirty years. Its reliability is not only questionable because of the great temporal span but also because of the presence of other, parallel memories with different contentual accents.[16] If one is to use Luther's self-testimonies at all to describe his early phase of development, then one ought to use only those coming from this time. That is the point of this investigation—understanding Luther's own understanding of faith in the Romans lectures.

## THE AUGUSTINIAN-PAULINE *SOLA FIDE*

Commentaries frequently repeat previous content. Thus, it ought not surprise us that the various commentaries on Romans frequently have featured passages emphasizing the central meaning of faith when explaining Romans 1:17.[17] This is true for the Romans commentaries of both Nicholas of Lyra (which Luther almost certainly had read) and, of special note, Peter Lombard. Luther never explicitly mentions this commentary, but Jun Matsuura has made clear that Luther's reference to a gloss on Romans 1:17 in his Sentences commentary was probably not referring to the *Glossa ordinaria*, which is insignificant at this passage,[18] but rather to Peter Lombard's explanation.[19] When we examine the context, then it does seem likely that Luther was really referring to this. We could thus take it as a clear indication that Luther did in fact know of Lombard's popular commentary on Romans.

Thus, we have a certain probability (but not absolute security) that Luther knew about Lombard's formulations, indicating that he and his reformational discovery had by no means departed fully from medieval patterns of thought and speech. "God's justice justifies the wicked freely through faith without works of the law," Lombard writes on Romans 1:17

16. Cf. Volker Leppin, "'*Omnem vitam fidelium penitentiam esse voluit*:' Zur Aufnahme mystischer Traditionen in Luthers erster Ablassthese," in *Transformationen: Studien zu den Wandlungsprozessen in Theologie und Frömmigkeit zwischen Spätmittelalter und Reformation*, 2nd ed. (Tübingen: Mohr Siebeck, 2018), 261–77, for more on Luther's dedication to Staupitz from 1518, which describes a similar self-discovery as the Grand Self-Testimony of 1545 but places *poenitentia* and not *iustitia* in the center.
17. Heinrich Suso Denifle points this out in his monumental collection of texts: *Quellenbelege: Die abendländischen Schriftausleger bis Luther über Justitia Dei (Röm 1, 17) und Justificatio*, ed. Heinrich Denifle (Mainz: Kirchheim, 1905), which is a helpful insight notwithstanding its polemical intententions.
18. Cf. PL 114:471D.
19. Luther, *Erfurter Annotationen*, 539:19, n. 3.

(with reference to Haimo of Auxerre),[20] and he explains somewhat later regarding Romans 3:22:

> I have said that justification is from God. This, however, is God's justice: that justification through which we are justified, is from God through faith in Jesus Christ, which means through faith through which one believes in Christ and which justifies the wicked. This faith does what the law demands. As this faith is not called faith of Jesus Christ because Christ believes it, in much the same way God's justice is not called God's justice because God is made just through it. Both belong to us, but is named after God or Christ because it is granted to us through God's justice as just. God's justice is therefore without the law.[21]

Lombard also employed Augustine, *De spiritu et littera*, for this statement. This makes it all the more understandable that his statements emphasize faith as a gift from God and make clear that, through Christ, the *iustificatio* also applies to the *impii* if they believe in him. These phrases indicate that Luther made reference to both Nicolaus of Lyra and to Lombard in some passages when trying to understand Romans. Lombard was very helpful for him, not least because his theology was not yet shaped by the thirteenth-century Aristotelian shift in theology. Lombard's influence is particularly obvious in the explanation of the phrase "ex fide in fidem" in Romans 1:17—Luther explicitly and clearly distances himself from Nicholas of Lyra's understanding,[22] who had explained this passage[23] along the lines of *fides informis* and *fides formata* as one reads by Thomas Aquinas.[24] Peter Lombard had explained it in a fashion far more commeasurate with Luther's own development, namely: "From the promising God's faith to the faith of the human who believes in him."[25] Anyone who sees *promissio*

---

20. Petrus Lombardus, *Glossa in epistolas Pauli* (Esslingen before September 8, 1473), on Rom 1:17: "*Iusticia dei est qua gratis iustificat impium per fidem sine operibus legis*"; cf. Denifle, *Quellenbelege*, 58.

21. Lombardus, Glossa zu Rom 3:22: "*dixi iusticiam esse ex deo. Haec autem iustitia dei, id est, haec iustificatio, qua iustificamur, a deo est per fidem Jhesu Christi, id est per fidem, qua creditur in Christum iustificatorem impiorum, que fides impetrat, quod lex imperat. Sicut autem ista fides Christi dicta est, non qua credit Christus, sic illa iusticia dei, non qua iustus est deus. Vtrunque enim nostrum est, sed ideo dei et Christi dicitur, quia iustum eius nobis largitate donatur. Justitia ergo dei sine lege est.*"; cf. Denifle, *Quellenbelege*, 62.

22. Cf. WA 56:133.13–14 with text-critical commentary on l.13.

23. Nicholas of Lyra, *Postilla super totam Bibliam* (Nuremberg: Anton Koberger, 1481), on Rom 1:17; cf. Denifle, *Quellenbelege*, 190.

24. This was based on *Summa theologiae II-II*, q. 4 a. 3 (Editio Leonina 8:46–47).

25. Lombard, *Glossa on Rom 1:17*; cf. Denifle, *Quellenbelege*, 58. The idea of *promissio* was anything other than uncommon in the twelfth century, as we see in an anonymous commentary on Paul: "*ex fide dei promitentis in fidem hominis qui credit ei*" Rolf Peppermüller, ed., *Anonymi*

as a strong moment of Luther's reformational development[26] will have to take this particular idea from Lombard into account.

Thus, in order to fully understand the horizon of thought in which Luther devoloped and expanded his understanding of faith during the Romans lectures, one really does need to examine more than his central memories of *iustitia activa/distributiva* in his Grand Self-Testimony. This terminology is derived from the *Nicomacean Ethics* (Eth. Nik. V, 5). Upon the arrival of Aristotle's works in Western-European theology during the High Middle Ages, the *iustitia* doctrine contained in his *Ethics* could be adopted in Christian theology.[27] The continuous copying and printing of older texts, such as Lombard's Romans commentary, established a persistence of Augustinian understanding of justice until well into the late Middle Ages. Luther's early explanations of Paul found material to work with there. The formulations, which are heavily dependent on Paul and Augustine, are the product of a harmony between the texts of the Bible and the Church Father, as well as isolated moments of medieval exegetical tradition. Luther produces a text corpus in the Romans lecture that strongly resembles what he will later describe as his reformational discovery. It is for this reason that many have believed they found this discovery in the years 1513–1515.

And Luther's explanation of Romans *does* seem to prophetically express his later language and theology. When explaining Romans 1:17, he explicitly states, "Only in the Gospel is the righteousness of God revealed . . . by faith alone, by which the Word of God is believed,"[28] and clearly demarcates faith in the Gospel from a justification from works.[29] The notes from his students indicate that he made this difference far clearer in his oral presentation than in his own lecture notes.[30] Accordingly, he resolves the difficulty of the formulation "ex fide in fidem" that justification

*auctoris saeculi XII Expositio in epistolas Pauli [Ad Romanos—II Ad Corinthios 12]* [Münster: Aschendorff, 2005], 38, 826).

26. Cf. Oswald Bayer, *Promissio: Geschichte der reformatorischen Wende in Luthers Theologie* (Göttingen: Vandenhoeck & Ruprecht, 1971).

27. Cf. Aquinas, *Summa Theologiae II-II*, q. 61 a. 2 (Editio Leonina 9: 35–36).

28. WA 56:171.28–172.1. Cited after LW 25:151; Reinhart Staats, "Augustins 'De spiritue et littera' in Luthers reformatorischer Erkenntnis," in *Der Durchbruch der reformatorischen Erkenntnis bei Luther. Neuere Untersuchungen*, ed. Bernhard Lohse (Wiesbaden: Zabern, 1988), 365–84 374, has pointed out the "noticably Lutheran" tone of these words.

29. WA 56:172.5–15.

30. WA 57 (I: Römerbrief):133.6–8. This constitutes a certain counterpoint to the correct observation of Schmidt-Lauber, *Vorlesung*, 62–64, who explains the absence of *"per solam fidem"* in the sense that "the new reformational understanding [did not enter the language] in such a clear fashion" (64). She in fact does highlight "that Luther emphasizes [. . .] the rejection of works

is found entirely in and out of faith. This becomes increasingly clear for him over time.[31] And yet, we can see just how ambivalent the term *sola fide* is at this point when Luther expressly attacks those individuals who want to get to God "by faith alone, but not through Christ."[32]

That this insight was not easily formulated (even though it was embedded in traditional patterns of explanation) can be seen in Luther's wrestling with the proper understanding of Augustine's "*De spiritu et littera*"[33] in the context of his interpretation of Abraham in Romans 3. In chaps. 13 and 22, Augustine famously writes about this difficult passage, "And accordingly, God speaks in the law of works: 'do what I command,'" and in the law of faith, it is said to God 'give what you command.'"[34] In his lecture notes, Luther adopts this formulation with the small addition, "namely in humble prayer . . . to God."[35] But this was still difficult for him, for he continued to add reflections about this, such as that the simple prayer "give

righteousness more strongly in his presentation than in his own preparations." (Schmidt-Lauber, *Vorlesung*, 155). My translations.

31. WA 56:73.8–9; cf. Ernst Bizer, *Fides ex auditu: Eine Untersuchung über die Entdeckung der Gerechtigkeit Gottes durch Martin Luther*, 1st ed. (Neukirchen-Vluyn: Neukirchener Verlagsanstalt, 1958), 23.

32. WA 56:298.25–26: "*sola fide, non per Christum.*" Cited after LW 25:286; cf. Bizer, *Fides ex auditu*, 1st ed., 27. One need not understand the emergence of *Sola fide* in a reformational sense in any particular case. It appears with some frequency before the Reformation, and even with a soteriological emphasis. Thus, Bernard writes: "*Quamobrem quisquis pro peccatis compunctus esurit et sitit iustitiam, credat in te qui iustifucas impium, et solam iustificatus per fidem, pacem habebit ad Deum*" (Bernard of Clairvaux, *Sämtliche Werke. Lateinisch/Deutsch*, ed. Gerhard B. Winkler, vol. 5 [Innsbruck: Tyrolia, 1994], 316, 15–17), and even with an explicit reference to Augustine and Ambrose in Ep. 77: "*credens et ipse sola fide hominem posse salvari*" (Bernard of Clairvaux, *Sämtliche Werke lateinisch/deutsch*, ed. Gerhard B. Winkler. Vol. 2 [Innsbruck: Tyrolia, 1992], 620, 17–18; cf. Else Marie Wiberg Pedersen, "The Significance of the *Sola fide* and the *Sola gratia* in the the Theology of Bernard of Clairvaux [1090–1153] and Martin Luther [1483–1546]," *Luther-Bulletin* 18 [2009], 20–43, 30). We also encounter this phrase with Thomas Brandwine, *THOMAE | BRADWARDINI | ARCHIEPISCOPI OLIM | CANTU-ARIENSIS | DE CAUSA DEI; | CONTRA PELAGIUM, | ET DE VIRTUTE CAUSARUM, | (. . .) LIBRI TRES* (1618; repr. Frankfurt, 1964), 394A–B: "*Bene igitur apostolus fidem praedicans gentibus, ut ostenderet non merito bonorum operum perveniri ad fidem, sed fidem sequi bona opera, dicit, hominem iustificari per fidem sine operibus legis; (. . .) sola fide sine operibus praecedentibus sit homo iustus*" (cf. Heiko Augustinus Oberman, *Werden und Wertung der Reformation*, 3rd ed. [Tübingen: Mohr, 1989], 84).

33. Cf. here also Staats, "Augustins 'De spiritue et littera'"; for a more extensive usage of Augustine, see Giancarlo Pani, "L'eredità di Agostino nella ,Römerbriefvorlesung' di Martin Lutero: La Expositio quorundam propositionum ex epistola ad Romanos," *Studi e materiali di storia delle religioni* 61 (1995): 83–97.

34. CSEL 60:175.21–23: ac per hoc lege operum dicit deus: 'fac, quod iubeo,' lege fidei dicitur deo: 'da quod Iubes'." My translation.

35. WA 56:257.2–4: "*sc. humili petitione . . . Deo.*" My translation.

what you command" (*Da quod iubes*) would by no means lead to grace but rather "we all believe, speak, confess and do works, but nevertheless we are not all justified."[36] Here we see an indication that faith really does not magically create salvation for Luther, despite some other statements that give this impression.[37] Especially where this is not the case, where faith does *not* provide the unquestionable, absolute assurance of salvation, then the question of certainty becomes a matter of urgency.[38] In the years after the Romans lectures, Luther found himself deeply troubled by the question of predestination and brought these troubles to his confessor Staupitz.[39] There are, in fact, certain tendencies toward predestination in the Romans lectures.[40] Luther devotes considerable attention to the worries associated with this in his *Scholion* to Romans 8:28. According to Luther, this verse provided "the matter of predestination and election" (*materia praedestinationis et electionis*).[41] In the exposition of these passages, Luther has four main concerns: (1) He wants to make clear that election does not take place "by necessity of the consequent" (*necessitate consequentis*) but rather "by necessity of the consequence" (*necessitate consequentiae*).[42] This meant that God's inscrutable decision necessarily means that the

36. WA 56 :257.17–18.
37. See the marginalia to Rom 1:16: "*I.e. est potentia ad salvandum omnes credentes, siue est verbum potens saluare omnes credentes ipsum. Et hoc per Deum et ex Deo. Sicut si dixeris: Ista gemma habet hanc virtutem ex Deo, Vt qui eam portat, non possit sautiari, Ita Euangelium ex Deo hoc habet, Vt qui ipsum crediderit, saluetur*" (WA 56:10.16–20).
38. One ought to also mention those passages that strongly emphasize certainty of salvation, found by Sven Grosse, "Heilsgewissheit des Glaubens: Die Entwicklung der Auffassungen des jungen Luther von Gewissheit und Ungewissheit des Heils," *Lutherjahrbuch* 77 (2010): 41–63, 44–45.
39. "*Ego semel conquerebar de sublimitate praedestinationis Staupitio meo. Respondit mihi: In vulneribus Christi intelligitur praedestinatio et invenitur, non alibi, quia scriptum est: Hunc audite. Der Vater ist zu hoch, sed dixit Pater: Ego dabo viam veniendi ad me, nempe Christum. Ite, credite, hengt euch an den Christum, so wirts sichs wol finden, quis sim, suo tempore. Das thun wir nicht, ideo Deus est nobis incomprehensibilis, incogitabilis; er wirt nicht begriffen, er will ungefast sein extra Christum*" (WA TR 2, No. 1490 [112, 9–16]).
40. When treating Rom 1:4 and 8:29, it was forced by the Latin text applying *praedestinatus* to Christ (WA 56:5.6. 18; 83.11–12. 25–26). For Rom 4:5, 8:28, and 9:12, Luther uses the term *praedestinatio* to explain the term *propositum* (WA 56:41.14; 83.8; 91.3); for Rom 5:6 to explain "*secundum tempus*" (WA 56:50.13; 309.17–18); for Rom 9:9 to explain *promissio* (WA 56:90.7); and for Rom 11:25 to explain *plenitudo gentium* (WA 56:113.13–14). For Rom 8:33, he uses *praedestinati* to explain *electi* (WA 56:85.1). For Rom 11:29, he explains "*dona et vocatio Dei*" with *praedestinare* (WA 56:114.10–11).
41. WA 56:381.17. Cited after LW 25:371.
42. WA 56:382.23–24.30–31; cf. Harry McScorley, *Luthers Lehre vom unfreien Willen nach seiner Hauptschrift De Servo Arbitrio im Lichte der biblischen und kirchlichen Tradition* (Munich: Kaiser, 1967), 220–21.

elect attain salvation. The elect attaining salvation is therefore utterly contingent in itself; there is nothing that a person can do, nor is there a point that they can insist on to attain salvation. They can only give thanks to God for his decision. (2) Luther is also concerned with how to deal with the fact that some people are not called and therefore not among the saved.[43] (3) Luther rejects the accusation against God that blames him for the bad outcome of the nonelected.[44] (4) He comforts those who doubt their election in that he sees the very humility, to which God promises salvation, in their fear.[45] He thereby explains assent to God's will as a sign of salvation.[46] Characteristically, this section is almost entirely missing in the notes of his students.[47] The section on "Da quod iubes" in the context of Romans 3 is as well. Taken together, these seem to confirm Schmidt-Lauber's insight that Luther avoided sensitive topics[48] in the lecture hall.[49]

These are all excurses, but they conspire together to undermine the basic thesis that grace is given *gratis* to the faithful[50] and that they attain justification without any merits or works.[51] This theological interpretation has a certain anti-Jewish moment in it, especially in the explanation of Abraham. According to Luther, Romans 4:10 (which argues against circumcision) provides an excellent argument against "the foolishness of the Jews" (*Iudeorum insipientia*).[52] If Abraham was justified without circumcision and works, then the Jews should not say that justification and works are necessary.[53] Luther clearly is embedded in a controversy with theologians of his age but is also confronting the basic religious convictions of the Judaism that he perceived. That Abraham "was justified through nothing except faith" is primarily directed against a purported

43. WA 56:383.35.
44. WA 56:383.27–29; 385.1–386.22.
45. WA 56:387.20–26.
46. WA 56:388.4–28.
47. The Scholion on Rom 8:28 is reduced to a small excerpt that speaks of a *propositum Dei*, but not from *praedestinatio* (WA 57 [I: Römerbrief]:195.7–16); the marginalia do provide an identification of *propositum* and *praedestinatio* (WA 77.7).
48. Schmidt-Lauber, *Vorlesung*, 156.
49. However, it is interesting to note that Luther told his students of a "trepidatio cordis" concerning the idea that God could change his mind (WA 56:48.18–24; 57:48.21–25).
50. WA 56:37, 26.
51. WA 56:42.3–4; 265.29–31.
52. Thus, the evaluation of Eduard Lohse, "Martin Luther und der Römerbrief des Apostels Paulus," *Kerygma und Dogma* 52 (2006): 106–25, 117, using Rom 9–11 is not valid for the entire lecture, which says that Luther spoke in the Romans lectures "not [. . .] polemically or with dishonoring words about the Jews." My translation.
53. WA 56:42.21–26.

Jewish conviction that Luther believes says that one is justified by works,[54] just as the idea of "the righteousness of works" without grace and Christ appears to be Jewish and insufficient to him.[55]

This is the context in which we must understand the clear statement, "that justification comes from faith but not by works."[56] This statement, and also its focus in the concept of "belief alone" (*sola credulitas*) as the basis for salvation,[57] only seems to disassociate itself from a thought structure assuming compensatory works. No matter how clear it is that no one can be given justification because of their works,[58] Luther's explanation to Romans 3:25 remains very decisive, "He does not give grace freely without demanding satisfaction, but rather he gave Christ to us as a satisfactor so that he gives grace freely to the satisfying through someone else."[59] The notes from Luther's students indicate that he augmented this satisfactory context in his oral presentation, "He does not give grace freely without demanding satisfaction, but rather he gave Christ to us so as a satisfactor and has accepted [him to give (grace) to] us freely, but not to Christ."[60] This statement is entirely consistent with Anselm's doctrine of satisfaction, the very stuff Luther was reading in Erfurt.[61] The precondition for the promise of grace is that Christ had fulfilled God's demands. It can only be said on this basis that "faith suffices without any work whatsoever."[62]

Luther's preferred attainment of grace through faith also places him in the lineage of scholastic thought. The terms *imputare* and *reputare*,

---

54. WA 56:40.26–28: "*non nisi ex fide Iustificatus fit.*" With considerations of the "new perspective" in Paul studies, Jens-Christian Maschmeier, "Glaube und Handeln bei Luther und Paulus. Kritische Anfragen an eine lutherische Paulusperspektive," *Kerygma und Dogma* 59 (2013): 21–44 demonstrates that "Paul and Luther are not identical in their determination of divine and human handling and thus in the central question of the relation between justification and justification by works." (29). My translation.
55. WA 56:99.9–10: "*iustitia operum.*" Cited after LW 25:89.
56. WA 56:41.21: "*Iustificationem ex fide, non autem ex operibus fieri.*"
57. WA 56:100.23.
58. WA 56:37.21–22.
59. WA 56:37.26–28: "*non sic gratis dat gratiam, vt nullam satisfactionem exegerit, Sed satisfactorem Christum pro nobis dedit, Vt sic satisfacientibus per alium ipsis tamen gratis gratiam daret.*" My translation.
60. WA 57 (I: Römerbrief):40.17–20: "*non sic dat graciam gratis, ut nullam satisfactionem exegerit, sed satisfactorem Christum pro nobis dedit et accepit et sic nobis quidem gratis, non autem Christo.*" My translation.
61. Cf. Luther, *Erfurter Annotationen*, 12–25. My translation.
62. WA 56:100.21: "*fides sufficit sine illis operibus.*"

which he read in Paul's letters, were interpreted by him with the *acceptio*-doctrine,[63] which had been in circulation since Duns Scotus and had continued to influence theologians until Gabriel Biel. In Sent I d. 17 q. 2, Biel presented the understanding of Ockham, according to which there was no contradiction in the idea that God would recognize a human act without any prior infusion of grace as being meritorious. He argued that meritous character depended on "the free will of God's grace which accepts it freely as a reward."[64] It was this very terminology that Biel had applied within a merit-theology framework,[65] which Luther (much like Nicholas of Lyra[66]) now adopted in order to interpret the *reputatio*-idea of Romans. "And so it is not he who works, but rather God who accepts his faith, who leads to justice."[67] is what Luther writes about Romans 4:3. This late-medieval *acceptatio*-theory is the framework behind Luther's understanding of Paul, which is why he can explain the following verse with both the formulation "that justification takes place out of faith, but not by works,"[68] and the remark, "This expresses only God's gracious acceptance, not the merits of a worker."[69] The mental moves made here are still entirely consistent with a medieval horizon, despite the clear resonances with later formulations. It also would spur him to further considerations that later would be perceived as strongly dissonant: the idea of a *simul* of justified

63. Cf. Werner Dettloff, *Die Entwicklung der Akzeptations- und Verdienstlehre von Duns Scotus bis Luther* (Münster: Aschendorff, 1963); this interdependence is overlooked by Bizer, *Fides ex auditu*, 3rd ed., 46–52.

64. Cf. Biel, *Collectorium*, I d. 17 q. 2 (Gabrielis Biel, *Collectorium circa quattuor libros Sententiarum. Prologus er Liber primus*, ed. Wilfried Werbeck and Udo Hofmann [Tübingen: Mohr 1973], 425, 8–9): "*ex sola Dei gratiosa voluntate eum libere ad praemiandum acceptante.*" My translation; cf. Biel, *Collectorium*, II d. 27 q. un. A. 3 dubium 2: "*Nam ratio meriti principlaissime convenit actui ex libera acceptatione divina.*" (Gabrielis Biel, *Collectorium circa quattuor libros Sententiarum. Liber secundus*, ed. Wilfried Werbeck and Udo Hofmann [Tübingen: Mohr, 1984], 520, 25–26), with a direct reference to Duns Scotus, Biel, *Collectorium*, lines 4–5.

65. Heiko Augustinus Oberman, *The Harvest of Medieval Theology: Gabriel Biel and Late Medieval Nominalism* (Cambridge: Harvard University Press, 1963), 176, neatly summarizes that for Biel, "justification is at once *sola gratia* and *solis operibus!*"

66. Nikolaus von Lyra, *Postilla zu Röm 3:21*; cf. Denifle, *Quellenbelege*, 191.

67. WA 56:41.3–4: "*Et ita est non operantis, Sed Dei acceptantis fidem ipsius ad Iustitiam*"; the students' notes are similar: "*dei acceptantis et ex gracia reputantis*" (WA 57 [I: Römerbrief]: 42.18–19). My translation.

68. WA 56:41.21: "*Iustificationem ex fide, non autem ex operibus fieri.*" My translation.

69. WA 56:41.21: "*Quod exprimit solam gratuitam Dei acceptationem et non meritum operantis.*" My translation.

and sinner.[70] We are "justified and unjust simultaneously,"[71] and it is this very justification that does not come from us, brought about "solely by the imputation of God,"[72] for sin never ceases in this life.[73] Thus, it can be said about the faithful, "They are actually sinners, but they are righteous by the imputation of a merciful God. They are unknowingly righteous and knowingly unrighteous; they are sinners in fact but righteous in hope."[74] It is this constitution of justice out of God's recognition (*reputatio*) that constitutes the actual difference between Luther's conception of justice in the Romans lectures and that of the philosophers.[75] Thus, what Luther recalls as the juxtaposition of everything he had learned turns out to be a critique of a certain scholastic position held by the likes of Thomas Aquinas. He makes this critique based on a different conception derived from the likes of Duns Scotus and very much at home in the *Via moderna*.

## EMBEDDEDNESS IN MYSTICAL SPIRITUALITY

The emphasis on God's reputation did lead to an unintended consequence: the form of justification was located entirely outside of the human person. The Romans lectures are not characterized by a tension between an imputational/forensic doctrine of justification or an effective

70. Cf. Otto Hermann Pesch, "Simul iustus et peccator: Sinn und Stellenwert einer Formel Martin Luthérs.—Thesen und Kurzkommentare," in *Gerecht und Sünder zugleich? Ökumenische Klärungen*, ed. Theodor Schneider and Gunther Wenz (Freiburg: Herder, 2001), 146–67, 150–52, who summarizes the "simul" in the Romans lectures. The idea was by no means disregarded in the Middle Ages, as Gregory of Rimini in particular demonstrates when he explains in Sent II d. 30–33 q.1 a. 4: "*Nam tollitur [peccatum originale] quoad reatum, non tollitur autem quoad essentiam, hoc est quod vitium illud sive qualitas illa, quae dicitur concupiscibilitas et est ante baptismum originale peccatum, manet quidem secundum essentiam suam etiam post baptismum, non manet autem ad reatum, id est non per eam est homo post baptismum reus damnationis aeternae, sicut erat ante baptismum*" (Gregorii Ariminensis, *OESA Lectura super primum et secundum Sententiarum*, ed. Damasus Trapp and Venicio Marcolino, vol. 6 [Berlin: De Gruyter, 1980], 194, 9–14; cf. Volker Leppin, "Aristotelisierung, Immediatisierung und Radikalisierung: Transformationen der Sündenlehre von Thomas von Aquin bis Martin Luther," in *Transformationen: Studien zu den Wandlungsprozessen in Theologie und Frömmigkeit zwischen Spätmittelalter und Reformation*, 2nd ed. (Tübingen: Mohr Siebeck, 2018), 303–31, 319–20. The exegetical basis does remain, however, problematic for today's readers (cf. Werner Georg Kümmel, *Röm 7 und die Bekehrung des Paulus* [Leipzig: Hinrichs, 1929]).
71. WA 56:269.21–22: "*simul [. .] Iusti et Iniusti*"—also in the notes: WA 57 (I: Römerbrief):164.6–7.
72. WA 56:269.1–2: "*ex sola Dei reputatione.*" Cited after LW 25:257.
73. WA 56:260.25–27.
74. WA 56:269.29: "*Re vera peccatores, Sed reputatione miserentis Dei Iusti; Ignoranter Iusti et Scientes inIusti; peccatores in re, Iusti autem in spe.*" Cited after LW 25:258.
75. WA 56:287.16–19.

understanding on the other.[76] The fact that every good thing in faith—namely Christ—is "extrinsecum" to the believing person[77] leads to the consideration of how these good things can be nevertheless the "property" of an individual and even "in us" ("*in nobis*"). The first clear answer is that all of these—wisdom, justice, sanctification, and salvation—"are not within us [. . .] when not through faith and hope in him."[78] This statement does not apply only to every member of the faithful but also to the saints, whose deeds are ultimately the works "of Christ in them" ("*Christi in eis.*")[79] Here we see a tendency to say that despite emphasis on the externality of the ascription of grace, there occurs no change in the faithful's essence but instead a radical change in status. Through faith, the believer receives the "*virtus Dei,*" which elevates them above all else.[80]

This paradoxical idea that a person can only be externally constituted is quite common to the previous generations of mystical pious literature,[81] and it should not surprise us when we see Luther expressing his ideas concerning the attainment of salvation primarily in the language of mysticism, even explicitly citing mystical literature.[82] When explaining

76. Berndt Hamm, "Pure Gabe ohne Gegengabe—die religionsgeschichtliche Revolution der Reformation," *Jahrbuch für Biblische Theologie* 27 (2012): 241–76, 261 thus restricts the understanding of justification in the Romans lectures down to the "not-guilty verdict" of God and thereby makes the reformational understanding of gifts too simple; for more on the general problem, cf. Risto Saarinen, "Justification by Faith: The View of the Mannermaa School," in *The Oxford Handbook of Martin Luther's Theology,* ed. Robert Kolb, Irene Dingel, and Ludomir Batka (Oxford: University Press, 2014), 254–63, 255; Mark Mattes, "Luther on Justifiaction as Forensic and Effective," in *The Oxford Handbook of Martin Luther's Theology,* ed. Robert Kolb, Irene Dingel, and Ludomir Batka (Oxford: University Press, 2014), 264–73. When one considers the aspects of effective justification, one repeatedly stumbles over while researching this stage; it does not seem to me advisable that one identifies Luther's real discovery as imputational justification. Martin Brecht, "Römerbriefauslegungen Martin Luthers," in *Paulus, Apostel Jesu Christi: FS Günter Klein,* ed. Michael Trowitzsch (Tübingen: Mohr 1998), 207–25, 208 has made the fascinating observation that Luther, while editing his new Bible translation in Coburg in 1530, "replaced the important and frequently occuring group of words *to justify justification* [*rechtfertigen, Rechtfertigung*] with the words *make just, justice.* [*gerecht machen, Gerechtigkeit*] [. . .] This new manner of expression does not convey the impression of an entirely imputational doctrine of justification." My translation.
77. WA 56:279.22–23.
78. WA 56:279.24–24: "*in nobis non [. . .] nisi per fidem et spem in ipsum*"; cf. WA 280.3–4.
79. WA 56:290.16.
80. WA 56:10.15; cf. 291.21.
81. Cf. Volker Leppin, "Externe Personkonstitution bei Johannes Tauler," in *Transformationen: Studien zu den Wandlungsprozessen in Theologie und Frömmigkeit zwischen Spätmittelalter und Reformation,* 2nd ed. (Tübingen: Mohr Siebeck, 2018), 127–36.
82. Albrecht Peters, "Luthers Turmerlebnis," in *Der Durchbruch der reformatorischen Erkenntnis bei Luther,* ed. Bernhard Lohse (Darmstadt: Wissenschaftliche Buchgesellschaft, 1968), 243–88, 271 has already drawn attention to the mystical horizon of many of Luther's

Romans 8:16, Luther cites Bernard's sermon *In annuntiatione Dominica*[83] and cites a passage here, which, according to Theo Bell, had "captivated him entirely":[84]

> I believe that this testimony consists of three parts. For it is necessary first of all to believe that you cannot have the remission of sins except through the kindness of God. Second, that you could not possess any good work unless

statements in the Romans lectures; cf. Peters, "Luthers Turmerlebnis," *Glaube und Werk: Luthers Rechtfertigungslehre im Lichte der Heiligen Schrift* (Berlin: Lutherisches Verlaghaus, 1967), 34.

83. Bernard of Clairvaux, *Sämtliche Werke. Lateinisch/Deutsch*, ed. Gerhard B. Winkler, vol. 8 (Innsbruck: Tyrolia, 1997), 96–129; for more on the "Bernard Renaissance" of the late Middle Ages, cf. Franz Posset, *The Real Luther: A Friar at Erfurt & Wittenberg. Exploring Luther's Life with Melanchthon as Guide* (Saint Louis: Concordia Publishing House, 2011), 86–90. The early literature about Luther was deeply aware of how important this sermon was for Luther. In his preface to the second volume of Luther's works (made famous because of its indication of a "theses posting"), Melanchthon describes a sort of spiritual conference in the cloister: "*Et senis cuiusdam sermonibus in Augustiniano Collegio Erphordiae saepe se confirmatum esse narrabat,cui cum consternationes suas exponeret, audivit eum de fide multa disserentem, seque deductum aiebat ad symbolum, in quo dicitur: credo remissionem peccatorum. Hunc articulum sic ille interpretatus erat, non solum in genere credendum esse, aliquibus remitti, ut et daemones credunt. Davidi aut Petro remitti, sed mandatum Dei esse, ut singuli homines nobis remitti peccata credamus. Et hanc interpretationem confirmatam dicebat Bernardi dicto, monstratumque locum in concione de Annunciatione, ubi haec sunt verba: sed adde, ut credas et hoc, quod per ipsum peccata TIBI donantur. Hoc est testimonium, quod perhibet Spiritus sanctus in corde tuo, dicens: dimissa sunt tibi peccata tua. Sic enim arbitratur Apostolus, gratis iustificari hominem per fidem*" (CR 6:159); Johannes Mathesius repeats this scene in his Luther biography (despite omitting the title "*de annuntiatione*"): "*Weil er aber tag und nacht im Kloster studiret vnd betet / vnd sich darneben mit fasten vnd wachen / kasteyet vnd abmergelt / war er stetig betrübt vnd trawrig / vnd all sein Meßhalten jm kein trost geben wolte / schickt jm Gott ein alten Bruder zu im Lloster / zum Beichtuatter ,/ der tröstet jn hertzlich / vnd weiset jn auff die gnedige vergebung der sünden im Symbolo Apostolorum, vnnd leret jn auß S. Bernhards Predigt / Er müste für sich selber auch glauben / das jhm der barmhertzig Gott vnnd Vatter / durch das einige Opffer vnnd blut seines gehorsamen Sones / vergebung aller sünden erworben / vnd durch den heiligen Geist inn der Apostolischen Kirche n / durchs wort der Absolution verkündigen ließ. Diß ist vnserm D. ein lebendiger vnd krefftiger trost in seinem hertzen gewesen.*" (*Historien /\ Von des Ehrwirdigen | in Gott seligen theuren Manns Got-| tes Doctoris Martini Luthers / anfang /\ Lere / leben / vnnd sterben /\ Alles ordenlich der Jarzal nach /\ wie sich alle sachen zu jeder zeit | haben zugetragen / | Durch den alten M. Johann Mathesium | gestelt / vnd für seinem Christlichen ende verfertiget (. . .)* (Nürnberg: Johann von Berg Erben, 1570), 5ʳ); cf. Theo Bell, *Divus Bernhardus: Bernhard von Clairvaux in Martin Luthers Schriften* (Mainz: Zabern, 1993), 91–92; Franz Posset, "Bernhard von Clairvaux's Meditation zu Psalm 31, 2 bei Martin Luther," *Lutherjahrbuch* 69 (2002): 71–78, 75–77. For information on Luther's knowledge of Bernard, cf. the overview from Ulrich Köpf, "Die Rezeptions- und Wirkungsgeschichte Bernhards von Clairvaux: Forschungsstand und Forschungsaufgaben," in *Bernhard von Clairvaux: Rezeption und Wirkung im Mittelalter und in der Neuzeit*, ed. Kaspar Elm (Wiesbaden: Harrassowitz, 1994), 5–65, 13–14.

84. Bell, *Divus Bernhardus*, 98.

God Himself gave it to you. And last, that you cannot earn eternal life by any of your works, unless it is given to you by grace.[85]

A Cictercian abbot thus tells Luther about the dependence on grace from God, the grounding of every good work in God, and the exclusion of any work or merit performed by oneself for eternal life. This comes to the formulation that this merit is given to the person "*gratis.*" Put differently, around the time of the Romans lectures, Luther clearly stumbles upon those statements that were so important for his understanding of justification in his reading of Bernard—and they even line up with those made by Paul and Augustine. They augment and complement each other. The monk and professor Martin Luther is thus able to bind his exegetical insights with the spiritual basis of monastic theology.[86]

This manner of Christ's presence in this mystically reflected context is essentially a pneumatic one, "Those who are Christians have the spirit of Christ and do rightly, even if they do not understand what we now say."[87] Such a formulation by no means excludes an effective dimension to the moment of justification. To the contrary in fact, it allows for a coherence of wills between that of God[88] and the believer, which results in a God-pleasing way of handling. The basis for this is a changed way of being—created through the relation to Christ. "Whoever believes with a full faith and trusts that they are God's son is God's son."[89]—Luther's marginal note justifies precisely this interpretation with Bernard's sermon

---

85. WA 56:370.1–5, "*hoc testimonium in tribus consistere puto. Necesse est enim primo omnium credere, quod remissionem peccatorum habere non possis nisi per indulgentiam Dei. Deinde, quod nihil prorsus habere queas boni operis, nisi et hoc dederit ipse. Postremo, quod eternam vitam nullis potest operibus promereri, nisi gratis detur et illa.*"; cf. Bernard, *Sämtliche Werke*, 8:96.9–13, which deviates only slightly. For more on how Luther uses this passage, cf. Bernhard Lohse, "Luther und Bernhard von Clairvaux," in *Bernhard von Clairvaux: Rezeption und Wirkung im Mittelalter und in der Neuzeit*, ed. Kaspar Elm (Wiesbaden: Harrassowitz, 1994), 271–301, 276–77. An overview of how Luther uses Bernard in the Romans lectures is offered by Bell, *Divus Bernhardus*, 83–99, who also reminds the reader "that Bernard of Clairvaux never had the position in Luther's theology which Augustine did" (Bell, *Divus Bernhardus*, 84). Cited after LW 25:359–60.

86. This combination is also present in the students' notes: WA 57 (I: Römerbrief):189.22–190.19.

87. WA 56:276.17–18: "*Qui sunt Christi, spiritum Christi habent et agunt recte, etiamsi non intelligunt, quod nos modo diximus.*"

88. WA 56:365.18–20: "*Non enim timendo, Sed amando fugitur ira Dei et miseria atque horror Iudicii et per conformitatem voluntatis Die quietatur conscientia.*" This formulation is entirely consistent with late-medieval spiritual literature: *conformitas* is a central concept in the theology of John Staupitz (cf. Markus Wriedt, *Gnade und Erwählung: Eine Untersuchung zu Johann von Staupitz und Martin Luther* [Mainz: Zabern, 1991], 146–51).

89. WA 56:79.2–3: "*Qui ergo plena fide credit et confidit se esse filium Dei, Est filius Dei*"—Cf. the notes of the students: WA 57 (I: Römerbrief):73.13–14.

*In annuntiatione Dominica.*[90] New being, which Luther now redescribes in a Pauline-Augustinian fashion, is reciprocal, just as we would expect from the Middle Ages. The believer is in Christ, and Christ is in them.[91]

The anthropology assumed by Luther here is entirely characterized by mystical thought. Luther relates being *secundum spiritum* in Romans 8:5 to the *interior homo* and thus with the idea that had occupied his attention during his Romans lectures, especially while reading John Tauler. Luther found several developed tracts on the idea "if thou wouldst become an interior man"[92] in Tauler's forty-second sermon and noted in the margins, "Become an internal human as it should be."[93] It is even more noteworthy that he had treated the topic of "innerness" in Tauler's previous sermon[94]—and he made an interesting note here as well. In the forty-first sermon, Tauler treats the woman searching for the lost coin (Luke 15:8–10) and says that there are two sorts of searching. "We must be both active and passive. We must be active, seeking; and we must be passive, being sought."[95] Luther interprets this with the concepts "*activa*" (for "real") and "*passiva*."[96] This terminology, according to which Luther explains his own remembered transformation in the Grand Testimony of 1545 while using *iustitia activa* and *passiva*, are steeped in mysticism, even where these terms appear in the Romans lectures. Here, Luther explains that human beings "are freed not from their own powers but actively through God and passively in themselves."[97] Tauler sees the passive character (*leidentlich*) in the context of the person going "into [their] own souls, into the very depths" (*seinen aygen grundt*).[98] Luther does not convey this mystical formulation exactly, but taken together, the various references make clear that a conflation of Paul and Tauler belongs to the many amalgamations found within the Romans lectures. This reaches its zenith in a comment on Tauler, "Therefore the the entirety of salvation consists

90. WA 56:79:15–17.

91. WA 56:74.5–6.

92. Johannes Tauler, *Sermones: des hoch\ geleerten in gnaden erleüchten do\ctoris Johannis Thaulerii sannt \ dominici ordens die da weißend \ auff den nächesten waren weg im \ gaist zů wanderen durch überswe\ bendenn syn. Von latein in teütsch \ gewendt manchem menschenn zů \ såliger fruchtbarkaitt* (Augsburg: Hans Otmar, 1508), fol. 102ᵛa: "*Wiltu ain inwennig mensch werdenn.*" Cited after: John Tauler, *The Sermons and Conferences of John Tauler*, ed. and trans. Walter Elliott (Washington, DC: Apostolic Mission House, 1910), 425.

93. WA 9:101.12–13: "*fieri hominem interiorem, quomodo oporteat.*"

94. WA 9:101.8–9.

95. Tauler, *Sermones*, 99ᵛb. Cited after: John Tauler, *Spiritual Conferences*, trans. and ed. Eric Colledge and M. Jane (Rockford, IL: Tan Books, 1978), 76.

96. WA 9:101.6–7.

97. WA 56:277.26–27: "*non ex Viribus suis, Sed per Deum active et in se passiue Liberatur.*" My translation.

98. Tauler, *Sermones*, 99ᵛb.

of resigning oneself in all things, both spiritual as well as temporal, as he teaches here. And in pure faith in God."[99] Thus, if we are going to speak of a "*Sola fide*" during the period of the Romans lectures, then it has to be a mystically colored one. The idea that the life in the spirit means a *mortificatio* of the old human also belongs here.[100] It is this very idea that Luther places on the title page of his *Theologia deutsch* when he published it in 1516 as his first-ever published work.[101] The Augustinian-Pauline theology of the Romans lectures is simultaneously a deeply mystical one, which is evenly familiar with Bernard of Clairvaux and John Tauler.[102]

## CONTEXTUALIZATION IN LUTHER'S MONASTIC ENVIRONS

This context also makes clear the *Sitz im Leben* of what Ernst Bizer has identified as a "theology of humility" in Luther's early writings.[103] Bizer used this concept as a foil to easily identify and isolate reformational theology. At least, that is what he wanted to do. The character of a "theology of humility" followed dogmatic catagories: in *humilitas*, one still ought to assume a limited degree of individual action on the part of the person. A more exact examination of this thesis would require a treatment of the concepts "humility," "humilitas," "humilis," etc. in the texts Bizer uses to argue for a reformational turn. For our purposes, it is enough to point out that *humilitas* is used within the Romans lectures[104] to relate Paul's text both conceptionally and existentially to that very monastic existence that shaped Martin Luther at this point.[105] That the

99. WA 9:102.34–36: "*Igitur tota salus est resignatio voluntatis in omnibus ut hic docet sive in spiritualibus sive temporalibus. Et nuda fides in deum.*"
100. WA 56:306.14–16; 416.8–9; Bizer, *Fides ex auditu*, 3rd ed., 36.
101. Cf. WA 1:153: "*Ein geistlich, edles Buchlein von rechter underscheid und vorstand, was der alt und neu mensche sei. Was Adams und was Gottes kind sei. Und wie Adam inn uns sterben unnd Christus ersteen soll.*"
102. Without this very concrete relation, *mortificatio* loses its meaning in an anthopological abstraction.
103. Bizer, *Fides ex auditu*.
104. Karl-Heinz zur Mühlen, *Nos extra nos: Luthers Theologie zwischen Mystik und Scholastik* (Tübingen: Mohr 1972), 44–45 has found clear results that a supposed juxtaposition between *humilitas* and Luther's understanding of faith (something Bizer also assumes) does not actually fit to Luther's intention since in *humilitas* the person no longer stands "under the omen of ascent, but rather under the existence under iuticium Dei." My translation.
105. Cf. the standard work Bernhard Lohse, *Mönchtum und Reformation: Luthers Auseinandersetzung mit dem Mönchsideal des Mittelalters* (Göttingen: Vandenhoeck & Ruprecht, 1963), as well as the portrayals of this existential situation by Ulrich Köpf, "Martin Luther als Mönch," *Luther* 55 (1984): 66–84; Lohse, "Monastische Traditionen bei Martin Luther," in *Luther—zwischen den*

faithful is "humble and small for and to themself" (*humilis et vilis sibiipsi*)[106] is fulfilled especially in monasticism. It is here that God finds those *humiliati* who are deserving of justification.[107] In the Romans lectures, Luther never programmatically portrays the special status of monasticism as a *via securior*,[108] but his thought (especially that pertaining to the preparation for justification) clearly develops a monastic ethos. That can be seen simply in the abundant emphasis placed on *humilitas*. This was a topic that had occupied Luther's own order for a while by this point. Jordan of Sachsen wrote a spiritual booklet for the Augustinian hermits called *vitasfratrum* where an entire chapter (II, 7) is devoted to *humilitas*.[109] Other comments from Luther have a consistent basic content. When he rejects lust, greed, and gluttony, he finds himself in good monastic company, just as when he criticizes pride[110] (Jordan gives the entirety of chapter II, 9 to that as well).[111] Of course, Jordan's recommendation of chastity[112] is a major topic for him, for he sees it as the means to retreat "from the flesh" (*a carne*).[113] Luther does the same thing when he counts his list of virtues, intended to distance the person from love of the "sensual" "*corporalia.*"[114] Luther envisions a journey of "self-cultivation" (*agricultura suiipsius*)[115] consisting in "praying intensively, learning intensively, working intensively, being chaste until that old [part of you] has been extinguished and a new will arises."[116] We would expect precisely this from monasticism. But not only the way of life, which is oriented toward asceticism, is interesting. The context in a theology of grace is as well. Those *agricultura* in the Romans lectures have a clear dispositional function: "Grace is not granted without that self-agriculture."[117] If we are to understand *Sola fide* in the sense that a human being may not attain salvation through their works nor prepare

---

Zeiten: Eine Jenaer Ringvorlesung, ed. Christoph Markschies and Michael Trowitzsch (Tübingen: Mohr, 1999), 17–35; and Christoph Burger, *Tradition und Neubeginn: Martin Luther in seinen frühen Jahren* (Tübingen: Mohr 2014), 45–54.

106. WA 56:264.11.

107. WA 56:36.23

108. Cf. Berndt Hamm, *Frömmigkeitstheologie am Anfang des 16. Jahrhunderts: Studien zu Johannes von Paltz und seinem Umkreis* (Tübingen: Mohr, 1982), 284–99.

109. Jordani de Saxonia, *Liber Vitasfratrum*, ed. Rudolph Arbesmann and Winfried Hümpfener (New York: Cosmopolitan Science and Art Service, 1942), 111–18.

110. WA 56:258.23–25.

111. Jordanus de Saxonia, *Vitasfratrum*, 125–29.

112. WA 56:258.25.

113. Jordanus de Saxonia, *Vitasfratrum*, 266.

114. WA 56:258.24.

115. WA 56:257.31.

116. WA 56:257.29–30: "*instanter orandum, instanter discendum, instanter operandum, castigandum, donec ista vetustas eradicetur et fiat nouitas in voluntate.*" My translation.

117. WA 56:257.28–31: "*Non enim dabitur gratia sine ista agricultura suiipsius.*" My translation.

themselves for salvation in any way, then we are faced with a Luther in the Romans lectures who wants to be understood in a manner very distinct from that! Further passages indicate that he did in fact believe in a preperatory development of a person before they would receive grace, even in those passages where he rejects a haughty understanding of good works. "Instead, all justified people do good works in grace, preparing themselves for the following perfection of their justification."[118] Toward this end, even Paul is interpreted in the sense of a dispositional understanding of works:

> Thus when the apostle says that a man is justified *apart from works of the Law* (v. 28), he is not speaking about the works which are performed in order that we may seek justification. Because these are no longer the works of the Law but of grace and faith, since he who performs them does not trust in them for his justification, but he wants to be justified.[119]

It is this desire for justification that shapes the entire life of Christians,[120] "even to the hour of death."[121] This framework is ultimately consistent with itself because full justification is attained only with a person's departure in death.[122]

When we look at it this way, the precondition for justification is not found in human works but rather in the monastic virtue of *humilitas*. God regards those who are humble, and this is identical with him satisfying their yearning for justification and ascribing his justice to them.[123] These statements alone appropriately contextualize *sola fide*. It is only possible to find a contradiction and inconsistency here if you examine these statements from the perspective of a mature Reformation and later Protestant culture that pits *sola fide* against anything that might appear as a meritous activity on the part of the person. For Luther and late-medieval piety, the *Sola* character of faith is decisive because it means a humble acceptance of God's judgement under the cross.[124] God makes a paradoxical move when

---

118. WA 56:259.14–14: "*Immo omnia opera Iusta et in gratia facta sunt praeparatoria ad sequentem profectum Iustificationis.*" My translation.
119. WA 56:264.21–25: "*Vnde Quando Apostolus dicit, Quod sine operibus legis iustificamur, Non loquitur de operibus, que pro Iustificatione querenda fiant. Quia hec iam non legis opera sunt, Sed gratie et fidei, cum qui hec operatur, non per hec sese Iustificatum confidant, Sed Iustificari cupiat.*" Cited after LW 25:252.
120. WA 56:264–35.
121. WA 56:264.18: "usque ad mortem." Cited after LW 25:252.
122. WA 56:258.13–14.
123. WA 56:259.19–20: "*Ideo Nullus sanctorum se Iustum putat aut confitetur, Sed Iustificari semper se petit et expectat, propter quod a Deo Iustus reputatur, quia respicit humiles.*" Cited after LW 25:37.
124. WA 56:266.11–12.

he considers those who have realized their own sinfulness to be just and damns those who consider themselves to be just on the basis of their own resources, doing so against the facts.[125] In this context, the exact relationship between works and faith loses its radicality. Luther's main contention is that works cannot suffice without faith[126] but simultaneously emphasizes that faith is what fulfills the law.[127] With this understanding, an ascetic life can very much serve as an expression of justification by demonstrating the consequences of faith:

> For circumcision is not given for the purpose of justification, but for a sign of the justification which has already been accomplished, just as also those who have been justified through faith are now commanded to perform good works, continually to circumcise themselves of evil lusts, and to mortify their flesh with its works and lusts. By these signs they demonstrate in a sense that they have faith and have been justified.[128]

Mortifying the flesh thus demonstratively signifies faith and belonging to the company of the justified. More than anything else, this is a theology to confirm monastic existence. The realization of faith and justification in dealings is by no means a trivial matter: whoever does not demonstrate their faith with deeds does not believe in Christ.[129] Deeds are thus a sure indication of faith and therefore for our justification. *Sine operibus* simply cannot be thought of in the sense that no works follow faith. Among other things, *Sola fide* denotes an event of justification preceding an ascetic disposition of the person. *Sola fide* assumes a ceaseless searching for justification. As soon as justification has been attained, it manifests concrete works. Such a *Sola fide* leaves a deep mark in Luther's monastic milieu and experience.

## CONCLUDING OUTLOOK

These investigations demonstrate to a certain extent just how badly those debates surrounding the dating of Luther's reformational insight missed the point. If we use "*Sola fide*" as our criterium, then yes, one can in fact

---

125. WA 56:259.23–24; cf. WA 41.11–12.
126. WA 56:263.19.
127. WA 56:263.17.
128. WA 56:43.17–21: "*Quia Circumsisio non in Iustificationem, Sed in figuram Iustificationis iam facta data, Sicut et modo per fidem Iustificatis precipitur, Vt operentur bonum et iugiter se circumcidant a prauis concupiscentiis et carnem mortificant cum operibus et concupiscentiiis suis. Quibus Velut signis probant sese habere fidem et Iustificatos esse.*" Cited after LW 25:37.
129. WA 56:103.13–15.

find it in the Romans lectures. But it is also clear that its usage at this point takes place in a spiritual context assuming the faithful to have somehow attained the proper disposition to be able to receive grace. Such a spirituality is considered necessary for *satisfactio*. This insight is still valid, even though Luther's theology of faith searching for *promissio* is already complete: "Faith and promise are related to each other."[130] It turns out that this has actually been passed down from Peter Lombard and cannot be considered a landmark moment in the development of reformational theology.

Thus, the Romans lectures are an amalgamation of various sources. Paul is brought into relation with Augustine, Lombard, Bernard of Clairvaux, and the self-evident milieu of monastic existence without the slightest hesitation. Taken together, these constitute a reference to the sources of Christian tradition before the grand reception of Aristotle in the thirteenth century. These sources are conveyed primarily in the form of Tauler. Luther makes a great effort to bring them into conformity with his own spiritual statements. The Romans lectures are thus the product of and—to a certain extent—the perfection of a particular strain of medieval theology and thus the root for a reformational theology soon to take wings. Therefore, there is indeed a *"Sola fide"* in Luther's Romans lectures—but it is still developing!

---

130. WA 56:45.15; 46.15–16: *"fides et promissio sunt relativa."* My translation.

# 5.

# *Sola scriptura*. The Genesis of the Reformation's Scriptural Principle. Observations Concerning Luther's Conflict with John Eck until the Leipzig Disputation

The main reason why the Leipzig disputation is interesting is because it asks whether councils can err. This debate, with enormous consequences for canon law, is only the most extreme expression of a hermeneutical confrontation.[1] This juxtaposition can be described using the main current of medieval positions,[2] with Eck representing the harmony model[3] and Luther representing the difference model. The latter would make a humanistic distinction between the original source and its further

---

1. Thomas Fuchs, *Konfession und Gespräch: Typologie und Funktion der Religionsgespräche in der Reformationszeit* (Weimar: Böhlau, 1995) has rightly drawn attention to this.
2. It would be too simple to explain medieval hermeneutics as being entirely determined by some model of harmony. Thus, Helmut Feld, *Die Anfänge der modernen biblischen Hermeneutik in der spätmittelalterlichen Theologie* (Wiesbaden: Zabern, 1977), 28–29 draws on the case (D. 20, 2) of treating the possible case of various exegetes coming to results different from the doctrine of the pope, explaining, "*aparet, quod divinarum scripturarum tractatores, etsi scientia Pontificibus premineant, tamen, quia dignitatis eorum apicem non sunt adepti, in sacrarum scripturarum expositinibus éis preponuntur, in causis uero diffiniendis secundum post eos locum merentur.*" (CICan 1:65).
3. One can follow Kurt-Victor Selge, *Normen der Christenheit im Streit um Ablaß und Kirchenautorität 1518 bis 1521. Erster Teil: Das Jahr 1518* (Heidelberg. Habilschrift, 1968), 91 in calling this a "balanced system of authorities" as he does while examining Cajetan. Wilbirgis Klaiber, *Ecclesia militans: Studien zu den Festtagspredigten des Johannes Eck* (Münster: Aschendorff, 1979), 25–26 points out that Eck's own attitude toward the relation between Scripture and tradition experienced a pronounced shift starting around 1525. While Eck gave priority to Scripture in the context treated here, he later gave priority to tradition.

development.[4] Where Eck perceived tradition and Scripture as mutually fortifying and explanatory authorities, Luther saw them as diverging. Thus, we see the formation of a polarity between Scripture and tradition. It would become a basic factor in reformational theology.[5]

The academic debate between Luther and Eck marked the end of a protracted distancing between the two. It arguably began in spring of 1517 when Eck sought the friendship of the Wittenberger.[6] From this point forth, the two would regard each other as irreconcilable enemies, each convinced of his own doctrinal correctness and of the other's heresy. This very public dispute, which began with and continued the theses on indulgence, was not only a collision of various firm opinions. It also occasioned significant developments in Luther's own thought.[7]

## *ASTERISCI* AND *OBELISCI*: THE HARMONY
## OF SCRIPTURE AND TRADITION

If we want to believe Eck, then he never wanted this fight.[8] He was only a doctrinal aide to Eichstatt's Bishop Gabriel of Eyb at the University of Ingolstadt, which is why he had to inform the bishop of Luther's indulgence theses. Upon hearing Eck's presentation, the bishop requested that

4. For basic information on the humanistic influence on Luther, cf. Helmar Junghans, *Der junge Luther und die Humanisten* (Göttingen: Vandenhoeck & Ruprecht, 1985).

5. Kurt-Victor Selge, "Das Autoritätengefüge der westlichen Christenheit im Lutherkonflikt 1517 bis 1521," *Historische Zeitschrift* 223 (1976): 591–617, 607, has recognized and convincingly written of the importance of this conflict between Luther and Eck.

6. Theodor Wiedemann, *Dr. Johann Eck, Professor der Theologie an der Universität Ingolstadt: Eine Monographie* (Regensburg: Pustet, 1865), 83 n. 23 uses a note from von Seckendorf "*Commentarius historicus et apologeticus de Lutheranismo*" to accept that Eck had already corresponded with Luther since Scheurl had put them in contact. The note reads, "*se theses suas anno 1518 edidisset, antequam Lutheri litera d.7. Jan. 1519 accepisset, et quandam cum hoc amicitiam per literas congtraxisse prius, quam eum vidisset ex commendatione Christophori Scheurlii*" (Viet Ludwig von Seckendorf and Louis Maimbourg, *VITI LUDOVICI a SECKENDORF | (…) | COMMENTARIU | HISTORICUS ET APOLOGETICUS | De | LUTHERANISMO,| Sive| DE REFORMATIONE | RELIGIONIS| ductu| D. MARTINI LUTHERI| (…)* [Leipzig: Johann Friedrich Gleditsch, 1694], l. 1:31). If one reads the phrase "*ex commendatione Christophori Scheurlii*" as applying to written correspondance and not a personal meeting (and Scheurl did in fact ensure the two were writing each other), the point of mediating contact nevertheless remains with Scheurl.

7. At this stage, it is called for to remind ourselves of a methodical remark from Selge, *Normen*, 33 to not interpret Luther in 1518 on the basis of later positions but rather to "understand him historically."

8. Also worth reading as a basis for reconstructing the events in Leipzig and the events leading up to it: Johann Karl Seidemann, *Die Leipziger Disputation im Jahre 1519: Aus bisher unbenutzten Quellen historisch dargestellt und durch Urkunden erläutert* (Dresden: Arnold, 1843).

he make a list of all the points where he diverged from Luther's opinions.[9] This resulted in Eck's *18 Theses*.[10] They took a circuitous route before reaching Luther;[11] when he read them, he counted thirty-one.[12] Luther recalled a comment from Eck himself[13] and gave these theses the name "*Obelisci*," (little spears),[14] to which he responded with his "*Asterisci*" (little stars).[15] Eck's critique of indulgences was never intended to start a public conflict about them. He sent them intentionally *privatim* to Wittenberg.[16] And Luther also did not have his answer—the *Asterisci*—printed.[17] Thus, in Eck's eyes, it was not Luther but rather Andreas Karlstadt who had

9. Johannes Eck, *Defensio contra amarulentes D. Andreae Bodenstein Carolstatini invectiones (1518)*, ed. Joseph Greving (Münster: Aschendorff, 1919), 36, 26–37, 1. It is difficult to say with any certainty when Eck first received the indulgence theses. The "*Conclusiones*" mentioned by Christoph Scheurl in a letter from November 5 are most certainly not the indulgence theses (Christoph Scheurl's *Briefbuch, ein Beitrag zur Geschichte der Reformation und ihrer Zeit*, ed. Franz von Soden and Joachim Karl Friedrich Knaake, vol. 2 [Potsdam: Gropius, 1872], 40 [n. 155]) since Scheurl wrote a complaint to Luther that he had not received them himself (WA Br 1:152, 7 [no. 62]) and then thanked Ulrich of Dinstedt on January 5, 1518, for giving them to him (Scheurl's *Briefbuch. Vol. 2*, 42 [n. 158]). The adressee in Ingolstadt, to whom Scheurl forwarded the theses (Scheurl, *Briefbuch*, 43 [n. 160]), was likely Eck (cf. Klemens Honselmann, *Urfassung und Drucke der Ablaßthesen Martin Luthers und ihre Veröffentlichung* [Paderborn: Schöningh, 1966], 90).
10. Eck, *Defensio* 37:2–4.
11. The points were conveyed by Bernard Adelmann of Adelmannsfelden, a cousin of the bishop who was open to the Reformation for a certain period, and the Nurnberg Humanist Circle (Wurm, *Johannes Eck* 97–98; Scheurl's *Briefbuch* 2, 47–48 [n. 165]). The final handover to Luther was carried out by Wenzeslaus Linck (WA Br 1:177, 3 [n. 76]).
12. WA 1:281–314.
13. WA 1:282.24.
14. WA 1:281.2.
15. WA 1:281.1. The terminology had been coined by Origin for text-critical classification. Petrus Mosellanus had mentioned this system in a recent publication: "*Origenes Hebræis literis instructus, siquid in interpretibus ab ipsis scripturæ fontibus uariaret, uel* ὀβελίσκοις *iugulauit, uel* ἀσερίσκοις *(sic) insignivit.*" (*ORATIO | DE VARIARVM LINGVA| RVM COGNITIONE PA| randa. Petro Mosella-|no Protogenese au/| tore. Lipsiæ in ma|gna eruditorum| corona pro/|nunciata* (Basel: Johann Froben, 1519), 35; cf. the note concerning this in WA 1:278 n. 1. There are also indications of this text in Erasmus in the *Adagia* I.V.57 (*Opera Omnia Desiderii Erasmi Rotterodami*, II, 1 [Amsterdam: Brill, 1993], 532, 344–533, 354; cf. DCL 1:401 n. 3).
16. Eck, *Defensio*, 37:4: Eck explicitly means that he did not have this text printed. It is precisely the same term used by Luther to describe the sending of his indulgence theses (cf. WA 1: 528, 18–26).
17. WA 1:279 emphasizes that a printed edition was missing by referring to WA Br 1:466, 39–41: "*Und so Doctor Ecken der Kützel so fast rühret, so sein dieselben obelisci noch vorhanden, wollen sie wohl an Tag bringen, die wir bisher, seiner Ehr verschonet, verhalten haben.*" As Luther's *Asterisci* were a direct commentary of Eck's *Obelisci*, it can be assumed that there was no printed edition at the time of this letter, August 18, 1519. The first printed edition of the *Asterisci* and *Obelisci* was provided in a heavily edited form of Luther's latin works (WA 1:280; for more on the editing, cf. WA 9:770–80).

given cause for a public fight by attacking the *Obelisci* in his *Apologeticae Conclusiones*.[18,19]

Part of the difficulty when trying to reconstruct the beginnings of this fight has to do with the style of the *Obelisci* themselves. They really do address individual theses but are written in such a way that it can be tricky to determine this context.[20] On the other hand, Luther's *Asterisci* are very clearly related to the *Obelisci*, meaning that we can easily reconstruct his opinions. The following passage will not address all topics of the debate. Eck gave special attention to the concept of penance,[21] canonical punishments,[22] purgatory,[23] the *thesaurus ecclesiae*,[24] papal authority to bind and loose,[25] obedience to the pope as a general governing instance,[26] and the atoning work of Christ.[27]

There is not enough space here to pursue the full scope of this argumentation. It would be worth doing so, though, since it presents an interesting exposition of the indulgence conflicts in the context of Karlstadt's position. But for our purposes, the writings about questions of authority are decisive. We see this in Eck's accusation (probably directed at theses 48 and 57[28]) that Luther did not demonstrate an adequate degree of honor toward the pope.[29] Luther answered that he had in fact provided sufficient recognition to the pope when he advised him that his prayers were more necessary for Christendom than money.[30] But thereafter, he changed tack and handled

---

18. D. Andree Carolstatini, *docto-| RIS ET ARCHIDIACONI VVITTEN-| BVRGENSIS: CCCLXX:ET APOLOGE-| ticę Conclusiones pro sacris literis & Vuitten-| burgen[sibus] ita editę vt & lectoribus | profuturę sint.* (Wittenberg: Johann Rhau-Grunenberg, 1518).

19. Eck, *Defensio*, 37, 4–7; WA Br 1:460.13–15; cf. Heiko Augustinus Oberman, "Wittenberg's War on Two Fronts: What Happened 1518 and Why," in *The Reformation: Roots and and Ramification* (Edinburgh: T&T Clark, 1994), 117–48, 130–31.

20. An essential resource here is the edition in DCL 1:401–47.

21. WA 1:282.8–10; 283.2–5, occurs frequently.

22. WA 1:283.25–26; 287.20–25, occurs frequently.

23. WA 1:293.33–36.

24. WA 1:307.35–36; 308.30–34; 309.28–33; 310.18–23, occurs frequently.

25. WA 1:296.17–20; 312.6–8, occurs frequently.

26. WA 1:305.18.

27. WA 1:307.7–9, occurs frequently.

28. Cf. DCL 1:202. Thesis 48 reads, "Christians are to be taught that the pope, in granting indulgences, needs and thus desires their devout prayer more than their money." (*Docendi sunt christiani, quod Papa sicut magis eget ita magis optat in veniis dandis pro se devotam orationem quam promptam pecuniam.*) (WA 1:235.32–33, cited after LW 31:29); Thesis 57: "*Temporales certe non esse patet, quod non tam facile eos profundunt, sed tantummodo colligunt multi concionatorum.*" (WA 236.12–13).

29. WA 1:305.18: "*At irreverentia in eis ponderenda est summi Pontificis sanctitati.*" For more of the crticism of the papacy in the indulgence theses, cf. Berndt Hamm, *The Early Luther*, 86–87.

30. WA 1:305.27–28; Luther is evoking Thesis 48 (cf. n. 28).

some more basic thoughts, writing: "The Pope is a human being, he can be tricked, especially by such clever and flattering freeloaders. But God is the truth which cannot err."[31] Luther clearly touches on the fallibility of the pope here, something that would not have raised too many eyebrows in the late-medieval context. While there had been long debates about papal infallibility by this point,[32] it had never been dogmatized and did not enjoy majority support in Christendom.[33] Thus, Luther's simultaneous emphasis on obedience to the pope while entertaining his fallibility was very consistent with late-medieval possibilities. But his emphasis on the humanity of the pope gets a bit more cheeky within the *Asterisci*, where he cites Romans 3:4 in the proem: "Everyone is a liar."[34] While he will start by using this statement in a rather affectedly humble first-person plural, his later reference to the pope as a mere man lent the statement both depth and zing. But he still remained nice and ecclesial, writing, "There is a difference between the Pope saying something or making a statute out of it, and there is an even bigger difference if the Pope makes a statute or a council orders it."[35] While the pope's own decisive authority was cast into doubt, the councils were brought into play as an approbatory instance.[36] But, they, too, were not granted the status of infallibility.

When we trace the development of Luther's thought, it is even more interesting to note which authorities he bound himself to in order to dislodge the infallibility of the pope. They were the Bible, the "doctors of the church" (*ecclesiastici Doctores*), and the "decrees of the fathers" (*Patrum decreta*).[37] The rejection is not directed primarily or exclusively at papal decisions but rather at the scholastic doctrinal opinions Luther now characterized as mere *opiniones* in contrast to his prefered doctrinal basis.[38]

31. WA 1:306.13–15: "*Homo est summus Pontifex, falli potest, praesertim a tam astutis et speciosis Gnatonibus. Sed veritas est Deus, qui falli non potest.*" My translation.
32. Cf. Brian Tierney, *Origins of Papal Infallibility 1150–1350: A Study on the Concepts of Infallibility, Sovereignity and Tradition on the Middle Ages* (Leiden: Brill, 1972).
33. For information on the dogmatization in the modern Roman Catholic Church, cf. DH 3074.
34. WA 1:281.15–16. My translation.
35. WA 1:308.25–26: "*Aliud est, Papam narrare, aliud statuere, Imo longe aliud Papam statuere, et Concilium approbare.*" My translation.
36. In 1518, Luther was clearly assuming a council would come to bear with the pope (cf. Selge, *Normen*, 32, with reference to WA 1:582.21–23).
37. WA 1:306.7.17.
38. WA 1:306.7. In light of this, the interpretation of the *Resolutiones* by Selge, *Normen*, 31 has to be questioned when he says that there was "basically no difference between the fathers and the Scholastics." Jens-Martin Kruse, *Universitätstheologie und Kirchenreform: Die Anfänge der Reformation in Wittenberg 1516–1522* (Mainz: Zabern, 2002), 165 has a better suggestion—that Scholasticism forms "the direct opposite to the theological approach of the Wittenbergers." My translations.

It was exactly this reduction that shaped Luther's perception of John Eck. As a matter of introduction, he wrote in his commentary to the first *Obeliscus*:

> First, I testify that I desire to say or maintain absolutely nothing except, first of all, what is in the Holy Scriptures and can be maintained from them; and then what is in and from the writings of the church fathers and is accepted by the Roman church and preserved both in the canons and the papal decrees. But if any proposition cannot be proved or disproved from them I shall simply maintain it, for the sake of debate, on the basis of the judgment of reason and experience, always, however, without violating the judgment of any of my superiors in these matters.[39]

It is interesting to note that the canons appear in the company of those authorities pitted against the mere opinions of the Scholastics. The canons will disappear understandably when Luther juxtaposes true authority to that of the pope since they owe their validity to papal promulgation. One cannot resolve this tension by simply focusing on the Bible, as we see when Luther explains his expectations concerning Eck: "I hoped that he would fight against me using the Bible or the church-fathers or the canons."[40] He also criticizes Eck's "name-dropping" reference to Scotus, Gabriel Biel, and other Scholastics.[41] The key to understanding Luther's position is most likely to be found in the phrase *decreta Patrum*, which serves as a *terminus technicus* to refer to those statements of the church fathers who had become relevant for canon law.[42] Understood thusly, the triple grouping of *Biblia*, *Patres*, and *canones* can correspond to the

---

39. WA 1:281.28–31. This order matches that of the *protestatio* to the *Resolutiones* of the indulgence theses: "*Primum protestor, me prorsus nihil dicere aut tenere velle, nisi quod in et ex Sacris literis primo, deinde Ecclesiasticis patribus ab Ecclesia Romana receptis, hucusque servatis et ex Canonibus ac decretalibus Pontificiis habetur et haberi potest. Quod si quid ex iis probari vel improbari non potest, id gratia disputationis duntaxat pro iudicio rationis et experientia tenebo, semper tamen in hiis salvo iudicio omnium superiorum meorum*" (WA 1:529.33–530.3, cited after LW 31:83); for more, cf. Selge, *Normen*, 12.

40. WA 1:282.1–2: "*Sperabam enim quod ex Bibliis vel eccelsiasticis Patribus aut Canonibus contra me pugnaret.*"

41. WA 1:282.3–4. This particular point of criticism on Luther's part is not entirely justified. In WA 1:298.14, Eck bases his arguments explicitly on Scripture (Job 19:21) with a verbal citation: "*Miseremini mei, saltem vos amici mei, quia manus Domini tetigit me.*" (WA 1:298.14–15; cf. Job 19:21 Vg.). This problem caught the attention of the sixteenth-century copy editors. A second hand added: "*non animarum in Purgatorio sed S. Hiob ad amicos suos haec vox est.*" (WA 9:775). The Wittenberg edition of Luther's Latin works kept this comment (WA 1:298.1).

42. Cf. the edition of *Decretum* under the title: *Decreta patrum siue concor-| dia discordantium canonum| Gratiani auctoris siue com|pilatoris: cum apparatibus| Johannis ac additionibus| Bartholomei brix-iensis* (Nürnberg : Anton Koberger, 1493).

*Scriptura/Biblia* and the *ecclesiastici Doctores/ Patrum decreta.* In both cases, papal decrees would have been implicated, in contrast to the later *protestatio* to the *Resolutiones.*[43] One can thus maintain that the *Asterisci* serves as a resume of Luther's position, where he sees a juxtaposition of authorities—Scripture and the church fathers (in the case where their thought took shape in canon law) square off against mere Scholasticism. This forms the springboard for his thought about authorities. This position, which Luther had put into written words in spring of 1519 (and definitely before May 19 of that year[44]), thus generally resembles the position formulated in the *Disputatio contra scholasticam theologiam.* Here, he defends Augustine from various criticism.[45] The composite of Scripture and church fathers as a basis of authority (expressed clearly in a letter to John Lang from May 18, 1517)[46] was still in effect in spring of 1518, and Luther expressed it here with special clarity: "It is egregiously oblivious to assert in the church or among Christians something which Christ did not teach (. . .) Where is that in the Bible? Where are the fathers? Where are the canons? Where anywhere in the whole world (with the exception of our master here)?"[47] The Bible, the church fathers, and the *canones* are not only listed as authorities here, but their authoritative character is derived directly from Christ's teachings, which is also to be found in ecclesial tradition. Luther's model stands in a long medieval lineage that saw a harmonious, albeit hierarchical blend of authorities. Scripture was emphatically the highest priority.[48] The other instances were not handled as contradictory but rather treated together with Scripture as forming a coherent stream of Gospel teaching proceding from Christ.

43. WA 1:529.35–530.1.
44. WA Br 1:178.17–21 (n. 77); WA 9:770 rightly states that the *misi* at this point is to be understood in its grammatically rigorous sense, meaning that Luther had already sent his *Asterisci* to Eck before writing this.
45. WA 1:224.7–8 and LW 31:9–10.
46. WA Br 1:99.10–13: "*Mire fastidiuntur lectiones sententiariae, nec est, ut quis sibi auditores sperare possit, nisi theologiam hanc, id est bibliam aut S. Augustinum aliumve ecclesiasticae autoritatis doctorem velit profiteri.*" Cf. LW 48:42: "It is amazing how the lectures on the *Sentences* are disdained. Indeed no one can expect to have any students if he does not want to teach this theology, that is, lecture on the Bible or on St. Augustine or another teacher of ecclesiastical eminence."
47. WA 1:308.9–14: "*Longe ergo impudentissima omnium temeritas est, aliquid in Ecclesia asserere et inter Christianos, quod non docuit Christus (. . .) Ubi hoc Biblia? ubi Patres? ubi Canones? (excipe Magistros nostros) ubi in toto mundo?*"
48. "It is absolutely traditional and unequivocal [. . .] when Luther time and again applys Scripture as the highest, absolutely true, divine authority in matters of the faith and arguments with it" (Selge, *Normen,* 30); cf. Selga, "Autoritätengefüge," 607. My translation.

As the *Resolutiones* state, they were to be read in "*catholico sensu.*"[49] The reformational point is that Christ-based authorities exclude Aristotle and Aristotle-shaped Scholasticism (also visible in the Lang letter). A harmony of Scripture and tradition based in Christ is still not questioned by the Wittenberg Reformer at this point in time.[50]

## THE LEAD-UP TO THE LEIPZIG DISPUTATION: SEPARATING PAPAL DOCTRINE FROM SCRIPTURE AND THE CHURCH FATHERS

In a letter to Cardinal Matthäus Lang from December 29, 1518,[51] Eck provided a vivid description of the path to the Leipzig Disputation. As we saw above, he saw Andreas Karlstadt as the ignitor of public dispute.[52] And in fact, he had suggested to Karlstadt in his *Defensio* in summer of 1518[53] that he submit the contentious matters to the review of the Holy See, "which merits its council in questions of faith,"[54] or to the Sapienza, the Sorbonne, or the University of Cologne.[55] This last offer is quite interesting in a number of ways. It is an expression of Eck's high estimation for

---

49. WA 1:625.28; cf. Selge, *Normen*, 30.

50. Karlstadt, *Apologeticae conclusiones* (unnumbered pages), *Preface*, also argues along these lines when he argues against interpreting Scripture with a blend of Aristotle. While he is still consistent with medieval teaching, he is even clearer than Luther at this point when he speaks of the priority of Holy Scripture: "i. *Textus Bibliae per ecclesiasticum doctorem allegatus / plus valet / ac vehementius vrget / quam dictum allegantis. (. . .) xij. Textus Biblie non modo vni / pluribusue ecclesie doctoribus / sed etiam tocius ecclesie acutoritati / prefertur,*" so that one can easily understand the verdict from Hermann Barge, *Andreas Bodenstein von Karlstadt*, vol. 1, *Karlstadt und die Anfänge der Reformation*, 2nd ed. (Nieuwkoop: De Graaf, 1968), 118–19: "The scriptural principle had never been stated so starkly until that point." The invective against Aristotle in the Heidelberg Disputation (cf. the standard work from Theo Dieter, *Der junge Luther und Aristoteles: Eine historisch-systematische Untersuchung zum Verhältnis von Theologie und Philosophie* [Berlin: De Gruyter, 2001]) also belongs in this tradition; the editors of Luther's Latin works rightly gave his preparations for this disputation the title "*Contra scholasticam sententiam*" (Martin Luther, *Studienausgabe*, ed. Hans-Ulrich Delius, vol. 1, 3rd ed. [Berlin: Evangelische Verlagsanstalt, 1987], 190, 1).

51. Vinzenz Pfnür's internet edition of Eck's letters translates "IIII. Kalendis Ianuarias" (WA 9:208.28) as "December 28," but the letter is correctly dated to December 29 ("Eck an Matthaeus Lang," Reformationsgeschichte, accessed March 31, 2023, http://ivv7srv15.uni-muenster.de/mnkg/pfnuer/Eckbriefe/N071.html).

52. WA 9:207.8–19.

53. Eck signs his postscript on August 1 (Eck, *Defensio*, 82, 16f); it was printed on August 14, 1518 (Eck, 83, 3–4); cf. Eck, 14.

54. Eck, *Defensio*, 81:12–3: "*quae in his, quae ad fidem attinent, merito consuli debetf*"; cf. WA 9:207:16–18.

55. Eck, *Defensio*, 81:12–16; cf. WA 9:207.18–19.

the University of Cologne; he described it in other writings as the "most noble university in Germany,"[56] which surely reflected his having studied there (as did Andreas Karlstadt[57]). But, as Heiko Augustinus Oberman has demonstrated to us, it is more important in this context that the University of Cologne had already supported Eck in the Southern German Rent Conflict (*Oberdeutsche Zinsstreit*);[58] Eck had experience with trusted allies there. But the fact that Eck treats the Apostolic See and the university lecture hall as being on par with each other ought to really surprise us. Eck is drawing on the authority of two legally distinct norms; presenting this matter to the Curia would have meant a doctrinal decision, while the universities would have brought forth an academic argument. The fact that he entertained the latter option when inviting Karlstadt indicates that he was not thinking about immediately classifying the Wittenberg reformers as heretics, even though he sees Luther as being close to Hussite thought in the *Obelisci*.[59] We thus see an openness in Eck starting to tend toward a strategy of demonstrating the conformity of this new reformational doctrine with the condemned doctrine of the previous century.

According to Eck, Karlstadt refused the offer of a disputation and instead published yet another defamatory book.[60] Eck was referring to Karlstadt's "*Defensio*," but he did stretch the truth a bit when he insinuated that Karlstadt was evading a disputation. Karlstadt's theses in this work explicitly appeal to the verdict of "each and every person,"[61] not those of

56. Cf. Joseph Greving, *Johann Eck als junger Gelehrter: Eine literatur- und dogmengeschichtliche Untersuchung über seinen Chrysopassus praedestinationis aus dem Jahre 1514* (Münster: Aschendorff, 1906), 36.

57. Barge, *Karlstadt 1*, 5–6.

58. Heiko A. Oberman, *Werden und Wertung der Reformation*, 2nd ed. (Tübingen: Mohr, 1979), 194.

59. WA 1:302.15–16; 305.6–7. Kurt-Victor Selge, "Der Weg zur Leipziger Disputation," in *Bleibendes im Wandel der Kirchengeschichte*, ed. Bernd Moeller and Gerhard Ruhbach (Tübingen: Mohr, 1973), 168–210, 174 n. 16 does not classify Eck's invective as an accusation of heresy, but this was definitely implied and Luther rightly read the insinuations as such. Earlier, Johann Tetzel had made the comparison between Luther, Wycliffe, and Hus. (DCL 1:342. 348. 354). The accusation of heresy was also an important topic in the communication between Eck and Karlstadt (cf. Karlstadt, *Conclusiones* [unnumbered pages], n. 148; Eck, *Defensio*, 54.16–21). For Luther's relation to Jan Hus, cf. Scott H. Hendrix, "'We Are All Hussites'? Hus and Luther Revisited," *Archiv für Reformationsgeschichte* 65 (1974): 134–61. Following the Leipzig Disputation, Luther worked hard to get to know Huss's writings better (cf. the letter from Wenzel of Rozdalowsky on July 17, 1519 [WA Br 1:419.19–21 [n. 186]]).

60. WA 9:207.19–208.2.

61. Andreas Karlstadt, *DEFENSIO | Andreę Carolostadii | aduersus | Eximii. D. Ioannis Eckii theologię | doctoris & ordinatii Ing.| Monomachiam | Patitur Carolostadius non modo Se.| A studiique Ro. In Italia/| Parisien. in Gallia / aut | Coloniensis in Ger-| mania iudicium/| sed etiam sin-| gulorum | & | omnium* (Wittenberg: Rhau-Grunenberg 1518). My translation.

the Apostolic See or the three named universities. Karlstadt thus added a further instance to Eck's rather strictly traditional heuristic ones: the literate public, which would have been quite limited in scope given that Latin was Karlstadt's language of choice. In the various appeals in this work, Karlstadt demonstrates his concept of a hermeneutical/scientific method for the church. It included internal church discourse concerning a decision about heresy and correct doctrine, an academic discourse with broad horizons of true and false, and the popular decision of the general public. That Eck would have interpreted Karlstadt's reaction as an evasion can be understood in the context of this methodical difference. His interpretation was doubtless an expression of real irritation. Eck would remain stubbornly with his plan of a disputation with the Wittenbergers and used the opportunity of Luther's distant proximity at the Augsburg Diet to attempt to bring this plan to fruition.[62] According to Eck, it was Luther who suggested Leipzig as the place to dispute.[63] Luther indicates in a writing from November 15 that Erfurt had also come into consideration,[64] but likely so that Eck's letter from December 4, 1518, to Duke Georg can be interpreted as granting Eck a free choice of universities.[65] This very letter documents that Eck decided to go to Leipzig with considerations of these possibilities. Accordingly, he wrote to Herzog Georg the Bearded and the University of Leipzig and its theology faculty, requesting their audience and their evaluation of the disputation.[66]

---

62. Eck sought to get the prince elector's attention in this matter six times (cf. WA Br 1:460, 51 [No. 192 Vorgeschichte]).

63. WA 9:208.7–12.

64. WA Br 1:231.5 (No. 109); In WA Br 1:314.33–34 (No. 140; Schreiben an Egran vom 2. Februar 1519); 316.6–8 (No. 142; Schreiben an Karlstadt vom 4. oder 5. Februar 1519), Luther does not mention Erfurt in this context. The sources do indicate that Eck was considering the costs and the distances (WA Br 1:321.48 [No. 142 Beilage]).

65. Seidemann, *Leipziger Disputation*, 113 (Beilage 6); slightly redacted in Felician Gess, ed., *Akten und Briefe zur Kirchenpolitik Herzog Georgs von Sachsen*, vol. 1 (Leipzig: Teubner, 1905), 47–49 (n. 62). Cf. the online edition of Eck's letter correspondance from Vinzenz Pfnür: "Eck an Hg. Georg von Sachsen," Reformationsgeschichte, accessed March 30, 2023, http://ivv7srv15. uni-muenster.de/mnkg/pfnuer/Eckbriefe/N068.html.

66. WA 9:208.13–20. Attaining the theological faculty's approval was no meager feat, as a notice of a planned answer indicates from February 1, 1519. (Seidemann, *Leipziger Disputation*, 128 [Beilage 20]; "Universitätskanzler Dr. Kochel (Leipzig)," Reformationsgeschichte, accessed March 30, 2023, http://ivv7srv15.uni-muenster.de/mnkg/pfnuer/Eckbriefe/N077.html. We can also see it in Eck's letter from February 19, 1519 (Seidemann, *Leipziger Disputation*, 127 [Beilage 19]; Gess, *Akten und Briefe*, 73–74 [No. 97], slightly redacted; cf. "Eck an die Leipziger Theologische Fakultät," Reformationsgeschichte, accessed March 30, 2023, http://ivv7srv15. uni-muenster.de/mnkg/pfnuer/Eckbriefe/N078.html; in which it is clear that Eck desired a disputation with Luther.

Part of the preparations for the disputation was the drafting of theses. Eck provided such a sequence of theses and took Luther by surprise in the process,[67] especially when the twelfth thesis (later the thirteenth due to an addition) attacked Luther in much the same way as he had previously attacked Karlstadt (due to Karlstadt's *conclusiones*). He homed in on the most neuralgic point, with the thesis reading:

> We negate that the Roman church was not superior to other churches before the time of Pope Sylvester but rather we have recognized always him who has the seat and faith of Saint Peter as the successor to Peter and the general.[68]

And thus, not only a personal feud had been expanded before the Disputation. Eck had now brought a new issue into focus that previously had not stood in the center of attention, despite his having touched it in the *Obelisci*: the question of the supremacy of the pope. He had found concrete reasons for this in one of Luther's indulgence theses, which, as Ernst Schäfer correctly states, had been done "entirely coincidentially":[69]

> For further proof of this, consider the Roman church as it was at the time of St. Gregory, when it had no jurisdiction over other churches, at least not over the Greek church.[70]

---

67. Cf. Luthers response, WA Br 1:316.6–9 (No. 142).

68. WA 9:209.41–210.2: "*Romanam ecclesiam non fuisse superiorem aliis ecclesiis ante tempora Sylvestri negamus, sed eum, qui sedem beatissimi Petri habuit et fidem, successorem Petri et vicarium Christi generalem semper agnovimus.*" According to Bernard Adelmanns of Adelmannsfelden, the attack was intensified by the fact that Eck sent these theses to Rome before Judica 1519 (in that year, April 10) (*DOCVMENTA| LITERARIA| VARII ARGVMENTI| IN LKVCEM PROLATA| CVRA | IOHANNIS HEVMANNI| (. . .)* [Altdorf: 1758], 174; cf. R. Albert, "Aus welchem Grunde disputirte Johann Eck gegen Martin Luther in Leipzig 1519," *Zeitschrift für die historische Theologie. NF* 37 [1873]: 382–441, 408). This process reveals Eck's participation in the condemnation of Martin Luther (cf. Peter Fabisch, "Johannes Eck und die Publikationen der Bullen 'Exsurge Domine' und 'Decet Romanum Pontificem'," in *Johannes Eck (1486–1543): Internationales Symposium der Gesellschaft zur Herausgabe des Corpus Catholicorum aus Anlaß des 500. Geburtstages des Johannes Eck vom 13. bis 16. November 1986 in Ingolstadt und Eichstätt,* ed. Erwin Iserloh [Münster: Aschendorff, 1988], 74–106). At the same time, he makes clear that Luther had good grounds to insist as conditions for the disputation, "that the minutes of this disputation not be sent to the Papal court in order to judge them." (WA Br 1:429.31–33 [No. 187 Beilage]; earlier, he had very much reckoned with the notes being sent to Rome [WA Br 1:318.82–83 [No. 142]).

69. Ernst Schäfer, *Luther als Kirchenhistoriker: Ein Beitrag zur Geschichte der Wissenschaft* (Gütersloh: Bertelsmann, 1897), 46.

70. WA 1:571.16–18: "*immo finge (. . .), Romanam ecclesiam esse, qualis erat etiam adhuc tempore B. Gregorii, quando non erat super alias ecclesias, saltem Graeciae.*" Cited after LW 31:152.

This argument was to serve as a supporting argument for Thesis 22, in which Luther ascertained that the pope could not remove the punishements of the souls from purgatory.[71] And this matter, which Luther would repeat in Augsburg,[72] really did pertain to those theses concerned with papal power in the context of penance. Using this focus of Luther, Eck was able to cleverly steer the debate toward ecclesiological matters. Eck *may* have been hoping to rope Luther into a further area, for one clear issue bound the difference between Luther's reference to the time of Gregory the Great and Eck's reference to the time before Pope Silvester: the Constantinian Donation.[73] This topic had become acute leading up to the Leipzig Disputation. The scholarly investigation from Lorenzo Valla,[74] which proved the fictitious nature of the Constantinian Donation, had been given two printings by Ulrich of Hutten, one in 1518 and one in 1519.[75] The fact that Eck was interested in disputing topics with a direct connection to this strongly suggests that he wanted to address this topic as well.

But Luther did not talk about it, likely because he may have only encountered Valla's text in 1520.[76] But he still had ample reasons to address matters pertaining to the papacy. And when we look at the chain of events, we see that his argument was actually a historical one.[77] He did not emphasize its theological volatility and may not actually have been aware of it. He merely argued that before Gregory the Great, the church of Rome was by no means the head of the churches in Greece and elsewhere. The way he made this argument shows just how self-evident this

---

71. WA 1:234.19–20: "*Quin nullam remittit animabus iun purgatorio, uqam in hac vita debuissent secundum Canones solvere.*"
72. WA 2:20.6–17.
73. Selge, "Weg zur Leipziger Disputation," 187–88 has made this clear; the observation has been adopted by Leif Grane, *Martinus Noster: Luther in the German reform movement 1518–1521* (Mainz: Zabern, 1994), 48–49. For the effects of the Donation of Constantine in the Middle Ages and the Reformation, cf. Volker Leppin, "Die Konstantinische Schenkung als Mittel der Papstkritik in Spätmittelalter, Renaissance und Reformation," in *Transformationen: Studien zu den Wandlungsprozessen in Theologie und Frömmigkeit zwischen Spätmittelalter und Reformation*, 2nd ed. (Tübingen: Mohr Siebeck, 2018), 189–210.
74. Lorenzo Valla, *De falso credita et ementita Constantini donatione*, ed. Wolfram Setz (Munich: Monumenta Germaniae Historica, 1986); cf. also Wolfram Setz, *Lorenzo Vallas Schrift gegen die Konstantinische Schenkung: De falso credita et ementita Constantini donatione: Zur Interpretation und Wirkungsgeschichte* (Tübingen: Niemeyer, 1975).
75. Cf. Ulrichi ab Hutten Equitis *Germani Opera quae extant omnia*, ed. Joseph Hermann Münch, vol. 2 (Berlin: Reimer, 1822), 408–09; for the context of Hutten's work, cf. Hutten, *Germani Opera*, 117–29.
76. WA Br 2:48.20–49.28 (No. 257).
77. Cf. Helmar Junghans, "Martin Luther und die Leipziger Disputation," in *Die Leipziger Disputation von 1519. Ein theologisches Streitgespräch und seine Bedeutung für die frühe Reformation*, ed. Markus Hein and Armin Kohnle (Leipzig: Evangelische Verlagsanstalt, 2019), 125–34, 132–33.

was for him. It was utterly natural for him to use it to demonstrate how limited the scope of papal jurisdiction had to be, including in its secular and temporal domain. He appears to have assumed that any proponents of a papal universalism would have been convinced by his arguments, which he did not seek to ground but rather accepted as being simply given. But Eck saw the explosive potential of questioning the historical verifiability of the papacy. He did this with his counterthesis, which relied on the biblical founding of papal primacy, namely the position of Peter. The church-historical question thus became a biblical one, and Luther was forced to meet Eck on this level and reflect on the biblical grounding of papal primacy.

The problem as such had become virulent at the Diet in Augsburg in 1518, during which Luther contested Cajetan's claim that the primacy of the pope could be derived from Matthew 16:18.[78] In this case, however, the matter could be temporarily silenced with a casual reference to the hiddenness of the Kingdom of God in Luke 17:20,[79] as well as by repeating the general historical observation in the *Resolutiones* that there had been a church in many places and times without Roman supremecy, with this being the standard case before Gregory the Great.[80] Importantly for the subsequent developments, Luther pointed to the necessity of a "judgment of God" (*divinum iudicium*).[81] The concept of divine right (*ius divinum*) would later become a central theme in reformational argumentation and appeared shortly after the Augsburg Diet in the appeal for a council on November 28 (although it was somewhat confusingly grouped together with *ius naturale* and *humanum*).[82] At this stage, the connection of *ius divinum* as a requisite basis and simultaneous contestation of the biblical grounding of papal primacy (which, we must remember, Luther still explicitly approved of at this point[83]) was not yet as explicit as it would

---

78. WA 2:19.30–20.6. It is characteristic for this matter that Luther used Matt 16:19 in other passages of the *Acta Augustana* to argue pertaining to the priestly authority to bind and loose (WA 2:13, 21–14, 4; LW 31:271).

79. WA 2:20.3–4.

80. WA 2:20.4–17.

81. WA 2:18.3, cited after LW 31:277.

82. WA 2:36.31–32.

83. WA 2:19.37–20.1 (and also after the Leipzig Disputation: WA 397, 3–4). Accordingly, in the Psalm Lectures, Luther clearly distanced himself from the Hussite teaching on papal primacy (and on the Eucharist) (WA 4, 345, 24–25). Selge, *Normen*, 27–28 points out that a reliance on Rom 13 in the reflection on papal primacy (WA 1:618.24–26; 621.12–18) actually gave a bit of a boost to papal primacy. The internal logic of Luther's letter to Spalatin WA Br 1:353.45–354.49 (No. 157): "*Si ergo posuissem, Quod Rhomana Ecclesia usque in hodiernum diem non omnibus Ecclesiis fuisset superior & quod contra Eccium staret hystoria Ecclesie usque ad nostros dies, vera dixissem, Sed nimis aperte & citra Insidias*" certainly does not state a blunt rejection of

become at the Leipzig Disputation. Eck expertly pushed Luther toward a reflected *ius divinum* concept with a clever exposition of the papal question in the twelfth (later thirteenth) thesis. Luther was forced to react to it.[84] He did so with the May 1519 publication of thirteen theses against Eck, the "*Disputatio et excusatio adversus criminationes D. Ioannis Eccii.*" They were accompanied by a preface that had the basic purpose of undoing the accusation of heresy. Luther did this in an extremely shrewd fashion:[85]

> So that you will not be harmed by the temptation of his poisonous riddle, my reader, you must know that among the articles of Jan Huss one among several is to be found in which he states that the pre-eminence of the papacy came from the emperor, as Platina plainly wrote. I, however, undertook to prove that this power was derived, not from imperial, but from papal decrees. The Lateran Church itself in an inscription sings about the origin and the extent of its authority, stating that by papal and imperial decrees it is the mother of churches etc. These little verses are well known. But what of it? It is necessary that the church itself also be Hussite to Eck and that he rekindle old ashes. Then by command of the pope and consent of the cardinals, the Lateran Church sings in this manner for all Rome and the universal church that it is no wonder that Eck loathes old ashes and according to his office of consecrator pants for a new holocaust to offer the Apostolic See, namely, to reduce the pope, the cardinals, and the Lateran Church itself to ashes anew. Thank God that then at least one person, Eck, will be left who has a Catholic taste, that most extraordinary persecutor of the most extraordinary, while all others are destroyed by the Bohemian virus.[86]

the church's claim to primacy (as Christopher Spehr, *Luther und das Konzil: Zur Entwicklung eines zentralen Themas in der Reformationszeit* [Tübingen: Mohr, 2010], 127 has it) but rather remains on a historical level that factually calls into question the papacy's universal validity.

84. It was actually the twelfth/thirteenth thesis that Eck used to open the conflict with Luther. The theses were not all "mainly directed against Luther" (see Fuchs, *Konfession und Gespräch*, 145).

85. The shrewdness of Luther's argumentation is found in the fact that he "did not position [himself] as a *rite et recte* condemned heretic of the Roman church," as Kaufmann, *Anfang*, 38 erroneously claims based on a false understanding of the Latin text. Luther avoids precisely this position. My translation.

86. WA 2:159.19–31: "*Nam ut venenati sui enigmatis scandalo non laedaris, scias, mi lector, inter articulos Ioannis Huss censeri etiam a nonnullis hunc, quod Romani Pontificis papalem excellentiam a Caesare esse dixerit, quod et Platina manifeste scribit. Ego vero non Caesareis, sed pontificiis decretis eandem monarchiam probari posui. Ita sane ipsamet Ecclesia Lateranensis in urbe de frontis suae peripheria cantat, dogmate Papali simul et Imperiali se esse matrem Ecclesiarum &c. noti sunt versiculi Quid igitur? Necesse est, ut ipsa quoque Ecclesia Eccio sit Hussita et igniat cineres. Deinde quia mandato Papae, consensu Cardinalium, totius Romae et universalis Ecclesiae illa sic cantat, nihil mirum, si Eccius fastidiat antiquos cineres et pro officio consecrationis suae consecrare anhelet novum holocaustum sedi Apostolicae, semel Papam, Cardinales ipsamque Ecclesiam Lateranensem in cineres novos redacturus. Deo gratia, quod unus saltem Eccius reliquus est, qui Catholice sapiat,*

Here, Luther utilizes various strategies to refute the accusation of Hussitism. On the one hand, he emphasizes that he argues in a different fashion than did Hus; on the other hand, he explained that Hus's opinions were, in fact, shared by others. The statement he had in mind was based on Jan Hus's statement in his magnum opus "*De ecclesia.*"[87] Condemned on July 6, 1415, in Constance,[88] the statement reads:

> Papal dignity originated with the emperor, and the primacy and institution of the pope emanated from imperial power.[89]

Luther cited this text rather imprecisely, and his vague *nonnulli* even masks—intentionally or otherwise—that this had to do with a condemned doctrinal statement. That he came to this sentence while treating Eck's thesis indicates that he understood exactly the context he was in, for Jan Hus had also derived papal power from Emperor Constantine—in the time of Pope Silvester.[90] But for his part, Luther emphasized that he did not share this heretic justification. He only used the papal decrees claiming to be a basis for papal power. Thus, his answer to the thirteenth thesis read:

> The very callous decrees of the Roman pontiffs which have appeared in the last four hundred years prove that the Roman church is superior to all others. Against them stand the history of eleven hundred years, the test of divine Scripture, and the decree of the Council of Nicaea, the most sacred of all councils.[91]

*singularissimus ille singularitatis persecutor, caeteris omnibus per virus Boemiae perditis.*" Cited after LW 31:315.

87. Hus, *De ecclesia*, 15D: "*Nam cesar Constantinus post trecentos annos papam instituit. Romanus enim pontifex fuit consocius aliis pontificibus usque ad dotacionem cesaris, cuius auctoritate cepit capitaliter dominari*" (Magistri Johannis Hus, *Tractatus de ecclesia*, ed. S. Harrison Thomson [Cambridge: Heffer, 1956], 122).
88. The papal confirmation of his condemnation occured on February 22, 1418.
89. DH 1209: "*Papalis dignitas a Caesare inolevit, et Papae praefectio et institutio a Caesaris potentia emanavit.*"
90. Cf. above, n. 130.
91. WA 2:161.35–37: "*Romanam Ecclesiam esse omnibus aliis superiorem, probatur ex frigidissimis Romanorum Pontificum decretis intra cccc annos natis, contra quae sunt historiae approbatae MC annorum, textus scripturae divinae et decretum Niceni Concilii omnium sacratissimi.*" Cited after LW 31:318. For more on the background of the accelerating papal critique, cf. Junghans, "Martin Luther und die Leipziger Disputation," 127. That Luther was now going down a well-trodden path can be seen in the reaction of his close comrades: Andreas Karlstadt wrote to Spalatin on February 24: "*Cæterum Rever. Patri Martino Luthero consuluerim abstinuisse à XII. conclusione, jam vero post editam evidentissimis rationibus loricandum; clam tum, & domi svasi, qvod sciam, Græcos scriptores S. Petro apicem & fastigium apostolatus concessisse.*" (SCRI-NIUM ANTIQUARIUM | iΔΓΟΧΕΙΡΑ| ANTIQVITATIS | FRAGMENTA,| SUMMORUM VIDELICET IN | ECCLES. ACAD. ET SCHOL. SUPE-| RIORE ÆVO VIRORUM,| (. .) M.

This actually lightly shifted Luther's line of argumentation. Now he was no longer referring to Gregory the Great but rather the time around 1100. In any case, he took a tack distinct from those of Eck and the condemmned Hus, who had both referred to the time of Constantine. Luther thus made clear that he would not submit himself to Eck's heresilogical rubric. At the same time, he started undermining it by demonstrating the broad acceptance of Hus's positions. On the one hand, he referred to Bartolomeo Platina and his "*Vita Christi ac omnium pontificum*," in which the vita of Benedict II describes the transfer of papal power via the Greeks through Constantine IV.[92] On the other, he recalled a verse written above the porticus of the Lateran Basillica:

> It is given through both papal as well as imperial teaching
> That I am the head and mother of the entire church.
> Here was the savior's heavenly kingdom
> Sanctified in the name of the creator as all was perfected.
> We implore, directed entirely to you in humble prayer,
> That this our house would be an elevated seat for you Christ.[93]

Luther pointed out the liturgical context of this poem and thus the active participation of the pope himself in its creation. He further underlined that a certain portion of the imperial origins of papal supremecy, which Hus incriminated, actually did have a broad ecclesial basis. Thus, leading up to the Leipzig Disputation, we see a general destruction of the accusation that Luther was a Hussite, although it is worth emphasizing that Luther

*JOH. GOTTFRID. OLEARIUS* [Halle: Saalfeld, 1691], 44; for more on Karlstadt's reluctance concerning the pope question, cf. Luther's writing to Lang in WA Br 1:368.19–24 [No. 167]); cf. Kruse, *Universitätstheologie*, 192–93.

92. Platina, *Platynae Historici Liber de vita Christi ac omnium pontificum (AA. 1- 1474)*, ed. Giacinto Gaida (Città di Castello: Lapi, 1932), 114, 9–11: "*Ad hunc Constantinus imperator hominis sanctitate permotus, sanctionem misit, ut deinceps quem clerus, populus, exercitusque Romanus in pontificum delegisset, eundem statim verum Christi vicarium esse omnes crederent: nulla aut Constantinopolitani principis, aut Italiae hexarchie expectata auctoritate, ut antea fiery consueverat.*"

93. See the claimed old version in the *Catalogo del Signorili* from around 1425 (Christian Hülsen, *Le chiese di Roma nel medio evo: Cataloghi et appunti* [Florenz: Olschki, 1927], 43: "*Dogmate papali datur simul imperiali / Quod sim cunctarum caput mater ecclesiarum. / Hinc Salvatoris celestia regna datoris / Nomine sanxerunt, cum cuncia peracta fuerunt. / Quaesumus ex toto conversi supplice voto / Nostra quod hec edes tibi Christe sit inclyta sedes*"; cf. also the slightly distinct citation (lacking a source citation) in WA 2:159 n. 2. The medieval inscription can only be seen in fragments today, but it was replaced with a similar baroque text (cf. Jürgen Krüger and Martin Wallraff, *Luthers Rom: Die Ewige Stadt in der Renaissance* [Darmstadt: Wissenschaftliche Buchgesellschaft, 2010], 167 n. 121).

never labeled himself to be on the side of the condemned heretic. He expressly confessed his support for the *consensus* of a worldwide church.[94]

And thus, we see that the *Disputatio et excusatio* neatly captures the significance of the pope question for the looming discussion between Eck and Luther. Luther published his own "*Resolutio super propositione sua decima tertia de potestate papae*" in June, where he handled the pope question with a broader investigation but generally returned to the argumentative basis he had used in the *Asterisci*. Depending on how one decides the above discussed question of the *canones*, this text was either a further degree of precision or a light change in tone of his earlier opinion. If we understand the *canones*, referred to by Luther in his *Asterisci*, as general canon law and papal decrees, then the *Resolutio* clearly rejects their theologically enforceable authority. But if one understands the church fathers as appropriated by the church, then the *Resolutio* sees Luther only qualifying the point that he distinguishes them from the rest of canonical law which is not binding. The leitmotif selected by Luther to determine authorities is the same one he used in his appeal to the council and would become decisive in the Leipzig Disputation: *ius divinium*, clearly distinguished from the *decreta hominum*.[95] Where the teachings of Christ had stood in the *Asterisci*, Luther now employed *ius divinum* in the same argumentative role. Luther first used this concept in a sermon held in early 1518 on the Zaccheus readings in Luke 19:8ff,[96] in which Luther presented his now mature understanding of penance as a comprehensive

94. WA 2:159.8–10.
95. WA 2:200.38.
96. This sermon has not been conclusively dated: Löscher dates it to 1517, and the WA settles on October 31, 1517, based on a remark made by Luther in his 1517 explanation of the Lord's Prayer (WA 1:94 n. 2). The day can be derived from the "*pridie Dedicationis*" (WA 1:94.6), which means the eve of the church consecration festival. But both Löscher and the WA assume that this festival pertained to the Castle Church. This is by no means certain: both January 17 for All Saints Church or May 31 for the City Church are quite plausible (cf. Norbert Flörken, "Ein Beitrag zur Datierung von Luthers Sermo de indulgentiis pridie Dedicationis," *Zeitschrift für Kirchengeschichte* 82 [1971]: 344–50, 349; in the same work, Flörken casts his vote for May 30, 1517). Given Luther's preaching role at this church, the latter date is the most likely. Martin Brecht argues for a date in March 1517 based on the remark in the Lord's Prayer explanation (Martin Brecht, *Martin Luther*, vol. 1, *His Road to Reformation 1483–1521* [Minneapolis: Fortress, 1985], 186), but this argument requires the conjecture that the date of the festival is pertinant to the Augustinian Church, whose unknown jubilee was in spring (the consequence derived from Brecht, *Martin Luther*, 506 n. 12). This construction is unnecessary for the simple reason that the connection to the Zachaeus sermon is only found in the printed edition prepared by Johann Agricola from 1518 (WA 9:133.8) and not in Luther's own printed edition from 1519 (WA 2:80–130). Thus, Löscher's date of October 31, 1517, would be possible. However, the connection Luther had to his preaching position still makes May 30 more likely.

human attitude.[97] He used Luke 3:8 to demand from the *Iuristae* to give him proof of "*de iure divino*," according to which oral confession and satisfaction were mandatory.[98] By this point (probably in May of 1517), *ius divinum* appears to have had a clear meaning as testimony from Holy Scripture,[99] juxtaposed with human rules. Luther described both with juristic language, but it is not possible to clearly position *ius divinum* within the established hierarchy of Bible, church fathers, and the legally relevant *canones*. Luther saw the latter as having not been created by human legal experts and a year later would name them the Teachings of Christ in the *Asterisci*. But in the *Resolutio*, we see *ius divinum* appear as a clearly distinct criterium. It is decisive for the development of his conflict with Eck that he no longer perceived himself as in conflict with the canonical lawyers but rather with the *decreta hominum* in general. The *Asterisci* had already emphasized the human side—and thus fallibility—of the pope. Much like in this text, he also employed Romans 3:4 in his appeal to the council on November 28, 1518—and the phrase *ius divinum* shows up there as well.[100] In this context of theological coagulation, it becomes clear to Luther that *ius divinum* is also to be distinguished from papal decrees.[101] Within the debate surrounding the Leipzig Disputation, this meant a further step toward clarification and a further degree of precision. It may have even meant a significant leap in Luther's own theology.

But even if the *hominum decreta* was now pitted against *ius divinum*, this did not mean a sharp separation between Scripture and tradition/ church fathers, notwithstanding the *ius divinum* reference in the Zacchaeus sermon. Instead, Luther's argumentation pertaining to the pope question indicates that he was still reading Scripture along the lines of patristic interpretation. The theological deliberations remained accompanied by a significant dose of historical argumentation, which provided a springboard for Luther's own objections. But he started molding these historical observations in a remarkably biblical fashion. For example, using Galatians 1:17–8 and 2:1, where Paul describes how he had spent three years in

---

97. For more on this development, cf. Volker Leppin, "'*Omnem vitam fidelium penitentiam esse voluit:*' Zur Aufnahme mystischer Traditionen in Luthers erster Ablassthese," in *Transformationen: Studien zu den Wandlungsprozessen in Theologie und Frömmigkeit zwischen Spätmittelalter und Reformation*, 2nd ed. (Tübingen: Mohr Siebeck, 2018), 261–77.

98. WA 1:98.31–36.

99. See also the parallel formulation when speaking of *ius divinum*: "*De privata nescio ubi Sciptura loquitur,*" in WA 1:98.31.

100. WA 2:37.12–15.

101. In much the same vein, Luther wrote to Willibald Pirckheimer on February 20, 1519: "*Res vergit, ut vides, in sacros canones, it es prophanas sacrarum literarum corruptelas,*" (WA Br 1:348.14–15 [No. 154]; cf. Grane, *Martinus Noster*, 50–51).

Arabia before going to Jerusalem a further fourteen years later to meet with Peter and the other pillars of the community there,[102] Luther deduced that the primacy of the papacy could not have been bound to Rome eighteen years after the resurrection.[103]

This argument is employed again in the Leipzig Disputation. But another line of thought took precedence: the thorough exegesis and explanation of the Bible passages used to ground the primacy of the pope. Luther did not fundamentally question the validity of the pope at this stage;[104] he emphasized that the pope was founded in God's will, even if he could not find a Bible passage to back up that statement.[105] It is right here that we see the truly decisive point in the argumentation. Luther analyzes two Bible passages commonly used to justify the papacy:[106] the *locus classicus* and main argument since the *Decretum Gratiani*,[107] Matthew 16:18, "You are Peter, and on this rock I will build my church,"[108] and John 21:17, "Feed my sheep," a Bible passage that had come into a central role for the justification of the papacy through the decrees of Gregory IX.[109] Throughout the entire Middle Ages, these two verses shaped the entire discussion about the primacy of the papacy, with their effect being felt well beyond canonical law.

As concerned Matthew 16:18, Luther stated that the canonical jurists no longer held a clear consensus that this passage actually justified the primacy of the pope.[110] He undermined this interpretation by referring to

102. In his 1519 Galatians commentary, which was concluded shortly before the Leipzig Disputation, Luther emphasized the independence of Paul and Peter using these verses (WA 2:472.1–27), as well as the fact that the apostles were not scattered throughout the world for thirteen years after the resurrection (WA 2:476.31–37). While his preface devotes considerable attention to the status of the *Romana ecclesia* (WA 2:443–50), he does not yet apply these passages to the primacy of Rome.

103. WA 2:190.29–40.

104. WA 2:185.13–16.

105. WA 2:186.5–12.

106. For more on the argumentation, see the presentation by Grane, *Martinus Noster*, 59–62.

107. For its usage in canon law, cf. D. 21 c. 2–3 (CICan 1:69–70).

108. Gerhard Ebeling, *Evangelische Evangelienauslegung: Eine Untersuchung zu Luthers Hermeneutik* (Munich: Lempp, 1942), 256 points out the "interesting chain of events" that Luther, purely coincidentially, held a sermon on Matt 16:13–19 in Leipzig on June 29, 1519, and thus could process "all of the material from the entire disputation" (WA 2:246.23) (the sermon in WA 2:246–49).

109. X 1.33.6 (CICan 2:198). Cf. Luther's reference to both Bible passages in the *Resolutiones* of the Leipzig Disputation, WA 2:397.15–16.

110. WA 2:188.4–6. Luther gives special attention here to the glosse in D. 50 c. 53. This reads: "*Preposuit. Hoc verbo pasce oues meas factus est princeps. ex de elec. significasti non illo: Tu es petra et super etc. quia illud fuit ei dictum ante passionem.*" (*Decretum Gratiani| Cum | Glossis domini Johannis theutonici prepositi alberstatensis et annotationibus Bartholomei brixiensis (. . .)* (Basel:

the explanation from the church fathers, considering their general insight as constituting valid precedence: "Secondly, the decrees apply this word of Christ inappropriately to Peter and the bishop of Rome alone. For the holy fathers have assured that Christ spoke these words to the church and all apostles in the person of Peter."[111] With the help of the patristic tradition (which he started with Jerome, neglecting further investigations), Luther could apply this verse to all of the apostles.[112] He also referred to passages from Chrysostom and Augustine.[113] This argumentation was consistent with the harmony model of exegesis where the church fathers paved the hermeneutical way for understanding Scripture. But Luther went further than the fathers, providing his own very extensive exegetical treatment of this passage, which he justified with the statement, "And why do we not consider the text and the words of Christ more, who has taught us more clearly through himself?"[114] Even if this did not mean fully juxtaposing Scripture and tradition (put another way, we cannot project the later model of difference onto this statement[115]), this little phrase is hermeneutically decisive, for it embraces the humanistically inspired method[116] of explaining a text using only the text itself. That in turn opens the possibility of explaining a passage either counter to the fathers or consistent with them with independent criteria. Luther's exegetical leitmotif was that Matthew 16:18 did not only apply to Peter but to all of the apostles. He did this by pointing out that Jesus's question of who the people thought he was also asked disciples themselves *as a group* (Matt 16:13–15).[117] Peter's answer

Johannes Amerbach und Johannes Froben, 1512), fol. 56ʳ a). His second reference is to a passage by Panormitanus. His commentary on X 1.6.4 (*Significasti*) reads: "*Tertio nota illa verba per quae christus constituit principem et papam beatum Petrum scilicet pasce oues meas etc. non autem per illa tu es petrus et super hanc petram etc. nam per illa verba christus promisit sibi pontificatum cum fuerit locutus in futurum etc.*" (Nicolaus de Tudeschis, *Lectura super quinque libros Decretalium. Pars prima super primo decretalium* [Venice, 1477], https://www.digitale-sammlungen.de/de/view/bsb00058048?page=162,163, numbered as fol. 80ᵛa); cf. Ian Christopher Levy, "The Leipzig Disputation: Masters of the Sacred Page and the Authority of Scripture," in *Luther at Leipzig: Martin Luther, the Leipzig Debate, and the Sixteenth-Century Reformations*, ed. Mickey L. Mattox et al. (Leiden: Brill, 2019), 115–44, 133.

111. WA 2:188.27–30: "*Secundo, quod idem verbum Christi male decreta aptant soli Petro et Rhomano potifici. Nam apud sanctos patres Christus hoc verbum dixisse ad ecclesiam et omnes Apostolos in persona Petri asseritur.*" My translation.

112. WA 2:188.31–32.

113. WA 2:188.34–189.9.

114. WA 2:189.10–11: "*Et cur non nos ipsi potius textum et verba Christi consyderamus, qui nos clarius per seipsum instruet.*" My translation.

115. Thus, it is still too early to speak of a "singular validity of Scripture" (Kruse, *Universitätstheologie*, 195) at this point in time. My translation.

116. Cf. Junghans, *Martin Luther*, 129.

117. WA 2:189.12–35.

in Matthew 16:16 was the unanimous opinion of all of the apostles.[118] Accordingly, calling Peter a "rock" also applied to all disciples.[119] His hermeneutical point of departure was that the context had to be taken into account.[120] Luther accordingly interpreted the passage of the keys (Matt 16:19) with a reference to the plural parallel in Matthew 18:18 as a statement for the entire church:[121] "I believe [. . .] that this authority of Matthew does not pertain to that of Peter or to his successor or to any one of the churches but rather to all churches."[122]

Luther found the *"pasce oves meas"* from John 21 to be more important. This can be seen in his references to the discussions within canonical law, whose late-medieval phase tended to grant this passage greater clout in justifying papal primacy than any other. Interestingly, Luther starts his explanation of this passage with the text itself, skipping the patristic tradition entirely. He exactly analyzes each concept, emphasizing that, in contrast to the mandate to go and baptize in Matthew 28:19, the mandate to pastor did not contain the *"omnes"* qualification. Thus, a supremecy over the entire church could not be justified by this passage.[123] Two careful philological observations joined this statement. Firstly, Luther emphasized that the verb *pascere* means something other than ruling and steering.[124] Secondly, he pointed to the context of John 21 where pastoring is written in the context of *diligere*.[125] This intellectual development constituted Luther's preparation for the Leipzig Disputation. In it, argumentation based solely on the biblical text becomes increasingly prominent, even though Luther has not yet drawn the principled conclusions that would become unavoidable in the aftermath of the Leipzig Disputation: the formation of the reformational Scriptural principle.[126]

---

118. WA 2:189.36–37.

119. WA 2:189.37–39.

120. WA 2:189.39–190.1.

121. WA 2:191, 1–20. Luther had at least a vague idea that Cyprian also supported this collective interpretation of Peter's mandate (WA 2:202.7–13).

122. WA 2:191.21–23: *"Credo (. . .), hanc Matthaei autoritatem neque ad Petrum neque ad successorem neque ad unam aliquam ecclesiam, sed ad omnes ecclesias pertinere."* My translation.

123. WA 2:194.24–28.

124. WA 2:195.16–28.

125. WA 2:195.29–37.

126. Gerhard Ebeling, "Luther II. Theologie," in *Religion in Geschichte und Gegenwart*, vol. 4, 3rd ed. (Tübingen: Mohr, 1960), 459–520, 503, stated: "From the beginning, Luther practiced a tacit 'Scriptural principle'." This statement can only be considered true if one understands the "Scriptural principle" to be the self-evident priority of Scripture with regard to all other authorities in the Middle Ages.

## THE LEIPZIG DISPUTATION: *SOLA SCRIPTURA*

After a year of building tensions, things came to head at the Leipzig Disputation, held in the Pleißenburg from June 27, 1519, until July 15, 1519.[127] For our purposes, the confrontation between Luther and Eck from July 4–13 is of greatest interest. It was here that these two delved into the nitty-gritty details of the office of the papacy.[128] Analyzing this office touched on every aspect of the interwoven tapestry of authorities within the church. Additionally, there were two other issues rumbling in the background of this debate. The first was Eck's early expression of suspicion that Luther might be guilty of Hussitism. Until this point, Eck had only hinted in this direction, but the question of the authority of conciliar decisions was dependent on it, and Luther *had* touched on this matter in the preface to his *"Disputatio et excusatio."* The second matter was the historical argumentation of the primacy of the papacy. Luther had taken this argumentation as a given until this point. It would be handled indirectly throughout the Leipzig Disputation.

The basis for the style of argumentation (and thus for the usage of authorities) were the *protestationes*, which the participants had formulated

127. Cf. on this Thomas Noack, "Der Ort der Disputation—die Pleißenburg," in Hein and Kohnle, *Leipziger Disputation*, 73–84.

128. Kurt-Victor Selge, "Die Leipziger Disputation zwischen Luther und Eck," *Zeitschrift für Kirchengeschichte* 86 (1975): 26–40, 30 rightly establishes that Eck did not behave in this case as would a strict papist. However, Oberman, "Wittenberg's War," 117–48, 130, 134 goes a bit too far in classifying Eck in the sense of "Papal Conciliarism" or a "Gersonist." Oberman, "Wittenberg's War," 133 refers to two passages from Eck's *Chrysopassus*. The first rejects the notion that the pope is some form of being placed between humanity and God (Johannes Eck, *CHRYSOPASSVS| A IOANNE MAIORIS ECKIO PROCANCELLARIO | AVRIPOLI ET CANONICO EISTETEM: LECTA EST | SVBTILIS ILLA PRAEDESTINATIONIS MATERIA | VVILHELMO ILLUSTRIS: PRINCIPE BAIOARIAM | GVBERNANTE. ANNO GRATIAE G. D. XII* (Augsburg: Johann Miller, 1514), C iiiiʳ; for evidence of this opinion in the Middle Ages, cf. Oberman, "Wittenberg's War," 133 n. 39). In the second, Eck gives a supportive reference to Johann Gerson's attitude toward *gratia confirmationis*, the decisions of the Council of Constance: *"assentimur domino cancellario* [i.e., Gerson] *in illa doctrina quam proclamauit in eo loco (puta in concilio Constantiae) vbi errores & schismata fuerunt extirpata: non seminata contra Caietanum."* (Eck, *Chrysopassus*, Gʳ). However, these two positions do not provide us with a comprehensive view into Eck's general views on conciliarism and papism—it is only clear that Eck wants to have nothing to do with the unreflected anticonciliarism of Prierias and Cajetan. One cannot really say that they "disagree sharply" (Oberman, "Wittenberg's War," 134); cf. the rightly critical reception of Obermans interpretation found in Remigius Bäumer, "Die Ekklesiologie des Johannes Eck," in *Johannes Eck (1486–1543): Internationales Symposium der Gesellschaft zur Herausgabe des Corpus Catholicorum aus Anlaß des 500. Geburtstages des Johannes Eck vom 13. bis 16. November 1986 in Ingolstadt und Eichstätt*, ed. Erwin Iserloh (Münster: Aschendorff, 1988), 129–54, 148–50. 153.

and whose content significantly diverged from each other. Andreas Karlstadt explained:

> We accord such honor to the Holy Scriptures that we do not want to claim or institute anything without them. In the other matters, however, which cannot be elucidated with their help, we grant only church authorities the first place.[129]

He thus stipulated a clear hierarchy of authorities (and gave a hint to his injured feelings). The first sentence explained the exclusive authority of Scripture when it came to strong claims and ordinances. It was clearly binding for Karlstadt. The second sentence opened a wide space for all of the cases in which a clear judgement could not be made on the basis of Scripture. In such cases, the ecclesially appropriated authorities were to be obeyed, but not in the sense of following an ordinance or law. This drove a wedge into the usual idea of a harmony between Scripture and tradition; leading up to this statement, Karlstadt had betrayed a clear priority of Scripture in his letters. For his part, Eck would remain entirely committed to the harmony model: "I am not inclined to say or assert anything which would be against Holy Scripture or the Holy Church."[130] "To say" (*dicere*) and "to assert" (*asserere*) apply to both church doctrine and Holy Scripture. There is no hint whatsoever of some difference being purported here. And this is what makes Luther's *protestatio* so outrageous: he clearly does not pick up on the different directions the other participants take in the Disputation. "I agree to the protest of both eminent Masters, Andreas Karlstadt and John Eck and follow them."[131] He clearly wanted to avoid being pigeonholed into a single model and left the matter unresolved to remain committed to the harmony model (as he had for quite some time) or join in developing the difference model.

In order to do justice to the Leipzig Disputation, we need to give brief attention to two matters accompanying this confrontation. The

129. WA 59:433.25–27: "*Sacris autem scripturis hunc honorem impendimus, quod nihil sine his aut asserere aut praecipere volumus. In caeteris autem, quae non liquide hinc doceri possunt, solis ecclesiasticis primas damus.*" My translation.

130. WA 59:434.34–35: "*non est animus mihi quicquam dicere vel asserere, quod vel sacrae scripturae vel sanctae ecclesiae esset adversum.*" Accordingly, on July 22, 1519, after the Disputation, Eck confided to the prince elector that Luther "rejects and negates the opinions and explanations of the Holy Fathers per se" and "thinks so highly of himself as if he might know the sense of Holy Scripture and how it pertains to the Holy Fathers." (WA Br 1:460.21–26 [No. 192 Vorgeschichte]). My translations.

131. WA 59:434.40–41: "*protestationem utriusque egregii domini et Andreae Carolstadii et Ioannis Eccii amplector et sequor.*" My translation.

Disputation would have very disparate effects on each of them. The first is the question of the historical evidence concerning the development of papal primacy, and the second is the question of Hussitism and the councils that would ultimately justify Luther's classification as a heretic. Lastly, we will examine the theological positioning of authorities.

First, while Luther and Eck did bounce a few arguments back and forth concerning the historical genesis of the papacy, they never delved into this matter with the same intensity as other questions. Luther retained the same arguments as before the Disputation: on the one hand, the Greeks did not recognize the pope as the highest bishop[132] and did not receive their consecration from him;[133] on the other hand, Peter had been in Jerusalem for eighteen years after the resurrection. The latter excluded for Luther any possibility of seeing the *ecclesia Romana* as the first and highest church on earth.[134] Eck dealt with these arguments prefunctorily. The eighteen years of Peter's absence from Rome were to be seen as further evidence that the primacy was not bound to the location but to the person of Peter. He only transferred his seat from Antioch to Rome at the command of Christ himself, thus according to divine law. A letter from Marcellus I,[135] which had been worked into the *Decretum Gratiani* (C. 24 q. 1 c. 15),[136] provided the source for this. Luther's Scripture-derived, historical argument was met with an argument from tradition coupled with the claimed authority of a divine mandate (*iubente Domino*).

Eck made even lighter work of the Greek matter. He conceded that the non-Roman bishops of the early church had, in fact, not been consecrated by the pope, but claimed that the pope still possessed authority over all priests.[137] Generally, he did not think that anything would be achieved by referring to the Greeks since they had fallen away from the pope and generally from Christendom.[138] While this matter was not developed extensively, we can see hints of an extensive diversion of ecclesiological understandings between him and Luther, since Luther considered the Greek church to be self-evidently Christian. Christ was clearly with the Greeks and not just with Rome.[139] All of these were excurses in the

132. WA 59:439.205–10.
133. WA 59:462.929–34.
134. WA 59:462.920–29.
135. As the brief papacy of Pope Marcellus II only started in 1555, Marcellus I was referred to simply as Marcellus by Gratian, Eck, and Luther.
136. CICan 1:970; WA 59:485.1623–36.
137. WA 59:468.1125–29.
138. WA 59:443.330–33.
139. WA 59:448.497–502.

discussion that congealed in Luther's mind to negate fully the papal claim to a long and uncontested primacy. He saw it as merely the product of recent decrees by the pope, based exclusively on human, non-divine conditions to boot.[140]

Second, Eck forced the legally and politically explosive question of Luther's alleged Hussitism into the Leipzig Disputation.[141] In the context of the Disputation, Eck catapulted this matter into prominence using the question of Roman primacy (recently brought into play by his contentious twelfth/thirteenth thesis). In accordance with his predecessors in Constance, he coupled the guilty verdict of Jan Hus with that of John Wycliffe:

> Thus among the damned and pestilant errors of John Wycliffe can be counted this one as well: "It is not necessary to salvation to believe that the Roman Church is supreme among the other [churches]"[142] Thus it is counted among the pestilant errors of Jan Hus: "Peter neither was nor is the head of the holy Catholic Church."[143] And also this one: "There is not the smallest sign of evidence that there should be one head ruling the Church in spiritual matters, [a head] who always abides and is preserved with the Church militant herself."[144] And this one: "Papal dignity originated with the emperor, and the primacy and institution of the pope emanated from imperial power."[145]

With the third condemned sentence, Eck brought Luther's argumentation within the *Resolutio* into central focus. By this point, it was clear to everyone involved that these three questions were really circling around the same matter: a church without a necessary dependency on the successor to Peter as its earthly head. And this brought the whole discussion about the papacy one step further, for until this point Luther had never fully questioned the papacy's right to earthly administration, only the pope's *ius divinum*. Eck made a rhetorical comparison of two quite distinct positions, on the one hand summarizing a long list of condemned positions by

---

140. WA 59:468.1100–05.
141. Here it must be said that Eck was not singularly focused on Hus. He also mentions the condemnation of the heresy of Lyon by Boniface VIII in "Unam Sanctam" (WA 59:461.888–91) and John XXII's condemnation of Marsilius of Padua (WA 59:461, 891, 894). The first may have contributed to Luther's apparent confusion when he associated the condemnation of Wycliffe and Hus with Boniface VIII (WA 59:466.1041–42). This insecurity had the unintended effect of Eck's clearly well-intended point of calling a council in the style of the medieval ones and did not achieve anything.
142. Cf. DH 1191.
143. Cf. DH 1207.
144. Cf. DH 1227.
145. Cf. DH 1209.

claiming that every Christian since the beginning of the church had been convinced of papal primacy not merely on the grounds of *iure humano*,[146] and on the other hand accusing Luther of playing into the hands of the Bohemians by contesting *iure divino* as a valid ground for papal primacy.[147]

Luther was forced to defend himself against this accusation and did so emphatically,[148] insisting that a schism would contradict Christian love.[149] But he substantially defended some of Eck's positions, certainly those that did not fundamentally question the pope's leadership of the church. That meant not contesting the salvific necessity of the supreme authority of the Roman church and the derivation of papal power from imperial decrees (addressed in the *Resolutio*). Firstly, the historical argument above had refuted his argument that there had been Christians in the past who attained salvation (such as Basilius of Caesarea or Gregory of Nazianz) without believing in papal supremecy.[150] But the dynamic of the debate cultivated a certain "hem and haw" in both partners. Despite the clarity of the historical argument, Luther still did not regard it as settled that the sentence "it is not necessary for salvation to believe that the Roman church is the highest among the others" was really heretical.[151] And the historical argument could also be used against the second point treated by Luther in the *Resolutio*, namely that Platina had argued that papal might was an emmanation of imperial might.[152] But during the debate, Luther went well past careful consideration and the rather playful language of the *Resolutio*.

And Luther doubled down on his new opinion on Hus. While he had distanced himself from Hus in the *Resolutio*, he had also made clear that Hus's opinions were shared by a great many Christians. Now, however, he explained with utter clarity:

146. WA 59:461.894–96.
147. WA 59:461.903–06.
148. WA 59:466.1043–44. Occasionally, the debate did get confrontational in an ugly way. Eck stated: "*Quod reverendus pater, honorem suum excusaturus, negat se Bohemorum patronum, si facta verbis responderent, magnificarent eum, at ultima primis non concordant, cum pestilentissimos Hussitarum errores non christiane dicat christianissimos. At de his posterius*" (WA 59:468.1107–10) and added that Luther was protecting the "*haereticorum (. . .) perfidiam*" (WA 59:468.1115–16). Luther then interrupted him with a *protestatio*: "*Protestor (. . .) coram vobis omnibus, quod egregius dominus doctor haec impudenter et mendaciter de me loquitur.*" (WA 59:468.1118–19). The question of heresy was doomed to bring a raw emotional side to the dispute—Luther surely knew at this point that such an identification with known heresy would eventually lead to a break with the church.
149. WA 59:462.913–15.
150. WA 59:466.1056–58.
151. WA 59:479.1459–61. My translation, cf. n. 142.
152. WA 59:467.1077–83.

Secondly, and this is certain, there are many articles among those of Jan Hus and the Bohemians which are completely Christian and Evangelical, which the general church cannot condemn. This is true for this and similar ones: "there is only one general church."[153]

For Luther, condemning this doctrine meant rejecting the ecumenical creeds.[154] Luther did not cite the condemned sentence entirely accurately, for, as Eck would later emphasize,[155] it had identified the church with the number of all those who are predestined to salvation (*numerus praedestinatorum*).[156] Here, we see an ecclesiological difference come into sharp focus. Its cause was to be found in the various interpretations of Augustine.[157] Luther emphasized that this sentence, when applied to the *numerus praedestinatorum*, was not Hussite but rather Augustinian.[158] At this point, Luther does not scold the councils. Eck would maneuver him into doing that later. But he does use the same argumentative figure as in the *Resolutio*, demonstrating that the condemned teaching of Jan Hus was actually promoted by those recognized as orthodox faithful, even teachers within the church. Eck countered this with the ecclesiological principle that the church also contains sinners,[159] which was excluded by the condemned teaching.[160] To put it somewhat bluntly, we see Hus and Luther emphasizing the concept of the invisible church and Eck emphasizing the visible church. It makes sense that the question of the papacy would lead here since—as we will see later in the question of biblical interpretation—the question of church leadership most certainly had to do with the distinction between invisible and visible instances. While Luther drew on 1 Corinthians to promote an ecclesiology fully oriented

---

153. WA 59:466.1048–50: "*Secundo, et hoc certum est, inter articulos Ioannis Huss vel Bohemorum multos esse plane christianissimos et evangelicos, quos non possit universalis ecclesia damnare, velut est ille et similis, quod tantum est una ecclesia universalis.*" For more on Prince Georg's reaction to the partial recognition of Hussitisim, cf. Heiko Jadatz, "Herzog Georg von Sachsen und die Leipziger Disputation," in Hein and Kohnle, *Leipziger Disputation*, 109–24, 109. 123. For Eck, this was one of the points that led him to file a legal accusation against Luther with the prince (WA Br 1:460, 26–29 [No. 192 Vorgeschichte]).
154. WA 59:466.1051–54.
155. WA 59:489.1755–62.
156. DH 1201.
157. Cf. the helpful heremeneutical considerations for Augustine interpretation from Christoph Markschies, "Taufe und Concupisentia bei Augustinus," in *Gerecht und Sünder zugleich? Ökumenische Klärungen*, ed. Theodor Schneider and Gunther Wenz (Freiburg: Herder, 2001), 92–108, especially 103–04.
158. WA 59:478.1423–26.
159. For the meaning of this teaching for Eck, cf. Bäumer, "Ekklesiologie," 140.
160. WA 59:489.1755–62.

toward Christ as the head of the church, Eck adhered to the opinion that this head was represented in the earthly instance of the pope.

Luther's difficulties with the condemnations at Constance were not restricted to the question of the papacy. Constance had also condemned the teaching: "The two natures, godly and human, are one Christ."[161] The editors of the *Enchiridion symbolorum* left the comment that this teaching is "a truncated article" and it is not entirely clear what "the point of objection" is.[162] Luther also saw it this way and thus simply remarked to this article: "I believe that Master John Eck confesses this article with me."[163] Luther was so certain his oppenents would agree to this christological teaching that he associated the question of the validity of this verdict with the status of the council's decision, even expressing his suspicion that this article had entered the council's files after it had concluded.[164] It cannot actually be determined if Luther really adhered to this opinion or if he was merely hoping to avoid the consequences of attacking the authority of the councils. In any case, Luther posed the question with stark clarity—and that was precisely what Eck wanted him to do. Eck skirted around the main issues Luther wished to talk about; they were, after all, condemned teachings and did not warrant further discussion. "May the honorable father not assiduate that I am judging these articles, for judgment has already been passed on them."[165] Eck made a big show of interpreting the dubiously condemned teachings on the two natures of Christ, stating that "godly" and "human" (*humanitas*) ought to be replaced by God and human being (*homo*).[166] This obviously missed the point of the condemned teachings. Eck found it to be more important to adhere to the fact that these were *condemned* teachings, citing the printed edition of the council's records (made in 1500 by Jerome of Croaria[167]) as proof that their condemnation was authentic.[168] From Eck's point of view, there was no room for Luther

161. DH 1204: "*Duae naturae, divinitas et humanitas, sunt unus Christus,*"; cf. WA 59:479.1441–43.

162. Footnote to DH 1204. The editors point out that the intended point of the condemnation was to be found in the fact that the sentence continued with an application: the church of the predestined was to be led by Christ.

163. WA 59:478.1429–30: "*Hos articulos, credo, confitetur mecum dominus Ioannes Eccius.*" My translation.

164. WA 59:479.1445.

165. WA 59:489.1749–50: "*Nec imponat mihi reverendus pater quos velim de illis articulis iudicare, quia iam iudicati sunt.*" My translation.

166. WA 59:489.1767–70.

167. For more on Luther's knowledge of this edition, cf. Schäfer, *Luther als Kirchenhistoriker*, 209.

168. WA 59:489.1737–40; cf. Council of Constance, *Acta Scitu dignissima docte|que concinnata Constantiensis | concilii celebratissimi* (Hagenau: Gran, 1500).

to maneuver here: to contest the decision of a council was to contest the nature of a council. And *that* is where Eck hit hard.

Eck accused Luther of arguing against the Council of Constance by affirming Hussite teaching as Christian.[169] The matter of councils had only been handled in passing before the Disputation, so Eck was raising a point here Luther was not prepared for—a topic in great contrast to the question of the papacy, which Luther had conducted extensive biblical analysis for. His immediate reaction to Eck's accusation was accordingly only a *protestatio*:

> Master Doctor Martin has protested at this point that it is not true that he spoke against the Council of Constance. Eck offers, however, that he prove this with writings and speech.[170]

This was not the first time that Luther interrupted his opponent, but it had a very large effect here. Luther's objection shows that he believed he had not yet cast the authority of the council into question until this point in the debate—even though he had contested its verdict. His reaction appears to convey a dreadful realization that these two things were not compatible with each other. He immediately seeks to establish the compatibility of his statements with an acceptable conciliar hermeneutic, pointing out that there were various degrees of verdict from the councils, with a difference being seen between articles that were "heretical, erroneous, blasphemous, risky and seditious" (*haeretici, erronei, blasphemi, temerarii, seditiosi*) and those that were "offensive to pious ears" (*piarum aurium offensive*).[171] While this may have deflected the accusation of heresy, Eck was still right in contesting[172] that it made the condemned articles *christianissimi*.

And thus, the disputants suddenly found themselves debating the fallibility of a council. Eck stated the stark truth: if the Council of Constance had really erred in those articles mentioned by Luther, then

---

169. WA 59:472.1230–36.

170. WA 59:472.1237–39: "*Protestatus est hoc loco dominus doctor Martinus, non esse verum, quod contra Constantiense concilium dixerit. Eccius contra offert se hoc probaturum ex scriptis et dictis.*" My translation.

171. WA 59:479.1446–48; cf. the verdict against Jan Hus on July 6, 1415: "*ex eis plures esse erroneos, alios scandalosos, aliquos piarum aurium offensivos, pluresque eorum esse temerarios et seditiosos, et nonnullos eorumdem esse notorie haereticos*" (Thomas Prügel, *Dekrete der Ökumenischen Konzilien*, ed. Josef Wolmuth, vol. 2, *Konzilien des Mittelalters* [Paderborn: Brill, 2000], 426.34–36). Luther had obviously informed himself very precisely about this verdict.

172. WA 59:489.1750–63.

the council's authority had been fundamentally called into question.[173] This was familiar territory for Luther, for in 1518 he debated Silvester Prierias and explained:

> I do not believe that the factual developments of the church are enough here (although there are no factual developments of the church in this case) because both the Pope and the Council can err as you find in Panormitanus when he most excellently treats Canon *X 1.6.4*.[174]

The main thrust went after the fallibility of the pope. In the process, it becomes clear that Luther understood the councils as being the essential representation of the church.[175] Notwithstanding this matter, he used the term "fallible" in the context of councils. But he had not yet cleared up what sorts of questions the councils were liable to fail in. Luther drew on a passage from a commentary on *Liber Extra* by Nicholas of Tudeschis, the former archbishop of Palermo (thus traditionally called "Panormitanus"), which he hoped would provide an example of the fallibility of councils.[176] It was not the best example as this passage does not pertain to dogma, arguing only for a ban on marriages between victims and perpetrators of rape.[177] We must consider this background when Luther speaks of the

173. WA 59:473.1250–52.
174. WA 1:656:30–33: "*Nec satis ibi esse credo etiam factum ecclesiae (quanquam hic non sit factum ecclesiae), quia tam Papa quam concilium potest errare, ut habes Panormitanum egregie haec tractantem li. i. de const. c. significasti.*" My translation.
175. WA 1:656.36–37.
176. Christopher Voigt-Goy, "'dictum unius privati:' Zu Luthers Verwendung des Kommentars der Dekretale Significasti von Nicolaus de Tudeschis," in *Orientierung für das Leben: Kirchliche Bildung und Politik in Spätmittelalter, Reformation und Neuzeit: FS Manfred Schulze*, ed. Patrik Mähling (Bern: Lit, 2010), 93–114, 104.
177. Panormitanus, *Commentary on X 1.6.4* ("*Significasti*") (Nicolaus de Tudeschis, *Lectura super quinque libros Decretalium. Pars prima super primo decretalium* [Venice, 1477], unnumbered pages, numbered as fol. 80ᵛb, accessed on March 31, 2023, https://www.digitale-sammlungen.de/de/view/bsb00058048?page=162,163); cf. Knut Wolfgang Nörr, *Kirche und Konzil bei Nicolaus de Tudeschis (Panormitanus)* (Köln: Böhlau, 1964), 104–6. The background of this statement has been explained by Voigt-Goy, "'dictum,'" 94–98. In C. 36 q. 2 c. 10–11, Gratian corrected those conciliar decisions, which banned marriage between rapists and their victims (which had referred to a passage by Jerome) (CICan 1:1291–92). This led to a lengthy discussion within canon law. Both the canonical discussion and the text by Nicholas of Tudeschis testify that Gratian had not only claimed the "possibility" but actually the facticity of a conciliar error ("*nam et concilium potest errare sicut alias errauit*" [Nicolaus de Tudeschis, *Lectura super*]), in the claim that the latter, as Bernd Moeller, "Luther und das Papsttum," in *Luther Handbuch*, ed. Albrecht Beutel 3rd ed. (Tübingen: Mohr, 2017), 131–40, 137, believes to see the decisive difference between Luther and Panormitanus. Instead, the difference has to do with the domain where the error took place.

fallibility of councils according to Panormitanus at the Leipzig Disputation.[178] He was thus moving within familiar territory for late-medieval law, especially as he began his statement in Leipzig by emphasizing that he did not want to touch the authority of the councils "*in his quae sunt fidei*."[179] Luther could have gone even further. The idea that councils can err in matters of the faith had been uttered by quite prominent voices of the Middle Ages. Pierre d'Ailly, whose work Luther famously knew very well, had used the argument: "A general council can err in matters of the faith. In fact, it has already actually erred as many examples demonstrate," in his discussion of the papacy in *Quaestio resumpta*. Pierre d'Ailly saw the most important example for this in the Council of Ephesus.[180]

Along with this basic affirmation of the councils, the Leipzig Disputation saw the growth of another viewpoint througout its course: the affirmation of the binding nature of the councils for matters of the faith was now associated with a mild restriction. Luther added to his previous statements: "I reserve this, as one must do, that a Council *has* erred and that it *can* err, especially (*praesertim*) in questions which pertain to faith."[181] The *praesertim* had the unintended effect of opening the possibility of an occasional error on the part of the councils, even in matters of the faith. This had the effect of fundamentally implying that the councils needed some sort of ratifying instance.[182] Such a statement went well beyond the citation of Panormitanus. The leitmotif for Luther in this matter was the special status of *ius divinum*, which he did not think could be used to grant authority to the councils.[183] Instead, the councils were to be understood as a "creation of this (divine) word" ("*creatura istius verbi*" [*dei*]).[184] The ecclesiologically explosive phrasing that the pope could fail because he was

---

178. WA 59:480.1466–67. Fuchs, *Konfession und Gespräch*, 178, rightly emphasizes that this reference to late-medieval canon law was deeply influenced and motivated by insights into scriptural hermeneutics.

179. WA 59:500.2080–81.

180. Pierre d'Ailly, *Quaestiones magistri Petri de | Alliaco cardinalis cameracenlsis super libros sententiarum* (Straßburg: Georg Husner, 1490), F6ʳ: "*concilium generale potest contra fidem errare. Immo de facto sic aliquando errauit sicut per multa exempla ostendunt.*"

181. WA 59:500.2081–83: "*Hoc solum mihi reservo quod et reservandum est, Concilium aliquando errasse et posse errare, praesertim in his quae non sunt fidei.*" My translation. Luther writes about this to Spalatin on July 20, 1519: "*I publicly acknowledged that some articles had been wrongly condemned* [by the Council of Constance], *articles which had been taught in plain and clear words by Paul, Augustine, and even Christ himself.*" (WA Br 1:422.71–73 [No. 137], cited after LW 31:322).

182. WA 59:480.1473–74.

183. WA 59:500.2083–84; 513.2484–86.

184. WA 59:479.1465. My translation.

just a human being like any other (already employed in the *Asterisci*) had now been extended to the councils.[185] He thus reached a concept that saw the representation of the church in the councils, but he now inverted the typical reasoning and critiqued them within this framework. If the councils were purely human endeavors, then the difference from *ius divinum* ought to be obvious and their theologically legitimated authority not justifiable.

Eck responded to this point by maintaining that, despite the fallibility of any individual person, a legitimately assembled council was led "not through human sense but by the divine spirit" ("*non humano sensu sed spiritu divino*").[186] The synodic character of the councils brought with it a dignity of its own, which was not the result of some special characteristic of the participants but rather of the mandate held in common by all of them. Eck could not fathom a council being so purely human as Luther claimed[187] since that would have knocked the support out from the entire medieval system of authorities.[188] Eck summarized this for Luther again:

> Therefore we must hold with the most constant faith which says that everything which the legitimately assembled councils have decided and defined is completely certain. In this way does Christ remain with us until the end of the world and "when two or three are assembled in my name etc."[189]

Eck had successfully maneuvered Luther into taking a position superficially against this one.[190] In the process, Luther was forced to hone thoughts he had been mulling on since at least early 1518. In this moment, the idea of conciliar fallibility became a certainty for him. He now demanded positive proof from Eck that a council could not err.[191] When he made his doubt

---

185. WA 59:480.1473–74.

186. WA 59:491.1795. My translation.

187. WA 59:490.1785–86. Luther's opinion is ultimately the consequence of developing an ecclesial concept in which the church was increasingly understood to be the orderly community of individuals. We can see this idea in development with William of Ockham (cf. Jürgen Miethke, *Ockhams Weg zur Sozialphilosophie* [Berlin: De Gruyter, 1969], 502–16). They also found their way into canon law, such as in the case of Panormitanus, utilized by Luther (cf. Voigt-Goy, "'dictum,'" 104).

188. For more on late-medieval approaches to claiming conciliar infallibility, cf. Volker Leppin, *Wilhelm von Ockham: Gelehrter, Streiter, Bettelmönch* (Darmstadt: Wissenschaftliche Buchgesellschaft, 2012), 220–21.

189. WA 59:490.1788–92: "*Unde potius hoc constantissima fide tenere debemus, quicquid concilia legitime congregata in iis quae sunt fidei determinaverint, definiverint, esse certissimum. Sic enim Christus manet nobiscum usque ad consummationem saeculi; et 'si duo congregati fuerint in nomine meo etc.'*" My translation.

190. Cf. Selge, "Leipziger Disputation," 36.

191. WA 59:508.2307.

public, Eck no longer regarded him as a Christian but as a heathen.[192] And thus, Eck and Luther found the threshhold case for heresy in the question of conciliar fallibility. Luther would never enjoy a home in his previous church from this point forth. But the positive theological ground for this separation lay even deeper in the precise definition of *ius divinum*. This became the sole standard by which Luther evaluated what was heresy and what was not.[193]

Third, the whole matter of *ius divinum* coupled the question of the pope to the definition of authorities and thus played a major role in the formation of reformational scriptural authority. Luther emphasized that he saw no problem in the papacy's factual validity: if a grand consensus of Christians found reason to elect a supreme bishop, this would be no problem. But this bishop could only enjoy his authority *iure humano*.[194] The basis for theologically binding statements could only be *ius divinum*, and Luther identified it with Holy Scripture at the Leipzig Disputation, responding to Eck:

> I marvel enough that the sublime Master Doctor has instituted that he wants to prove divine right but has until today failed to employ a single syllable of Scripture but only those of sayings and works of the fathers, and these contradict each other.[195]

This definition makes the further development of Luther's thought with regard to the *Asterisci* clear. If one has to see *ius divinum* as being in the accordance to Christ's teachings (and they had always struggled to see any other relation between these two concepts), Luther now made the definition substantially more exact. A year prior, Luther still understood

---

192. WA 59:511.2415–18; for more on the meaning of this controversy, cf. Lohse, "Luther und Huß," 73.

193. WA 59:508.2308–11.

194. WA 59:439.205–10. The Schmalkald Articles also see Luther considering the possibility of recognizing the papacy under *iure humano* but concludes, "Summa. Er kans nicht thun" (WA 50:215.14–216.15); consider also the famous note by Melanchthon's signature on the Schmalkald Articles: "*Ich Philippus Melanthon halt dise obgestelte artikel auch fur recht und christlich. Vom babst aber halt ich, so ehr das evangelium wolte zulassen, das yhm umb fridens und gemeiner einikeit willen der jenigen christen, so auch unter yhm sind und kunfftig sein möchten, sein superioritet uber die bischove, die ehr hatt iure humano, auch von uns zuzulassen sey*" (*Die Bekenntnisschriften der Evangelisch-Lutherischen Kirche. Quellen und Materialien*, vol. 1, *Von den altkirchlichen Symbolen bis zu denKatechismen Martin Luthers*, ed. Irene Dingel [Göttingen: Vandenhoeck & Ruprecht 2014], 803.9–18).

195. WA 59:463.960–62: "*Satis miror, egregium dominum doctorem instituisse probare ius divinum, et usque hodie ne unam syllabam quidem scripturae inducit, sed tantum dicta et facta patrum eademque sibi ipsis repugnantia*"; for more on the clear centering in Scripture, cf. WA 59:437.146–55.

the teachings of the *patres* and the *canones* as falling under *ius divinum*.
Not anymore! This meant the resolution of a long tradition of ambivalence
and vagueness in medieval thought, for there was a canonical tradition of
interpreting Scripture as *divina lex*[196] in contrast to the results of councils.
A prominent example can be found in our favorite case of the *Decretum
Gratiani*, where Panormitanus concluded the fallibility of the councils.[197]
In a comment to C. 36 q. 2 c. 11, Gratian gave the following explanation of conciliar statements: "This authority does not prejudge that of
Jerome, especially since his is based on the authority of the divine law."[198]
It was precisely at this point that consensus was lacking. Panormitanus
felt comfortable with the idea that the pope created *ius divinum*.[199] That
meant that Luther was employing a passage of dogmatic history that had
not yet been legally clarified. His *Asterisci* begin within a broad, medieval
interpretive spectrum, but in the course of the Leipzig Disputation, his
theology homed in on Scripture as the basis for the church's authority.

Here, he voted indisputably for the predominance of Scripture, which
was held by virtually all medieval thinkers, including Panormitanus. Eck
did not see any reason to contradict this, granting Luther in the strife
concerning papal primacy that biblical citations were to be regarded as
*divinum* in contrast to those of the church fathers.[200] But the theologian
from Ingolstadt could also explain: "The monarchy and a singular leadership within the church has been instituted by divine right and by Christ.
Therefore the texts of Holy Scripture and the certified history do not
contradict it,"[201] which meant somehow integrating the church fathers into
*ius divinum*.[202] As he did this within a harmony model, he therefore saw no
contradiction of terms. Only if one were to go as far as Luther in seeing
a real possibility of hermeneutical difference between the church fathers
and Scripture did the question of how one was to position these authorities
to each other arise. Where Luther saw a potential friction—and certainly

<hr>

196. For more on the interchangeability of *ius divinum* and *lex divina,* cf. Jean Gerson, *Oeuvres
complètes*, ed. P. Glorieux, vol. 3 (Paris: Desclée, 1962), 135.
197. For more on this context, see n. 150–51 above and Voigt-Goy, "dictum.'"
198. CICan I:1292: "*Hec auctoritas non preiudicat auctoritati Ieronimi, maxime cum illa testimonio
diuinae legis nitatur.*" My translation.
199. Commentary on *Liber Extra*, l. 5, tit. 7, c. 7 (CICan 2:779): "*Papa potest inducere novum articulum
fidei declarando illud ius divinum*" (Niccolò, *ABBATIS| PANORMITANI | COMMENTARIA
| In Quartum & Quintum Decretalium Libros. | (. . .)* (Venedig: 1617), 117ʳa; cf. also Nörr, *Kirche
und Konzil*, 124–25).
200. WA 59:443.338.
201. WA 59:435.72–73: "*Monarchia et unus principatus in ecclesia dei est de iure divino et a Christo
institutus, quare textus sacrae scripturae vel historiae approbatae ei non adversantur.*" My translation.
202. Cf. Selge, "Leipziger Disputation," 32.

the exclusive superiority of Scripture over the fathers—Eck continued to remain within the harmony model, which Luther had been gradually leaving behind him since 1518. This was proving easy for him to do, for he had already excised papal decrees from the harmonious cooperation of the Middle Ages. The church fathers would only enjoy authority to the extent that their statements were compatible with those of Scripture. Luther referred to the *regula Augustini* for this basic statement, according to which it applied "that the statements of all scriptures are to be judged according to divine scripture."[203]

The juxtaposition of two different hermeneutics—one of harmony, one of difference—for classifying Scripture and patristic sources became extremely acute when the conversation turned toward the matter of the head of the church. For Luther's argument that Christ was the head of the church, he employed 1 Corinthians 15:24f along with Augustine's explanation,[204] as well as 1 Corinthians 3:5.[205] Eck could only accept this on a systematic level with his harmony-based thought that Christ was the head of the mystical body but the pope led the head of the *ecclesia militans* as his representative.[206] He made reference to Jerome, who purportedly explained that the pope had been instituted in order to fend off precisely those schisms as we see in 1 Corinthians 3:5. At this moment, Luther made a statement that would prove to be decisive for the future order of authorities:

> I cannot suffer that I am diverted from higher authorities by lower ones. And Jerome is not so important that we depart from Paul because of him.[207]

This sentence contains the decisive shift away from the harmony model toward the difference model. Seeing Paul and Jerome as being a higher (*maior*) and lower (*minor*) authority was entirely unproblematic. But that Luther saw the danger of the lower authority suspending the power of the higher—that he no longer saw the possibility of harmonious cooperation between them but only difference—was a new move on his part. Eck's answer made this difference of viewpoints very clear:

---

203. WA 59:509.2351–52: "*quod omnium sciptorum dicta iudicanda sunt per divinam scripturam.*" My translation. Luther repeatedly referred to the *regula Augustini* in D. 9 c. 5 in this context (CICan 1:17), cited by Luther in WA 59:466.1066–467.3; cf. WA Br 1:468.104–C5 (No. 192).
204. WA 59:437.131–38.
205. WA 59:437.152–55.
206. WA 59:441.282–442.285.
207. WA 59:445.397–98: "*Non patior propter minorem auctoritatem inductam me divelli a maiore, nec tantus est Hieronymus ut propter eum Paulum deseramus.*" My translation.

And when he rightly gives Paul preference to Jerome, it is nevertheless necessary to piously believe that Jerome understood Paul's statement well at this point.[208]

As willing as Eck was to follow his Wittenberg colleague in classifying the authorities, he was not at all willing to understand this classification as a parallel or an outright conflict. In his mind, the lower authority served to help understand the higher and was to be read generally with broad trust.

The controversy concerning the status of a citation from Jerome may be the starkest exposition of the debators' difference, but they also wrestled with an apatristic explanation of Scripture. This occurred within the same horizon of divergence between models of difference and harmony. Eck cited John 5:19 to justify his understanding of the papacy, "Very truly, I tell you, the Son can do nothing on his own, but only what he sees the Father doing; for whatever the Father does, the Son does likewise," and interpreted this in the sense that the earthly church was to be considered a true image of the heavenly one.[209] This idea was obviously going in the direction of the church as *corpus Christi*. Luther contested it, emphasizing that the passage was not speaking of the church as an *ecclesia triumphans* (church triumphant) and *ecclesia militans* (church militant) but rather exclusively about the relation between God Father and God Son.[210] Eck responded with a reference to Bernard of Clairvaux's interpretation of the passage in *De consideratione ad Eugenium*,[211] which has a strong ecclesiological bent to it and uses the biblical passage along with a host of others to intensify the idea of ecclesial hierarchy.[212] As much as Luther held Bernard in high regard,[213] Eck read the Cistercian abbot along the same lines as he read Jerome: as an aide to understand the sense of Scripture. Luther contested this role, at least as concerned Eck's intended exclusivity:

> I honor the divine Bernard and do not despise his statement but one must accept the genuine and characteristic sense of scripture in a contentious case.[214]

208. WA 59:450.566–68: "*Et quamquam merito Paulum praeferat Hieornymo, pie tamen credendum est Hieronymum eo loco sententiam Pauli bene intellexisse.*" My translation.
209. WA 59:435.75–79.
210. WA 5, 438.155–61.
211. WA 59:441.267–81; cf. Bernhard of Clairvaux, *Sämtliche Werke. Lateinisch/Deutsch*, ed. Gerhard B. Winkler, vol. 1 (Innsbruck: Tyrolia, 1990), 730.7–18.
212. Bernhard, *Sämtliche Werke*, I:18–22.
213. Cf. Theo Bell, *Divus Bernhardus. Bernhard von Clairvaux in Martin Luthers Schriften* (Mainz: Zabern, 1993); Franz Posset, *The Real Luther: A Friar at Erfurt & Wittenberg* (St. Louis: Concordia, 2011).
214. WA 59:445.411–14: "*divum Bernardum veneror et eius sententiam non contemno, sed in contentione accipiendus est sensus genuinus et proprius scripturae.*" My translation.

Just like with 1 Corinthians, Luther pitted a genuine sense of Scripture against the exegesis of a father. The argument in the *Resolutio* that one ought to regard Scripture without external sources was not applied here in complement to patristic explanation but actually replaced them altogether. The reactions of the two debators at this stage indicate just how far they had diverged from each other.

Not only did they disagree on the extent of interpreting the church fathers: other hermeneutic rules were equally contentious.[215] When addressing 1 Corinthians 3:5 and 1:12f—the very passages Luther had used to contest the primacy of Peter—Eck pointed out that the passage did not speak generally about primacy but only about individual persons. But Luther retorted:

> I am moved more by that text of Paul than by such a violent and forced distinction because he is supported by no authorities even though he wants to argue according to divine law.[216]

And thus the Wittenberg Reformer had rejected the classic scholastic means of *distinctio* as an instrument of exegesis, at least as pertained to this case. Instead, he preferred the simple reference of authorities. He was not alone in this, for Eck went on to accuse him of arguing with *sophisticae cautelae*.[217] In the heat of the moment, both could agree that one ought not to overburden the biblical text with scholastic interpretation.

Before the Disputation, Luther found the meat of the matter in the biblical passages of Matthew 16:18 and John 21:17. The hermeneutical discussion led to them at this point in the Disputation. Leading up to the Disputation, Luther questioned to what extent the Matthew passage could actually be applied; he was not entirely sure if one could regard it as *ius divinum* for the *status quaestionis* at hand. Eck did use the passage as *ius divinum*.[218] What followed was a characteristic discussion between him and Luther about the relation between *ius divinum* (in this case understood as Scripture by both of them) and the church fathers. Eck provided a blizzard

---

215. In this context, the confrontation between Eck and Karlstadt becomes all the more fascinating. Karlstadt contended: "*Scire sanctam scripturam non est multas auctoritates memoriter recitare, sed spiritum introclusum in literis et dominum nostrum Christum quaerere et gustare, insuper auctoritates ex intentione scribentium proferre*" (Otto Seitz, ed., *Der authentische Text der Leipziger Disputation (1519)* [Berlin: Schwetschke, 1903], 26)—a frequently neglected early form of Luther's "*Christum predigen vnd treyben*" (WA DB 7:384.25–26).

216. WA 59:455.709–11: "*Me plus movet ipse textus Pauli, quam tam violenta et extorta distinctio, quia nulli prorsus innititur auctoritati, cum tamen velit e divino iure arguere.*" My translation.

217. WA 59:458.815–17; cf. similar accusations, WA 486.1660–67.

218. WA 59:459.830–33; cf. WA 494.1874–75.

of citations from the church fathers and marginalia to bolster his interpretation of Matthew 16:18. They were the same ones Luther had cited:
Jerome, Chrysostom, and Augustine.[219] When Luther accused Eck of not
arguing with Scripture but with references to the church fathers,[220] Eck
claimed to not be deriving *ius divinum* from the church fathers but only to
be demonstrating how they were of the opinion that the primacy of Peter
was justified *iure divino*.[221] Eck had emphatically supported his harmony
model by using the church fathers as a tool to discern the true sense of
Scripture. It could not have been more different from Luther's difference
model, made especially clear by Luther's explanation in this context:

> Even if Augustine and all fathers understood Peter [Petrum] to be the stone
> [petram], I nevertheless resist them alone by calling upon the authority of the
> Apostle Paul, who writes in 1 Cor. 3[:11]: "For no one can lay any foundation
> other than the one that has been laid; that foundation is Jesus Christ," and
> upon the authority of Peter, who calls Christ in 1 Peter 2[:4–6]: "a living
> stone" and a "cornerstone" and teaches that we are built into a spiritual
> house upon it. If accordingly Peter really was the foundation of the church,
> the church would fall to the voice of a single servant girl at the watch and
> certainly would not overcome the gates of hell. [cf. Matt 26:69–70]. It thus
> follows that when the holy fathers call Peter [Petrum] the rock [petram] at
> this place, then they either suffer from human weakness or have some other
> understanding which I will not mention here.[222]

Where Eck understood Scripture through the fathers, Luther understood Scripture through a concordant search of Scripture. Luther was
moving steadily toward a disassociation of Scripture from tradition. Eck
enquired by what authority Luther could claim the clarity of Scripture
for his explanation. According to Eck, it was a truly Bohemian (which
was to say Hussite) error to believe that one understood Scripture better
than the popes, councils, scholars, and universities.[223] Where Luther

---


219. WA 59:459.835–460.377.

220. WA 59:463.960–62.

221. WA 59:470.1161–64.

222. WA 59:465.1004–14: "*Quodsi etiam Augustinus et omnes patres Petrum intellexerint per petram,
resistam ego eis unus auctoritate apostoli Pauli, id est divino iure, qui scribit primae ad Corinthios
3.: 'Fundamentum aliud nemo ponere potest, praeterquam quod positum est, quod est Iesus Christus,'
et auctoritate Petri, primae 2., ubi Christum lapidem vivum et angularem appellat, docens, ut super-
aedificemur in domum spiritualem. Alioquin si Petrus esset fundamentum ecclesiae, lapsa fuisset
ecclesia ad unius ancillae ostiariae vocem, quam tamen nec portae inferorum expugnare poterunt.
Sequitur ergo, quod sancti patres, quando Petrum appellant petram hoc loco, vel humana patiuntur
vel aliquem alium sensum habent, de quo non pronuncio.*" My translation.

223. WA 59:470.1176–81.

claimed that only *sacra scriptura* could shape doctrine, Eck claimed that an interpretive instance for all Christians could only be found in the authority of a council or a pope.[224] Eck met Luther's claim to a proper and clear understanding of Scripture with the preponderance of tradition and institutional security. This argument had a lot of power since Luther was not only trying to distinguish *ius divinum* from a context of tradition but was also undertaking a hierarchial classification within divine law. When Eck accused him of supporting the Bohemians, Luther responded:

> The Bohemians have acted wrongly by separating themselves from our unity by their own authority, even if divine right is on their side, for the highest divine law is charity and unity of the Spirit.[225]

This comment came at a relatively early point in the Disputation and demonstrated an important accentuation for its further development: *ius divinum* filling the vacuum of papal primacy was also *ius divinum* in the sense of a love that unified the church. Luther would not manage to resolve the tension between these points throughout the Disputation.

The difference in interpretive approaches to Matthew 16 was also felt in interpreting John 21:17. Again, Eck used the church fathers to argue that the primacy of Peter was founded here[226] and emphasized that this citation was *ius divinum*.[227] Luther agreed with him,[228] but the interpretation of the passage remained contentious. Luther proclaimed that he had found the *sensus evangelicus*.[229] Eck accused him of arguing against the interpretation of fathers, popes, and councils.[230] Luther read "pasture/tend" (*pascere*) in the same way he did in the *Resolutio*: it did not mean administration or government but teaching, preaching, remonstrating, praying, and leading by example.[231] Additionally, this mandate was conditioned by a love of Christ, meaning that no primacy per se could be established here but only one that stood continuously under an external condition.[232] The

---

224. WA 59:473.1253–54.
225. WA 59:462.913–15: "*inique faciunt Bohemi, quod se auctoritate propria sepɔrant a nostra unitate, etiamsi ius divinum pro eis staret, cum supremum ius divinum sit charitas et unitas spiritus.*"
226. WA 59:486.1077–487.1093.
227. WA 59:494.1877–78.
228. WA 59:497.1988–90.
229. WA 59:497.1990–498.2002.
230. WA 59:494.1880–83.
231. WA 59:497.1990–498.2002.
232. WA 59:498.2025–26.

hermeneutic difference between the two men became most clear in the interpretation of *pascere*. Again, Luther read this word exclusively in the sense employed by Scripture.[233] Eck referred to an interpretation of the fathers[234] and, even more characteristically, to the etymological observation that *pastor*—and thus an office—was derived from *pascere*.[235] The latter observation demonstrated the effect of humanistic education in early Modern society. Eck had had enough contact with it to employ its argumentation,[236] but he did so very differently than did Luther. Luther had learned to understand a text in its historical context and stringently applied this method to the normative text of *ius divinum*. Eck did not start his argumentation with backgrounds and contexts but with the normative consequences. One of them was to be found in the attributes of the pastoral office.

This stage of the debate further demonstrates how the two positions were drifting apart. Eck saw an intermediate result of the debate as a confirmation of papal primacy:

> Therefore I want to bring this to conclusion presently that I believe that Saint Peter has received the primacy of the entire church from Christ because of the promise given to him in Matt 16[:18], just as Jerome, Cyprian, Augustine and others have understood [. . .] And the other arguments lead me to believe that this conclusion, which has been affirmed by all fathers and most recently by the Council of Constance, is true. I do not want to support this opinion with my own intelligence but rather want to submit it to the judgment of other ordained judges, be they the Holy See or other wise and good men.[237]

The Ingolstadt professor was fully convinced that each individual had a duty to submit to the church's tradition as represented by fathers and the

233. WA 59:509.2355–59.
234. WA 59:506.2254–60.
235. WA 59:512.2441–44. My translation.
236. Johann Peter Wurm, "Johannes Eck und die Disputation von Leipzig 1519. Vorgeschichte und unmittelbare Folgen," in Hein and Kohnle, *Leipziger Disputation*, 159–73, 159. For more on Eck's own education, cf. Wiedemann, *Eck*, 3–27. Wiedemann's biography of Eck remains the best to the present day.
237. WA 59:520.2700–02. 2713–18: "*Unde et ego istam conclusionem volo finire in praesentia, quod reputem sanctum Petrum primatum totius ecclesiae a Christo tenuisse ex promissione ei facta, Matthaei xvi., sicut intelligit Hieronymus, Cyprianus, Augustinus et alii [. . .] Et per alia superius adducta reputo conclusionem illam a tot sanctis patribus et novissime per concilium Constantiense comprobatam, esse veram. Nolo tamen inniti propriae prudentiae, paratus captivare intellectum meum in his et quibuscunque aliis iudicio iudicum ordinandorum, sedis apostolicae et aliorum prudentium et bonorum virorum.*" My translation.

councils. The authority question found its answer in an ecclesiology-oriented harmony model that could only see one moment of difference: that which existed between the authorities and the reasoning of an individual. If necessary, the latter would have to conform to the prior in faithful obedience.[238]

Luther stated his opinion with equal clarity:

> It is not in the power of the Roman Pontif or of an inquisitor of heretical evil to found new articles of the faith. They have only to judge according to them. Faithful Christians cannot be brought to accept anything beyond what is contained in Holy Scripture, which is the proper divine law, even if a new and proven revelation arises. Instead, we are prohibited from believing by divine law whatever is not proven, no matter through the divine scriptures or a purely immanent revelation.[239]

This was not yet a fully formulated scriptural principle. That can be seen in the indication of a "manifest revelation," which had roots in the late-medieval discussion[240] and provided a certain amount of space for the expansion of biblical source material.[241] And Luther had not yet offensively proclaimed such a clear scriptural principle. On August 18, 1519, he described his position to the prince elector. It was completely conformed to medieval theology:

> Next to the text of the Bible, I have held one doctor against another, and have introduced Doctor Eck alone without the Bible, and I want to do this for the rest of my life and not relent.[242]

238. For the history of this formulation, cf.: Luca Bianchi, "'Captivare intellectum in obsequium Christi'," *Rivista critica di storia della filosofia* 38 (1983): 81–87.

239. WA 59:466.1059–64: "*Nec est in potestate Romani pontificis aut inquisitoris haereticae pravitatis, novos condere articulos fidei, sed secundum conditos iudicare. Nec potest fidelis christianus cogi ultra sacram scripturam, quae est proprie ius divinum, nisi accesserit nova et probata revelatio. Immo ex iure divino prohibemur credere, nisi quod sit probatum, vel per scripturam divinam vel per manifestam revelationem.*" The background of this idea of justifying new ideas can be seen in Panormitanus's commentary to *Liber Extra*, l. 5, tit. 7, c. 7: "*Papa potest inducere novum articulum fidei declarando illud ius divinum*" (cf. n. 152). My translation.

240. Luther himself refers to Gerson, who bound the *lex divina* to *revelatio* in his *Liber de vita spirituali animae lectio 2 corollarium 5* (Gerson, *Oeuvres*, 3, 135); This is seen even more clearly in the tendency of a possible special revelation for William of Ockham (cf. Leppin, *Ockham*, 248–49).

241. In much the same way, Grane, *Martinus Noster*, 85, maintains with consideration of the Leipzig Disputation: "It would be a misunderstanding to talk about a 'Scripture principle.'" For the significance of Luther's statement, cf. also Spehr, *Konzil*, 149.

242. WA Br 1:467.71–73 (No. 192). "*(. . .)ich hab wohl etwa einen doctorem neben dem Text der Bibel wider einen andern, den Doctor Eck bloßnackt ohn Bibel einführet, gehalten und will mein Lebtag das zu tun nit abstehn.*" My translation.

However, he added:

If I had a clear text, then I would remain with it, even if meant disagreeing with the explanations of the teachers.[243]

In this case, Luther was referring to a statement by Nicholas of Tudeschis, who had argued that an individual could override the opinion of the pope if they had a clear scriptural reference,[244] thus constituting a juxtaposition of Scripture and tradition for certain cases. There were a lot of loose threads in these two statements, and Luther had clearly not yet bound them together in a solid *Sola scriptura* principle. But the fact that Luther is arguing with the first sentence with the prince elector is quite important. The criterium for theologically legitimate statements in Leipzig would be clearer and more decisive than in 1518 and would not be reliant on a secondary "confession" of intent—only those arguments rooted in Scripture could be considered mandatory. Church fathers and proper councils could only serve and affirm them. But they could not be used to understand scriptural arguments. This statement marks a significant departure from Luther's earlier thought as we see portrayed in the *Asterisci* and preserved in Eck's own argumentation during the Leipzig Disputation. With this departure, Luther created a foundation for a difference model in handling Scripture and tradition.

## WIDE-REACHING EFFECTS: MELANCHTHON'S BACCALAUREATE THESES AND THE PRINCIPLE *SOLA SCRIPTURA*

Within about a year, Luther had come a long way indeed. He had begun with a harmony model, which saw the will of Christ expressed equally in Scripture, fathers, and *canones*. Leading up to the Leipzig Disputation, the question of papal primacy and Luther's doubt concerning its age led to the papal *canones* being removed from the network of authorities. Throughout this year, Luther began interpreting Scripture out of Scripture. He would only take the consequences of that to their full extent while under pressure

---

243. WA Br 1:468.113–14 (No. 192). "*Wo ich einen klaren Text hätte, wollt ich dabei bleiben, wann schon der Lehrer Auslegung dawider wäre.*" My translation.

244. Panormitanus, *Commentary on X 1.6.4* ("*Significasti*"): "*nam in concernentibus fidem etiam dictum vnius priuati esset preferendum dicto pape si ille moueretur melioribus et auctoritatibus noui et ueteris testamenti quam Papa*" (Nicolaus de Tudeschis, *Lectura super quinque libros Decretalium. Pars prima super primo decretalium* [Venice, 1477], fol. 80ᵛb, https://www.digitale-sammlungen.de/de/view/bsb00058048?page=162,163); cf. Voigt-Goy, "dictum.'"

from his deft opponent Eck at the Leipzig Disputation. But it is safe to say that he was not inventing anything completely new there, only finding the courage to draw the conclusions of what he had been ruminating on in the previous months. From this point forth, Scripture would constitute the singular source of the church's teachings. Contesting the verdict of Jan Hus in Constance was intimately connected to the question of *ius divinum* but did not actually constitute an active application of the scriptural principle to the church's teachings. Instead, the course of the Disputation had forced Luther into contesting the church's authority for this case, something he did not really want to do. He likely did not forsee the consequences for himself.[245]

This further development was carried out by Philipp Melanchthon and the rest of the Wittenberg community. On September 9, 1519, while disputing his twenty-four theses to acquire the theological baccalaureate,[246] he spoke using material from the Leipzig Disputation: "It is only necessary for a Catholic to believe in those articles testified in Scripture, but not others."[247] That meant critiquing the valid doctrine of the church. For Melanchthon, contesting the Doctrine of Transsubstantiation from 1215 would no longer be considered heretical.[248] There was no going back now: the *Sola scriptura* principle was formulated and established.[249] It had been discovered by Luther during his confrontation with Eck, where the comfortably medieval harmony model of authorities was still assumed. He gradually distanced himself from that harmony model and developed a difference model, which ultimately gave birth to the reformational conviction of *Sola scriptura*.

245. For the great significance of the Leipzig Disputation for the further development of the Reformation, cf. Volker Leppin and Mickey L. Mattox, "The Leipzig Debate: A Reformation Turning Point," in *Luther at Leipzig: Martin Luther, the Leipzig Debate, and the Sixteenth-Century Reformations*, ed. Mickey L. Mattox et al. (Leiden: Brill, 2019), 11–30.
246. Concerning the question of authorship, cf. Wilhelm Maurer, *Der junge Melanchthon zwischen Humanismus und Reformation*, vol. 2 (Göttingen: Vandenhoeck & Ruprecht, 1996), 102.
247. Melanchthons, *Werke*, vol. 1, *Reformatorische Schriften*, ed. Robert Stupperich (Gütersloh: Gütersloher Verlagshaus, 1951), 24.29–30. "*Catholicum prater articulos, quorum testis est scriptura, non est necesse alios credere.*" My translation. For more on this interpretation of the Baccalaureate theses, cf. Kruse, *Universitätstheologie*, 227.
248. Melanchthon, *Werke*, 1:25.1–2.
249. Cf. Maurer, *Melanchthon*, 102–03. Another result of the Leipzig Disputation was the conviction that the pope was the antichrist, at least when his power was explained as Eck did (WA 6:429.33–430.6). Earlier, Luther had believed that the antichrist committed his foul work in Rome but had expressed this only as suspicions in letters (WA Br 1:270.11–13 [No. 121]; 359.28–30 [No. 161]). That Luther had as a goal of the "Disputation [. . .] to reveal the primacy claim of the Roman Bishop as the work of the Antichrist" (Schubert, "Libertas disputandi," 426) is not supported by the sources. My translations.

# 6.

# How Does Luther See Scripture Explaining Scripture? A Look at Luther's Pneumatic Hermeneutics

Ever since Gerhard Ebeling subjected Luther to a thorough study in the middle of the twentieth century,[1] Luther has been increasingly appreciated as a hermeneutical thinker. His special contribution to the history of Christian theology has its ground in an intensive study of Scripture. He made the meaning of Scripture into his own agenda. However, as Wolfhart Pannenberg has diagnosed in his "Crisis of the Scriptural Principle,"[2] modern Protestantism has distanced itself significantly from Luther as concerns scriptural hermeneutics. This new approach to hermeneutics cannot be qualified simply as being modern but rather must be carefully and thoughtfully analyzed in relation to its medieval roots. This chapter will start by examining Luther's programmatic hermeneutic of "self-explaining Scripture" (*scriptura sui ipsius interpres*).

---

1. See especially Gerhard Ebeling, *Evangelische Evangelienauslegung: Eine Untersuchung zu Luthers Hermeneutik* (Munich: Lempp, 1942), as well as his magnificent studies assembled in Ebeling, *Lutherstudien*, vol. 1 (Tübingen: Mohr, 1971).
2. Wolfhart Pannenberg, "The Crisis of the Scripture Principle," in *Basic Questions in Theology: Collected Essays*, vol. 1 (Minneapolis: Fortress Press, 2008), 20–33.

163

# HOW *"SCRIPTURA SUI IPSIUS INTERPRES"* EMERGED: THE QUESTION OF THE INTERPRETER

Luther first writes the phrase *"sui ipsius interpres"* as applied to Scripture in his *"Assertio omnium articulorum."*[3] This establishes a clear context for the emergence of this discovery:[4] The bull *Exsurge Domine* not only condemned a large number of Luther's articles but also, in its own way, addressed the question of hermeneutic. Calling upon the Lord to "rise up" in the title[5] made it clear that Leo X understood himself to be the head of the church with a responsibility to and an authority from God himself. Tucked away in this prayer was an understanding of scriptural exegesis and hermeneutics. After calling upon Christ and Rome's saints Peter and Paul, there was a lengthy supplicatory prayer—held in the subjunctive rather than the imperative (*"Exsurgat"*)—of "the universal church of all saints and others" (*omnis sanctorum ac reliqua universalis ecclesia*).[6] This contained an accusation against those heretics who ignored the *interpretatio* of those saints and instead explain Holy Scripture according to the standards of the Holy Spirit and "their own, self-glorifying, ambitious understanding" (*proprius sensus ambitionis*).[7] The target was obviously Luther, but the implicit hermeneutical statement saw scriptural understanding through the Holy Spirit being carried out in conversation with the saints' history

3. Luther, *Assertio omnium articulorum* (WA 7:97.23); cf., however, the very similar formulation: *"Also ist die schrifft jr selbs ain aigen liecht"* (Luther, *Predigten des Jahres 1522*, WA 10/III:238.10).

4. The horizon of discovery naturally goes back further: the question as to what extent the interpretation of Scripture ought to be based solely in Scripture or dependent on some third resource had occupied Luther's attention since his interrogation from Cajetan in 1518; cf. Luther, *Acta Augustana* (WA 2:17.6–9): *"Et qui tam vigilanter Extravagantem contra me observarat, satis pulchre dissimulabat Canonem illum, quo prohibet Ecclesia, ne quis proprio ingenio scripturas interpretetur, et iuxta Hilarium non afferendas sed referendas esse ex sacris literis intelligentias."* (And while he so readily used the *Extravagante* against me, he cleverly pretended not to know that canon on the basis of which the church prohibits anyone from interpreting the Scriptures solely on his own authority. According to Hilary, one should not read a meaning into the Holy Scriptures, but extract it from them.) Cited after LW 31:276; for more, cf. Richard P. Bucher, *The Ecumenical Luther. The Development of His Doctrinal Hermenutic* (Saint Louis: Concordia Publishing House, 2003), 45.

5. Leo X, *Exsurge Domine*, encyclical letter, June 15, 1520, DCL 2:364.

6. Leo X, *Exsurge Domine*, DCL 2:366. My translation. The forms of *exsurgere* written here without "s".

7. Leo X, *Exsurge Domine*, DCL 2:366. In his impressive attempt to explain the formulation "sui ipsius interpres" within the context of the *Assertio*, Walter Mostert, "Scriptura sacra sui ipsius interpres. Bemerkungen zum Verständnis der Heiligen Schrift durch Luther," *Lutherjahrbuch* 46 (1979): 60–96, 62–63 neglects precisely this context of the text, which brings into consideration that rejecting the *propria* cannot be considered a genuine expression of Martin Luther's hermeneutics.

of exegesis. Luther was portrayed as a lone spirit who positioned himself against the overwhelming tradition of interpretation constituted in the communion of saints.

Luther protested against exactly this in his *Assertio*, which he probably wrote on commission from the Prince Elector of Saxony.[8] The first folio of this text had been printed as early as the beginning of December,[9] and the entire text had been printed by January 16, 1521 at the latest, for it was on this date that Luther sent the text to Spalatin "now complete."[10] Within the context of reformational history, this meant that Martin Luther knew while writing this text that the sixty-day grace period within the bull had passed.[11] He now faced the very real risk of excommunication. Of course, he had burned the bull upon receiving it, so it was clear that he was not going to allow his opinion to be changed.[12] Luther had likely not even heard of his own excommunication (which took place on January 3, 1521), so his answer was not an effort to stave off excommunication but rather to justify his own position within the distance to the pope. Of course, we must assume that the prince elector's court was thrumming with interest for arguments to bring to the coming audition at the Imperial Diet (which the prince elector had arranged personally).[13] This makes the text extremely complex when evaluating its effect on Luther's trial. Legally speaking, showing up at the Imperial Diet with an exposition of the *Causa Lutheri* likely would not have led to his being classifed as holding the true faith in the sense of the "legal question" (*quaestio iuris*). The Diet was not interested in that anyway. The "question of the factual events" (*quaestio facti*) was definitely interested in finding out if Luther had actually said what he was accused of saying. The title of Luther's *Assertio* ought to have answered the question for everyone, and he was compromising his legal position enormously. He may not have actually been aware of this as he still hoped to establish his orthodoxy in the form of a disputation in the Diet of Worms.

8. Cf. Luther to Spalatin, November 29, 1520: "*Articulos singulos damnatos a Bulla mox aggrediens suscipio defendendos singulos, sicut scripsisti, et a me peti intelligo.*" (WA Br 2, 220 [No. 355, 5–6]).
9. This can be deduced from the fact that Luther wrote to Spalatin on December 7, 1520, that he could no longer remove the dedication of the text to the recently deceased Fabian of Felitzsch since the text had been printed "*ea parte*" (Luther to Spalatin, December 7, 1520 [WA Br 2:229 [No. 359.7–8]]).
10. Luther to Spalatin, January 16, 1521 (WA Br 2:249 [No. 368.9]).
11. Leo X, *Exsurge Domine*, DCL 2:398. 400.
12. For more, cf. Leppin, *A Late Medieval Life*, 50.
13. For more, cf. Armin Kohnle, *Reichstag und Reformation. Kaiserliche und ständische Religionspolitik von den Anfängen der Causa Lutheri bis zum Nürnberger Religionsfrieden* (Gütersloh: Gütersloher Verlagshaus, 2001), 90–95.

Thus, we must consider the legal horizon when interpreting certain statements within the *Assertio*. But regardless, the preface to the text lays the groundwork for a unique hermeneutic. Luther interpreted the damnation of scriptural explanation according to *"proprius sensus ambitionis"* in the sense of a general canonical rule, according to which "Holy Scriptures are not to be interpreted according to one's own understanding."[14] Reinhard Schwarz has plausibly assumed that Luther is referring to C. 24 q. 3 c. 27, which uses a formulation from Jerome to define a heretic as someone whose approach to Scripture is described as follows: "He interprets Scripture differently than how the understanding of the Holy Spirit requires."[15] This had the effect of focusing the question on the matter of how the Holy Spirit actually works during the explanation of Scripture. The bull believed, of course, that ecclesial consensus was necessary. But now there were other options in the room, although they still needed to be determined.

For his part, Luther explained the ban bull as demanding him "to follow and believe the commentary of humans while neglecting the Holy Scriptures."[16] Where the bull assumed an interlock between Scripture and interpretation, Luther described a (rather fanciful) juxtaposition in the sense that the commentaries were being used instead of Scripture itself. While this was certainly polemical, it makes it clear that Luther's main point was a rather simple one: one should not begin the process of scriptural explanation with the typical medieval approach of immediately applying the *Glossa ordinaria*. This is actually the first and very simple answer to the question of how one is to lay out Scripture using Scripture—look at Scripture first and leave everything else out to begin with. To state it in Luther's words, by "neglecting the Holy Scriptures."[17] As Albrecht Beutel has aptly summarized, "the principle upon which Luther sees biblical

14. Luther, *Assertio*, WA 7:96.10–11: *"Non esse scripturas sanctas proprio spiritu interpretandas."* My translation.

15. CICan 1:998: *"aliter (. . .) intelligit quam sensus Spiritus sancti flagitat."* My translation; treated by Luther in his commentary on Galatians from 1519 in WA 2:590.29–31; cf. Reinhard Schwarz, *Martin Luther: Lehrer der christlichen Religion* (Tübingen: Mohr, 2015), 34 n. 32; Martin Ohst, "Luthers 'Schriftprinzip,'" in *Luther als Schriftausleger: Luthers Schriftprinzip in seiner Bedeutung für die Ökumene*, ed. Hans Christian Knuth (Erlangen: Martin-Luther-Verlag, 2010), 21–39, 21–22.

16. Luther, *Assertio* (WA 7:96.36–37): *"ut sepositis sacris literis intendamus et credamus hominum commentariis."* My translation. The juxtaposition of Scripture and commentaries indicates that Luther was approaching the hermeneutic much more fundamentally with his *sui ipsius interpres* formulation than merely attacking the fourfold sense of Scripture; fore more on the debate surrounding this, especially with Emser, cf. Randall C. Gleason, "'Letter' and 'Spirit' in Luther's Hermeneutics," *Bibliotheca Sacra* 157 (2000): 468–85.

17. Luther, *Assertio* (WA 7:97.5).

hermeneutics being founded [means] that the interpreter is given the task of giving the self-explanation of Scripture an unimpeded space to unfold and therefore to allow one's own spirit with its tendency of commenting on Scripture *proprio spiritu* to be overcome by the spirit of Scripture."[18]

Luther contrasts the practice of drawing on other commentaries with the observation that Scripture is "completely certain from itself, easily understood, entirely open, provider of its own explanation, proof for all things, judging and illuminating."[19] As concerns the contrast to the commentaries, the decisive phrase here is "from itself" (*per sese*). Luther insists that any and all stroke of insight concerning Scripture must and will come from Scripture itself. He referred to Psalms 119 (Vulgate 118):130: "The explanation, or, as the Hebrew properly reads: The unfolding of your words gives light; it imparts understanding to the simple"[20] to justify this power of *illuminatio*.

Exegesis can *understand* plausibility of this self-confiding power of Scripture, but that does not mean that it *attains* the self-confidence of Scripture. Much in the spirit of Jerome, Luther provides a pnematological-hermeneutic ground for that—Scripture can only be understood through the Holy Spirit, "spirit cannot be found anywhere more present and alive than those very Holy Scriptures which he wrote."[21] The Spirit is therefore the sponsor of—and in a strict sense, the author—of the Holy Scriptures,[22] and it is through this that the Holy Spirit is present and alive. In fact, the Holy Spirit is even more present and alive than anywhere else. The phrase "those very Holy Scriptures which he wrote" makes clear that we have to


18. Albrecht Beutel, "Erfahrene Bibel: Verständnis und Gebrauch des verbum dei scriptum bei Luther," in *Protestantische Konkretionen: Studien zur Kirchengeschichte* (Tübingen: Mohr 1998), 66–103, 79. My translation.
19. Luther, *Assertio* (WA 7:97.23–24): "*per sese certissima, facillima, apertissima, sui ipsius interpres, omnium omnia probans, iudicans et illuminans.*" My translation.
20. Luther, *Assertio* (WA 7:97): "*Declaratio seu, ut hebraeus proprie habet, Apertum seu ostium verborum tuorum illuminat et intellectum dat parvulis.*" My translation.
21. Luther, *Assertio* (WA 7:97.2–3): "*qui spiritus nusquam praesentius et vivacius quam in ipsis sacris suis, quas scripsit, literis inveniri potest.*" My translation. For more on the hermeneutical effect of the Holy Spirit, cf. Luther, *Crucigers Sommerpostille*: "Darumb ist die Schrifft ein solch Buch, dazu gehret nicht allein lesen und predigen, sondern auch der rechte Ausleger, nemlich die offenbarung des Heiligen Geistes" (WA 21:230.21–23); cf. Volker Stolle, "Gottes Name und Gottes Wort: Anstöße Luthers zu einer theologischen Hermeneutik," *Lutherische Theologie und Kirche* 33 (2009): 33–68, 40. Stolle brings his interpretation (which, incidentally, has broad parallels with the above material) of Luther's hermeneutics to this formulation: "The sanctified and sanctifying reader and interpreter of Holy Scripture" (Stolle, "Gottes Name," 53).
22. Cf. Stolle, "Gottes Name," 58: "The Holy Spirit is not only the primary author of Scripture (which is why Scripture can be called Holy), but also simultaneously the primary interpreter and communicator of Scripture (which is why its recipients can be called holy)." My translation.

do with a special form of authorship where the author gives himself into the texts he creates. Accordingly, the *spiritus scripturae* can only be found in Scripture itself.[23] Thus, Luther's own pneumatology takes on a moment very heavy in the theology of Scripture. He pits this new scriptural pneumatology against the ecclesiological pneumatology in the ban bull. He incorporates the ecclesiological dimension by emphasizing that the *spiritus fidei* that rules in the church is necessarily the same throughout all time, including in the *ecclesia primitiva*, in which there were no commentaries from the likes of Augustine or Aquinas.[24] Put another way, if the church had managed to interpret Scripture before tradition, then the church in later times must be able to operate with the same degree of certainty, simplicity, openness, and self-understandability as back then. Of course, other approaches are not to be excluded, but Scripture remains the *primum principum* as concerns the first principle and the "judgment over all words" (*omnium verborum iudicum*) for its application.[25] Luther reads the position of the ban bull as if it were to claim that other instances—commentators, fathers, scholastics—had the responsibility to pass a verdict on Scripture. He wants to turn this situation on its head. Only the *verba divina* could be the *prima principia* for Christians, but human words could only be understood as *conclusiones* derived from them. Such human statements must be derived from Scripture and be proven by them.[26]

This approach has not yet departed from the dominant framework of the Middle Ages. We see this with Thomas Aquinas when he describes four distinct theological authorities: Scripture, Holy Doctrine, human arguments, and philosophical authorities. Only those arguments derived from Scripture are granted the attributes proper (*proprius*) and necessary (*necessarius*). Holy Doctrine is assumed to be proper but only is allowed the status of probability. The other two have an even weaker status.[27] The difference between these two positions is constituted not by the priority of Scripture but rather Luther's heavy emphasis on pneumatological hermeneutics, which must have looked pretty individualistic from the viewpont

---

23. Luther, *Assertio* (WA 7:97.8–9); nevertheless, God naturally remains fundamentally distinct from Scripture: "*Duae res sunt Deus et Scriptura Dei, non minus quam duae res sunt, Creator et creatura Dei*" (WA 18:606.11–12) (God and the Scripture of God are two things, no less than the Creator and the creature are two things.) Translation after LW 33:25; cf. Stolle, "Gottes Name," 40.
24. Luther, *Assertio* (WA 7:97.16–19).
25. Luther, *Assertio* (WA 7:97.31–32). My translation.
26. Luther, *Assertio* (WA 7:98.4–5).
27. Aquinas, *Summa I q. 1 a. 8 ad 2* (*Editio Leonina* 4:23); cf. Hermann Schüssler, *Der Primat der Heiligen Schrift als theologisches und kanonistisches Problem im Spätmittelalter* (Wiesbaden: Zabern, 1977), 275.

of his opponents who had a long tradition of coupling pneumatology with the church; anyone in the sixteenth century who believed they understood Scripture in the same way as those in the first centuries had a fundamental problem with the church and its historical development. This viewpoint was onto something: for Luther, trusting in the hermeneutical competence of the church for understanding Scripture would mean trusting in human competencies and powers, not the spirit.

## AMBIVALENCE IN LUTHER'S ARGUMENTATION

The context of Luther's discovery of the formulation *scriptura sui ipsius interpres* makes it clear that the main thrust of Luther's argumentation was the rejection of exclusive papal competence in explaining Scripture. Starting with the Leipzig Disputation, the point of scriptural explanation becomes a central moment of his argument that the pope is the antichrist.[28] In his treatise *To the Christian Nobility of the German Nation*, he attacked papal supremecy in exegesis as being one of the walls behind which the pope hid in the face of Luther's critique: if you pushed the pope with Scripture, the pope would claim that you did not have the authority to explain Scripture.[29] As the question of interpretive competencies started to heat up, *Exsurge Domine* must have seemed like a stark confirmation of what everyone suspected or firmly believed. And the pope *did* do exactly what Luther had accused him of: he rejected Scripture as an argumentative basis for critiquing papal teaching and action. Strictly speaking, he did not actually insist on his own interpretive authority but rather on the communion of the church throughout the centuries.

But Luther saw every single one of these attempted proofs as unbiblical. As we have seen in the previous chapter, Luther developed a difference model for scriptural hermeneutics that rejected human interpretation, including that of the Roman harmony model, with its reliance on patristic and ecclesial interpretive history.[30] Luther saw the danger of an argument to the point of absurdity: if you are supposed to listen to the popes and the teachers, then you may as well skip Scripture altogether. Since the pope and the teachers trusted the Scholastics, then you may as well just listen to them. If you followed this chain of reasoning further, you ended

---

28. Cf. Volker Leppin, *Transformationen: Studien zu den Wandlungsprozessen in Theologie und Frömmigkeit zwischen Spätmittelalter und Reformation*, 2nd ed. (Tübingen: Mohr Siebeck, 2018), 473.
29. Luther, *An den christlichen Adel* (WA 6:411.8–9, 33–36).
30. For more on the juxtaposition of these two models, cf. in this volume p. 119.

up just listening to Aristotle.[31] These are hot polemics, but they do give us an insight into Luther's general development as a theologian. He had begun with questioning the dominance of Aristotle in theology[32] and had then expanded his scope of confrontations to other areas of spirituality and church. Understanding Scripture as explanation through Scripture seems to be the stringent application of this very line of reasoning.

The front against the church fathers appears secondary to that against the pope and the Scholastics.[33] Besides the argument of a basic bond between Spirit and Scripture, Luther argues against following the fathers because they contradict each other and affected the integrity of Scripture.[34] Once again, we see a polemical rhetoric in the last point. But the frustration with incoherence among the fathers was general to the Middle Ages. Peter Abelard made something of a hermeneutical principle out of this with his "*Sic et non*," but Luther likely did not know of it.[35] But that notwithstanding, the contradiction and plurality of the fathers in the Middle Ages was such a hot topic that John Altenstaig dedicated a reflection to it in his 1517 *Vocabularius*. Under the keyword "*opinio*," he questioned, "Que autem opinio est magis sequenda quando discordant doctores?"[36] ("Which opinion should be followed more strongly when the doctors disagree?"). Altenstaig found an answer for himself in the decision of the pope.[37] But the question shows that Luther's insight was by no means new. In fact, Altenstaig's consideration may have even provided Luther with a confirmation of his dreaded papal centering in doctrinal authority beyond the Bible. In any case, this is an indication that the argument against the fathers was not his invention but was a common one.

31. Luther, *Assertio* (WA 7:100.27–33).
32. Leppin, *A Late Medieval Life*, 28–29.
33. And yet, it appears to Taras Khomych that Luther's scepticism toward the church fathers undergoes a further development with the *Assertio*. However, this should not be seen as a sudden break in Luther's attitude but the culmination of a lengthy and nuanced development reflection on the part of Luther concerning the question of legitimate authority in theology. Taras Khomych, "Luther's Assertio: A Prelimary Assessment of the Reformer's Relationship to Patristics," *Annali di storia dell'esegesi* 28 (2011): 351–63, 356; cf. the various studies in *Reformatorische Theologie und Autoritäten. Studien zur Geschichte des Schriftprinzips beim jungen Luther*, ed. Volker Leppin (Tübingen: Mohr, 2015).
34. Luther, *Assertio* (WA 7:98.27–32).
35. The first publication of this work only took place in the nineteenth century: *Ouvrages inédits d'Abélard*, ed. Victor Cousin (Paris: Impr. Royale, 1836).
36. Johann Altenstaig, *Vocabularius Theologie com- | plectens vocabulorum descriptiones / diffinitiones et significa| tus ad theologiam vtilium (. . .) magno cum labore et diligentia | compilata a Joanne Altenstaig Min|delhaimensi / sacre scriptu-|re vero ama-|tore* (Hagenau: 1517), fol. 169ᵛa; cf. Schüssler, *Primat*, 276.
37. Altenstaig, *Vocabularius Theologie*.

And yet, his focus was certainly not placed on destroying the fathers. He continued to refer to them positively, seeing excellent role models in how to conduct theology by using Holy Scripture.[38] Their method spoke directly against papal claims to authority. Luther could refer to a citation from a letter from Augustine to Jerome that expressly treated this matter. It was adopted into the *Corpus Iuris Canonici* D. 9 c. 5:

> I have learned to honor only those books which are called canonical because I believe firmly that none of their authors have erred. I read the others, however, notwithstanding their holiness and doctrine, such that I do not consider them to be true because they have any particular opinion, but only if they can convince me through the canonical Scriptures or probable rational argumentation.[39]

Luther drew on this citation as early as his defense against Prierias.[40] He drew on it once again to demonstrate to the pope that both canonical law and the fathers stood on his side. Luther contended with tradition for the absolute priority of Scripture, including its self-interpretation. Indeed, most of tradition did stand on his side—but his specific development was the pneumatic hermeneutic.

## SPIRITUAL EXPLANATION OF SCRIPTURE

With these considerations, it becomes clear that self-explaining/self-confiding Scripture has the essential function of shaping and emphasizing the Reformation's developing scriptural principle. But we have not actually confronted the question of how this self-explanation actually takes place. The negative aspect and the clear hierarchy of authorities are both evident. Scripture is to be explained on its own terms; if commentaries are used, then they should be used in a late stage and in such a fashion that their arguments can be easily discerned as derivate from those of Scripture. But the real question is how an interpreter can explain the independently standing Holy Scriptures such that the present and living Holy Spirit comes into effect. Put differently, the question of *Exsurge Domine* becomes quite

<hr>

38. Luther, *Assertio* (**WA** 7:98.7–10).
39. Luther, *Assertio* (**WA** 7:99.5–10): "*Ego solis eis libris, qui canonici dicuntur, eum deferre honorem didici, ut nullum eorum scriptorem errasse firmiter credam, caeteros vero, quantalibet sanctitate doctrinaque praepolleant, ita lego, ut non ideo verum credam, quia ipsi sic senserunt, sed si per Canonicas scripturas aut ratione probabili mihi persuadere potuerunt.*" My translation. Cf. CICan 1:17; the citation is found in *Epistola* 82 from Augustine to Jerome (CSEL 6:354).
40. Luther, *Ad dialogum Silvestri Prierati* (**WA** 1:647.22–24).

relevant at this stage, even though it has a somewhat different profile. Can an individual actually shut off their own *spiritus* and replace it with the divine when interpreting Scripture without being embedded in the church's tradition? Both sides actually accused the other of the same thing, with Luther accusing the pope of bringing human opinions into play when he referred to the fathers,[41] and the pope accusing Luther of bringing his own individual human side into play when interpreting Scripture. Both sides were concerned with securing the authority of the Holy Spirit and its connection to Holy Scripture. The question was how this actually takes place. *Exsurge Domine* had a clear answer: a secure, reliable connection could be established in the ancient interpretive community of the church as could be seen in the fathers and the church's approbations.

Luther thus had the task of describing a pneumatically adequate interpretation without needing the church's resources. We see the beginnings of this in the *Assertio* with his reference to Mary who, according to Luke 2:19, "pondered" all these words "in her heart."[42]

Luther had a good platform to explain his new understanding of theology, including his scriptural hermeneutics, in his 1539 edition of his German texts. This came nearly two decades after he wrote the *Assertio*[43] and, if we follow the very plausible suspicion of Marcel Niedens, was not only targeted toward professional theologians but "perhaps even all literate Christians."[44] However, so many formulations and questions pertain to the debates from 1520 to 1521 that it would be a methodical error to bring Luther's explanatory statements of the theology of the *Assertio* from this later standpoint into consideration. These explanations can only be considered a continuation of his earlier thought.[45]

---

41. Luther, *Assertio* (WA 7:100.14–15): "*Sint sancti viri et Ecclesiarum patres, sed homines et Apostolis atque prophetis impares.*"
42. Luther, *Assertio* (WA 7:99.21–22).
43. Martin Nicol, *Meditation bei Luther*, 2nd ed. (Göttingen: Vandenhoeck & Ruprecht, 1991), 98 rightly demonstrates with a plethora of references that this understanding of theology was a development that started early with Luther.
44. Marcel Nieden, "Anfechtung als Thema lutherischer Anweisungsschriften zum Theologiestudium," in *Praxis Pietatis: Beiträge zu Theologie und Frömmigkeit in der Frühen Neuzeit: FS Wolfgang Sommer*, ed. Hans-Jörg and Marcel Nieden (Stuttgart: Kohlhammer, 1999), 83–102, 84.
45. An extensive study, which we cannot undertake here, would establish intermediate stages, such as the statement concerning pneumatically guided hermeneutics in Luther, *Crucigers Sommerpostille*: "*Aber zu solcher offenbarung gehoeren auch rechte Schüler, die sich gerne leren und weisen lassen (wie diese frome einfeltige Juenger), nicht Klüglinge und eigensinnige Geister seien und Selbsgewachsene Meister, die da mit jrer klugheit weit uber den Himel reichen, Denn es ist auch ein solche lere, die da wil unser Weisheit zur Nerrin machen und der Vernunfft die Augen ausstechen, wo sie anders sol gegleubt und verstanden werden, Denn sie kompt auch nicht aus Menschen weisheit*

This is also true for Luther's new reflections on the relation between fathers and Scripture. Towards the beginning of the preface, he gave the following explanation in the sense of a *captatio benevolentiae* that emphasized his own missing righteousness:

> Although it has been profitable and necessary that the writings of some church fathers and councils have remained, as witnesses and histories, nevertheless I think, "*Est modus in rebus*," and we need not regret that the books of many fathers and councils have, by God's grace, disappeared. If they had all remained in existence, no room would be left for anything but books; and yet all of them together would not have improved on what one finds in the Holy Scriptures.[46]

He used the following lines to describe his understanding of theology with a "nearly canonical"[47] tripole of *oratio, meditatio,* and *tentatio*. The singular basis of all theology is an individual's occupation with "studying and reading of the Scriptures" (*des studirens und lesens in der Schrifft*).[48] Everything else should point to Scripture alone. Much as in the *Assertio*, Luther justified this with Augustine's writing to Jerome (cited above),[49] further evidence that he was thinking still in much the same manner as earlier. It becomes clear that the psalm Luther uses to justify the "correct way of studying theology" (*rechte weise in der Theologia zu studirn*)[50] is the

---

wie ander lere und Kûnst auff Erden, so aus der Vernunfft geflossen und die men weder darein fassen kan" (WA 21:230.29–37).

46. Luther, *Vorrede deutsche Werke* (WA 50:657.12–17): "*Und wiewol es nuetzlich und notig ist, das etlicher Veter und Concilien schrifft blieben sind als Zeugen und Historien, So dencke ich doch: Est modus in rebus, und sey nicht schade, das vieler Veter und Concilien buecher durch Gottes Gnade sind untergangen. Denn wo sie alle hetten sollen bleiben, solte wol niemand weder ein noch ausgehen koennen fur den Buechern, und wuerdens doch nicht besser gamacht haben, denn mans in der heiligen Schrifft findet.*" Cited after LW 34:283: "Preface to the Wittenberg Edition of Luther's German Writings."

47. Marcel Nieden, *Die Erfindung des Theologen: Wittenberger Anweisungen zum Theologiestudium im Zeitalter von Reformation und Konfessionalisierung* (Tübingen: Mohr 2006), 81.

48. Luther, *Vorrede deutsche Werke* (WA 50:657.20). Cited after LW 34:248.

49. Luther, *Vorrede deutsche Werke* (WA 50:658.21–24). Luther does not cite Augustine word for word but he is clearly intending him: "*Und folge hierin dem Exempel S. Augustin, der unter andern der erst und fast allein ist, der von aller Veter und Heiligen Buecher will ungefangen allein der heiligen Schrifft unterworffen sein, Und daruber kam in einen harten straus mit S. Hieronymo, der jm furwarff seiner Vorfaren buecher.*" (Herein I follow the example of St. Augustine, who was, among other things, the first and almost the only one who determined to be subject to the Holy Scriptures alone, and independent of the books of all the fathers and saints. On account of that he got into a fierce fight with St. Jerome, who reproached him by pointing to the books of his forefathers.) Cited after LW 34:285.

50. Luther, *Vorrede deutsche Werke* (WA 50:658.29). Cited after LW 34:285.

very psalm to which Luther had referred to in the *Assertio*: Psalm 119.[51] The reformer wants to develop the steps of theological study from what he considers to be David's words.

The first step is *oratio*, praying to God that he would grant instruction and guidance. This is how a person assures themself that they are not turning reason into their doctrinal authority.[52] This is the decisive step in order to prevent a person from mixing their own content into the explanation of Scripture.

The second step is *meditatio*. Again, we see the connection to the statements in the *Assertio* and the fact that the word moves the heart. Luther goes quite far with this:

> Secondly, you should meditate, that is, not only in your heart, but also externally, by actually repeating and comparing oral speech and literal words of the book, reading and rereading them with diligent attention and reflection, so that you may see what the Holy Spirit means by them.[53]

Meditation thus has the character of a continuous back-and-forth motion in conscious life. This is similar language to the Wartburg Postille, where Luther speaks of comparing the words "against each other and against Scripture." Luther thus emphasizes that this has to do with a lengthy process that does not immediately lead to some imagined goal.[54] Meditation is characterized by its lengthy nature and thus to a maturation of insight.

Finally, studying the Bible leads to the situation of *tentatio*, temptation, "which teaches you not only to know and understand, but also to experience how right, how true, how sweet, how lovely, how mighty, how comforting God's Word is, wisdom beyond all wisdom."[55]

---

51. Luther, *Vorrede deutsche Werke* (WA 50:659.3). Ps 119 could have played a significant role in the transformation of the medieval framework (cf. Nieden, *Erfindung*, 82–83; Oswald Bayer, "Oratio, Meditatio, Tentatio: Eine Besinnung auf Luthers Theologieverständnis," in *Lutherjahrbuch* 55 (1988): 7–59, 18–22).

52. Luther, *Vorrede deutsche Werke* (WA 50:659.13–21). Accordingly, Oswald Bayer, *Martin Luther's Theology: A Contemporary Interpretation* (Grand Rapids: Eerdmans, 2008), 17 can emphasize while referring to WA TR 3:312.11–13 (No. 3425) that the *gratia spiritus* stands at the beginning of the process of scriptural explanation.

53. Luther, *Vorrede deutsche Werke* (WA 50:659.22–25): "*Zum andern soltu meditirn, das ist: Nicht allein im hertzen, sondern auch eusserlich die muendliche rede und buchstabische wort im Buch jmer treiben und reiben lesen und widerlesen, mit vleissigem auffmercken und nachdencken, was der heilige Geist damit meinet.*" Cited after LW 34:286; for more on this "definition" of meditation, cf. Nicol, *Meditation*, 62.

54. Luther, *Vorrede deutsche Werke* (WA 50:659.25–29).

55. Luther, *Vorrede deutsche Werke* (WA 50:660.1–4): "*die leret dich nicht allein wissen und verstehen, sondern auch erfaren, wie recht, wie warhafftig, wie suesse, wie lieblich, wie mechtig, wie troestlich*

As Martin Nicol has emphasized,[56] this most intense step[57] of the encounter with Holy Scripture indicates the spiritual background of the early Luther's occupation with mysticism. In the *Operationes in Psalmos*, Luther designated Tauler as an *expertus* who had experienced much *tribulatio* and demonstrates that God does not encounter his children anywhere more graciously, lovingly, sweetly, and in more trust as after the trial of tribulation."[58] In fact, temptation *is* a central concept for John Tauler's theology[59] and became essential for Luther's as well. Luther's description of theological steps demonstrates an intense transformation of his mystical-monastic formation from his early years. We see this in his three steps. These steps strongly remind us of *lectio, meditatio, oratio,* and *contemplatio,* which had been developed with special zeal in the *Scala claustralium* by Guigo (II) the twelfth century Carthusian.[60] For him, these four branches constitute the monk living in solitude, "through which they are elevated from earth to heaven."[61] However, Luther made a significant change to

*Gottes wort sey, weisheit uber alle weisheit.*" Cited after LW 34:287; for a thorough introduction to the significance of temptation for Luther's theology, cf. Michael Weinrich, "Die Anfechtung des Glaubens. Die Spannung zwischen Gewißheit und Erfahrung bei Martin Luther," in *Jesus Christus als die Mitte der Schrift: Studien zur Hermeneutik des Evangeliums,* ed. Christof Landmesser, Hans-Joachim Eckstein, and Hermann Lichtenberger (Berlin: De Gruyter, 1997), 127–58, 134–40; cf. especially Luther, *Auslegung des 118. Psalms* (WA 31/1:95.10–15): "*Sonst lerneten wir nimer mehr nicht, was glaube, Wort, geist, gnade, sunde, tod odder teufel were, wo es ymer friede, vnd on anfechtung solte zugehen, damit wurden wir denn Gott selbs nimer mehr kennen lernen, kurtz vmb, wir wurden nimer mehr rechte | Christen, kundten auch nicht Christen bleiben, Not vnd angst zwingt vns da zu vnd behellt vns fein ym Christenthum*" (cf. Weinrich, "Die Anfechtung des Glaubens," 147).

56. Nicol, *Meditation,* 95.
57. For a comparison of the medieval *contemplatio* in a paradigm of meditation, cf. Nicol, *Meditation,* 92.
58. Luther, *Operationes in Psalmos* (WA 2:17–20): "*deum suis filiis non esse unquam gratiorem, amabiliorem et dulciorem ac familiariorem quam post tribulationis probationem.*" My translation. Cf. also Luther, *Adventspostille*: "*Wer aber diße leutt sind, kan ich noch nit sagen, es were denn, das es die seyn sollten, die mit der hohen anfechtung des todts und der hellen tzu schaffen haben, da der Taulerus von schreybt, denn dieselbige anfechtung vortzehret fleysch und blut, ia marck und beyn, und ist der todt selbs, das sie niemant ertragen kan, er werde denn wunderbarlich erhalten*" (WA 10/1/2:105.26–106.1); cf. for more on the *Operationes* passage Thorsten Dietz, *Der Begriff der Furcht bei Martin Luther* (Tübingen: Mohr, 2009), 148.
59. Dietz, *Furcht,* 149–53. A thorough study on this is provided by the dissertation from Bernd Moeller, "Die Anfechtung bei Johann Tauler" (Diss., typewritten manuscript, Universität Mainz, 1956). However, it is discernably influenced by reformational viewpoints, such as when it is claimed of Tauler's critique of works: "But if we follow such expressions to their root, then it becomes evident that the good works are not condemned per se but rather the improper attitude of the person to them" (15), and at the end, when compared with Luther, the negative dogmatic conclusion is drawn: "It appears to me that his understanding of overcoming temptation is ultimately orthodox Catholic" (72). My translations.
60. Guigo, *Scala claustralium* (PL 184:475–84). My translation; cf. Nicol, *Meditation,* 19.
61. Guigo, *Scala claustralium* (PL 184:475C): "*qua de terra in coelum sublevantur.*"

this paradigm: by placing prayer at the beginning, he made clear that the process was not human motion and achievement toward heaven. Rather, it necessarily had its origin in God's succour.[62] As he makes clear in the *Assertio* with a phrase borrowed from Psalms 119:105, God's *illuminatio* is necessary for the word to permeate through the person. It is also characteristic that Luther does not see the culmination of this process in *contemplatio*.[63] Encountering God does not reach fulfillment in a direct adoration of God. It reaches it in Scripture itself. Therefore, *lectio* is not just one step among many but the central basic activity with a strong concentration in *meditatio*.[64]

This is the thorough development of Luther's early claim that the Spirit is present and alive in Scripture. As the soul draws ever deeper in prayer, meditation, and temptation, it encounters the Spirit in Scripture. In his later years, Luther developed his pneumatic hermeneutics much more strongly than he did in his early transformation of monastic and, in a narrow sense, mystical tradition. His early formation with medieval mysticism[65] lets us assume that he was moved by the mystical tradition as he separated himself from papal and scholastic interpretation. But the development reaches its zenith in the preface to his German works. Here, he does not diminish his proximity to mysticism and to monastic praxis, he underlines it. The authorities he uses and the examples of the *scriptura sui ipsius interpres* from the *Assertio* also make clear that what the late Luther was describing was essentially the same thing as what the young Luther described as the self-explanation of Holy Scripture. When these are brought together, we see that the faithful person is given a methodically consistent path for spiritual fulfillment. The central element of this method is the direction toward God through commandments and an experiential dimension that Luther understands as a "Pruefestein" (touchstone).[66] "Not only to know and understand, but also to experience" is the goal of pneumatic scriptural exegesis.[67] The full discovery of the Holy Spirit in Scripture only occurs in the faithful, existential application of Scripture to one's life. This is the ultimate sense of Luther's famous formulation

---

62. Cf. Nieden, "Anfechtung," 85.
63. Cf. Nieden, "Anfechtung," 86.
64. Cf. Nicol, *Meditation*, 91.
65. For a more comprehensive study, see Volker Leppin, *Die fremde Reformation: Luthers mystische Wurzeln*, 2nd ed. (Munich: Beck, 2017).
66. Luther, *Vorrede deutsche Werke* (WA 50:660.1).
67. Luther, *Vorrede deutsche Werke* (WA 50:660.2): "*nicht allein wissen und verstehen, sondern auch erfaren.*" Translation after LW 34:287; cf. Bayer, "Oratio, Meditatio, Tentatio," 52–53.

from the table talk, delivered to us by Veit Dietrich: "Yet experience alone makes the theologian."[68]

## THE EDUCATED COMMUNICATING COMMUNITY: LUTHER'S PROTECTION OF PNEUMATIC HERMENEUTICS AGAINST SUBJECTIVISM

Today, we must remind ourselves continuously of a well-known fact: Luther's fundamental hermeneutic should not be compared directly with the Enlightenment's historical-critical exegesis. A thinker such as Erasmus of Rotterdam, who was deeply committed to the early church, has much more in common with Enlightenment exegesis than did Wittenberg's Reformer.[69]

Luther's pneumatic exegesis has a deeply existential component missing in an objectivity-focused, scholarly approach to the Old and New Testaments. However, this does not mean that Luther's scriptural explanation can be written off as mere subjectivity, even though *Exsurge Domine* accused him of precisely that. Luther secured his pneumatic hermeneutics against this in various ways.[70] Perhaps the most important is that the interpreting subject must always stand in an ecclesial community of communication, which is why Oswald Bayer can speak of an "ecclesiological understanding of theology."[71] Thus, it is interesting to see how Luther takes the idea of the words stirring Mary's heart (see above) and develops them even further about a year after the *Assertio*. In the Wartburgpostille, he explains the good news of Christmas with this very passage and explains in all clarity:

> The Christian Church contains all of God's Word in its hearts and weighs them, measures them against each other and against Scripture. Therefore

58. WA TR 1:16.13 (No. 46): *"Sola autem experientia facit theologum."* Cited after LW 54:7; for more on the significance of *experientia* for Luther's understanding of theology, cf. Bayer, *Martin Luther's Theology*, 21–22, 37; Gerhard Ebeling, "Lehre und Leben in Luthers Theologie," in *Lutherstudien*, vol. 3 (Tübingen: Mohr, 1985), 3–43, 27.

69. Cf. Peter Walter, *Theologie aus dem Geist der Rhetorik: Zur Schriftauslegung des Erasmus von Rotterdam* (Mainz: Matthias-Grünewald-Verlag, 1991). It is an interesting idea that Peter Neuner and Friedrich Schröger, "Luthers These von der Klarheit der Schrift," *Theologie und Glaube* 74 (1984): 39–58, 42 understand Luther's *sui ipsius interpres* to be an expression of a humanistic attitude, regardless of the later conflict between Luther and Erasmus.

70. Scott H. Hendrix, "Luther against the Background of the History of Biblical Interpretation," *Interpretation* 37 (1983): 229–39, 236, has emphasized this basic interdependence of scholarly analysis of the biblical text and a spiritual appropriation.

71. Bayer, "Oratio, Meditatio, Tentatio," 58–59.

whoever would find Christ must find the Church first. Who can find out who Christ is supposed to be and what faith in him is if they did not know where his faithful are? And whoever wants to know something about Christ must trust themselves or build their own bridge into heaven by means of their own reason but rather go to the church and attend it and question it.[72]

Now, it *would* be sloppy to project this content back onto the *Assertio* as, more significantly than the temporal separation, a very dense chain of developments lay between that document and this theological formulation. But that Luther was thinking already about the incorporation of his individually executed pneumatic hermeneutics into an ecclesial context around the time of the *Assertio* can be seen in the fact (which is typically missed in the hermeneutical discussion) that Luther renewed his appelation for a general council of the church just a few weeks after the *Assertio*.[73] This meant that he clearly hoped for the victory of truth by means of such a legitimately assembled council of the church,[74] even though he had by now long condemned the idea of infallibility of councils.[75] However, such a synod appeared to constitute an appropriate path in order to punch through the authoritarian executive structure working against him in *Exsurge Domine*. Perhaps it could even clear the path for a collective implementation of pneumatically led exegesis.

Of course, Luther would immediately agree with the idea that such pneumatic interpretation requires scholarly support. *Oratio, meditatio*, and *tentatio* may well have constituted the real path to theology, but that did not render their teaching and study in an academic sense obsolete. In fact, his letter to the councilmen of all cities in Germany contains a vociferous appeal for learning ancient languages, especially the biblical ones:

72. Luther, *Kirchenpostille 1522* (WA 10/I/1:140.7–13): "*Die Christlich kirche behellt nu alle wort gottis ynn yhrem hertzen unnd bewigt dieselben, hellt sie gegennander und gegen die schrifft. Darumb wer Christum finden soll, der muß die kirchen am ersten finden. Wie wollt man wissen, wo Christus were und seyn glawbe, wenn man nit wiste, wo seyn glawbigen sind? und wer ettwas von Christo wissen wil, der muß nit yhm selb trawen noch eyn eygen bruck ynn den hymel bawen durch seyn eygen vornunfft, ßondernn tzu der kirchen gehen, dieselb besuchen und fragen.*"
73. Luther, *Appellatio* (WA 7:75–82).
74. Cf. Christopher Spehr, *Luther und das Konzil: Zur Entwicklung eines zentralen Themas in der Reformationszeit* (Tübingen: Mohr, 2010), 234–54.
75. Cf. the investigations from Spehr, *Luther und das Konzil*, 64: The first claim against Prierias that the councils were infallible was valid "only with regard to church praxis (. . .), not, however, concerning doctrintal matters." It was only in the Leipzig Disputation that Luther arrived at the opinion that the church could also err in matters of the faith (Spehr, *Luther und das Konzil*, 149–53).

Although the gospel came and still comes to us through the Holy Spirit alone, we cannot deny that it came through the medium of languages, was spread abroad by that means, and must be preserved by the same means. . . . In proportion then as we value the gospel, let us zealously hold to the languages. For it was not without purpose that God caused his Scriptures to be set down in these two languages alone—the Old Testament in Hebrew, the New in Greek. Now if God did not despise them but chose them above all others for his word, then we too ought to honor them above all others. . . . And let us be sure of this: we will not long preserve the gospel without the languages. The languages are the sheath in which this sword of the Spirit [Eph 6:17] is contained; they are the casket in which this jewel is enshrined; they are the vessel in which this wine is held; they are the larder in which this food is stored; and, as the gospel itself points out [Matt 14:20], they are the baskets in which are kept these loaves and fishes and fragments. If through our neglect we let the languages go (which God forbid!), we shall not only lose the gospel, but the time will come when we shall be unable either to speak or write a correct Latin or German.[76]

With such an appeal for Greek and Hebrew and a matching philological education in the sense of humanism, Luther doubled down on his opinion that the effect of the Holy Spirit was contained immediately in Holy Scripture, but in such a fashion that it required human comprehension. This is consistent with the statements contained in the *Assertio*, not by claiming that human interpretive faculties are a necessary assumption for salvation, but rather that language and grammar are instrumental and necessary for understanding the semantic sense and content of biblical texts. Oswald

76. Luther, *An die Ratherren aller Städte deutschen Landes* (WA 15:37.3–6. 16–22; 38.7–15): "*Denn das konnen wir nicht leucken, das, wie wol das Euangelion alleyn durch den heyligen geyst ist komen und teglich kompt, so ists doch durch mittel der sprachen komen und hat auch dadurch zugenomen, mus auch da durch behallten werden. (. . .) So lieb nu alls uns das Euangelion ist, so hart last uns uber den sprachen hallten. Denn Gott hat seyne schrifft nicht umb sonst alleyn ynn die zwo sprachen schreiben lassen, das allte testament ynn die Ebreische, das new ynn die Kriechische. Welche nu Gott nicht veracht, sondern zu seynem wort erwelet hat fur allen andern, sollen auch wyr die selben fur allen andern ehren. (. . .) Und last uns das gesagt seyn, Das wyr das Euangelion nicht wol werden erhallten on die sprachen. Die sprachen sind die scheyden, darynn dis messer des geysts stickt. Sie sind der schreyn, darynnen man dis kleinod tregt. Sie sind das gefess, darynnen man disen tranck fasset. Sie sind die kemnot, darynnen dise speyse ligt. Und wie das Euangelion selbs zeygt, Sie sind die koerbe, darynnen man dise brot und fische und brocken behellt. Ja wo wyrs versehen, das wyr (da Gott fur sey) die sprachen faren lassen, so werden wir nicht alleyn das Euangelion verlieren, sondern wird auch endlich dahyn geratten, das wir wider lateinisch noch deutsch recht reden odder schreyben kuenden.*" Cited after LW 45:358–59, 359, 360: *To the Councilmen of All Cities in Germany That They Establish and Maintain Christian Schools*. Bucher, *Ecumenical Luther*, 46 rightly classifies this effort of Luther into the horizon of his insistence for the literal sense of Scripture; for more on the significance of grammatical textual understanding, cf. Bayer. "Oratio, Meditatio, Tentatio," 33.

Bayer rightly emphasized that Luther's formulation of *oratio, meditatio*, and *tentatio* shaped Orthodoxy, Pietism, and parts of the Enlightenment in equal measure, as long as it was "not opposed abstractly by the scholarly nature of theology as the result of human ingenuity."[77]

Luther sees the "internal and external clarity" (*claritas interna* and *externa*) of Holy Scripture[78] as constituting the theological background for the double buffer against subjectivism, ensured by both a scholarly understanding and an ecclesial consensus. He presents this programmatically in *De servo arbitrio*:

> To put it briefly, there are two kinds of clarity in Scripture, just as there are also two kinds of obscurity: one external and pertaining to the ministry of the Word, the other located in the understanding of the heart. If you speak of the internal clarity, no man perceives one iota of what is in the Scriptures unless he has the Spirit of God.[79]

The office of public proclamation is responsible for the external clarity,[80] while the actual *cognitio cordis* means a deeply personal and spiritual appropriation of the content. As Eilert Herms emphasizes, this always assumes "the reality of the external existence of this clarity."[81] Thus, there is both an ecclesial dimension to the community of communication in Luther's pneumatic hermeneutics and a thorough theological formation

77. Bayer, "Oratio, Meditatio, Tentatio," 8.
78. Cf. the classification of both aspects to "a *scholarly* and a *spiritual* element" in Wilfried Härle, "Wer hat die Kompetenz zur (richtigen) Schriftauslegung? Überlegungen im Anschluss an Luther und Schleiermacher," in *Solo verbo. FS Hans Christian Knuth*, ed. Knut Kammholz (Kiel: Lutherische Verlagsgesellschaft, 2008), 147–68, 149 (italics in Härle); for the significance of the *claritas* from *De servo arbitrio* for the preface from 1539, cf. Bayer, "Oratio, Meditatio, Tentatio," 25.
79. Luther, *De servo arbitrio* (WA 18:609.4–7): "*Duplex et claritas scripturae, sicut et duplex obscuritas, Una externa in verbi ministerio posita, altera in cordis cognitione sita, Si de interna claritate dixeris, nullus homo unum iota in scripturis videt, nisi qui spiritum Dei habet.*" Cited after LW 33:28: *The Bondage of the Will*.
80. Cf. also Neuner and Schröger, "Luthers These," 51: "Clarity obviously has more to do with church structures than a first meets the eye." Thus, it is insufficient to simply compare Luther's hermeneutics to the binding of authoritative scriptural explanation in Roman Catholic theology (thus Härle, "Kompetenz," 155–56). A principled reflection remains necessary concerning how this office of public proclamation with a theological education creates a special instance for not only clarity but also the explanation of the true sense of biblical texts. The self-explanation is primarily a spiritual event and thus to be classified as *claritas interna*.
81. Eilert Herms, "Äußere und innere Klarheit des Wortes Gottes bei Paulus, Luther und Schleiermacher," in *Jesus Christus als die Mitte der Schrift: Studien zur Hermeneutik des Evangeliums*, ed. Christof Landmesser, Hans-Joachim Eckstein, and Hermann Lichtenberger (Berlin: De Gruyter, 1997), 3–72, 10; cf. a similar phrae in Neuner and Schröger, "Luthers These," 48. My translation.

for the office of proclamation, without which pneumatic exegesis runs the risk of missing the real sense of Scripture.

While both the communication community and philology remain easily understandable criteria, Luther pushes a further hermeneutical regulation into prominence: Luther's own trust in his insights derived from his own occupation with Scripture, which become an immovable basis for any scriptural insight. Ultimately, Luther follows a circular process where insights are to be derived from Scripture, which then become principles for making further insights into Scripture.

This can be seen in the prefaces to James and Jude in his translation of the Bible. Here, he states that only those texts that "push Christ" (*Christum treyben*)[82] are to be regarded as apostolic. This formulation can be found as early as Luther's first edition of the New Testament (*September Testament*) and is thus close in time to the *Assertio*. One can thus assume that the formulation can serve the purpose of providing a bit more form to the *Assertio*'s principle of Scripture's self-interpretation. Both the person of Christ and his saving work serve as the content, thus making justification through grace and faith alone, without human works,[83] to the central matrix for understanding Scripture.

Here, Luther created a clear guideline for his scriptural hermeneutics,[84] which he makes methodically accountable through the differentiation between law and gospel. In his commentary on Galatians from 1535, he makes this his greatest theological guideline: "Therefore whoever knows well how to distinguish the Gospel from the Law should give thanks to God and know that he is a real theologian."[85] And in fact, he drew heavily upon this argumentation in the *Assertio* for his argumentation against *Exsurge Domine*:

---

82. Luther, *Vorrede auf die Episteln Sanct Jacobi und Judas* (WA DB 7:384.27). A study of this famous passage in the context of Luther's prefaces to the Bible has been undertaken by Jörg Armbruster, *Luthers Bibelvorreden: Studien zu ihrer Theologie* (Suttgart: Deutsche Bibelgesellschaft, 2005), 142–44; cf. also Luther, *Von Menschenlehre zu meiden* (WA 11/II:73.15–16): "*Denn das ist ungetzweyfflet, das die gantze schrifft auff Christum allein ist gericht*"; for more on Luther's christological centering of his understanding of Scripture, cf. Johannes Brosseder, "Luthers Hermeneutik und ihre gegenwärtige ökumenische Bedeutung," *Communio viatorum* 43 (1991): 220–43, 229–30.

83. Luther, *Vorrede auf die Episteln Sanct Jacobi und Judas* (WA DB 7:384.9–18).

84. One can follow August Twesten in differentiating between a material principle and a formal principle, and many do. I am not sure if this helps us to better understand Luther's concerns though.

85. Luther, *In epistolam Pauli ad Galatas Commentarius* (WA 40/I:207.17–18): "*Qui igitur bene novit discernere Evangelium a lege, is gratias agat Deo et sciat se esse Theologum.*" Cited after LW 26:115, *Lectures on Galatians*. Cf. also the numerous other citations for this provided by Ebeling, "Lehre und Leben," 34, n. 99.

There are namely two Words of God, one is the command, the other is the promise. It is not comprehensible that the promise could be fulfilled by some work without faith.[86]

However, the proximity to the fundamentals of pneumatic hermeneutics becomes all the more evident when one considers that there is a transformation of the basic mystical conviction of the destruction and reconstitution of the human being through God taking place here. Now, it takes place according to a theology of the word.[87] This can be heard loud and clear in one of the first defining approaches to the difference between law and gospel in Luther's first lecture on the Psalms. When explaining the phrase "what the Lord God will speak in me" in Psalms 84(85):9, he expounds:

> This touches the difference between Law and Gospel. For the Law is the Word of Moses [that comes up] to us (*adnos*), while the Gospel is the Word of God [that comes] into us (*in nos*). The former remains outside and speaks of figures and visible shadows of things to come, but the latter comes inside and speaks of internal, spiritual, and true things. It is one thing to speak into us, and another to speak to us. [When He speaks] into us, He is effective and captures us, but not at all [when He speaks] to us. Thus the Word of faith like a two-edged sword (Heb. 4:12) penetrates into the inner parts and instructs and sanctifies the spirit. But the Word of the Law trains and sanctifies only the flesh.[88]

While writing the *Dictata*, Luther did not yet know Tauler, who would go on to become of central importance for him. But he was moving clearly within a mystical-monastic world and took the Gospel to be an internal, spiritual thing, which he then juxtaposed to the Law. He would later

---

86. Luther, *Assertio* (WA 7:120.9–11): "*Duo enim sunt verba dei, alterum est praeceptum, alterum promissio: praeceptum opera, promissio fidem exigit, nec est cogitabile, quomodo promissio impleri sine fide per opus quodcunque possit.*" My translation.

87. Leppin, *Transformationen*, 408–12; for more on the significance of Luther's accent on the word in contrast to the previous mystical paradigms, cf. Berndt Hamm, *The Early Luther*, 211–13.

88. Luther, *Dictata super Psalterium* (WA 4:9.28–35): "*In hoc tangitur differentia euangelii et legis. Quia lex est verbum Mosi ad nos, Euangelium autem verbum dei in nos. Quia illud foris manet, de figuris loquitur et umbris futurorum visibilibus: istud autem intus accedit et de internis, spiritualibus et veris loquitur. Aliud enim est in nos, aliud ad nos loqui. In nos enim efficax est et capit nos, ad nos autem nequaquam. Ita verbum fidei penetrat ut gladius anceps in interiora et spiritum erudit et sanctificat. Verbum autem legis tantum carnem erudit et sanctificat.*" Cited after LW 11:160, *First Lectures on the Psalms*. As Forde concedes, it appears to be an artificial alternative in this context if one attempts to locate the origin of the distinction between law and gospel in the conscience or in hermeneutics (Gerhard O. Forde, "Law and Gospel in Luther's Hermenutic," *Interpretation* 37 [1983]: 240–52, 243).

change this juxtaposition a bit, but the way he orients these two entities toward each other indicates a rootedness in a spiritual reflection performed by the internal person. And thus, the circle is complete. The assumptions of pneumatic hermeneutics lead the believer into a world of existential experience with and through the biblical text.[89] That Scripture explains itself means for the human interpreter that they must allow themself to be taken into an experience with God while working with Scripture. This experience teaches the interpreter to distinguish properly between law and gospel within Scripture.[90]

Luther's pneumatic hermeneutic is deeply rooted in mystical-experiential theology. As a hermeneutic of the biblical text in both intention and effect, it is a genuine expression of Martin Luther's reformational theology. Therefore, it is strongly contrasted with historical-critical explanation, which emerges with the Enlightenment. It stands much closer to the monastic-mystical spirituality of the Middle Ages, transforming it according to the theology of the word.

89. For the meaning of experience for Luther's biblical hermeneutics, cf. Eberhard Jüngel, ". . . unum aliquid assecutus, omnia assecutus . . . Zum Verständnis des Verstehens—nach M. Luther, De servo arbitrio (WA 18:605 = BoA 3, 100)," in *Jesus Christus als die Mitte der Schrift: Studien zur Hermeneutik des Evangeliums*, ed. Christof Landmesser, Hans-Joachim Eckstein, and Hermann Lichtenberger (Berlin: De Gruyter, 1997), 73–99, 91–92.
90. For a thorough study of this distinction, cf. Schwarz, *Luther Lehrer*, 187–262.

# 7.

# "For the Letter Kills, but the Spirit Gives Life." Interpreting 2 Corinthians 3:6 in the Middle Ages and the Reformation Era

When Martin Luther started disclosing his theological insights, he did not meet universal agreement even within Wittenberg itself.[1] Among his first adversaries was his colleague Andreas Karlstadt, who bought an edition of Augustine in 1517 specifically to prove Luther's misapprehension of the church father and his own accurate understanding.[2] The attempt failed completely; moved by a recently published book by John of Staupitz, presumably *De executione aeternae praedestinationis*,[3] Karlstadt changed his mind, now being convinced that he needed correction rather than Luther. To develop his new persuasion, he worked hard on understanding Augustine's *De spiritu et littera*. He did so, presenting a lecture on the book at Wittenberg University and swiftly having it printed.

This episode teaches something about the hot intellectual atmosphere during those days in Wittenberg and indicates the attention the issue of letter and spirit gained in the early Reformation. The theme was not only addressed in Augustine's work, but foremost in in 2 Corinthians 3:6: "for the letter kills, but the Spirit gives life" (*littera enim occidit Spiritus autem vivificat*). The sentence leads to the question of hermeneutics, obviously a

---

1. This hitherto unpublished paper has originally been written in English. I am grateful to Lukas Odgen for linguistic advice and help in writing this paper. A revision has been made by this volume's translator, Samuel Brandt.
2. Ernst Kähler, *Karlstadt und Augustin. Der Kommentar des Andreas Bodenstein von Karlstadt zu Augustins Schrift De spiritu et littera. Einführung und Text* (Halle: Max Niemeyer, 1952), 5, 4–7.
3. Köhler, *Karlstadt und Augustin*, 4.

matter of high relevance in the early Reformation. To Gerhard Ebeling, the doyen of German Luther research, the interpretation of this very verse made a core difference between Luther and his medieval predecessors.[4] Despite admitting some exceptions,[5] he outlines a sketch of medieval hermeneutics elaborating the fourfold sense of Scripture on the basis of the Pauline quotation.[6] Its literal sense had been neglected since the days of Origen, and the verse served to establish the difference between the literal sense and the three kinds of spiritual senses. That was, according to Ebeling, exactly what Luther broke away from, bringing the verse back to its primordial understanding—the distinction of Law and Gospel.[7] The aim of the following will be to reconsider this dominating view on the history of exegesis by comparing Luther's approach with the medieval one.

## MARTIN LUTHER: LAW AND GOSPEL

There is no question that for Luther, the correct understanding of 2 Corinthians 3:6 was critically important. Here he saw one of the decisive differences between new and old theology. This becomes obvious in his usage of the distinction in the "Anti-Latomus," written in Wartburg Castle in 1521 against the Leuven theologian Jacob Latomus. The latter had thoroughly argued against Luther's anthropology, and the reformer provided a comprehensive answer to him in this text. When he reached the issue of justification, he stressed that this should come only from grace and not from any human deeds or from observing the law, underpinning this conviction with the biblical circumscription: "It is obvious then, that the killing letter is the Law, while the life-giving Spirit is grace in Christ's faith."[8] Life is a life in the Spirit, and life in the Spirit is life in the grace of the Gospel. That seems to be, in short, what Luther says here. So, the biblical allegation does not lead to any exegetical rules—it leads to the center of Christian life, the basis of any hermeneutics.

4. Gerhard Ebeling, *Evangelische Evangelienauslegung: Eine Untersuchung zu Luthers Hermeneutik* (Munich: Albert Lempp, 1942), 279.
5. Ebeling, *Evangelienauslegung*, 279 n. 13. Ebeling does not make clear what passage of Paul of Burgos he is referring to here, but as Wilfried Werbeck, *Jacobus Perez von Valencia. Untersuchungen zu seinem Psalmenkommentar* (Tübingen: Mohr Siebeck, 1959), 94 n. 2 reveals, the section in question is his addition to Nicholas of Lyra's prologue (referred to in Ebeling, *Evangelienauslegung* 133–34 n. 89).
6. Gerhard Ebeling, *Luther. Einführung in sein Denken* (Tübingen: Mohr Siebeck, 2006), 109–10.
7. Ebeling, *Evangelienauslegung*, 279.
8. Luther, *Rationis Latomi confutatio* (WA 8:71.12–13): "*Claret ergo, literam occidentem esse universam legem, spiritum vivificantem autem gratiam in fide Christi.*"

Luther's understanding of 2 Corinthians 3:6 seems quite clear at this stage in his development, forming a marker of difference to the medieval faith in an extremely sensitive phase of the history of the Reformation, shortly after the reformer had been excommunicated and outlawed. His reasoning about the verse had started much earlier. In his first lecture on the Psalms he simply followed the standard hermeneutical line by putting the historical sense as the killing letter opposed to the life giving spirit in the three other senses and stressing that one side would not be fruitful without the other.[9] The leitmotif here in discerning both was outward and inward like in the mystical tradition: Anyone who would read "have dominion" (*dominabitur*) in Psalms 72(71):8 in the sense of temporal government would be reduced to the killing letter, while those who would see the spiritual kingdom of God here would follow the life-giving Spirit.[10] Luther can even sum this up in an overall rule: "It is best in the Holy Scriptures to discern the Spirit from the letter. This in particular really makes a theologian."[11] Ebeling finds this "already totally reformatory" even if "not decisive."[12] This observation is typical for the transformative way of Luther's development: We cannot starkly distinguish medieval and reformatory thinking in Luther the way former generations have done. There was no abrupt break with the Middle Ages but an incremental transition from the early medieval beginning to the late reformer, never loosing all ties to his roots.

This is also true for the very peculiar issue of letter and spirit in 2 Corinthians 3:6. While we can see the exegetical use of it in the first lectures on the Psalms, we can also observe Luther connecting the opposition of letter and Spirit with the one of Old Testament and New, thereby creating the basis for the dialectics of Law and Gospel. This brought a distinct anti-Jewish overtone into debate when Luther argued that some exegetes had come only to the historical sense following the "Hebrew wrong-writers [falsigraphi] of the Rabbis and the figments of Jewish vanities."[13] The killing letter, we see here, to him meant a biblical reading without Christ as the clue for its understanding, because he was the one to send the

---

9. Luther, *Dictata super Psalterium* (WA 55/I:7–24).

10. Luther, *Dictata super Psalterium* (WA 55/I:27–32).

11. Luther, *Dictata super Psalterium* (WA 55/I:25–26): "*In Scripturis Sanctis optimum est Spiritum a litera discernere, hoc enim facit vero theologum.*"

12. Ebeling, *Evangelienauslegung*, 279 n. 14: "This early formulation, highly evocative of the Reformation [. . .] is not without ambivalence." My translation.

13. Luther, *Dictata super Psalterium* (WA 55/I:13.1–2): "*quosdam Rabim hebræos falsigraphos et figulos Iudaicarum vanitatum.*"

life-giving Spirit "after the killing letter."[14] Thus, we have both together here in his earliest lecture: the hermeneutic application of 2 Corinthians 3:6, as well as an understanding led by the teaching of justification.

As time went by, the latter understanding of the verse would dominate and become exclusive in the reformer's approach to this verse. The exclusion of exegetical understanding was made shortly before Luther wrote the Anti-Latomus, but in a similarly Anti-Roman context. Prior to leaving Wittenberg for the Diet of Worms that would lead him to flee to Wartburg Castle, Luther answered a polemic from Jerome Emser. Here, he clearly formed the critique which Ebeling would underpin with his telling the story of exegesis:

> Consequently, Paul's sentence in 2 Cor 4, 'For the letter kills, but the Spirit gives life,' matches those two senses, literal and spiritual just as well as Emser's head matches philosophy and theology. I will not comment here on how and why Origen, Jerome and some other Fathers have drawn and bent the sentence this way.[15]

This makes clear that Luther saw himself not only in opposition to the Catholic side, but even to considerable church fathers, what is much less usual to him. It also requires us to take a closer look at the tradition.

## THE BASIS: AUGUSTINE, *DE SPIRITU ET LITTERA*

As the case of Karlstadt shows, the reformers knew that they were not the first to relate 2 Corinthians 3:6 to the dialectics of law and gospel or, a bit more simplified, Old and New Testament. The first to do so, obviously, had been Augustine in his *De spiritu et littera*. We cannot follow his entire argument here, leading to the broader issue of justification and free will. Instead, we will concentrate on the exegesis of the verse in question, which we find in the chapters IV.6 to VI.10 of *De spiritu et littera*. This excurse is founded on a short definition that turns the juxtaposition in the Pauline text into a correlation: "The letter is killing if not accompanied by the life-giving Spirit".[16] This might appear to be only a slight modification of

---

14. Luther, *Dictata super Psalterium* (WA 55/2:953.1783): "*post literam occidentem.*"

15. Luther, *Auf das Buch Emsers Antwort* (WA 7:653.1–5): "*Darumb der spruch Pauli 2. Cor. 4. 'Der buchstabe der toedtet, der geyst lebendigt' reymet sich eben ßo woll zu dissen tzween synnen, schrifftlich und geystlich, als Emßers kopff sich zu der philosophia und Theologia reymett. Wie aber unnd warumb Origenes, Hieronymus und ettlich mehr vetter dissen spruch auch alßo tzogen und tzwungen haben, laß ich itzt anstehen.*"

16. Augustine, *De spiritu et littera* IV.6 (CSEL 60:157.26): "*littera est occidens, nisi adsit uiuificans spiritus*".

the original but carries a huge impact. With Augustine, there is no way to abandon the letter itself, but the letter is part of a nexus in which the Spirit clearly prevails without the letter completely vanishing.

That laid the basis for applying the biblical distinction to the correlation of both the Old and the New Testament. Another Pauline passage became decisive for this, namely Romans 7, where Paul in v. 11 speaks about the killing sin and connects this with the commandments of the law.[17] The law, according to Augustine, is summarized in forbiddance: "You shall not covet." This is right and good, according to Augustine, but it cannot be ever fulfilled without the Holy Spirit replacing bad desire with good.[18] The Bishop of Hippo also reflects an anthropological reason for why the interdiction on its own is not enough to abandon sin, in the line of Romans 7: The commandment itself only induces knowledge of sin but cannot help avoiding it. Hence, it enlarges sin instead of procuring it.[19]

The issue of sin and redeeming from sin leads Augustine to the broader context of both: the story of salvation as given in the Old and New Testament, in law and gospel, or grace. He sums up his reflection on 2 Corinthians 3:6 with the confession that righteousness never could have been reestablished by the law but solely through faith in Jesus Christ (*nisi per fidem Iesu Christi*).[20] Even in its wording, this comes quite close to the reformers' concept of justification and might have inspired the use of 2 Corinthians 3:6 we find in Luther.

This concludes what the reformers could pick up from Augustine. However, this is not everything that can be drawn from him. While Luther (at least in 1521) was inclined to exclude an application of 2 Corinthians 3:6 to an allegorical reading of Scripture, his paragon Augustine did not do so. To him, the verse (e.g., in the case of the Song of Songs) also applied to the figurative method of interpretation,[21] even if this was not the bishop's preferred use of the verse. Rather, he presupposed that his reader already knew this application of it and attempted to broaden what he saw as a traditional understanding, introducing the reasonings referred to above. Thus, the reformers were right somehow to reference him arguing for their relating the verse to the connection of law and gospel.

<hr>

17. Augustine, *De spiritu et littera* IV.6 (CSEL 60:158.10–21).

18. Augustine, *De spiritu et littera* IV.6 (CSEL 60:158.22–24).

19. Augustine, *De spiritu et littera* V.8 (CSEL 60:160.13–154).

20. Augustine, *De spiritu et littera* VI.10 (CSEL 60:162.16–20).

21. Augustine, *De spiritu et littera* IV.6 (CSEL 60:158.1–3): "*neque enim solo illo modo intelligendum est quod legimus: littera occidit, spiritus autem uiuificat, uta liquid figurate scriptum, cuius est absurda proprietas, non accipimis sicut littera sonat.*" The Song of Songs is mentioned as an example in line 7.

But they were not totally right in doing so for their refusing its exegetical use. Augustine obviously preferred relating the verse to law and gospel:

> I want in particular [. . .] to demonstrate what the apostle says: The statement, "the letter kills, but the spirit gives life," is not about figures of speech, even if it can be applied to them congruently, but more about the Law evidently prohibiting what is bad.[22]

There is a slight but important concession: "Even if it can be applied to them congruently." This makes it obvious that Augustine did not like this application but admitted it instead of ruling it out completely. The reformers would do exactly what he was reluctant to do: exclude the exegetical use.

In other cases, we can observe a reformatory style of thinking in differences or exclusions contrasting to a kind of looking for harmonies we encounter in the Middle Ages. Here, at least, Augustine was more on the medieval side than on that of the reformers. He did not totally exclude the understanding of 2 Corinthians 3:6 in terms of exegesis like the reformers would do, while relegating it somehow in relation to a preferred interpretation. With this, he laid the basis for medieval theology to adopt both ways.

## MEDIEVAL TRADITION

When Luther spoke about the exegetical use of 2 Corinthians 3:6, he did not refer to Origen by accident. The Alexandrian father was the founder of spiritual exegesis of the Bible, and he occasionally used 2 Corinthians 3:6 to justify this spiritual approach.[23] So, Luther had reason to blame him for many of the same things he blamed Jerome for: in his *Commentaria in Iob*, Origen used exactly the Pauline verse to justify an allegorical interpretation of the numbers of animals Job was said to possess.[24] For Luther, this was a distraction from the main point of the text.

22. Augustine, *De spiritu et littera* V.7 (CSEL 60:159.7–10): "*uolo enim [. . .] demonstrare illud, quod ait apostolus: littera occidit, spiritus autem uiuificat, non de figuratis locutionibus dictum, quamuis et illic congruenter accipiatur, sed potius de lege aperte quod malum est prohibente.*"
23. Cf. Origen, *Commentary to the Gospel of Matthew* (GCS 40/2:353).
24. Gerome, *Commentaria in Ijob* c. 42 (PL 26:800A-C): "*Dominus autem benedixit novissimis Iob magis quam principio eius. Et facta sunt ei quatuordecim millia ovium, et sex millia camelorum, et mille iuga boum, et mille asinae. Principia Christi Dei, et Domini nostri, Legis Moysi exordia esse significantur. Novissima vero eius Evangelium esse monstratur. Unde Ecclesiastes ait: Meliora sunt novissima sermonis, quam initium eius. Proinde meliora sunt mysteria Evangelii revelata in Christo, Legis significationibus et figuris: meliora sacrificia cordium contritorum, quam holocaustomata*

In any event, neither of these fathers are as decisive for the medieval understanding of letter and spirit in hermeneutics as was Gregory the Great. In many respects, he was as tremendous an impact for medieval spirituality as he was for hermeneutics. In the *Prooemium* to his *Commentary on the Song of Songs*, he developed his own understanding of biblical interpretation. The Pauline quote in question took on a very central place here. He used the distinction of letter and spirit to introduce another closely related distinction: the one of words (*verba*) and sense (*sensus*).[25] Their relation, he said, is similar to that between straw and corn: while the one was to feed the animals, the latter was to be enjoyed by humans.[26] To have the right nutrition, then, the humans should explore the mysteries hidden beneath the letters,[27] leading them to deeper insight and higher salvation. Gregory made these remarks to introduce his interpretation of the Song of Songs, the book Augustine had referred to as well while talking about allegorical interpretation. This similarity did not occur by coincidence. The Song of Songs always caused the most severe problems for a literal interpretation of the Bible. The amazing oriental love songs collected in it could not easily be included in a Christian macro-interpretation. But seeing them just as dead straw, with Gregory using here the word *palea*, verbally meaning "the bedding of the plants," could make it possible to dodge the interpretative difficulties and to read Christian doctrines into the text. Gregory demonstrated this with his allegorical interpretation of the text that would fulfill every wish for the hermeneutics of spiritual senses.

The connection of 1 Corinthians 3:6 with allegorical interpretation has also found its place in one of the most important textbooks used in the High Middle Ages: the *Didascalion* of Hugh of St. Victor. This book, dating from the twelfth century, intended to introduce an appropriate reading of the Holy Scripture in the context of universal wisdom, showing how a student or a monk had to approach Scripture. In book 6, Hugh dealt with the senses of Scripture, passing over the eschatological or anagogical

*pecudum. Melior manifestatio veritatis in Evangelio, quam allegoriarum umbra in veteri Testamento. Sic itaque benedixit Dominus novissimis Iob magis quam principio eius, ut in utroque populo, Iudaeorum et gentium, gratia abundaret: quos populos secundum morum qualitates, quasi sub diversorum animalium nominibus haec Scriptura voluit appellare. Quam vero significationem eadem animalium in se vocabula contineant, in principio operis istius dixisse me memini. Duplicatum vero horum animalium numerum, propter utrumque populum puto, sive propter abundantiorem gratiam Evangelii, ut iam diximus, de qua Apostolus ait: Sufficientia nostra ex Deo est: qui et idoneos nos fecit, et ministros novi Testamenti, non littera, sed spiritu: littera enim occidit: spiritus autem vivificat."*
25. Gregory the Great, *Super Cantica Canticorum Expositio. Prooemium* (PL 79:473D).
26. Gregory the Great, *Super Cantica Canticorum Expositio. Prooemium* (PL 79:474A).
27. Gregory the Great, *Super Cantica Canticorum Expositio. Prooemium* (PL 79:474A).

sense and just concentrating on the historical or literal sense, the allegorical sense, and the tropological or moral sense. This is only surprising for those who think the Middle Ages were bound to rigid conceptional patterns. They were not, but they gave some material to play with, as did Hugh.

He cited the Pauline verse in his paragraphs on allegory. After establishing a historical basis, he saw the verse as necessary to lead the reader of the Bible into the mysteries of the Trinity and incarnation. Following Hugh, this was the reason why Paul spoke about the life-giving spirit:[28] insight into those mysteries was required for eternal life. Hugh called them the *sacramenta*, not yet using *sacramentum* as a technical term for particular rites but more in the broader sense of something sacred. As would be the case centuries later in Luther, Hugh connected this foundation of spiritual exegesis with some anti-Jewish remarks. The "old people" (*antiquus ille populus*), according to him, were repudiated because they only followed the killing letter, missing the life-giving spirit.[29] Hugh was also aware of another problem that would bring up some discussion later in the Reformation era. Spiritual understanding could lead to arbitrariness in interpretation, with everyone following their own presuppositions.[30] To avoid this, obedience to the fathers was required.[31] Life-giving spirit, then, did not mean uncontrolled playing with the text. It meant letting the fathers lead to God's secrets by means of allegorical method.

It is thus safe to say that 2 Corinthians 3:6 was widely used to underscore the method of allegorical interpretation in the Middle Ages. So far, Ebeling was right in contrasting Luther's view of exegesis to the medieval one. This connection was not unquestioned, though. Nicholas of Lyra in his *Postilla* both concentrated on the literal sense in general and also contributed to the understanding of 2 Corinthians 3:6 in the course of his exposition. And he did so in an Augustinian sense, including several opinions instead of excluding some: "The letter, without the Spirit coming to help, kills."[32] Even more, he outlines Augustine's argument that the commandment as a letter alone would not lead to life, while the "law of faith" (*lex fidei*) would

---

28. Hugh of St. Victor, *Didascalion* 6 (Hugonis de Sancto Victore, *operum Editio auspiciis Gulduini abbtis procurata et IV voluminibus digessa*, vol. 1, ed. Rainer Berndt and José Luis Narvaja [Münster: Aschendorff, 2017] 420, 22–24).
29. Hugh of St. Victor, *Didascalion* 6 (Hugo, Opera 1:420.26–27).
30. Hugh of St. Victor, *Didascalion* 6 (Hugo, Opera 1:420.28–421. 2).
31. Hugh of St. Victor, *Didascalion* 6 (Hugo, Opera 1:421.3–10).
32. Look for this and the following: Biblia, *Sexta pars biblie cum | glosa ordinaria et expsotione lyre litteralle et morali necnon additionibus et replicis* (Basel: Petri, 1498), and 2 Cor 3:6: "*littera sine spiritu adiuvante occidit.*"

do so, as Lyra says. Quoting Augustine from *"contra Faustum,"* he adds: "Letter and Spirit are also called law and grace."[33] This interpretation of Augustine lacks an explicit depreciation of the hermeneutic application of the verse as we could find in Augustine's *De spiritu et littera*.

This is astonishing, especially when we take Nicholas' preference of the literal sense into account. It is no wonder, that Paul of Burgos, who wrote additions to Lyra's *Postilla*, connected the dots and drew the consequences for what he saw as a correct understanding of 2 Corinthians 3:6, one hundred years before the Reformation:

> First, one has to say: When the apostle says, 'The letter kills, but the spirit gives life', he does not intend to distinguish literal and spiritual sense, which is the issue here, but [he distinguishes] the Old Law, which was given in written letters, as in the tablets of the Decalogue or in the books of the Mosaic Law, and the New Law that was given in the Spirit, namely in the hearts [. . .]. Therefore, the Old Law is called the law of the letter, while the New Law is called the law of the Spirit.[34]

Here, we find less harmony than in Augustine. Paul obviously comes close to the reformatory approach, drawing 2 Corinthians 3:6 completely into the field of the correlation of Old and New Testament. His inspiration by Augustine becomes clear by his following argument, when he speaks about the cognition of sin through the Old Testament,[35] hence following the argument of Romans 7 we found in Augustine. This makes him neither a kind of pre-reformer nor, like Ebeling wanted to see him,[36] an exception. He just shows that the Augustinian heritage was rich and varied in the Middle Ages.

This becomes clear when we look at the many more authors who saw in 2 Corinthians 3:6 the distinction of Old and New Testament or law and gospel. Long before Paul of Burgos, they had a strong basis in the spiritual culture of the eleventh century. Here we can also see that the

---

33. *"Littera et spiritus aliomodo dicuntur lex et gratia"*; The Augustine text Lyra seems to refer to reads: *"intellegit, quid distet inter litteram et spiritum, quae duo dicuntur alio modo, lex et gratia"* (Augustine, *Contra Faustum* XV, 8 [CSEL 25/1:432–8–9]).

34. Paul of Burgos, *Additio ad Prologum Postillae* (PL 113:47C).

35. Paul of Burgos, *Additio ad Prologum Postillae* (PL 113:47C): *"Ad primum, dicendum, quod Apostolus dicit: 'Littera occidit, spiritus autem vivificat', non intendit distinguere inter sensum litteralem et spiritualem, de quibus hic agitur: sed inter legem veterem, quae fuerat data in litteris scriptis, scilicet, in tabulis decalogi, et in libris Mosaicae legis; et inter legem novam, quae fuit data in spiritu, scilicet in cordibus (. . .) unde lex vetus dicitur lex litterae, et lex nova, lex spiritus."*

36. Ebeling, *Evangelienauslegung*, 270 n. 13; cf. above p. 3.

difference between the two modes of interpreting 2 Corinthians 3 need not be seen as separated as the Reformation polemics suggest. Bruno of Segni, who served as a bishop in the time of Papal reform of the eleventh century, explains the mention of wine and oil in Revelation 6:6 in his exposition of the Revelation of John:

> The wine signifies the Law's austerity, the oil the Gospel. The one makes drunken, the other cures. The one distorts sin, the other calls the insane back to sin. "For the letter kills, but the Spirit gives life"[37]

Bruno's manner of interpretation is ingenious. He uses the allegorical method to direct the reader's understanding to the correlation of law and gospel, which to him is far more a juxtaposition than it was in Augustine. Even if this might indicate that he did not follow the church father completely, it also shows the broad impact of the latter's writings in general. Accordingly, Bruno was by no means the only one to follow the Augustinian pattern here. In the very same eleventh century, we even find an ascetic monk connecting the verse with justification. In his *Exposition on the Psalms*, Brun the Carthusian wrote with an all too familiar anti-Jewish emphasis:

> "Because I did not perceive that the letter would not justify." This means: The "mine" [my people] will perceive that the letter of the Law could not justify anyone. "For the letter kills." This means to say: They will identify that it was wrong for the Jews to affirm that someone could be justified through the Law. Because the law only indicates the sin, but it does not help dodging it. And perceiving through the letter alone cannot justify.[38]

Again, we see the Augustinian heritage in the allusion to the law making us know the sin, thus combining 2 Corinthians 3:6 and Romans 7. This means that the reformers' interpretation looks far less innovative than Luther himself wanted it to be seen or likely thought it to be.

One would be mistaken to see all this as just exceptions at the fringes of the church. Not only was Brun himself exceedingly influential but even

---

37. Bruno of Segni, *Expositio in Apocalypsim VI* (PL 165:636A): "*Vinum legis austeritatem, oleum Evangelium significant: illud inebriat, hoc sanat; illud mentem evertit, hoc dementes ad mentem revocat: 'Littera enim occidit, spiritus autem vivificat.'*"

38. Bruno the Carthusian, *Expositioin Psalmos. Ps 70* (PL 152:986 C-D): "*Quoniam non cognovi litteram esse iustificantem, id est, mei cognoscent litteram legis veteris non posse aliquem iustificare. 'Littera enim occidit'. Quod est dicere: Cognoscent illud esse falsum, quod Iudaei affirmabant aliquem ex lege iustificari posse. Lex enim solummodo peccatum indicat. Non etiam ad abstinendum adiuvat. Et cognoscendo per litteram non posse iustificari.*"

more prominent thinkers joined him in his Augustinian approach to the letter-spirit disjunction. For example, the famous late-eleventh-century Archbishop of Canterbury Lanfranc combined in his *Commentary on Second Corinthians* the different approaches to the verse in a similar manner as Bruno of Segni had done, but he did so with a bit more caution with regard to the four senses. He related the life-giving spirit to the "*spiritualiter intellecta*," which might be referred to as a spiritual sense in the Scripture but does not need to be. He placed more weight on the opposition of the Old Testament Law, in particular mentioning circumcision and Sabbath, to the Law of Faith, based in Christ.[39] No wonder that his even more illustrious adherent and twofold successor—in the Monastery of Bec, as well as on the sede of Canterbury—Anselm also followed the Augustinian line here. He did so in one of his less-well-known treatises. In the beginning of the twelfth century, he wrote his *Epistola de sacrificio azimi et fermentati* about the question of azymes, the use of unleavened bread in the Eucharist that was controversial between the churches of the East and the West. The Western rite of using the unleavened bread, according to Anselm, was argued by the Greeks by means of the very verse 2 Corinthians 3:6: Using sour dough in the Eucharist to them meant introducing the Old Testament and Jewish rites into the Christian ones, and hence being killed by the pure letter.[40] Obviously, the Greek argument led directly to the relation of Old and New Testament, and consequently Anselm argued against it by referring to Augustine, again combining the verse with Romans 7. The letter only kills, Anselm argued, when it sticks to sin, showing it and so provoking it, as long as it is not accompanied by the grace that would help avoiding sin.[41] If anywhere, here the Augustinian argument seems well preserved, not in the manner of handing over a tradition but rather by becoming relevant for theological debate.

If there is any more need to show that the Middle Ages never had forgotten this Augustinian understanding of 2 Corinthians 3:6, a final view of two figures who were decisive for scholastic education should thoroughly convince us. The first is Peter Lombard. Famous for his *Book of the Sentences*, widely used at universities in the Middle Ages for basic theological lectures, he also wrote some biblical commentaries. If his Pauline

---

39. Lanfrank, *Commentarius in Pauli Epistolas* (PL 150:224B).

40. Anselm, *Epistola de sacrificio azimi V* (Anselmi Cantuariensis Archiepiscopi, *Opera Omnia*, vol 2, ed. Franz S. Schmitt (Stuttgart: Fromann Holzboog, 1968), 229.3–7.

41. Anselm, *Epistola de sacrificio azimi V* (Anselm, *Opera Omnia*, 2:229.8–18).

exegesis had not become part of a recension of the *Glossa ordinaria*,[42] it would not have had the same impact as *Book of the Sentences*, but nevertheless it was considerably influential. Like Augustine, Peter Lombard developed a dialectic of law and gospel when he came to interpret 2 Corinthians 3:6. Again, it was the law separated from the Spirit that Peter depicted as the killing letter. The spirit helped promote spiritual understanding and fulfilling of what the letter prescribed.[43] By this interpretation, together with that of Nicholas of Lyra, the Augustinian sense of 2 Corinthians 3:6 was handed over to future generations in the late Middle Ages, as well as in the Reformation era. This can also be seen in the *Summa theologiae* of Thomas Aquinas. When dealing with the question of whether the new law justifies (which really meant the law of the gospel), Aquinas returned explicitly to Augustine's *De spiritu et littera* and the explanation of 2 Corinthians 3:6 found in it. Following this line, the distinction of inward and outward was decisive to Aquinas. The letter killed as long as it was just an outwardly spoken letter not grasped by inner faith. In this sense, even the gospel could be a killing letter if grace had not arrived in the inner human being.[44]

* * *

There was some reason for Luther to claim that what he propagated was totally different to former generations. This made his message powerful, even if he obviously was exaggerating. Stating this does not mean litigating that there was something new in his message. There was sufficient originality, if only looking at the new combinations of spiritual insights and ecclesiastical reform we can observe in him. But the new did not come as a sudden break as Luther himself would have us believe. It came as a slow transformation.

Coming back to the case study here, this means Luther was not the first to return to Augustine's interpretation of 2 Corinthians 3:6, contrary to what he himself suggested. This is true for two reasons: First, he was not simply returning to Augustine. He radicalized the church father by setting his harmonizing approach aside and separating what the ancient bishop had bound together. And second, he was not the first to retrieve

42. Marcia L. Colish, "From *Sacra pagina* to *theologia*: Peter Lombard as an Exegete of Romans," *Medieval Perspectives* 6 (1991): 1–19.
43. Peter Lombard, *Commentary on 2 Corinthians* (PL 192:23D–24A).
44. Thomas Aquinas, *Summa theologiae* I–II q. 106 a. 2 res (Editio Leonina 7: 274).

the relation of 2 Corinthians 3:6 to the law and gospel dialectics. Even more, those preceding him were more than just exceptions, in contrast to what Ebeling suggested. There was a strong line of Augustinian interpretation of the verse in the Middle Ages, including such famous names as Lanfranc, Anselm of Canterbury, Peter Lombard, and Thomas Aquinas. When Luther strengthened this interpretation against the use of the verse for the fourfold sense of Scripture, he did not separate himself from tradition but rather transformed it, himself becoming a substantial part of it.

# Bibliography


Abelard, Peter. *Ouvrages inédits d'Abélard*. Edited by Victor Cousin. Paris: Impr. Royale, 1836.

———. *Ethics: An Edition with Introduction*. English translation and notes. Edited by D. E. Luscombe. Oxford: Clarendon Press, 1971.

Altenstaig, Johann. *Vocabularius Theologie com- | plectens vocabulorum descriptiones / diffinitiones et significa| tus ad theologiam vtilium (…) magno cum labore et diligentia | compilata a Joanne Altenstaig Min\delhaimensi / sacre scriptu-\re vero ama-\tore*. Hagenau, 1517.

Anon. *Das ist ein schonner | Passion von dem leyden vnsers | lieben herren Jhesu Christi|*. Nuremberg: Hieronymus Huber, 1504.

Anon. *Das leben vnsers erle | digers Jesu Christi / nach lauttung des hey-\lligen Ewangeli / mit vil andechtiger be-\ trachtung / Auch mit beylauffung des | lebens der junckfrawen Marie / von | einem Parfuesser der obseruantz | Also zusamen gezetz / von anfang | der kindthait Cristi / biß auff | sein himelfart / vol suesser | vnd andechtiger leer | vnd betrachtung*. Nuremberg: Stuchs, 1514.

Aquinatis, S. Thomae. *Scriptum super Sententiis*. Vol. 4, edited by Maria Fabian Moos. Paris: P. Lethielleux, 1947.

Bernhard von Clairvaux. *Sämtliche Werke. Lateinisch/Deutsch*. Edited by Gerhard B. Winkler. Vol. 1, Innsbruck: Tyrolia, 1990. Vol. 2, Innsbruck: Tyrolia, 1992. Vol. 5, Innsbruck: Tyrolia-Verlag, 1994. Vol. 6, Innsbruck: Tyrolia Verlaganstalt, 1995. Vol. 8, Innsbruck: Tyrolia, 1997.

Biblia. *Sexta pars biblie cum | glosa ordinaria et expsotione lyre litteralle et morali necnon additionibus et replicis*. Basel: Petri & Froben, 1498.

Biel, Gabriel. *Gabrielis Biel Collectorium circa quattuor libros Sententiarum. Liber secundus*. Edited by Wilfired Werbeck and Udo Hofmann. Tübingen: Mohr, 1984.

———. *Collectorium circa quattuor libros Sententiarum. Libri quarti pars prima (dist. 1–14)*. Edited by Wilfried Werbeck and Udo Hofmann. Tübingen: Mohr, 1975.

———. *Collectorium circa quattuor libros Sententiarum. Liber tertius*. Edited by Wilfried Werbeck and Udo Hofmann. Tübingen: Mohr, 1969.

———. *Collectorium circa quattuor libros Sententiarum. Liber secundus*. Edited by Wilfried Werbeck and Udo Hofmann. Tübingen: Mohr, 1984.

———. *Collectorium circa quattuor libros Sententiarum. Prologus er Liber primus*. Edited by Wilfried Werbeck and Udo Hofmann. Tübingen: Mohr, 1973.

Brandwine, Thomas. *THOMAE | BRADWARDINI | ARCHIEPISCOPI OLIM | CANTUARIENSIS | DE CAUSA DEI; | CONTRA PELAGIUM, | ET DE VIRTUTE CAUSARUM, | (. . .) LIBRI TRES*. London: Johannes Billius, 1618.

Council of Constance. *Acta Scitu dignissima docte|que concinnata Constantiensis | concilii celebratissimi*. Hagenau: Gran, 1500.

D'Ailly, Pierre. *Quaestiones magistri Petri de | Alliaco cardinalis cameracen|sis super libros sententiarum*. Straßburg: Georg Husner, 1490.

*Decreta patrum siue concor-| dia discordantium canonum| Gratiani auctoris siue com|pilatoris: cum apparatibus| Johannis ac additionibus| Bartholomei brixiensis*. Nürnberg: Anton Koberger, 1493.

*Decretum Gratiani| Cum | Glossis domini Johannis theutonici prepositi alberstatensis et annotationibus Bartholomei brixiensis (. . . .)*. Basel: Johannes Amerbach und Johannes Froben, 1512.

Denifle, Heinrich Suso. *Quellenbelege: Die abendländischen Schriftausleger bis Luther über Justitia Dei (Röm 1, 17) und Justificatio*. Edited by Heinrich Denifle. Mainz: Kirchheim, 1905.

Denzinger, Heinrich, ed. *Compendium of Creeds, Definitions, and Declarations on Matters of Faith and Morals*. 43rd ed. Edited by Peter Hünermann, Robert Fastiggi, and Anne Englund Nash. San Francisco: Ignatius Press, 2012.

*DOCVMENTA| LITERARIA| VARII ARGVMENTI| IN LKVCEM PROLATA| CVRA | IOHANNIS HEVMANNI| (. . .)*. Altdorf, 1758.

Doering, Matthias. *Continuatio Chronici Theodorici Engelhusii*. In | *Scriptores | rervm | Germanicarvm | praecipve | Saxonicarvm*. Vol. 3, edited by I. B. Menckenii. Leipzig, 1730.

Eck, Johannes. *AVDI LECTOR | johannes Eccij Theologi In-| goldstadiensis. orationes accipe tres non | inelegantes (. . .)*. Augsburg: Miller, 1515.

————. *CHRYSOPASSVS| A IOANNE MAIORIS ECKIO PROCAN-CELLARIO | AVRIPOLI ET CANONICO EISTETEM: LECTA EST | SVBTILIS ILLA PRAEDESTINATIONIS MATERIA | VVILHELMO ILLUSTRIS: PRINCIPE BAIOARIAM | GVBER-NANTE. ANNO GRATIAE G. D. XII.* Augsburg: Johann Miller, 1514.

————. *Disputatio Joan. Ec|kij Theologi Viennae Pannoniae ha-| bita cum Epistola ad Reuerendis-| simum Episcopum Ei-|stettensem.| (. . .).* Augsburg: Miller 1517.

————. "Universitätskanzler Dr. Kochel (Leipzig)." Reformationsge-schichte. Accessed March 30, 2023. http://ivv7srv15.uni-muenster. de/mnkg/pfnuer/Eckbriefe/N077.html;).

————. *ENCHI-| RIDION LOCO-| RVM COMMVNIVM IOAN-| nis Eckij, aduersus Martinum Lu-| therum & asseclas eius (. . .)| Interiecta sunt passim quaedam ha| ctenus impressa (. . .) per ve-| nerabilem virum F. Tilmannum Siber-| gensem (. . .).* Köln: Fuchs & Quentel, 1532.

————. *ENCHI| RIDION LOCORVM | communium adversus Lu| therum & alios ho-| stes ecclesiæ.| Ioan. Eckio authore.| AVTHUR IAM SEPTI-| mo recognouit & pluribus lo-| cis illustrauit, adnotatonib.| P. Tilmanni acco-| modatis.* Augsburg: Weissenhorn, 1536.

————. *De indulgentiis in Enchiridion locorum | communium aduersus Lut-teranos.| joanne Eckio Autore.* Landshut: Weißenburger, 1525.

————. *Defensio contra amarulentes D. Andreae Bodenstein Carolstatini invectiones (1518).* Edited by Joseph Greving. Münster: Aschen-dorff, 1919.

————. *Disputatio Viennae Pannoniae habita (1517).* Edited by Therese Virnich. Münster: Aschendorff, 1923.

————. *Enchiridion. Handbüchlin gemainer stell unnd Artickel der jetzt schwe-benden Neuwen leeren. Faksimile-Druck der Ausgabe Augsburg 1533.* Edited by Erwin Iserloh. Münster: Aschendorff, 1980.

Eckhart, Meister. *Werke.* Vol. 2, edited by Nikolaus Largier. Frankfurt: Klassiker-Verlag, 1993.

Erasmus of Rotterdam. *NOVVM IN-| strumentum omne, dilgienter ab ERASMO ROTERDAMO| recognitum et emendatum non solum ad græcam ueritatem, ue-| rumetiam ad multorum utriusque linguæ codi-cum, eorumque ue-| terum simul et emendatorum fidem (. . .).* Basel: Froben, 1516.

————. *Ausgewählte Schriften.* Edited by Wener Welzig, Vol. 2. Darm-stadt: Wissenschaftliche Buchgesellschaft, 1975.

Geiler, Johannes. *Das schiff des heils| Auff das aller kürtzest hie vß geleget |
Nach der figur die doctor Johannes von Eck gemacht hat zů Ingolt| stat.
bewegt auß den predigten des wirdigen Herren doctor Johannes gei-| ler
von Keisersperg . . .]*. Straßburg : 1512.

Gerson, Jean. *Oeuvres complètes*. Edited by P. Glorieux. Vol. 3, Paris:
Desclée, 1962. Vol. 7/2, Paris: Desclée, 1968. Vol. 9, Paris: Desclée,
1973.

———. *Quarta pars operum Johan-| nis Gerson prius non impressa*. Stras-
bourg: 1502.

Gess, Felician, ed. *Akten und Briefe zur Kirchenpolitik Herzog Georgs von
Sachsen*. Vol. 1, *1517–1524*. Leipzig: Teubner, 1905.

Hugo de Sancto Victore. *Hugonis de Sancto Victore operum Editio auspiciis Gulduini abbatis procurata et IV voluminibus digessa*. Vol. 1,
edited by Rainer Berndt and José Luis Narvaja. Münster: Aschendorff, 2017.

Hus, Jan. *Historia | et | monumenta | joannis hus | atque | hieronymi | pragen-
sis*. Vol. 1. Nürnberg: Montanus, 1715.

———. *Tractatus de ecclesia*. Edited by S. Harrison Thomson. Cambridge:
Heffer, 1956.

John Duns Scotus. *Ioannis Duns Scoti Opera omnia*. Vol. 13. Vatican: Typ.
Polyglottis Vaticanis, 2011.

Johann Ruchrath von Wesel. *De indulgentiis*. In *Reformtheologen des 15.
Jahrhunderts: Johann Pupper von Goch, Johann Ruchrath von Wesel,
Wessel Gansfort*. Edited by Gustav Adolf Benrath. Gütersloh: Güt-
ersloher Verlagshaus, 1968. 39–60.

Johannes of Dorsten. *De celebratione missae*. Erfurt: c.1488.

Johannes von Paltz. *Werke*. Vol. 1, *Coelifodina*, edited by Christoph
Burger and Friedhelm Stasch. Berlin: De Gruyter, 1983.

———. *Werke*. Vol. 3, *Opuscula*. Berlin: De Gruyter, 1989.

"Joint Declaration on the Doctrine of Justification." Lutheran World
Federation. Accessed April 1, 2023. https://www.lutheranworld.
org/content/resource-joint-declaration-doctrine-justification.

Jordanus de Saxonia. *Liber Vitasfratrum*. Edited by Rudolph Arbesmann
and Winfried Hümpfener. New York: Cosmopolitan Science and
Art Service, 1942.

Karlstadt, Andreas. *DEFENSIO | Andreę Carolostadii | aduersus | Eximii.
D. Ioannis Eckii theologię | doctoris & ordinatii Ing.| Monomachiam |
Patitur Carolostadius non modo Se.| A studiique Ro. In Italia/| Parisien.
in Gallia / aut | Coloniensis in Ger-| mania iudicium/| sed etiam sin-|
gulorum | & | omnium*. Wittenberg: Rhau-Grunenberg, 1518.

————. *D. Andree Carolstatini docto-| RIS ET ARCHIDIACONI VVIT-| TEN-| BVRGENSIS: CCCLXX:ET APOLOGE-| ticę Conclusio-nes pro sacris literis & Vuitten-| burgensibus] ita editę vt & lectoribus | profuturę sint.* Wittenberg: Johann Rhau-Grunenberg, 1518.

————. *Karlstadt und Augustin. Der Kommentar des Andreas Bodenstein von Karlstadt zu Augustins Schrift De spiritu etr littera. Einführung und Text.* Edited by Enrst Kähler. Halle: Max Niemeyer, 1952.

————. *Kritische Gesamtausgabe der Schriften und Briefe Andreas Bodensteins von Karlstadts.* Vol. 1/1, ed. Thomas Kaufmann. Gütersloh: Gütersloher Verlagshaus, 2017. Vol. 3, Gütersloh: Gütersloher Verlagshaus, 2020.

Kolde, Dietrich. *Der Christenspiegel des Dietrich Kolde von Münster.* Edited by Clemens Drees. Werl: Dietrich-Coelde-Verlag, 1954.

Seitz, Otto, ed. *Der authentische Text der Leipziger Disputation (1519).* Berlin: Schwetschke, 1903.

Lombardus, Petrus. *Sententiae in IV libris distinctae.* Vol. 2. Grottaferrata Rom: Coll. S. Bonaventurae Ad Claras Aquas, 1981.

von Landskron, Stephan. *Die Hymelstrazs: Mit einer Einleitung und vergleichenden Betrachtung zum Sprachgebrauch in den Frühdrucken.* Augsburg: Gerardus Johannes Jaspers, 1484, 1501, 1510; Amsterdam: Rodopi, 1979.

Luther, Martin. *Erfurter Annotationen 1509–1510/11.* Edited by Jun Matsuura. Köln: Böhlau, 2009. **AWA 9.**

————. *Studienausgabe.* Vol. 1, edited by Hans-Ulrich Delius. Berlin: Evangelische Verlagsanstalt, 1987.

Magnus, Albertus. *Opera Omnia.* Vol. 33, edited by Steph., Caes., Aug., and Borgnet. Paris: Vivès, 1895.

Maillard, Olivier. *Sacre theologie magistri: necnon | eloquii preconis celeberrimi | fratris oliuerii ordinis mi|norum professoris opus quadragesimale | perutilissimum.* Paris: 1508.

Maior, John. *Quartus Sententiarum Johannis Maioris.* Paris: 1509.

Mathesius, Johann. *Historien /| Von des Ehrwirdigen | in Gott seligen theuren Manns Got-| tes Doctoris Martini Luthers / anfang /| Lere / leben / vnnd sterben /| Alles ordenlich der Jarzal nach /| wie sich alle sachen zu jeder zeit | haben zugetragen / | Durch den alten M. Johann Mathesium | gestelt / vnd für seinem Christlichen ende verfertiget (. . .).* Nürnberg: Johann von Berg Erben, 1570

Melanchthons. *Werke.* Vol. 1, edited by Robert Stupperich. Gütersloh: Gütersloher Verlagshaus, 1951. Vol. 5, Gütersloh: Gütersloher Verlagshaus, 1965.

Myconius, Friedrich. *Geschichte der Reformation.* Edited by Otto Clemen (Leipzig: Voigtländer, 1954).

Nikolaus of Lyra. *Postilla super totam Bibliam.* Nuremberg: Anton Koberger, 1481.

Oldecop, Johann. *Chronik des Johan Oldecop.* Edited by Karl Euling. Tübingen: Litterarischer Verein, 1891.

Olearius, Gottfried. *SCRINIUM ANTIQUARIUM | ΙΔΡΟΧΕΙΡΑ | ANTIQVITATIS | FRAGMENTA,| SUMMORUM VIDELI-CET IN | ECCLES. ACAD. ET SCHOL. SUPE-| RIORE ÆVO VIRORUM,| (. . .) M. JOH. GOTTFRID. OLEARIUS.* Halle: Saalfeld, 1691.

Panormitanus. *ABBATIS| PANORMITANI | COMMENTARIA | In Quartum & Quintum Decretalium Libros. | (. . .).* Venedig: 1617.

———. *Nicolaus de Tudeschis, Lectura super quinque libros Decretalium. Pars prima super primo decretalium.* Venice: 1477.

Peppermüller, Rolf. *Anonymi auctoris saeculi XII Expositio in epistolas Pauli Ad Romanos—II Ad Corinthios 12.* Münster: Aschendorff, 2005.

———. *Glossa in epistolas Pauli.* Esslingen before September 8, 1473.

Petrus Mosellanus. *ORATIO | DE VARIARVM LINGVA| RVM COG-NITIONE PA| randa. Petro Mosella-|no Protogenese au/| tore. Lipsiæ in ma|gna eruditorum| corona pro/|nunciata.* Basel: Johann Froben, 1519.

Platina. Platynae Historici *Liber de vita Christi ac omnium pontificum (AA. 1- 1474).* Edited by Giacinto Gaida. Città di Castello: Lapi, 1932.

Prügel, Thomas. *Dekrete der Ökumenischen Konzilien.* Vol. 2, *Konzilien des Mittelalters,* edited by Josef Wolmuth. Paderborn: Brill, 2000.

Rapp, Ludwig. "Die Statuten der ältesten bekannten Synode von Brixen im Jahre 1511." *Zeitschrift des Ferdinandeums für Tirol und Vorarlberg* 22 (1878): 1–46.

Scheurl, Christoph. *Briefbuch, ein Beitrag zur Geschichte der Reformation und ihrer Zeit.* Vol. 2, edited by Franz von Soden and Joachim Karl Friedrich Knaake. Potsdam: Gropius, 1872.

von Seckendorf, Viet Ludwig, and Louis Maimbourg. *VITI LUDOVICI a SECKENDORF | (...) | COMMENTARIU | HISTORICUS ET APOLOGETICUS | De | LUTHERANISMO,| Sive| DE REFOR-MATIONE | RELIGIONIS| ductu| D. MARTINI LUTHERI| (...).* Leipzig: Johann Friedrich Gleditsch, 1694.

Seuse, Heinrich. *Deutsche Schriften.* Edited by Karl Bihlmeyer. Stuttgart: Kohlhammer 1907.

————. *Heinrich Seuses Horologium Sapientiae*. Edited by Pius Künzle. Freiburg: Universitätsverlag, 1977.

Suso, Henry. "Little Book of Eternal Wisdom." In *The Exemplar, with Two German Sermons*. Edited and translated by Frank Tobin. Mahwah, NJ: Paulist Press, 1989.

Stapulensis, Faber. *QVINCVPLEX | Psalterum | G allicum. | R omanum. | H ebraicum. | V etus. | C onciliatum*. Paris: Henricus Stephanus, 1509.

von Staupitz, Johann. "Salzburger Predigten: Eine textkritische Edition." Edited by Wolfram Schneider-Lastin. Diss., Phil. Tübingen, 1990.

————. *Sämtliche Schriften*. Vol. 2, *Lateinische Schriften II*, edited by Lothar Graf zu Dohna, Richard Wetzel, and Albrecht Endriss. Berlin: De Gruyter, 1979.

————. *Johann von Staupitzens sämmtliche Werke/Iohannis Staupitii Opera, quae reperiri potuerant omnia*. Edited by Joachim Carl Friedrich Knaake, Erster Band: Deutsche Schriften. Postdam: A. Krausnick, 1867.

Tauler, John. *Sermones: des hoch| geleerten in gnaden erleüchten do|ctoris Johannis Thaulerii sannt | dominici ordens die da weißend | auff den nächesten waren weg im | gaist zů wanderen durch überswe| bendenn syn. Von latein in teütsch | gewendt manchem menschenn zů | såliger fruchtbarkaitt*. Augsburg: Hans Otmar, 1508.

————. *Sermons*. Translated by Maria Shrady. Classics of Western Spirituality. Mahwah, NJ: Paulist Press, 1985.

————. *The Sermons and Conferences of John Tauler*. Edited and translated by Walter Elliott. Washington, DC: Apostolic Mission House, 1910.

Thomas of Kempen. *Thomae Hemerken a Kempis Opera Omnia*. Vol. 2, edited by Joseph Pohl. Freiburg: Sumptibus Herder, 1904.

Ulrich of Hutten. *Ulrichi ab Hutten Equitis Germani Opera quae extant omnia*. Vol. 2, edited by Joseph Hermann Münch. Berlin: Reimer, 1822.

Valla, Lorenzo. *De falso credita et ementita Constantini donatione*. Edited by Wolfram Setz. München: Monumenta Germaniae Historica, 1986.

William of Ockham. *Guilelmi de Ockham Opera Theologica*. Vol. 7, *Quaestiones in librum quartum sententiarum Reportatio*. Edited by Rega Wood and Gedeon Gál. St. Bonaventure: St. Bonaventure University, 1984.

Wyclif, Iohannis. *Tractatus de ecclesia*. Edited by Johann Loserth. London: Trübner, 1886.

## Studies

Albert, R. "Aus welchem Grunde disputirte Johann Eck gegen Martin Luther in Leipzig 1519." *Zeitschrift für die historische Theologie. NF* 37 (1873): 382–441.

Allgaier, Walter. "Der "fröhliche Wechsel" bei Martin Luther: Eine Untersuchung zu Christologie und Soteriologie bei Luther unter besonderer Berücksichtigung der Schriften bis 1521." Diss., Erlangen, 1966.

Angenendt, Arnold. "Seuse Lehre vom Ablaß." In *Reformatio ecclesiae: FS Erwin Iserloh*, edited by Remigius Bäumer, 143–54. Paderborn: Aschendorff, 1980.

Arand, Charles P., Robert Kolb, and James A. Nestingen. *The Lutheran Confessions: History and Theology of The Book of Concord*. Minneapolis: Fortress Press, 2012.

Armbruster, Jörg. *Luthers Bibelvorreden: Studien zu ihrer Theologie*. Suttgart: Deutsche Bibelgesellschaft, 2005.

Assel, Heinrich, and Bruce McCormack, eds. *Luther, Barth, and Movements of Theological Renewal (1918–1933)*. Berlin: De Gruyter, 2020.

Assmann, Jan. *Religion and Cultural Memory: Ten Studies*. Stanford: University Press, 2005.

Bagchi, David. "Luther's Ninety-Five Theses and the Contemporary Criticism of Indulgences." In *Promissory Notes on the Treasury of Merits. Indulgences in Late Medieval Europe*, edited by Robert N. Swanson, 331–55. Leiden: Brill, 2006.

Barge, Hermann. *Andreas Bodenstein von Karlstadt*. Vol. 1, *Karlstadt und die Anfänge der Reformation*, 2nd ed. Nieuwkoop: De Graaf, 1968.

Bäumer, Remigius. "Die Ekklesiologie des Johannes Eck." In *Johannes Eck (1486–1543): Internationales Symposium der Gesellschaft zur Herausgabe des Corpus Catholicorum aus Anlaß des 500. Geburtstages des Johannes Eck vom 13. bis 16. November 1986 in Ingolstadt und Eichstätt*, edited by Erwin Iserloh, 129–54. Münster: Aschendorff, 1988.

Bayer, Oswald. "Das Wort ward Fleisch. Luthers Christologie als Lehre von der Idiomenkommunkation." In *Jesus Christus—Gott für uns*, edited by Friedrich-Otto Scharbau, 58–101, 61f. Erlangen: Martin-Luther-Verlag, 2003.

———. "Oratio, Meditatio, Tentatio: Eine Besinnung auf Luthers Theologieverständnis." *Lutherjahrbuch* 55 (1988): 7–59.

————. *Martin Luther's Theology: A Contemporary Interpretation*. Grand Rapids: Eerdmans, 2008.

————. *Promissio: Geschichte der reformatorischen Wende in Luthers Theologie*, 2nd ed. Darmstadt: Wissenschaftliche Buchgesellschaft, 1989.

Bedouelle, Guy. "Lefèvre d'Étaples et Luther: Une recherche de frontières. 1517–1527." *Revue d'histoire et de philosophie religieuses* 63 (1983): 17–31.

Bell, Theo. *Divus Bernhardus: Bernhard von Clairvaux in Martin Luthers Schriften*. Mainz: Zabern, 1993.

Beutel, Albrecht. *Protestantische Konkretionen: Studien zur Kirchengeschichte*. Tübingen: Mohr, 1998.

Bianchi, Luca. "Captivare intellectum in obsequium Christi," *Rivista critica di storia della filosofia* 38 (1983): 81–87.

Bizer, Ernst. *Fides ex auditu: Eine Untersuchung über die Entdeckung der Gerechtigkeit Gottes durch Martin Luther*. Neukirchen-Vluyn: Neukirchener Verlagsanstalt, 1958; 3rd ed., 1966.

Brecht, Martin. "Luthers neues Verständnis der Buße und die reformatorische Entdeckung." *Zeitschrift für Theologie und Kirche* 101 (2004): 281–91.

————. "Luthers reformatorische Sermone." In *Fides et pietas: Festschrift Brecht, Martin zum 70. Geburtstag*, edited by Christian Peters and Jürgen Kampmann, 15–32. Münster: Lit, 2003.

————. "Römerbriefauslegungen Martin Luthers." In *Paulus, Apostel Jesu Christi: FS Günter Klein*, edited by Michael Trowitzsch, 207–25. Tübingen: Mohr, 1998.

————. *Martin Luther.* Vol. 1, *His Road to Reformation 1483–1521*. Minneapolis: Fortress, 1985.

Breul, Wolfgang. "Luthers Visitation im Augustinerkloster Grimma und seine frühe Ablasskritik: 'Nun will ich der Pauke ein Loch machen.'" *Herbergen der Christenheit* 32/33 (2008/2009): 7–27.

Brinkmann, Bodo, ed. *Cranach der Ältere*. Ostfildern: Hatje Cantz Verlag, 2007.

Brosseder, Johannes. "Luthers Hermeneutik und ihre gegenwärtige ökumenische Bedeutung." *Communio viatorum* 43 (1991): 220–43.

Bruin, Cebus C. de. "Ist Geert Groote der Verfasser des Büchleins *De imitatione Christi*? Kritische Randbemerkungen zu Van Ginnekens Hypothese betreffs der Autorschaft der Imitatio." In *Altdeutsch und altniederländische Mystik*, edited by Kurt Ruhe, 462–96. Darmstadt: Wissenschaftliche Buchgesellschaft, 1964.

Brush, Jack E. *Gotteserkenntnis und Selbsterekenntnis. Luthers Verständnis des 51. Psalms.* Tübingen: Mohr, 1997.

Bucher, Richard P. *The Ecumenical Luther. The Development of His Doctrinal Hermenutic.* Saint Louis: Concordia Publishing House, 2003.

Burger, Christoph. "Die Passionsharmonie des Augustinereremiten Johannes von Paltz (ca. 1445–1511)." In *Evangelienharmonien des Mittelalters*, edited by Christoph Burger, 123–38. Asson: Royal Van Gorcum, 2004.

———. *Tradition und Neubeginn: Martin Luther in seinen frühen Jahren.* Tübingen: Mohr, 2014.

Colish, Marcia L. "From *Sacra pagina* to *theologia*: Peter Lombard as an Exegete of Romans." *Medieval Perspectives* 6 (1991): 1–19.

Courtenay, William J. *Capacity and Volition: A History of the Distinction of Absolute and Ordained Power.* Bergamo: Pierluigi Lubrina, 1990.

Delius, Hans-Ulrich. *Augustin als Quelle Luthers: Eine Materialsammlung.* Berlin: Evangelische Verlagsanstalt, 1984.

Dettloff, Werner. *Die Entwicklung der Akzeptations- und Verdienstlehre von Duns Scotus bis Luther.* Münster: Aschendorff, 1963.

Dieter, Theo. *Der junge Luther und Aristoteles: Eine historisch-systematische Untersuchung zum Verhältnis von Theologie und Philosophie.* Berlin: De Gruyter, 2001.

Dietz, Thorsten. *Der Begriff der Furcht bei Martin Luther.* Tübingen: Mohr, 2009.

Ebeling, Gerhard. *Evangelische Evangelienauslegung: Eine Untersuchung zu Luthers Hermeneutik.* München: Lempp, 1942.

———. *Lutherstudien.* Vol. 1, Tübingen: Mohr, 1971; Vol. 3, Tübingen: Mohr, 1985.

Evangelische Kirche in Deutschland, ed. *Rechtfertigung und Freiheit. 500 Jahre Reformation 2017. Ein Grundlagentext des Rates der Evangelischen Kirche in Deutschland (EKD).* Gütersloh: Gütersloher Verlagshaus, 2014; 4th ed., 2015.

Evangelische Kirche in Deutschland and Deutsche Bischofskonferenz, eds. *Erinnerung heilen—Jesus Christus bezeugen. Ein gemeinsames Wort zum Jahr 2017.* Hannover: Linden, 2016.

Evener, Vincent. *Enemies of the Cross: Suffering, Truth, and Mysticism in the Early Reformation.* Oxford: University Press, 2021.

Evener, Vincent, and Ronald K. Rittgers, eds. *Protestants and Mysticism in Reformation Europe.* Leiden: Brill, 2018.

Fabisch, Peter. "Johannes Eck und die Publikationen der Bullen 'Exsurge Domine' und 'Decet Romanum Pontificem'." In *Johannes Eck (1486–1543): Internationales Symposium der Gesellschaft zur Herausgabe des Corpus Catholicorum aus Anlaß des 500. Geburtstages des Johannes Eck vom 13. bis 16. November 1986 in Ingolstadt und Eichstätt*, edited by Erwin Iserloh, 74–106. Münster: Aschendorff, 1988.

Feld, Helmut. *Die Anfänge der modernen biblischen Hermeneutik in der spätmittelalterlichen Theologie.* Wiesbaden: Zabern, 1977.

Flörken, Norbert. "Ein Beitrag zur Datierung von Luthers Sermo de indulgentiis pridie Dedicationis." *Zeitschrift für Kirchengeschichte* 82 (1971): 344–50.

Forde, Gerhard O. "Law and Gospel in Luther's Hermenutic." *Interpretation* 37 (1983): 240–52.

Fuchs, Thomas. *Konfession und Gespräch: Typologie und Funktion der Religionsgespräche in der Reformationszeit.* Weimar: Böhlau, 1995.

Georges, Tobias. *Quam nos divinitatem nominare consuevimus: Die theologische Ethik des Peter Abaelard.* Leipzig: Evangelische Verlagsanstalt, 2005.

Gleason, Randall C. "'Letter' and 'Spirit' in Luther's Hermeneutics." *Bibliotheca Sacra* 157 (2000): 468–85.

Gradl, Stefan. "Inspektor Columbo irrt: Kriminalistische Überlegungen zur Frage: Kannte Luther Thomas?" *Luther* 77 (2006): 83–99.

Grane, Leif. "Christus finis omnium: Eine Studie zu Luthers erster Psalmenvorlesung." In *Caritas Dei: Beiträge zum Verständnis Luthers un der gegenwärtigen Ökumene*, edited by Oswald Bayer, 170–91. Helsinki: Luther-Agricola-Gesellschaft, 1997.

———. *Contra Gabrielem: Luthers Auseinandersetzung mit Gabriel Biel in der Disputatio Contra Scholasticam Theologiam 1517.* Copenhagen: Gyldendal, 1962.

———. *Martinus Noster: Luther in the German reform movement 1518–1521.* Mainz: Zabern, 1994.

Greving, Joseph. *Johann Eck als junger Gelehrter: Eine literatur- und dogmengeschichtliche Untersuchung über seinen Chrysopassus praedestinationis aus dem Jahre 1514.* Münster: Aschendorff, 1906.

Grosse, Sven. "Heilsgewissheit des Glaubens: Die Entwicklung der Auffassungen des jungen Luther von Gewissheit und Ungewissheit des Heils." *Lutherjahrbuch* 77 (2010): 41–63.

Haas, Alois Maria. *Nim din selbes war: Studien zur Lehre von der Selbsterkenntnis bei Meister Eckhart, Johannes Tauler und Heinrich Seuse.* Freiburg: Universitätsverlag, 1971.

Hägglund, Bengt. "Luther und die Mystik." In *Kirche, Mystik, Heiligung und das Natürliche bei Luther: Vorträge des Dritten Internaionalen Kongresses für Lutherforschung*, 84–93. Göttingen: Vandenhoeck & Ruprecht, 1967.

Hamm, Berndt. "Art. Staupitz, Johannes von." *Theologische Realenzyklopädie* 32 (2001): 119–27.

———. "Johann von Staupitz (ca. 1468–1524)—spätmittelalterlicher Reformer und 'Vater' der Reformation." *Archiv für Reformationsgeschichte* 92 (2001): 6–41.

———. "Pure Gabe ohne Gegengabe—die religionsgeschichtliche Revolution der Reformation." *Jahrbuch für Biblische Theologie* 27 (2012): 241–76.

———. "Wollen und Nicht-Können als Thema der spätmittelalterlichen Bußseelsorge." In *Spätmittelalterliche Frömmigkeit zwischen Ideal und Praxis*, edited by Berndt Hamm and Thomas Lentes, 111–46. Tübingen: Mohr, 2001.

———. *Ablass und Reformation: Erstaunliche Kohärenzen*. Tübingen: Mohr, 2016.

———. *Frömmigkeitstheologie am Anfang des 16. Jahrhunderts: Studien zu Johannes von Paltz und seinem Umkreis*. Tübingen: Mohr Siebeck, 1982.

———. *Promissio, Pactum, Ordinatio: Freiheit und Selbstbindung Gottes in der scholastischen Gnadenlehre*. Tübingen: Mohr, 1977.

———. *Religiosität im späten Mittelalter: Spannungspole, Neuaufbrüche, Normierungen*, edited by Reinhold Friedrich and Wolfgang Simon. Tübingen: Mohr Siebeck, 2011.

———. *The Early Luther: Stages in a Reformation Reorientation*. Minneapolis: Fortress Press, 2017.

Härle, Wilfried. "Wer hat die Kompetenz zur (richtigen) Schriftauslegung? Überlegungen im Anschluss an Luther und Schleiermacher." In *Solo verbo. FS Hans Christian Knuth*, edited by Knut Kammholz, 147–68. Kiel: Lutherische Verlagsgesellschaft, 2008.

Helmer, Christine, ed. *The Medieval Luther*. Tübingen: Mohr, 2020.

Helmer, Christine. *The Trinity and Martin Luther*. 2nd rev. ed. Bellingham: Lexham, 2017.

Hendrix, Scott H. "Luther against the Background of the History of Biblical Interpretation." *Interpretation* 37 (1983): 229–39.

———. "Luther." In *Cambridge Companion to Reformation Theology*, edited by David Bagchi and David Steinmetz, 39–56. Cambridge: Cambridge University Press, 2004.

————. "'We Are All Hussites'? Hus and Luther Revisited." *Archiv für Reformationsgeschichte* 65 (1974): 134–61.

Herms, Eilert. "Äußere und innere Klarheit des Wortes Gottes bei Paulus, Luther und Schleiermacher." In *Jesus Christus als die Mitte der Schrift: Studien zur Hermeneutik des Evangeliums*, edited by Christof Landmesser, Hans-Joachim Eckstein, and Hermann Lichtenberger, 3–72. Berlin: De Gruyter, 1997.

Holm, Bo Kristian, and Peter Widmann, eds. *Word—Gift—Being*. Tübingen: Mohr Siebeck, 2009.

Honselmann, Klemens. *Urfassung und Drucke der Ablaßthesen Martin Luthers und ihre Veröffentlichung*. Paderborn: Schöningh, 1966.

Hülsen, Christian. *Le chiese di Roma nel medio evo: Cataloghi et appunti*. Florenz: Olschki, 1927.

Iserloh, Erwin. "Sacramentum et exemplum—ein augustinisches Thema lutherischer Theologie." In *Reformata reformanda: Festgabe für Hubert Jedin zum 17. Juni 1965*, edited by Erwin Iserloh and Konrad Repgen, 247–64. Münster: Aschendorff, 1965.

Jadatz, Heiko. "Herzog Georg von Sachsen und die Leipziger Disputation." In *Die Leipziger Disputation 1519*, edited by Markus Hein and Armin Kohnle, 109–24. Leipzig: Evangelische Verlagsanstalt, 2011.

Johnson, Anne Marie. *Beyond Indulgences. Luther's Reform of Late Medieval Piety, 1518–1520*. Kirksville: Truman State University Press, 2017.

Jüngel, Eberhard. ". . . unum aliquid assecutus, omnia assecutus . . . Zum Verständnis des Verstehens—nach M. Luther, De servo arbitrio (WA 18:605 = BoA 3, 100)." In *Jesus Christus als die Mitte der Schrift: Studien zur Hermeneutik des Evangeliums*, edited by Christof Landmesser, Hans-Joachim Eckstein, and Hermann Lichtenberger, 73–99. Berlin: De Gruyter, 1997.

————. *Justification. The Heart of the Christian Faith: A Theological Study with an Ecumenical Purpose*. London: Bloomsbury, 2014.

Junghans, Helmar. "Martin Luther und die Leipziger Disputation." In *Die Leipziger Disputation von 1519. Ein theologisches Streitgespräch und seine Bedeutung für die frühe Reformation*, edited by Markus Hein and Armin Kohnle, 125–34. Leipzig: Evangelische Verlagsanstalt, 2019.

————. *Der junge Luther und die Humanisten*. Göttingen: Vandenhoeck & Ruprecht, 1985.

Kaufmann, Thomas. *Der Anfang der Reformation: Studien zur Kontextualität der Theologie, Publizistik und Inszenierung Luthers und der reformatorischen Bewegung*. Tübingen: Mohr Siebeck, 2012.

Khomych, Taras. "Luther's Assertio: A Prelimary Assessment of the Reformer's Relationship to Patristics." *Annali di storia dell'esegesi* 28 (2011): 351–63.

Kjeldgaard-Pedersen, Steffen. *Gesetz, Evangelium und Buße: Theologiegeschichtliche Studien zum Verhältnis zwischen dem jungen Johann Agricola (Eisleben) und Martin Luther.* Leiden: Brill, 1983.

Klaiber, Wilbirgis. *Ecclesia militans: Studien zu den Festtagspredigten des Johannes Eck.* Münster: Aschendorff, 1979.

Klitzsch, Ingo. *Die "Theologien" des Petrus Abaelardus: Genetisch-kontextuelle Analyse und theologiegeschichtlich Relektüre.* Leipzig: Evangelische Verlagsanstalt, 2010.

Kohnle, Armin. *Reichstag und Reformation. Kaiserliche und ständische Religionspolitik von den Anfängen der Causa Lutheri bis zum Nürnberger Religionsfrieden.* Gütersloh: Gütersloher Verlagshaus, 2001.

Kolde, Theodor. "Wittenberger Disputationsthesen aus den Jahren 1516–1522." *Zeitschrift für Kirchengeschichte* 11 (1890): 448–71.

Köpf, Ulrich. "Martin Luther als Mönch." *Luther* 55 (1984): 66–84.

———. "Monastische Traditionen bei Martin Luther." In *Luther—zwischen den Zeiten: Eine Jenaer Ringvorlesung*, edited by Christoph Markschies and Michael Trowitzsch, 17–35. Tübingen: Mohr, 1999.

———. "Wurzeln reformatorischen Denkens in der monastischen Theologie Bernhards von Clairvaux." In *Reformation und Mönchtum*, edited by Athina Lexutt, Volker Mantey, and Volkmar Ortmann, 29–56. Tübingen: Mohr Siebeck, 2008.

———. *Frömmigkeitsgeschichte und Theologiegeschichte: Gesammelte Aufsätze.* Tübingen: Mohr, 2022.

Körner, Ferdinand. *Tetzel, der Ablaßprediger: Sein Leben und sein Wirken für den Ablaß seiner Zeit, mit besonderer Rücksicht auf katholische Anschauungen neu untersucht und möglichst nach den Quellen, mehrfach nach bisher noch ungedruckten, dargestellt.* Frankenberg: Roßberg, 1880.

Kreuzer, Michael. *"Und das Wort ist Fleisch geworden:" Zur Bedeutung des Menschseins Jesu bei Johannes Driedo und Martin Luther.* Paderborn: Bonifatius, 1998.

Krüger, Jürgen, and Martin Wallraff. *Luthers Rom: Die Ewige Stadt in der Renaissance.* Darmstadt: Wissenschaftliche Buchgesellschaft, 2010.

Kruse, Jens-Martin. *Universitätstheologie und Kirchenreform: Die Anfänge der Reformation in Wittenberg 1516–1522.* Mainz: Zabern, 2002.

Kümmel, Werner Georg. *Röm 7 und die Bekehrung des Paulus*. Leipzig: Hinrichs, 1929.

Selga, Kurt-Victor. "Das Autoritätengefüge der westlichen Christenheit im Lutherkonflikt 1517 bis 1521." *Historische Zeitschrift* 223 (1976): 591–617.

Kyndal, Erik. "Christus, 'Sakrament' und 'Gabe.' Einer terminologische Präzisierung von Luthers Christologie 1521." In *Kirche zwischen Heilsbotschaft und Lebenswirklichkeit: Festschrift für Theodor Jørgensen zum 60. Geburtstag*, edited by Dietz Lange and Peter Widmann, 197–216. Frankfurt: Lang, 1996.

Leclercq, Jean. *The Love of Learning and the Desire for God: A Study of Monastic Culture*. New York: Fordham University Press, 1961.

Leppin, Volker. "Der Primat des Papstes im langen 15. Jahrhundert." In *Die Päpste der Renaissance. Politik, Kunst und Musik*, edited by Michael Matheus et al., 353–80. Regensburg: Pustet, 2017.

———. "Does Ockham's Concept of Divine Power Threaten Man's Certainty in His Knowledge of the World?" *Franciscan Studies* 55 (1998): 169–80

———. "Der Verlust des Menschen Luther: Zu Ebelings Lutherdeutung." *Journal for Early modern Christianity* 1 (2014): 29–50.

———. "Hermeneutik und Seelsorge. Gerhard Ebelings Vermächtnis für die Lutherforschung." In *Neige dein Ohr... Beiträge zur ökumenischen Theologie: FS Christian Schad*, edited by Paul Metzger, Andreas Rummel, and Wolfgang Schumacher, 123–30. Leipzig: Evangelische Verlagsanstalt, 2021.

———. *Die fremde Reformation. Luthers mystische Wurzeln*. 2nd ed. München: Beck, 2017.

———. *Martin Luther*. Darmstadt: Wissenschaftliche Buchgesellschaft 2006; 3rd ed., 2017.

———. *Martin Luther: A Late Medieval Life*. Grand Rapids: Baker Academic, 2017.

———. *Transformationen: Studien zu den Wandlungsprozessen in Theologie und Frömmigkeit zwischen Spätmittelalter und Reformation*. 2nd ed. Tübingen: Mohr Siebeck, 2018.

———. *Wilhelm von Ockham: Gelehrter—Streiter—Bettelmönch*. 2nd ed. Darmstadt: Wissenschaftliche Buchgesellschaft, 2012.

———. "Der Einfluss Johannes Ecks auf den jungen Luther." *Luther* 86 (2015): 135–47.

Leppin, Volker, ed. *Reformatorische Theologie und Autoritäten. Studien zur Geschichte des Schriftprinzips beim jungen Luther*. Tübingen: Mohr, 2015.

Leppin, Volker, and Dorothea Sattler, eds. *Reformation 1517–2017. Ökumenische Perspektiven*. Göttingen: Vandenhoeck & Ruprecht, 2014.

Leppin, Volker, and Mickey L. Mattox. "The Leipzig Debate: A Reformation Turning Point." In *Luther at Leipzig: Martin Luther, the Leipzig Debate, and the Sixteenth-Century Reformations*, edited by Mickey L. Mattox et al., 11–30. Leiden: Brill 2019.

Leppin, Volker, and Stefan Michels, eds. *Reformation als Transformation? Interdisziplinäre Zugänge zum Transformationsparadigma als historiographische Beschreibungskategorie*. Tübingen: Mohr Siebeck, 2022.

Leppin, Volker, and Timothy Wengert. "Posting of the Ninety-Five Theses." *Lutheran Quarterly* 29 (2015): 373–98.

Levy, Ian Christopher. "The Leipzig Disputation: Masters of the Sacred Page and the Authority of Scripture." In *Luther at Leipzig: Martin Luther, the Leipzig Debate, and the Sixteenth-Century Reformations*, edited by Mickey L. Mattox et al. 115–44. Leiden: Brill, 2019.

Lexutt, Athina. "Christologie als Soteriologie: Ein Blick in die späten Disputationen Martin Luthers." In *Relationen—Studien zum Übergang vom Spätmittelalter zur Reformation. Festschrift zu Ehren von Karl-Heinz zur Mühlen*, edited by Wolfgang Matz and Athina Lexutt, 201–16. Münster: Lit., 2000.

Lienhard, Marc. *Martin Luthers christologisches Zeugnis: Entwicklung und Grundzüge seiner Christologie*. Göttingen: Vandenhoeck & Ruprecht, 1979.

Lohse, Bernhard. "Luther und Bernhard von Clairvaux." In *Bernhard von Clairvaux: Rezeption und Wirkung im Mittelalter und in der Neuzeit*, edited by Kaspar Elm, 271–301. Wiesbaden: Harrassowitz, 1994.

———. *Evangelium in der Geschichte: Studien zu Luther und der Reformation*, edited by Leif Grane et al., 11–30. Göttingen: Vandenhoeck & Ruprecht, 1988.

———. *Mönchtum und Reformation: Luthers Auseinandersetzung mit dem Mönchsideal des Mittelalters*. Göttingen: Vandenhoeck & Ruprecht, 1963.

Lohse, Bernhard, ed. *Der Durchbruch der reformatorischen Erkenntnis bei Luther*. Darmstadt: Wissenschaftliche Buchgesellschaft, 1968.

———. *Der Durchbruch der reformatorischen Erkenntnis bei Luther: Neuere Untersuchungen*. Stuttgart: Zabern, 1988.

Lohse, Eduard. "Martin Luther und der Römerbrief des Apostels Paulus." *Kerygma und Dogma* 52 (2006): 106–25.

Markschies, Christoph. "Taufe und Concupisentia bei Augustinus." In *Gerecht und Sünder zugleich? Ökumenische Klärungen*, edited by Theodor Schneider and Gunther Wenz, 92–108. Göttingen: Vandenhoeck & Ruprecht, 2001.

Martin Honecker. "Martin Luthers Theologie im Reformationsgedenken." *Theologische Rundschau* 81 (2016): 35–47.

Maschmeier, Jens-Christian. "Glaube und Handeln bei Luther und Paulus. Kritische Anfragen an eine lutherische Paulusperspektive." In *Kerygma und Dogma* 59 (2013): 21–44.

Massaut, Jean-Pierre. "Lefèvre d'Étaples d'exérgèse au xvi^e siècle." *Revue d'histoire ecclésiastique* 78 (1983): 73–78.

Maurer, Wilhelm. *Der junge Melanchthon zwischen Humanismus und Reformation.* Vol. 2. Göttingen: Vandenhoeck & Ruprecht, 1996.

McScorley, Harry. *Luthers Lehre vom unfreien Willen nach seiner Hauptschrift De Servo Arbitrio im Lichte der biblischen und kirchlichen Tradition.* München: Kaiser, 1967.

Miethke, Jürgen. *Ockhams Weg zur Sozialphilosophie.* Berlin: De Gruyter, 1969.

Moeller, Bernd. "Luther und das Papsttum." In *Luther Handbuch*, 3rd ed., edited by Albrecht Beutel, 131–40. Tübingen: Mohr, 2017.

———. "Thesenanschläge." In *Luthers Thesenanschlag—Faktum oder Fiktion*, edited by Joachim Ott and Martin Treu, 9–31. Leipzig: Evangelische Verlagsanstalt, 2008.

———. "Die Anfechtung bei Johann Tauler." Diss., Universität Mainz, 1956. Typewritten manuscript.

———. *Die Reformation und das Mittelalter: Kirchenhistorische Aufsätze.* Edited by Johannes Schilling. Göttingen: Vandenhoeck & Ruprecht, 1991.

Morerod, Charles. "Le manque de clarté de Gabriel Biel et son impact sur la Réforme." *Nova et Vetera* 75 (2000): 15–32.

Morrow, C. "Reconnecting Sacrament and Virtue: Penance in Thomas's Summa Theologiae." *New Blackfriars* 91 (2010): 304–20.

Mostert, Walter. "Scriptura sacra sui ipsius interpres. Bemerkungen zum Verständnis der Heiligen Schrift durch Luther." *Lutherjahrbuch* 46 (1979): 60–96.

Mourin, Louis. *Jean Gerson, Prédicateur français.* Brugge: De Tempel, 1952.

Neuner, Peter, and Friedrich Schröger. "Luthers These von der Klarheit der Schrift." *Theologie und Glaube* 74 (1984): 39–58.

Nicol, Martin. *Meditation bei Luther.* 2nd ed. Göttingen: Vandenhoeck & Ruprecht, 1991.

Nieden, Marcel. "Anfechtung als Thema lutherischer Anweisungsschriften zum Theologiestudium." In *Praxis Pietatis: Beiträge zu Theologie und Frömmigkeit in der Frühen Neuzeit: FS Wolfgang Sommer*, edited by Hans-Jörg and Marcel Nieden, 83–102. Stuttgart: Kohlhammer, 1999.

————. *Die Erfindung des Theologen: Wittenberger Anweisungen zum Theologiestudium im Zeitalter von Reformation und Konfessionalisierung.* Tübingen: Mohr, 2006.

Noack, Thomas. "Der Ort der Disputation—die Pleißenburg." In *Leipziger Disputation,* edited by Markus Hein and Armin Kohnle, 73–84. Leipzig: Evangelische Verlagsanstaldt, 2011.

Nörr, Knut Wolfgang. *Kirche und Konzil bei Nicolaus de Tudeschis (Panormitanus).* Köln: Böhlau, 1964.

O'Kane, Martin. "Picturing the 'Man of Sorrows': The Passion-Filled Afterlives of a Biblical Icon." *Religion and the Arts* 9 (2005): 62–100.

Oberman, Heiko Augustinus. "Simul gemitus et raptus: Luther und die Mystik." In *Kirche, Mystik, Heiligung und das Natürliche bei Luther: Vorträge des Dritten Internaionalen Kongresses für Lutherforschung.* Göttingen: Vandenhoeck & Ruprecht, 1967, 20–59.

————. "Wir sein pettler. Hoc est verum. Bund und Gnade in der Theologie des Mittelalters und der Reformation." In *Die Reformation: Von Wittenberg nach Genf.* Göttingen: Vandenhoeck & Ruprecht, 1986, 90–112.

————. *The Harvest of Medieval Theology: Gabriel Biel and Late Medieval Nominalism.* Cambridge: Harvard University Press, 1963.

————. *The Reformation: Roots and and Ramification.* Edinburgh: T&T Clark, 1994.

————. *Werden und Wertung der Reformation: Vom Wegestreit zum Glaubenskampf.* 2nd ed. Tübingen: Mohr, 1979.

Ohly, Friedrich. "Geistige Süße bei Otfried." In *Schriften zur mittelalterlichen Bedeutungsforschung.* Darmstadt: Wissenschaftliche Buchgesellschaft, 1977, 93–127.

————. *Süße Nägel der Passion: Ein Beitrag zur theologischen Semantik.* Baden-Baden: Koerner, 1989.

Ohst, Martin. "Luthers 'Schriftprinzip.'" In *Luther als Schriftausleger: Luthers Schriftprinzip in seiner Bedeutung für die Ökumene,* edited by Hans Christian Knuth, 21–39. Erlangen: Martin-Luther-Verlag, 2010.

Otto, Henrik. *Vor- und frühreformatorische Tauler-Rezeption: Annotationen in Drucken des späten 15. und frühen 16. Jahrhunderts.* Gütersloh: Gütersloher Verlaghaus, 2003.

Ozment, Stephen. *The Serpent and the Lamb: Cranach, Luther, and the Making of the Reformation.* New Haven: Yale University Press, 2011.

Pani, Giancarlo. "L'eredità di Agostino nella ‚Römerbriefvorlesung' di Martin Lutero: La Expositio quorundam propositionum ex epistola ad Romanos." *Studi e materiali di storia delle religioni* 61 (1995): 83–97.

Pannenberg, Wolfhart. *Basic Questions in Theology: Collected Essays.* Vol. 1. Minneapolis: Fortress Press, 2008.

———. "'Extra nos'—Ein Beitrag Luthers zur christlichen Frömmigkeit." In *Weg und Weite: Offene Wege: Festschrift für Karl Lehmann,* edited by Albert Raffel, 197–205. Freiburg: Herder, 2001.

Paulus, Nikolaus. *Die deutschen Dominikaner im Kampfe gegen Luther (1518–1563).* Freiburg im Breisgau: Herder, 1903.

———. *Geschichte des Ablasses am Ausgang des Mittelalters.* 2nd ed. Darmstadt: Wissenschaftliche Buchgesellschaft, 2000.

———. *Johann Tetzel, der Ablaßprediger.* Mainz: Kirchheim, 1899.

Pesch, Otto Hermann. "Neuere Beiträge zur Frage nach Luthers 'Reformatorischer Wende'." *Catholica. Jahrbuch für Kontroverstheologie* 37 (1983): 259–87; 38 (1984): 66–133.

———. "Simul iustus et peccator: Sinn und Stellenwert einer Formel Martin Luthers.—Thesen und Kurzkommentare." In *Gerecht und Sünder zugleich? Ökumenische Klärungen,* edited by Theodor Schneider and Gunther Wenz, 146–67. Freiburg: Herder, 2001.

———. "Zur Frage nach Luthers reformatorischer Wende: Ergebnisse und Probleme der Diskussion um Ernst Bizer, Fides ex auditu." *Catholica. Jahrbuch für Kontroverstheologie* 20 (1966): 216–43, 264–80.

Peters, Albrecht. *Glaube und Werk: Luthers Rechtfertigungslehre im Lichte der Heiligen Schrift.* Berlin: Lutherisches Verlaghaus, 1967.

Peura, Simo. "Die Teilhabe an Christu." In *Luther und Theosis: Vergöttlichung als Thema der abendlandischen Theologie,* edited by Simon Peura and Antti Raunio. Helsinki: Luther-Agricola-Gesellschaft, 1990.

Poschmann, Bernhard. *Handbuch der Dogmengeschichte IV/3: Buße und Letzte Ölung.* Freiburg: Herder, 1951.

Posset, Franz. "Bernhard von Clairvaux's Meditation zu Psalm 31, 2 bei Martin Luther." *Lutherjahrbuch* 69 (2002): 71–78.

———. "Preaching the Passion of Christ on the Eve of the Reformation." *Concordia Theological Quarterly* 59 (1995): 279–300, 282–95.

———. *The Front-Runner of the Catholic Reformation: The Life and Works of Johann von Staupitz.* Aldershot: Ashgate, 2002, 135–156.

———. *The Real Luther: A Friar at Erfurt & Wittenberg.* St. Louis: Concordia, 2011.

Ratzinger, Joseph. "Kommentar zu *Dei verbum* Kap. 1–2." In *Lexikon für Theologie und Kirche. Ergänzungsbd. 2,* edited by Heinrich Suso Brechter et al., 497–528. Freiburg: Herder, 1967.

Reinert, Jonathan. *Passionspredigt im 16. Jahrhundert: Das Leiden und Sterben Jesu Christi in den Postillen Martin Luthers, der Wittenberger Tradition und altgläubiger Prediger.* Tübingen: Mohr, 2020.

Rieger, Reinhold. *Von der Freiheit eines Christenmenschen / De libertate christiana.* Tübingen: Mohr Siebeck, 2007.

Rittgers, Ronald R. "Embracing the 'True Relic' of Christ: Suffering, Penance, and Private Confession in the Thought of Martin Luther." In *A New History of Penance,* edited by Abigail Firey, 377–93. Leiden: Brill, 2008.

———. *The Reformation of Suffering: Pastoral Theology and Lay Piety in Late Medieval and Early Modern Germany.* Oxford: University Press, 2012.

Rix, H. "Luther's Debt to the Imitatio Christi." *Augustiniana* 28 (1978): 91–107.

Rosin, Robert. "Reformation Christology: Some Luther Starting Points." *Concordia Theological Quarterly* 71 (2007): 147–68.

Ruh, Kurt. *Geschichte der abendländischen Mystik. Vierter Band: Die niederländische Mystik des 14. bis 16. Jahrhunderts.* Munich: C. H. Beck, 1999.

Saarinen, Risto. *Gottes Wirken auf uns: Die transzendentale Deutung des Gegenwart-Christi-Motivs in der Lutherforschung.* Stuttgart: Steiner Verlag Wiesbaden, 1989.

———. "Justification by Faith: The View of the Mannermaa School." In *The Oxford Handbook of Martin Luther's Theology,* edited by Robert Kolb, Irene Dingel, and Ludomir Batka, 254–63. Oxford: University Press, 2014.

Schäfer, Ernst. *Luther als Kirchenhistoriker: Ein Beitrag zur Geschichte der Wissenschaft.* Gütersloh: Bertelsmann, 1897.

Schauerte, Heinrich. *Die Bußlehre des Johannes Eck.* Münster: Aschendorff, 1919.

Schmidt-Lauber, Gabriele. *Luthers Vorlesung über den Römerbrief 1515/16: Ein Vergleich zwischen Luthers Manuskript und den studentischen Nachschriften.* Köln: Böhlau, 1994.

Schneider, Florian. *Christus praedicatus et creditus: Die reformatorische Christologie Luthers in den Operationes in Psalmos (1519–1521), dargestellt mit beständigem Bezug zu seiner Christologie.* Neukirchen-Vluyn: Neukirchener, 2004.

Schüssler, Hermann. *Der Primat der Heiligen Schrift als theologisches und kanonistisches Problem im Spätmittelalter.* Wiesbaden: Zabern, 1977.

Schusterm Susanne. *Aemilie Juliane von Schwarzburg-Rudolstadt und Ahasver Fritsch: Eine Untersuchung zur Jesusfrömmigkeit im späten 17. Jahrhundert*. Leipzig: Evangelische Verlagsanstalt, 2006.

Schwarz, Reinhard. *Martin Luther: Lehrer der christlichen Religion*. Tübingen: Mohr, 2015.

———. *Vorgeschichte der reformatorischen Bußtheologie*. Berlin: De Gruyter, 1968.

Seeberg, Reinhold. *Die religiösen Grundgedanken des jungen Luther und ihr Verhältnis zu dem Ockhamismus und der deutschen Mystik*. Berlin: De Gruyter, 1931.

Seidemann, Karl. *Die Leipziger Disputation im Jahre 1519: Aus bisher unbenutzten Quellen historisch dargestellt und durch Urkunden erläutert*. Dresden: Arnold, 1843.

Seitz, Manfred. "Luthers Christologie in seinen Predigten." In *Jesus Christus—Gott für uns*, edited by Friedrich-Otto Scharbau, 43–57. Erlangen: Martin-Luther-Verlag, 2003.

Selge, Kurt-Victor. "Der Weg zur Leipziger Disputation." In *Bleibendes im Wandel der Kirchengeschichte*, edited by Bernd Moeller and Gerhard Ruhbach, 168–210. Tübingen: Mohr, 1973.

———. "Die Leipziger Disputation zwischen Luther und Eck." *Zeitschrift für Kirchengeschichte* 86 (1975): 26–40.

———. "Mittelalterliche Traditionsbezüge in Luthers frühe Theologie." In *Die frühe Reformation in Deutschland als Umbruch*, edited by Bernd Moeller, 149–56. Gütersloh: Gütersloher Verlagshaus, 1998.

———. *Normen der Christenheit im Streit um Ablaß und Kirchenautorität 1518 bis 1521. Erster Teil: Das Jahr 1518*. Heidelberg. Habilschrift, 1968.

Setz, Wolfram. *Lorenzo Vallas Schrift gegen die Konstantinische Schenkung: De falso credita et ementita Constantini donatione: Zur Interpretation und Wirkungsgeschichte*. Tübingen: Niemeyer, 1975.

Soukup, Pavel. "Jan Hus und der Prager Ablassstreit von 1412." In *Die mittelalterlichen Ablasskampagnen: Luthers Thesen von 1517 im Kontext*, edited by Andreas Rehberg, 485–500. Berlin: De Gruyter, 2017.

Spehr, Christopher. *Luther und das Konzil: Zur Entwicklung eines zentralen Themas in der Reformationszeit*. Tübingen: Mohr, 2010.

Stamm, Rainer, ed. *Lucas Cranach der Schnellste*. Bremen: Hachmannedition, 2009.

Steinmetz, David. *Luther and Staupitz: An Essay in the Intellectual Origins of the Protestant Reformation.* Durham: Duke University Press, 1980.

Stolle, Volker. "Gottes Name und Gottes Wort: Anstöße Luthers zu einer theologischen Hermeneutik." *Lutherische Theologie und Kirche* 33 (2009): 33–68.

Stracke, Ernst. *Luthers großes Selbstzeugnis 1545 über seine Entwicklung zum Reformator historisch-kritisch untersucht.* Leipzig: Eger & Sievers, 1926.

Tacke, Andreas. *Der katholische Cranach: Zu zwei Großaufträgen von Lucas Cranach d.Ä., Simon Franck und der Cranach-Werkstatt (1520–1540).* Mainz: von Zabern, 1992.

Tierney, Brian. *Origins of Papal Infallibility 1150–1350: A Study on the Concepts of Infallibility, Sovereignty and Tradition on the Middle Ages.* Leiden: Brill, 1972.

Tomlin, Graham. "The Medieval Origins of Luther's Theology of the Cross." *Archiv für Reformationsgeschichte* 89 (1998): 22–40.

Totten, Mark. "Luther on *unio cum Christo*: Toward a Model for Integrating Faith and Ethics." *Journal of Religious Ethics* 31 (2003): 443–62.

Twesten, August Detlev Christian. *Vorlesungen über die Dogmatik der Evangelisch-Lutherischen Kirche, nach dem Compendium des Herrn Dr. W. M. L. de Wette.* 3rd ed. Hamburg: Friedrich Perthes, 1834.

Ufer, Joachim. "Luther und Tetzel." *Blätter für pfälzische Kirchengeschichte und religiöse Volkskunde* 46 (1979): 166–76.

Ullmann, Carl. *Reformatoren vor der Reformation: Vornehmlich in Deutschland und den Niederlanden.* 2nd ed. Gotha: Perthes, 1866.

Ulrich Köpf. "Die Rezeptions- und Wirkungsgeschichte Bernhards von Clairvaux: Forschungsstand und Forschungsaufgaben." In *Bernhard von Clairvaux: Rezeption und Wirkung im Mittelalter und in der Neuzeit,* edited by Kaspar Elm, 5–65. Wiesbaden: Harrassowitz, 1994.

van den Berg, Marinus K. A. "Thomas van Kempen." *Ons Geestelijk Erf* 77 (2003): 9–29.

van Dijk, Rudolf. "Spiritualität der 'inicheit.' Mystik und Kirchenkritik in der Devotio Moderna." In *Die Kirchenkritik der Mystiker: Prophetie aus Gotteserfahrung,* vol. 2, edited by Mariano Delgado, 9–38. Stuttgart: Kohlhammer, 2005.

Viladesau, Richard. *The Triumph of the Cross: The Passion of Christ in Theology and the Arts, from the Renaissance to the Counter-Reformation.* Oxford: Oxford University Press, 2008.

Vogel, Lothar. "Zwischen Universität und Seelsorge: Martin Luthers Beweggründe im Ablassstreit." *Zeitschrift für Kirchengeschichte* 118 (2007): 187–212.

Vogelsang, Erich. *Die Anfänge von Luthers Christologie nach der Ersten Pslamenvorlesung insbesondere in ihren exegetischen und systematischen Zusammenhängen mit Augustin und der Scholastik dargestellt.* Berlin: De Gruyter, 1929.

Voigt-Goy, Christopher. "'dictum unius privati:' Zu Luthers Verwendung des Kommentars der Dekretale Significasti von Nicolaus de Tudeschis." In *Orientierung für das Leben: Kirchliche Bildung und Politik in Spätmittelalter, Reformation und Neuzeit: FS Manfred Schulze*, edited by Patrik Mähling, 93–114. Bern: Lit, 2010.

Volz, Hans. *Martin Luthers Thesenanschlag.* Weimar: Böhlau, 1959.

Walter, Peter. *Theologie aus dem Geist der Rhetorik: Zur Schriftauslegung des Erasmus von Rotterdam.* Mainz: Matthias-Grünewald-Verlag, 1991.

Weinrich, Michael. "Die Anfechtung des Glaubens. Die Spannung zwischen Gewißheit und Erfahrung bei Martin Luther." In *Jesus Christus als die Mitte der Schrift: Studien zur Hermeneutik des Evangeliums*, edited by Christof Landmesser, Hans-Joachim Eckstein, and Hermann Lichtenberger, 127–58. Berlin: De Gruyter, 1997.

Wengert, Timothy J. "Martin Luther's First Major Publication." *Lutheran Quarterly* 36 (2022): 166–80.

Wetzel, Richard. "Staupitz und Luther. Annäherung an eine Vorläufer-Figur." In *Blätter für pfälzische Kirchengeschichte und religiöse Volkskunde* 58 (1991): 369–95.

Wiberg Pedersen, Else Marie. "The Significance of the *Sola fide* and the *Sola gratia* in the the Theology of Bernard of Clairvaux [1090–1153] and Martin Luther [1483–1546]." *Luther-Bulletin* 18 (2009): 20–43.

Wiedemann, Theodor. *Dr. Johann Eck, Professor der Theologie an der Universität Ingolstadt: Eine Monographie.* Regensburg: Pustet, 1865.

Williams, Thomas. "Introduction: The Life and Work of John Duns the Scot." In *The Cambridge Companion to Duns Scotus*, edited by Thomas Williams, 1–14. Cambridge: University Press, 2003.

Winterhager, Wilhelm-Ernst. "Martin Luther und das Amt des Provinzialvikars in der Reformkongregation der deutschen Augustiner-Eremiten." In *Vita religiosa im Mittelalter: Festschrift für Kaspar Elm zum 70. Geburtstag*, edited by Franz J. Felten and Nikolas Jaspert, 707–38. Berlin: Duncker & Humblot, 1999.

————. "Ablaßkritik als Indikator sozialen Wandels vor 1517: Ein Beitrag zu Voraussetzungen und Einordnung der Reformation." *Archiv für Reformationsgeschichte* 90 (1999): 6–17.

Workman, Herbert B. *John Wylif: A Study of the English Medieval Church.* Vol. 2. Oxford: Clarendon, 1926.

Wriedt, Markus. *Gnade und Erwählung: Eine Untersuchung zu Johann von Staupitz und Martin Luther.* Mainz: von Zabern, 1991.

Wurm, Johann Peter. "Johannes Eck und die Disputation von Leipzig 1–519. Vorgeschichte und unmittelbare Folgen." In *Leipziger Disputation,* edited by Markus Hein and Armin Kohnle, 159–73. Leipzig: Evangelische Verlagsanstaldt, 2011.

Ziegenaus, Anton. *Umkehr, Versöhnung, Friede: Zu einer theologisch verantworteten Praxis von Bußgotttesdienst und Beichte.* Freiburg: Herder, 1975.

zu Dohna, Lothar Graf. "Staupitz und Luther. Kontinuität und Umbruch in den Anfängen der Reformation." *Pastoraltheologie* 74 (1985): 452–65.

Zumkeller, Adolar. *Erbsünde, Gnade, Rechtfertigung und Verdienst nach der Lehre der Erfurter Augustinertheologen des Spätmittelalters.* Würzburg: Echter Verlag, 1984.

zur Mühlen, Karl-Heinz. *Nos extra nos: Luthers Theologie zwischen Mystik und Scholastik.* Tübingen: J. C. B. Mohr, 1972.

# Index

*Living by Faith: Justification and Sanctification,* by Oswald Bayer (2003).

*Harvesting Martin Luther's Reflections on Theology, Ethics and the Church,* essays from *Lutheran Quarterly,* edited by Timothy J. Wengert, with foreword by David C. Steinmetz (2004).

*A More Radical Gospel: Essays on Eschatology, Authority, Atonement, and Ecumenism,* by Gerhard O. Forde, edited by Mark Mattes and Steven Paulson (2004).

*The Role of Justification in Contemporary Theology,* by Mark C. Mattes (2004).

*The Captivation of the Will: Luther vs. Erasmus on Freedom and Bondage,* by Gerhard O. Forde (2005).

*Bound Choice, Election, and Wittenberg Theological Method: From Martin Luther to the Formula of Concord,* by Robert Kolb (2005).

*A Formula for Parish Practice: Using the Formula of Concord in Congregations,* by Timothy J. Wengert (2006).

*Luther's Liturgical Music: Principles and Implications,* by Robin A Leaver (2006).

*The Preached God: Proclamation in Word and Sacrament,* by Gerhard O. Forde, edited by Mark C. Mattes and Steven D. Paulson (2007).

*Theology the Lutheran Way,* by Oswald Bayer (2007).

*A Time for Confessing,* by Robert W. Bertram (2008).

*The Pastoral Luther: Essays on Martin Luther's Pastoral Theology,* edited by Timothy J. Wengert (2009).

*Preaching from Home: The Stories of Seven Lutheran Women Hymn Writers,* by Gracia Grindal (2011).

*The Early Luther: Stages in a Reformation Reorientation,* by Berndt Hamm (2013).

*The Life, Works, and Witness of Tsehay Tolessa and Gudina Tumsa, the Ethiopian Bonhoeffer,* edited by Samuel Yonas Deressa and Sarah Hinlicky (2017).

*The Wittenberg Concord: Creating Space for Dialogue,* by Gordon A. Jensen (2018).

*Luther's Outlaw God: Volume 1: Hiddenness, Evil, and Predestination*, by Steven D. Paulson (2018).

*The Essential Forde: Distinguishing Law and Gospel*, by Gerhard O. Forde, edited by Nickolas Hopman, Mark C. Mattes, and Steven D. Paulson (2019).

*Luther's Outlaw God: Volume 2: Hidden in the Cross*, by Steven D. Paulson (2019).

*Minister's Prayer Book: An Order of Prayers and Readings, Revised Edition*, edited by Timothy J. Wengert, Mary Jane Haemig, Chris Halverson, and Robert Harrell (2020)

*The Augsburg Confession: Renewing Lutheran Faith and Practice*, by Timothy J. Wengert (2020).

*Luther's Outlaw God: Volume 3: Sacraments and God's Attack on the Promise*, by Steven D. Paulson (2021).

*Stories from Global Lutheranism: A Historical Timeline*, by Martin J. Lohrmann (2021).

*Teaching Reformation: Essays in Honor of Timothy J. Wengert*, edited by Luka Ilić and Martin J. Lohrmann (2021).

*Experiencing Gospel: The History and Creativity of Martin Luther's 1534 Bible Project*, by Gordon A. Jensen (2023).

*Face to Face: Martin Luther's View of Reality*, by Robert Kolb (2024).

*A New Song We Now Begin: Celebrating the Half Millennium of Lutheran Hymnals 1524–2024*, edited by Robin A. Leaver (2024).

*Sola: Christ, Grace, Faith, and Scripture Alone in Martin Luther's Theology*, by Volker Leppin (2024).

The translations in this volume are based on the following publications, all used by permission.

Chapter 1: Volker Leppin, "Ablasskritik im späten Mittelalter," in *Der Wert des Heiligen: Spirituelle, materielle und ökonomische Verflechtungen*, ed. Andreas Biler et al. (Stuttgart: Steiner, 2020), 153–165.

Chapter 2: Volker Leppin, "'Solus Christus': Von der spätmittelalterlichen Passionsfrömmigkeit zum reformatorischen Glauben," in *Transformationen: Studien zu den Wandlungsprozessen in Theologie und Frömmigkeit zwischen Spätmittelalter und Reformation*, 2nd ed. (Tübingen: Mohr, 2018), 279–301.

Chapter 3: Volker Leppin, "Das ganze Leben Buße: Der Protest gegen den Ablass im Rahmen von Luthers früher Bußtheologie," in *Die mittelalterlichen Ablasskampagnen: Luthers Thesen von 1517 im Kontext*, ed. Andreas Rehberg (Berlin: de Gruyter, 2017), 523–564.

Chapter 4: Volker Leppin, "Sola fide und monastische Existenz: Die Amalgamierung von Paulus und Mystik in Luthers Römerbriefauslegung," in *Transformationen: Studien zu den Wandlungsprozessen in Theologie und Frömmigkeit zwischen Spätmittelalter und Reformation*, 2nd ed. (Tübingen: Mohr, 2018), 333–354.

Chapter 5: Volker Leppin, "Die Genese des reformatorischen Schriftprinzips: Beobachtungen zu Luthers Auseinandersetzung mit Johannes Eck bis zur Leipziger Disputation," in *Transformationen: Studien zu den Wandlungsprozessen in Theologie und Frömmigkeit zwischen Spätmittelalter und Reformation*, 2nd ed. (Tübingen: Mohr, 2018), 355–397.

Chapter 6: Volker Leppin, "Wie legt sich nach Luther die Schrift selbst aus? Luthers pneumatische Hermeneutik," in *Sola Scriptura 1517–2017: Rekonstruktione-Kritiken–Transformationen–Performanzen*, ed. Stefan Alkier (Tübingen: Mohr, 2019), 83–102.